VERDUN

VERDUN

———❧———

THE LONGEST BATTLE OF
THE GREAT WAR

PAUL JANKOWSKI

OXFORD
UNIVERSITY PRESS

OXFORD
UNIVERSITY PRESS

Oxford University Press is a department of the University of Oxford.
It furthers the University's objective of excellence in research,
scholarship, and education by publishing worldwide.

Oxford   New York
Auckland   Cape Town   Dar es Salaam   Hong Kong   Karachi
Kuala Lumpur   Madrid   Melbourne   Mexico City   Nairobi
New Delhi   Shanghai   Taipei   Toronto

With offices in
Argentina   Austria   Brazil   Chile   Czech Republic   France   Greece
Guatemala   Hungary   Italy   Japan   Poland   Portugal   Singapore
South Korea   Switzerland   Thailand   Turkey   Ukraine   Vietnam

Oxford is a registered trade mark of Oxford University Press
in the UK and certain other countries.

Published in the United States of America by
Oxford University Press
198 Madison Avenue, New York, NY 10016

Library of Congress Cataloging-in-Publication Data
Jankowski, Paul, 1950–
Verdun: the longest battle of the Great War /Paul Jankowski.
pages   cm
Includes bibliographical references and index.
ISBN 978-0-19-931689-2
1. Verdun, Battle of, Verdun, France, 1916. I. Title.
D545.V3J36   2014
940.4'272—dc23   2013013998

1 3 5 7 9 8 6 4 2

Printed in the United States of America
on acid-free paper

In Memoriam
Richard Cobb 1917–1996
Maurice Keen 1933–2012
Historians and Tutors at Balliol

CONTENTS

TIMELINE

―――――・◆◆◆・―――――

1914

August 3: Germany declares war on France.

September: Following the German defeat on the Marne, General Erich von Falkenhayn succeeds Helmuth von Moltke as Chief of the German General Staff.

September–October: The German Fifth Army of Crown Prince Wilhelm surrounds Verdun on three sides.

1915

August: General Joseph Joffre, Chief of the French General Staff, removes most French artillery from the forts near Verdun and creates a "Fortified Region" relying instead on forces in the field.

September: French offensive against the German Third Army in Champagne fails to break through its second lines.

December: Falkenhayn presents the Kaiser with a plan to attack Verdun.

1916

February 21: The German Fifth Army, still under Crown Prince Wilhelm, attacks French positions on the right bank of the Meuse near Verdun. Operation *Gericht* begins.

February 21–March 1: Some French units surrender or retreat, while others, notably the chasseurs of Colonel Driant in the Bois des Caures, resist tenaciously.

February 25: Germans take the fort of Douaumont.

February 26: General Philippe Pétain assumes command of the French Second Army, which succeeds the "Fortified Region" of Verdun.

March 6: Germans begin successive attacks on the left bank of the Meuse.

April 10: *Ordre du jour* of Pétain: "Courage, on les aura!"

May 1: Pétain leaves Verdun for Bar-le-Duc to assume command of the Groupe d'Armées du Centre, which encompasses the Second Army. General Robert Nivelle succeeds him at the head of the Second Army.

May 22: Failed French attempt to retake Douaumont.

June 4: Beginning of Brussilow offensive in the East, requiring German intervention to rescue their Austrian allies.

June 7: The Germans take Fort Vaux.

Late June: With successive offensives in the Fleury-Souville sector, the Germans come closer to Verdun than ever. As some French units yield or break, Pétain considers withdrawing to the left bank of the Meuse.

Late June–early July: The German advance is halted.

1 July: Anglo-French offensive on the Somme begins.

August 27: Romania enters the war on the side of the Entente.

August 28: General von Falkenhayn is relieved. General Paul von Hindenburg succeeds him as Chief of the German General Staff, with General Erich Ludendorff as Quartermaster General.

October 24: The French retake the Fort of Douaumont.

November 2: The French retake the Fort of Vaux.

October–December: Signs of German morale crisis, in particular mass surrenders, as French retake ground on the right bank lost in February.

December 12: Joffre is relieved as Chief of the General Staff, receiving honorific functions and the title of Maréchal de France. Nivelle succeeds him, and is himself succeeded at Verdun by General Guillaumat.

December 15: The French retake much of the terrain on the right bank conquered by the Germans in February.

1917

April 6: United States declares war on Germany.

April 16: First day of Nivelle's failed offensive at the Chemin des Dames, in the Aisne.

April 29: Pétain succeeds Nivelle as Chief of the French General Staff.

August 22: The French retake the remaining heights on the left bank of the Meuse (Le Mort-Homme and Côte 304) from the Germans at Verdun.

1918

March 21: German spring offensives begin in the West, only to be stopped by July.

August 8: "Black day of the German army."

Late September: The American Expeditionary Force launches the Meuse-Argonne offensive, centered at Verdun.

November 11: Armistice signed at Rethondes.

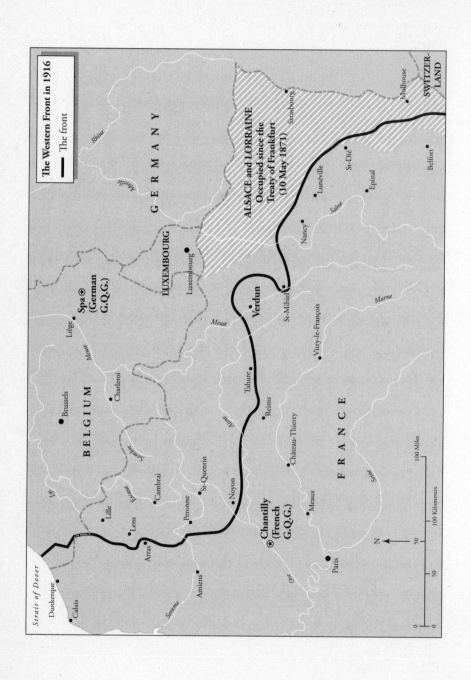

The Western Front in 1916

— The front

ALSACE and LORRAINE
Occupied since the
Treaty of Frankfurt
(10 May 1871)

SWITZER-
LAND

GERMANY

LUXEMBOURG

BELGIUM

FRANCE

Strait of Dover

Rhine

Moselle

Meuse

Meuse

Sambre

Lys

Escaut

Aisne

Oise

Somme

Saône

Marne

Seine

Mulhouse

Strasbourg

St-Dié

Belfort

Lunéville

Épinal

Nancy

St-Mihiel

Verdun

Vitry-le-François

Tahure

Reims

Château-Thierry

Meaux

Paris

Noyon

Péronne

St-Quentin

Cambrai

Lens

Lille

Arras

Amiens

Calais

Dunkerque

Brussels

Charleroi

Liège

Spa ⊗
(German
G.Q.G.)

Luxembourg

Chantilly
(French
G.Q.G.) ⊗

N

0   50   100 Miles

0   50   100 Kilometers

Verdun

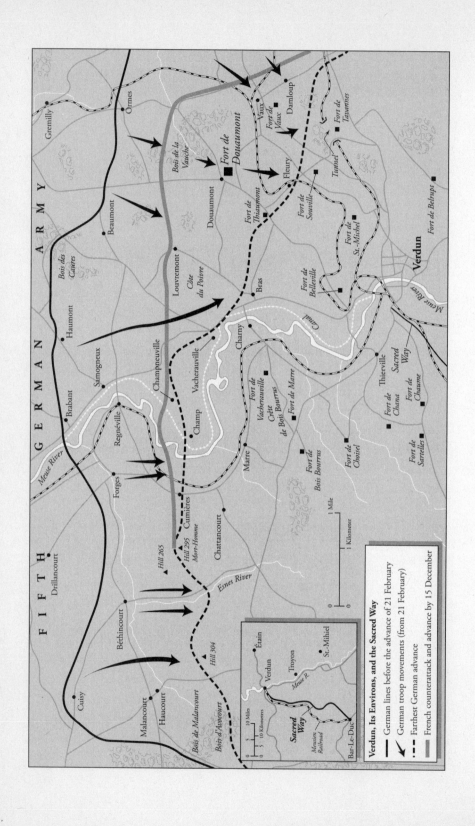

Verdun, Its Environs, and the Sacred Way

FIFTH GERMAN ARMY

Gremilly

Ormes

Bois de la Vauche

Fort de Douaumont

Vaux

Fort de Vaux

Damloup

Fort de Tavannes

Beaumont

Bois des Caures

Douaumont

Fort de Thiaumont

Fleury

Fort de Souville

Tunnel

Fort de St-Michel

Fort de Belrupt

Haumont

Louvremont

Côte du Poivre

Bras

Fort de Belleville

Verdun

Samogneux

Champneuville

Vacherauville

Charny

Canal

Meuse River

Thierville

Sacred Way

Brabant

Champ

Fort de Vacherauville

Crête de Bois Bourrus

Fort de Marre

Fort de Chana

Fort de Chaume

Regnéville

Forges

Cumières

Mort-Homme

Hill 295

Marre

Fort de Bois Bourrus

Fort de Choisel

Fort de Sartelles

Hill 265

Drillancourt

Chattancourt

Esnes River

Hill 304

Éfain

Verdun

Troyon

St-Mihiel

Béthincourt

Malancourt

Haucourt

Meuse R.

Cuisy

Bois de Malancourt

Bois d'Avocourt

Sacred Way

Meuse Railroad

Bar-Le-Duc

10 Miles

5   10 Kilometers

1 Mile

1 Kilometer

German lines before the advance of 21 February
German troop movements (from 21 February)
Farthest German advance
French counterattack and advance by 15 December

Introduction

ON THE 21ST OF FEBRUARY 1916, eighteen months into the first world war, German forces attacked French positions north and northeast of Verdun, the ancient stronghold on the Meuse River in eastern France, and opened what the novelist and war veteran Maurice Genevoix called "the battle-symbol of the entire 1914–1918 war." The ten-month-long positional battle called "Verdun" conferred grandeur upon the place, and even before it had ended the ruined city and its environs were giving off intimations of posthumous fame. Some cities in wartime transcend whatever strategic significance they can boast, and acquire the enduring quality of legend. Saragossa in 1808 and Stalingrad in 1942–1943 each endowed their defenders with the aura of national saviors. So did Verdun, a place where so many French and Germans died—300,000 in all—that the vast ossuary that went up there after the war could hold only a fraction of their shattered and scattered remains. Genevoix did not need to explain what he meant. No one would wish to pierce the consensual halo that surrounded the martyred city.[1]

At first sight the stature of Verdun among the French appears unimpeachable. It lasted longer than any other battle of the war—at least until December of 1916, when the French recaptured most of the ground they had lost in February. Even then the fighting did not stop: the battle reflected the interminable and monotonous bloodletting of the war itself. Second, it was a defensive battle, one the French had not started, which seemed to capture their position in a war they had not started either. And third, it was a solitary battle, fought by the French without any allies. The British were preparing their own offensives in a different sector of the Western Front, the Russians and the Italians were fighting on distant fronts, and the Americans did not enter the war until months after Verdun was over. This set it apart from most of the other great battles and incarnated another reality of World War One: during its course the French lost far more men than their allies on the Western Front, almost twice as many as the British, and more than a dozen times as many as the Americans. Verdun was indeed emblematic of the French experience of the war.

Embedded in French history, Verdun's stature transcends it. "Verdun will go down in history as the slaughterhouse of the world," an American ambulance driver wrote after arriving there in August 1917, as the French recaptured the crests of Côte 304 and le Mort-Homme from the Germans for the last time. Yet a more dispassionate gaze makes its celebrity seem a little surprising, even from a French perspective. It was not a decisive battle—not a Waterloo, a Sedan, a Kursk, each representing a moment when one side lost the initiative, never to retrieve it. The earlier Battle of the Marne had ended more decisively and saved the country more dramatically; it had stopped the invading German armies in their tracks and even pushed them back. So did the counteroffensives of 1918, which fathered as well the country's postwar military doctrines, envisaging long war and methodical battle, in ways that Verdun never did. The modern strategic importance of the place appeared doubtful to some of its defenders even as they were defending it.

Neither the French nor the Germans ever recovered from their losses at Verdun. Nonetheless, in war everything is relative: had the battle weakened one side more than the other? The answer, supposed to come later in the year on the Somme, turned out to be less than obvious. It was not the bloodiest episode of the war either, elevated above others by the magnitude of the carnage. Many more died in the war of movement around the Ardennes and the Belgian border in August and September 1914. French casualty rates during their offensives before—in Champagne in 1915, and after in the Aisne in 1917—at times exceeded those at Verdun. "For reasons that are not very difficult to find," as he put it, Jules Romains had placed Verdun at the narrative center of *Men of Good Will*, his immense historical epic of a novel. The closer you look at it, however, the harder it is to locate those reasons, and the preeminence of Verdun can appear anything but self-evident.[2]

Verdun did not have any drastic political impact. It did not save or dispatch a regime—it was no Bouvines in 1214, which strengthened one French monarch, Philippe Auguste, or Rossbach in 1757, which helped weaken another, Louis XV, or Waterloo in 1815 or Sedan in 1870, which dethroned two others—Napoleon and then his nephew. As a regime the Third Republic remained much the same after the Battle of Verdun as before. The Prime Minister (or Président du Conseil, as he was then called), Aristide Briand, held on, and so did the head of state, Raymond Poincaré. The battle did weaken the position of General Joseph Joffre, chief of the General Staff, accused by his critics in the Chamber of Deputies of having left Verdun poorly defended. Yet in the end the disappointing Franco-British offensive on the Somme in the summer and autumn of the same year did more to send Joffre on his way than Verdun. Verdun did briefly advance the career of General Robert Nivelle, who succeeded Joffre, but who remained at the helm only until his disastrous offensive at the Chemin des Dames in the spring of 1917. Politically, the long battle was neutral.

If Verdun "made" France, it was not through any immediate military or political impact, a capitulation or a resignation, a crisis or an upheaval from which a new and different country emerged. It happened slowly, over the decades, with the accretion of meanings that succeeding generations bestowed upon it. Its hold on national consciousness developed over time because only gradually did it emerge that Verdun would be the last great victory in battle of French arms. Nothing like it would ever happen again, not in 1917 or 1918, not between 1939 and 1945, and certainly not during the messy wars of decolonization that followed. Such standing elevated it even above the Great War itself. The messengers that transmit or mediate what is loosely termed collective memory—more precisely, public history—consistently transfigured Verdun, extracting it from its temporal context. The schoolbooks, political speeches, press and audio-visual reports, commemorations, popular histories, films, novels, and songs, the vehicles that convey the sense of an event to the millions who know little of it, spoke of "union," "people," "fatherland," "resistance," "soil," as though of a moment of regeneration. Verdun became a high point of reference for anyone attempting to argue, as many did in the years and decades after 1918, that the country was losing its way. No other battle, recent or remote, served such a purpose. In this sense asking how Verdun "made" France is tantamount to asking what France made of Verdun. A second question would be, how far did this construction depart from the battle itself?

The Germans dwell on Verdun too, almost brood over it, more than the Somme, where the outcome was more to their advantage. They suffered almost as many casualties there as the French, under conditions just as harrowing if not more so: their soldiers, unlike the French, had few forts in which to take shelter from the shell fire, the shrapnel, and the weather. No less than the French, the Germans extracted from the slaughter a parable of human resolution. Verdun, unlike the Somme, produced no Ernst Jünger, author of the celebrated trench memoir *Storm of Steel*. And across the Rhine it never generated anything like the literature and documentation it did in France, making for a poverty of sources worsened for the historian by the destruction of the archives of the Imperial German Army in an Allied bombing raid over Potsdam in 1945. But it nonetheless inspired a heroic literature of its own, mythologizing the common soldier there. Fictional and semi-fictional accounts celebrated his resolution, or his comradeship, or the inner voice of the nation resounding above the din of battle. Sometimes, unlike the French, these accounts did not so much celebrate union as castigate betrayal—of the common soldier by the high command or the home front; and sometimes official rhetoric— nationalist, revanchist, or more ominously National Socialist—eagerly seized on such themes. Through them ran a leitmotiv, suggesting that for them too Verdun was a symbol of the entire war: of tragic or of noble failure.[3]

Beyond the national protagonists, in the press and popular histories by British and American writers in particular, Verdun came to occupy still another symbolic niche. To them it came to seem a uniquely grim battle, perhaps the grimmest of all, in one popular account.[4] Others in the same vein beheld an archetypal battle of materiel, a technocratic Moloch devouring its children, "the symbol almost without parallel of the awfulness of modern industrial conflict."[5] From factory to trench, into the narrow theater ringed by fuming or flaming ridges, flowed the bumper crop of weaponry, all that national inventiveness and productivity could yield, leading another British author many years later to describe it as "an entirely new battle: one of annihilation." Such renderings elevate Verdun into national and historical limbo, symbolizing the futility of industrial war and even sometimes of war itself.[6]

"From the symbol we need to extract the substance," as a French historian once wrote, and Verdun is no exception. No design to exploit the battle for partisan motives, to impose consent or silence dissent, need drive all these transfigurations of Verdun or indeed of any other battle of its magnitude. Nor need they reflect some violence performed by the present upon the past, as though to attribute meaning in retrospect is unfailingly anachronistic. Legend has its reality, the battle has its own, and the history of the first not only invites the history of the second: it requires it.[7]

That is the point of this book. A great many histories of Verdun exist. Books or pamphlets about the battle began appearing even before it had ended and never stopped coming. They varied widely in conception, from popular narratives to more analytical studies relying on military archives, with each genre providing fine exemplars or archetypes—most obviously Alastair Horne's *The Price of Glory* and Gérard Canini's *Combattre à Verdun*, respectively. Between 1983 and 1998 over a quarter of all French publications about the battles of the Great War were about Verdun. Ever since the 1920s, it seems, such attentions in print coincided with decennial anniversaries of 1916. They all confirm an unquenchable thirst among readers for details of the ordeal. What happened there, they wondered.[8]

But by the 1980s and 1990s battles were losing ground as objects of interest among historians, whatever eminence Verdun might enjoy among them. So were traditional military histories, classically preoccupied with tactics, command, logistics, and all the proximate or remote reasons for an outcome in the field. By then the home front and all its civilians, the colonies and all theirs, the minds and bodies of the soldiers, the experience of war and above all its cultural afterlife were filling the agendas of younger scholars. In France new centers and professional organizations reoriented and rejuvenated the study of the war, drawing on this or that battle or engagement or sector of the front, but tending more often than not to deny to a Marne or a Somme or a Verdun its earlier status as an object worthy of study in itself. "Battle-history," sometimes derided among British and American historians as "drums and trumpets" history, began disappearing from the shelves of the academy, relegated by its most disdainful critics to the coffee tables of suburban homes.

Yet battle history remains the foundation of it all, grounding and enabling the more rarified considerations that might follow from it— the "anthropology of the soldier," debates about cultural "memory," the reordering of gender relations; without the day—or, as at Verdun, the months—and its facts and realities there would be no other questions to dissect. Historians now typically pose these and other questions about the war individually rather than as a whole, but ideally they should be asked all at once. And where else than in the event that brings them together, the battle? The event lends itself to the newer questions, if only they are put to it alongside the more fundamental questions about the why and the how. The ambition of this book is to tell the story of Verdun by mixing the old history with the new, the cold calculus of terrain gained and shells expended and lives lost with the depths of human experience on both sides. It aims to give the total history of a battle.

Numbers can help quantify the battle in objective terms, but are all but useless at recapturing moods and mentalities. These leave traces, occasionally allowing some speculation—about disenchantment revealed in desertion rates, for example, or the waning and waxing of postwar memory suggested by the frequency of visitors. But the subjective dimensions of the battle only offer themselves to the historian through discreet personal episodes scattered across the regiments and the months. Wellington, who was comfortably adept at both, remarked that a battle was like a ballroom dance, suggesting diversity as well as repetition, and through most of the sources for the Battle of Verdun patterns of experience emerge that historians can recognize but rarely measure. To quantify the feelings and experiences of those who lived and died at Verdun on either side of the Meuse, for months on end, would be pedantic and pointless. Their words survive, conveyed here almost a hundred years later in an effort to bring the reader as close as possible to what they faced at Verdun.

I

The Three Hundred Days of Verdun

FEBRUARY 1916: ALL MONTH, FOG, RAIN, AND SNOW had covered the Champagne and Argonne fronts. On the night of the 19th an east wind brought back stars and moonlight and, in the morning, cloudless blue skies.[1] The next day, Monday the 21st, the earth began to shake. To the north soldiers in their dugouts in the Aisne could hear the dull roar and feel the ground rumble, more powerfully than when they had attacked in Artois the year before. That night they watched the southeastern horizon glow with multicolored flashes, and the next day they learned that the Germans were attacking Verdun, 60 miles away. Beyond it, far to the south of the town, a distant drum roll, punctuated by regular shocks, echoed in the Vosges Mountains. Closer by, above Bar-le-Duc, an ambulance driver heard sinister noises, quite unlike anything that French artillery gave off, and the barn where he slept that night trembled as though from seismic shocks or volcanic eruptions.[2]

Twelve hundred German guns had begun firing in unison on French positions in and around Verdun minutes after seven o'clock that morning, preceded by isolated volleys during the night. At four a.m. a stray giant, a 380 mm shell weighing nearly 1,700 pounds, had pierced the darkness, knocked some stone off the cathedral and fallen into the presbytery. It was the latest affront in the serial sacrilege that had defiled places of worship in Belgium during the very first days of the war, and the archpriest preserved the shell casing in his garden. As the morning wore on the shelling intensified, and German observers watched from observation platforms as the French earthworks and command posts began to vanish from view in drifting clouds of smoke and dust. The piles of shells slowly grew shorter, the heaps of smoking cartridges taller. An artillerist registered a "real pleasure," a rhythmic delight—"we fired, fired, fired, without letting up," blow after blow, shell after shell, hour after hour, and the sweat ran down his face in the winter air. Towards noon the din deepened as trench mortars began to pound, and at four o'clock, when the most intense shelling, the *Trommelfeuer*, set in and the batteries began firing every 15 seconds, it rose to a climactic and unholy crescendo. An hour later it faded. The annals of war had never recorded anything like it. A million shells had fallen that day alone, the first day of the battle of Verdun.[3]

To an artist seated in a German plane 6,500 feet overhead, the detonations seemed so loud, so proximate, that he believed they were under enemy fire. But the shells came from their own guns. He had come along to sketch the scenes below. The Meuse and its flooded banks reflected the bright winter sun; the German guns along their wooded arc flashed; the tiny town in the distance, obscured by four thick clouds of smoke, meant little to him until the forward gunner gave up shouting the name above the roar of the twin propellers and pointed to "Verdun" on the map.

Balloons and sausage-shaped dirigibles floated below them, and squadrons of their own aircraft darted about through evanescent puffs of smoke and bursts of shrapnel. By the afternoon, fires were burning in the town. Shells fell by the bridges and into the river, sending up columns of spray through the blue-gray banks of smoke. But otherwise the sky seemed busier, more crowded with the antics and projectiles of airborne humans, than the earth below. Had three-dimensional warfare already taken the place of the linear variety, so manifest in the war of movement of 1914 and the offensives of 1915? The artist in the sky, peering through binoculars, discerned no French soldiers on the ground anywhere; and later, when he signed the watercolors that embodied his impressions of the day, no uniforms in horizon blue dotted his canvasses.[4]

This was understandable: the French *poilus*—as soldiers in the general infantry were known, partly for their often unshaven appearance, and much to their initial irritation—were for the most part underground or under cover of some kind, lost from view, isolated from their commanders, isolated from one another. At the headquarters of 30th Corps* in the Bois de la Chaume, northeast of Verdun, the wooded hills and ravines to the north appeared ablaze along a front of about eight miles, and before ten o'clock that morning they had lost all contact with the units there. Cables snapped, runners and cyclists disappeared, light signals faded in smoke and dust. The supply services could not reach the men with food, water, or ammunition either; even if access had been open, planes flying at will were bombing rail stations in Verdun, Chagny to the north, and Revigny to the south, and trains bearing their precious freight had prudently come to a halt farther away, well out of range.

And meanwhile the French artillery remained silent, mostly. A rich variety of enemy poison gas had spread a strong odor of chlorine, ether, and burnt almond among the batteries positioned in the woods and slopes between the Bois d'Haumont to the north and Vacherauville by the Meuse. The artillerists buried their noses and mouths in cotton wool and covered their eyes with chauffeurs' goggles, untroubled by such hindrances to their aim, for the ambient smoke and flames had already precluded accurate firing. At first some of them had tried firing gas shells of their own at the German guns, but had found them too numerous or too far to spot. Besides, munitions could not easily reach the guns: in Cumières, on the left bank, a driver of heavy artillery shells found himself flat on his stomach, covering himself with foliage and branches as best he could. Short of shells and ignoring what the coming days might ask of them, the artillerists heeded the strict orders from corps headquarters to economize. The infantry would have to fend for themselves for the moment.[5]

And they did. Cut off from their divisional and regimental command posts, deprived of supplies or reinforcements, they huddled in trenches, dugouts, and makeshift shelters in the half-dozen forested enclaves along

---

* Between 1914 and 1918 French and German infantry units were generally organized as follows: four companies to a battalion, three battalions to a regiment, two regiments to a brigade, two brigades to a division, two divisions to a corps. An active division, including other services such as artillery or engineering, numbered 17,286 in the French army and 16,650 in the German (on paper). At the beginning of the offensive the 5th German army—the army at Verdun—consisted of six corps, each of two divisions, with another nine regiments in reserve; by early March the reinforced French Second Army had 18.5 divisions in line, organized in five corps: *Weltkrieg*, X, 69; Bernède, *Verdun*, 363; Laparra, *Machine*, 50–51; Werth, *Verdun*, chart on 66–67.

the line separating French from German forces. The shell fire at first swept the sector methodically, like a giant reaper, visiting them every fifteen minutes or so with thunder and earthquake; later it rose to a continual mechanical pounding, a *Trommelfeuer* that shook them to their entrails and left them trembling and witless. They heard the savage concert of two-ton shells piercing the earth and heavy mortars leveling trenches and shattering dugouts; they smelled their nauseating acidic odor; they saw the parabolas of the 380s and the 420s, behemoths of chromed steel whose fragments sliced like razors through the thickest tree trunks—they saw them cross the paths of lesser missiles, the 210s that still hit with the shock of a train traveling at 50 miles an hour and finally come to rest amid mountains of earth. "Imagine if you can," wrote Marc Stéphane, "a steadily growing storm raining only paving stones, only building blocks. . . ."[6]

Their huts and dugouts danced, or rose and fell, or caved in. Towards ten o'clock the first wounded began to stream into the Bois des Caures. A *chasseur*, an infantryman with a head wound, went mad and had to be tied up. There and in the adjoining woods men watched and listened as their fellows disappeared beneath collapsing walls and roofs of earth and foliage. Another chasseur in the Bois des Caures, a battle-hardened corporal, eyed four stretcher-bearers, the survivors of a single volcanic explosion that had destroyed their refuge a dozen feet below ground, pour through the "wolves' hole," the aperture, of his already overpopulated lair—"now there are sixteen of us." The corporal disliked the fugitive Samaritans, the way they shook and their teeth chattered, the way they jostled one another in a primordial search for shelter.[7]

Soon the Bois des Caures, the Bois d'Haumont, and the Bois de Ville above and beyond them no longer deserved their names—by nightfall, reduced to a tangled mass of tree trunks and barbed wire, they resembled the refuse heaps of forlorn lumber mills. Collapsed parapets, severed trees, mangled branches and menacing craters underfoot made the trenches impassable. The hillsides might have belonged to some undulating lunar surface but for the wreckage of fortifications and plant life that covered them, a spectacle both demonic and *sui generis*.[8]

A few minutes after 5 o'clock, when the German guns lengthened their range or ceased firing, the shattered woods began to crawl with well-armed intruders. The Germans had emerged from their own woods and dugouts and were advancing slowly in the gathering darkness. Some had been waiting in waterlogged trenches or frigid dugouts for days, and the night before the sounds of song and accordion had wafted from their lines to some of the French trenches. Others had left encampments to the north and west at dawn and marched across a snowy landscape, inflamed by a blood-red sunrise. One of them, a machine-gunner, had listened with a growing sense of confidence to the shelling that echoed through the surrounding hills and valleys.[9]

In groups of 50 or 60 they began to reconnoiter the terrain that separated them from the French lines 2,500 feet away, to widen breaches in the barbed wire with cutters and burn away the debris of dugouts and the fallen trunks and branches with blowtorches. So confident were they already of the path ahead that some did not trouble to free their rifles from their shoulder slings. For the next two days they moved ahead in wavelets, in columns, in small and irregular formations, even alone or in pairs. They slipped through the intervals between blockhouses or what was left of them, jumped from crater to crater; they skirted the flanks of ruined trenches or hacked and bored their way through them. Some carried grenades but no rifles, some wielded knives and hatchets, some wore yellow masks and carried flamethrowers with tanks of flammable liquid and hoses that spurted jets of fire six-feet long. Pioneers, the indispensable engineers of the German army, worked to rebuild trenches and link shell-holes into passable ditches. When the men encountered resistance they held up, as they had been ordered, and waited while officers with revolvers launched white rockets to call in artillery fire. Once the fire moved on, so did they, into enemy territory, sometimes at a run.[10]

Inspired by the promise of a promenade, they nonetheless moved on prudently and deliberately, encountering dazed survivors who surrendered in small groups. A French captain, crazed perhaps by the day's blows to his senses or by the prospect of his would-be captors, shot himself with a rifle in front of them. In wrecked dugouts they found white bread, chocolate, wine, blankets, straw mattresses—unmistakable signs of sudden flight; and from the ruins of Haumont village they watched crowds of French soldiers fleeing from the heights of Brabant to the north, toward the town of Samogneux on the river. By six o'clock most of the first-line trenches and outposts in the woods had fallen. That night the German infantrymen listened in their conquered dugouts to the howls and impacts of shells and the explosions of munitions dumps, and watched the sky and the villages flame.[11]

But they had run into resistance that day as well. "I think the Germans had a nasty surprise," one of the French chasseurs recalled many years later. "They expected to find nothing before them and found survivors instead." By nightfall French artillery began firing into them, and isolated and outnumbered groups of survivors in the Bois des Caures and the Bois d'Haumont took up defensive positions amid the wreckage of trees and the ruins of hamlets wherever they could, even as they pulled back. This stunned the attackers. In Haumont village, clambering through craters and over walls, the only signs of life that greeted them at first came from survivors mentally unhinged by the daylong shell fire and unable to defend themselves. But from the ruins of the church and its cemetery above, from cellars and reverse slopes beyond that descended to the Meuse, came rifle and machine gun fire from an enemy still hidden, still capable. Now the attackers here and elsewhere were vulnerable, exposed against all expectations to an unseen foe. Their miracle-working artillery had let them down, and the very functions of their own weaponry turned against them: flamethrowers, intended to clean out the last helpless occupants of subterranean refuges, now became portable bombs that once pierced by hostile bullets incinerated their own bearers. Some withdrew and abandoned the evening's precious gains. And in the next few days, as reinforcements began to arrive, French resistance gradually stiffened. It would cost the French; one division, the 72nd, would lose over half its men, killed, wounded, or missing; but with their lives they bought time.[12]

Time for what? Did Verdun matter so mightily? A French lieutenant stationed on another front wrote to his mother that something important was happening that day in the distance, toward Verdun, but he wondered why the Germans had chosen to attack there. Even if the ancient town on the Meuse fell, he mused, it would only mark a moral victory of sorts.[13]

Crown Prince Wilhelm, heir to the imperial throne and commander of the German Fifth Army that was attacking Verdun, enthusiastically thought so. But no one, other than General Erich von Falkenhayn, the chief of the German General Staff, could answer the question. And perhaps not even he: he managed to leave not only his enemy but also his compatriots, his contemporaries, and all of posterity in the dark about his intentions that day. What vision had inspired his undertaking? Or, perhaps, competing visions—for Falkenhayn would not have been the first commander to envisage variable outcomes to a project. Among the French, General Herr, the commander of the fortified region of Verdun who had been warning from his headquarters of an attack for a month and more, could not deduce German designs that day from German shelling. And at Chantilly, in the chateau within easy reach of Paris where the General Staff of the French Army had set up its permanent headquarters in November 1914 once the front finally stabilized, General Joseph Joffre doubted the Germans as well. A week earlier, on the 15th, he had conceded grudgingly what he and his staff had denied in January, that they might attack at Verdun. But they might equally well attack at Nancy, or in Champagne, or the Nord, or somewhere else along the 600-mile front that had stretched since the autumn of 1914 from the North Sea to the mountains of the Swiss border. Joffre suspected a diversion at Verdun, intended to deflect his forces from the point of some later enemy offensive elsewhere, or perhaps a psychological blow aimed at his countrymen's morale but devoid of military consequence.[14]

Why attack a place of uncertain strategic and imaginary symbolic significance, and attack it so fiercely? For many years after the war, Falkenhayn's motives would pit his friends against his foes and divide the most impartial of historians. But the French reasons for defending Verdun, for committing an entire army—the Second Army, under Philippe Pétain—appear scarcely less perplexing than the Germans' for attacking it. For 18 months they had almost starved it of guns and men, as though to belittle the once mighty ring of forts, built before the turn of the century and well before the new war of trenches and stationary artillery, until the omens of assault grew unmistakable. Then they resolved to defend every inch of land there, dismissing military considerations that might have demanded a partial withdrawal, or an elastic defense, or even a strategic retreat. But still, like their adversaries, they would husband their resources there, parsimoniously, for they had aspirations elsewhere. Where was the consistency, the calculus of interest and of gain in all this? This, too, hung in the air on the night of the 21st of February.

Such questions hinted at the disturbing possibility that human choice might not count for as much in the course of this battle as in some others. Perhaps, on the 21st of February, both Falkenhayn and Joffre contemplated Verdun as a secondary theater, and perhaps forces beyond their control turned it into a primary one. But such conjectures never preoccupied the students of Verdun or the historians of the war, or survived the serial solemnities of national memories. In the re-creations and the retellings, the stakes became self-evidently crucial, for could so many have died for an ancillary cause? "Verdun was the gateway," the veteran at Verdun tells the visiting boy scouts at the beginning of Léon Poirier's 1931 film *Verdun Souvenirs d' histoire*. "Once the enemy broke through Verdun, he would be among us. Six hundred thousand Frenchmen died here to stop them." The German memoirists and raconteurs had no quarrel with this. "At Verdun France either stood or fell," Paul Ettighoffer, a German survivor, declared on the first page of his own account in 1936. But on February 21, 1916, to Falkenhayn who attacked and to Joffre who defended, Verdun was something less than the place of destiny.[15]

That day it did not appear to either of them as the precious symbol of centuries of struggle, one that concentrated the tribal emotions of the protagonists. Falkenhayn believed the French would sacrifice much to defend it, but had he scoured the front for some immemorial or totemic marker of national identity he might more astutely have fixed on Reims, gathered around its battered cathedral full of the ghosts of 30 anointed kings, or even Nancy, a sop the Germans tossed to France after they took Alsace and much of Lorraine in 1871. He did not mention Verdun's past. Neither did Joffre. But soon, as though to marginalize strategic considerations that appeared mysterious in any case, Verdun found itself dignified with historical roles it had not conspicuously enjoyed before.[16]

For centuries, the chroniclers began to recall, Latins and Teutons had battled each other here. Morale, in this war, was all, and morale required that it resist—that Virodunum, the Roman outpost on the site of a Celtic hill fort, protected by armed bishops since the fourth century, fortified by Vauban in the seventeenth, besieged by Prussian invaders in the eighteenth and again in the nineteenth, hold out once more when they returned in the twentieth, on February 21, 1916. For their part, some of the invaders' compatriots began claiming it as a symbol of their own— claiming, in fact, to be repossessing a national site. For centuries, the German newspapers reminded their readers in the early days of the battle, the bishopric had been theirs, a Free City attached to the Holy Roman Empire, until the French wrenched it back by force in the sixteenth century and finally by treaty in the seventeenth. How many of his compatriots, a German major, a veteran of the battle, still wondered after the war, sang their national anthem "Von der Maas bis an die Memel" (from the Meuse to the Memel) without knowing that the splendid fields of "der Maaslandschaft" had been German until the Treaty of Westphalia in 1648? In 1916 Verdun briefly became in the hands of Germany's myth producers what Tannenberg more lastingly had become in 1914—the battle in which the German Eighth Army destroyed the Russian Second Army: the invented site of history's revenge. There, in the East, they had affixed with toponymic sleight of hand one of the two place-names—Tannenberg or Grunwald—of a Germanic defeat by Poles and Lithuanians in 1410 to their own defeat of the Russians nearby at the outset of the present Great War. Here, in the West, they discerned in the attack on Verdun the chance to avenge almost as old a historical wrong. Nothing could have been further from the minds of Joffre and Falkenhayn that morning than protecting or redeeming some uniquely sacred site of national memory.[17]

In its sound and fury the 21st of February had shaken the land as in some hallucinatory prophecy. The rest of the year and more played out that day, in a deluge of steel and shrapnel that violently fissured the front, severed the front from the rear and one part of the army from the other, and left resistance, like survival, to personal initiative. It presaged, as well, the diminishing returns that each offensive brought as time wore on, and the tendency towards equilibrium that only an overwhelming superiority in men and materiel could upset. It hinted at the iron logic of stalemated warfare, soon to find its human face not in Falkenhayn or Joffre but in Philippe Pétain, symptom and spirit of limited ambitions.

The day posed as well the conundrum of novelty. The German Fifth Army had attempted a novel use of artillery, massive and intensive and comparatively brief, and some cautiously creative infantry tactics to accompany it—probing, tentative, the very opposite, in fact, of those that had served both armies so poorly in 1914. Would they work? The day's developments gave no very clear answer. And would the troops on both sides suffer more terribly, fight more tenaciously, shirk more sullenly, than anywhere else on the Western Front? That day most of the French had fought. But some had fled, and others had surrendered, and the disparities raised the inescapable mystery of motivation, soon to be drowned by memory and reverence in a congratulatory chorus of thanks. Why men fought, and what if not for whom they believed themselves to be fighting, seemed so self-evident to the historians of both sides that they rarely worried themselves about any insubordination or indiscipline here, or, if defense of home and hearth explained French tenacity, about the compulsions driving the equally dogged perseverance of their adversaries, or about the anxiety, resignation, or incomprehension with which civilians east and west of the Rhine greeted the news of this strangest of battles.

In retrospect, the day presaged muddle and enigma. But in the hands of artists and assorted celebrants it easily lent itself to symbolic or allegorical overload. In Poirier's 1931 film, technocracy attacked rusticity that morning; it juxtaposed the giant guns of one side with the humble villages of another, the imposed discipline of the *Feldgrau* with the spontaneous gaiety of the *poilu*, and sent the morning's first shell onto the roof of a defiant cottager. Even Heinz Paul's German film, released the same year as the spoken version of Poirier's and criticized by the Nazis for its sober depictions of defeat rather than glory, skipped over the eight-hour-long bombardment to dwell instead on a buoyant and vocal German infantry, attacking a waiting, desultory foe, luckily reprieved by a weather-induced delay. The films turned their cameras on the human surge, the epic element. And Jules Romains, who devoted almost a third of his 1938 novel *Verdun* to the 21st of February, knowingly telescoped the entire battle and indeed the entire war into a certain vision of the day, made of industrial slaughter, valiant foot soldiers, and blasé commanders in remote chateaux and pleasure-domes.[18]

But by sundown the day made little sense to contemporaries, and the next days' cryptic communiqués on both sides alluded only to intense artillery activity in the sector, to prisoners taken and positions captured or lost or retaken. No one could know that the day of 21st February only mattered as the first of 300 and more to follow—days of siege and counter-siege, and of a battle that from a historian's distance gives every appearance of running itself according to its own infernal logic.

"This battle of Verdun can drag itself out more than any other battle, longer than Mukden for instance," Maurice Barrès was already writing on the 26th of February. The nationalist author, resigned by now to remote rather than proximate victories, raised the specter of the Russo-Japanese war in 1904–5, when firepower and manpower had unexpectedly expanded the duration as well as the carnage of modern battle. The Russians abandoned the town of Mukden after two months, and ceded

Port Arthur after five. Both sides suffered huge losses, but neither—this Barrès did not say—won a conclusive victory on land.

How long did the battle of Verdun last? Until July, when the Germans ceased major offensive operations? Or September, when they formally renounced them? Until October, when the French recaptured Fort Douaumont, or December, when they took back most of the other positions they had lost in February, or August of the following year, when they finally expelled the Germans from one that still remained, atop the crest of le Mort-Homme? Even in November 1916 positions taken from the French in February still stood in enemy hands, and an observer could only call the battle "essentially over."[19] False endings staggered the battle, until it imposed upon the chroniclers and the record-keepers its singularity: Verdun was the longest, longer by far than Mukden.

The answer to how many died there, how many were wounded or disappeared into captivity, depended upon dates and sources and definitions; different ways of counting losses allowed inflated estimates and treacherous comparisons. In time Verdun lost its mythical status as the most murderous battle of the Western Front, and even of history, but the numbers still hid a crude secret: the losses rose so high because the battle lasted so long.

A battle ends when one side imposes its will or the other voluntarily leaves the scene. It becomes endless when advance is impossible but withdrawal unthinkable, when pauses cannot last and truces cannot hold, when the protagonists can neither attain nor renounce their goals yet the men and materiel and life blood of war still flow their way. The battle sustains itself.

An *attaque brusquée*, a sudden drive to rupture the French lines, soon stalled, and for ten months and more the battle of Verdun repeated as though in slow motion the episode again and again in both directions. In the end the outcome—negative, wanting in finality, a Borodino rather than a Waterloo—mattered less than the feat of survival. The French had triumphed more over adversity than over adversaries, and the adversities were many: an initial loss of maneuver room, a defensive position that found them astride a river and pressed into a salient; supply lines from the hinterland so constricted that only an unprecedented resort to trucks, to the internal combustion engine instead of the locomotive, saved the day; an inferiority in heavy artillery; and the diabolical conspiracy of circumstance. To have held out and taken the offensive on the Somme in July

1916 as well spoke volumes to an enemy whose hubris undermined his method: Falkenhayn, whatever else he may have counted on, believed the French had reached their limit. They were spent, he thought, by Verdun. And he had always regarded them as a second-rate military power, in any case. Not for the first and not for the last time, the German military mind had underestimated the enemy.[20]

Anxiety and worse gripped the army of Verdun by the 24th, as the enemy pushed it back to its second arc of concentric positions, spread along a radius of about six miles out from the town. Slowed but not stopped by counterattacks from the shreds of the 72nd Infantry Division still in its path, the *Feldgrauen* overran the Bois des Fosses, the Bois des Chaumes, the Bois des Caurières, encircled the village of Louvemont, forced open a pathway to the village of Douaumont and the hulking but disarmed and pitifully garrisoned fort by the same name. The next day the fort fell. Facing renewed encirclements, troops evacuated the hills to its north and west, the Côte du Poivre and the Côte du Talou, and the open plain of Woëvre to its south. But the promenade of the attackers' dreams did come to grief, ruined by the rival projects of newly arrived defenders. Masters of the fort, the Germans could not take the village of Douaumont until their shells had obliterated and their men had assaulted it ten times. Even then, by the 6th of March, they could progress no farther, nailed to their positions there and elsewhere on the hillsides of the Côtes de Meuse by increasingly assertive adversaries. Pushed by a restive government, the French General Staff had by now resolved to defend Verdun, and had sent steady reinforcements, as well as Generals Castelnau and then Pétain, to do so. No one expected some providential victory here, some improbable Rocroi or Austerlitz; they harbored instead the more modest wish to leave the enemy's larger appetites unsatisfied by methodical obstruction. "The mission of the 2nd army is to frustrate at any cost the effort the enemy is making," Pétain had said upon arriving at Verdun, in resolute but sober words that conveyed patience instead of élan and limits instead of visions.[21]

Unable to exploit its successes of the first few days on the right bank, the German Fifth Army resolved to attack on the left. Through the weeks of March and April it tried over and over to conquer commanding heights on both sides of the river, heights below which Verdun would lie at its mercy. Over and over, it failed. Usually, exhausted or bled white by renewed assaults on the village of Vaux, the hilltops of le Mort-Homme or the Côte 304, the Bois des Corbeaux or the Bois d'Avocourt, the Germans would fall back and cling to wretched gains where they could, to cratered slopes, blasted woods, and rubble-strewn cellars. "So we won't enter Verdun until 1920 at the earliest!" the German commander on the left bank, General Max von Gallwitz, exclaimed: Côte 304, he had understood, presaged much more to come. Defenders became attackers, exchanging roles with macabre reciprocity, leaving assailants in possession one day only to be driven out the next, sometimes after close-quarter fighting that left streets and hillsides littered with corpses. On the 9th of April eleven German regiments attacked along a seven-mile front on the left bank, between Avocourt and Cumières; once again the French held or retook most of the line, losing one of the summits atop le Mort-Homme but keeping the village of Cumières after repelling ten successive German attacks. The day provoked Pétain's most celebrated exhortation, his "Courage! on les aura" (we'll get them!), the words of many a poster and many a call to buy war bonds, even though then, six weeks into the battle, the end was nowhere in sight.[22]

A de facto attritional struggle, the condition that this war's commanders, including Falkenhayn, habitually and conveniently claimed to have intended all along, set in, made of local attacks and counterattacks and a usually unfounded conviction that casualties inflicted exceeded casualties suffered. Falkenhayn and Joffre began to show signs of impatience with the local commanders, who in turn lamented their parsimonious dispensations of men and materiel. Late in May machine guns drove French assailants off the roofs of Douaumont; two weeks later the Germans took the neighboring fort of Vaux by flushing out its garrison of feverish, parched defenders on the seventh day of their siege with grenades and toxic fumes fed through apertures and ventilation systems. Flame-throwers had done the rest. Such local triumphs and tragedies might have perpetuated the bloody but inconclusive battle of Verdun had not the unmistakable omens of the coming Allied offensive on the Somme induced the German high command to bring matters to a head. In the last week of June, as British and French guns began shelling the German Third Army on the Somme, the Fifth Army made its last desperate bid to prevail on the Meuse. Six divisions attacked along a two-and-a-half mile front on either side of the ridge that ran southwest from Douaumont to Froideterre. Bavarian units captured part of the village of Fleury and submerged parts of the fort of Souville, only three miles from Verdun. Their corpses covered the ravin du Bazil and the ravin de Chambitoux, inert testimony to the vanity of the enterprise, for in July and August French counterattacks—some from the air—expelled the survivors from the ditches and outworks of Souville and from the ruins of Fleury. It was the closest the Fifth Army would ever come to Verdun. From then on its men and its guns began slowly moving west and north, to fields on the Somme where the fighting surpassed the scope but rarely the intensity of the Maasmühle, the mill on the Meuse.

By late summer, at Verdun, the surge was moving the other way. It reversed direction without any sudden convulsion or spasm, only with sluggish and uncertain motion, across a landscape bereft of vegetation and even of the barbed wire that men had implanted here earlier in the year. A ton of shells, by most calculations, had laid waste each yard of the front. Nothing remained to uproot. For three months the troops fought each other from hole to hole, mounted small raids, in a hail of grenades, without shelter, without rest, sometimes without food or water, on continual alert, deprived by now even of the protections they had contrived for themselves in the winter. But the momentum was shifting. The French began to plan and execute with meticulous method partial offensives that left little to chance and that recaptured Fort Douaumont in late October, Fort Vaux in early November, and the Bois des Caures and the neighboring woods in mid-December. At the end of the year the lines ran more or less where they had when the Germans had sprung operation *Gericht* in February; and in a battle of attrition the defender wins in a stalemate.[23]

It seemed a fine revenge. For three days in October French heavy artillery pounded the German defenders of Douaumont, setting off fires in the fort and destroying their dugouts in the stone quarries of Hardomont to the right and the batteries of Damloup to the left. In a new mass air war, French Nieuports and Farmans patrolled the skies, as unchallenged as the German Fokkers and Drachens of February and March had been. In good order, directed by compass and preceded by a rolling artillery barrage, three divisions of infantry advanced by the clock through fog, until the first battalions submerged the fort and its demoralized defenders. "The enemy has no monopoly over method," an observer noted simply, and the recapture of Douaumont, followed by that of Vaux two weeks later, seemed to confirm what some limited successes on the

Somme that summer had already presaged: the French, sooner than the British, had entered the age and grasped the war of materiel.[24]

In December a French pilot flying low watched as Zouaves—their distinctive red Fez replaced now by Adrian helmets—climbed in and out of craters and moved on, followed by aircraft and support troops. Desultory German artillery fire, weak and imprecise, greeted the methodical advance of the French troops. The army that had seized these ridges and ravines with élan in February showed little inclination to hold them now. Its morale was poor, so poor that thousands had surrendered that month alone, and the pilot watched them come down from Douaumont in long columns, guarded by the walking wounded, their French captors. The view from the air, like that in February when the German planes owned the skies and the terrestrial roles were reversed, suggested that enough materiel might indiscriminately wear down even the most tenacious and practiced defenders, especially if the scent of success accompanied its deployment.[25]

Nine months later, in August 1917, the French recaptured the remaining observation points the Germans still held on the left bank, atop the Côte 304, le Mort-Homme, and the Côte du Talou. They overwhelmed the defenders not with one ton of steel for each square yard but six, nor with 50 artillery pieces for every half-mile or so of front as at Champagne in 1915 or 70 as at Verdun or on the Somme the year before, but with almost 150. The guns neutralized the inferior German artillery with powerful gas attacks at dawn, the infantry rapidly seized its objectives, 100 enemy guns and 10,000 prisoners came their way. Now the debris of battle littered the landscape, strewn for miles on end, an inert tempest of shoes, grenades, empty bottles, signal rockets, pierced helmets, rifles, decaying corpses, and body parts that glowed with phosphorescence by night.[26]

Falkenhayn and Joffre, who had rarely visited the scene anyway, had long since departed. The year before, at the end of August, Field Marshal Paul von Hindenburg and General Erich Ludendorff had ousted their rival. Nothing, in 1916, had gone his way. Before Verdun he had pronounced Russia *hors de combat*, France on the verge of exhaustion, England likely to mount premature counterattacks, Rumania unlikely to enter the war against them. Instead Russia had attacked in June, England had waited until July to mount an offensive with France that was anything but premature, Verdun had neither fallen nor crippled the French, and now Rumania had entered the war on the side of Germany's enemies. Hindenburg and Ludendorff immediately prevailed upon the Kaiser to call off any plans of resuming the Verdun offensive. Joffre left the command of the General Staff in December, hastened on his way by the disappointments of the Somme offensive, called off the month before. Each had left with dignity, keeping up appearances, but Verdun had helped their enemies and rivals send them on their way, reproaching the German with a failed attack, the Frenchman with a precarious defense.

But did any of the critics understand the meaning of what had happened here? Understand that without allies rich in resources, neither could ever hope to win such a war, then or in the future, against an industrial power or coalition of powers dwarfing their own capabilities? The heavy caliber German guns had violently put the question on the 21st of February, and it remained open at the end of the year—remained open, in fact, long after the war itself had ended.

A few years later some of the shell craters, overlapping in chains, filled in, vegetation and even flowers grew again here and there, and a few villages began rising from their ruins. A temporary ossuary housed the remains of the nameless dead, who awaited their permanent home in the grand edifice that would go up at the end of the decade and dominate the surrounding country. Tourists, veterans, and families of the fallen came by, some out of curiosity, the way they might visit the ruins of Carthage or Pompeii. And two officers, two majors newly assigned from the postwar army, helped reconstruct for them the happenings here in 1916.[27]

A problem remained. Which, of the 300 and more days to choose from, should the town or the nation select to commemorate the battle? In the early years, for the nation, only the start of the war on the 4th of August and its end on the 11th of November made good their hold on the collective national memory. The war was too recent, the profusion of individual recollections too immediate, to allow consensus to settle on any other occasion of moment, and Verdun had lasted so long, and seen so many enter and emerge in their ceaseless flow, that what proved difficult for the war proved doubly so for the battle.[28]

In time a habit formed. Of all the dates to commemorate the great battle, none imposed itself as consistently as the 21st of February. Over time the French slowly retired the days of success or revenge at Verdun, days when they had stopped the enemy's forward movement or recaptured

Fort Douaumont or pushed the Germans back to their original lines, and instead recalled to life a day of disaster and despair, the first. Even in years when dignitaries came in June or July or November, the town, the newspapers, the radio and television stations observed the event on the 21st of February, more often than not, as though by common and tacit consent, as though fright and suffering enjoyed a staying power that success lacked. Jules Romains ended his *Verdun* with the French counterattack on le Mort-Homme on the 9th of April and with Pétain's exhortation the same day. But he devoted to it only a fraction of the space he had to the battle's first day in the opening chapters. So it was with the habits that public recollection slowly came to adopt. There is no official Verdun-day in France. But if there were, it would by now fall on the 21st February.[29]

Even before the end of the war, the songster hired by the government to compose and perform at the front and at home, Theodore Botrel, had anointed the day in the second stanza of his "Les chasseurs de Driant":

A murderous 'spray'
Drenches the dark grove
The twenty-first of February
Of nineteen sixteen.

On that date in 1920, at the Trocadéro in Paris, veterans gathered to recall "the terrible hours of the Bois des Caures" and to hear André Maginot, by then minister of pensions, tell them that "France still needs you." The following year, on the same day at the same place, Louis Barthou marked the fifth anniversary by reminding the assembled veterans that he stood before them not only as Minister of War but also as the father of a son killed at the front. Grief, in this war, never strayed far from commemoration. Five years later, on the same day but this time in the Bois des Caures, the deputy and minister Désiré Ferry recalled the fighting there at the start of "the greatest battle of the war" and gloomily asked his listeners: "Combatants of Verdun, what have they done to your victory?"[30]

This day in particular struck chords. It seemed to evoke not the dash of sudden victory but the stoicism of protracted siege, oddly archaic in this most modern of landscapes, lending itself to a tradition of melancholic rather than triumphal national communion and to a familiar but unarticulated question: Why?[31]

2

Verdun under German Eyes

AT FIRST, THERE WAS, STRICTLY SPEAKING, no Battle of Verdun.
German and French newspapers offered their readers confused and contradictory explanations of the why and the wherefore of the violent events
taking place there, unable to discern much sense in them, unable, even, to
give them a name.

Circumstances had hobbled them from the start. Torn between a professional desire to expose the facts and a patriotic one to inspire their
readers, journalists had to operate as well under the heavy hand of military and civilian authority. Especially the French, more regimented than
their German counterparts: Strict censorship, already in place by the 5th
of August 1914, had hardly let up by the time of Verdun. To tighten the
vise, almost no French journalists were allowed at the front before 1917.
They had to rely for information on official communiqués, encounters
with officers and men at rest or on leave, and foreign newspapers.[1]

In the dark themselves, French war correspondents could scarcely
enlighten their readers. At first they faithfully reproduced military communiqués about artillery activity in the region of Verdun and on the Côtes
de Meuse and about enormous enemy losses. On the 25th of February—
four days after the initial bombardment—typesetters began inserting the
words "battle of Verdun" or the "battle for Verdun" into the headlines.
But editors then provided multiple and often contradictory explanations.
In the same issue *Le Gaulois* suggested in one article that Verdun itself
was a major target, in another that it was not, and in a third that it was
all about German confidence. *Le Matin* spoke ominously of a "supreme
effort against France" but then attributed it chiefly to the enemy's worries
about German domestic opinion. *Le Petit Journal* thought it likely that
the enemy had some major objective in mind, but declined to identify it.

L'Humanité and others warned of imminent offensives elsewhere. Verdun mattered to the enemy. Why, they could not say.[2]

Even if some of the French military communiqués mentioned Verdun, the German ones did not, preferring to give pride of place to the forts rather than the town. Who could know, the *Frankfurter Zeitung* wondered on the 24th of February, whether this was some purely local event or a major operation long in the making: the German General Staff, the *Oberste Heeres Leitung* (OHL), would not and could not say. The paper surmised that the Fifth Army, the German army in the area, had decided to eliminate the obtrusive salient in its front, and the same day two other dailies, the *Berliner Tageblatt* and the *Münchner Neueste Nachrichten*, imagined equally geometrical justifications for their countrymen's arms—to straighten out the line along the front in the area, as they already had at Arras and on the Somme. Ever since 1914 the Fifth Army commanders had been demanding no less.[3]

To believe Erich von Falkenhayn, the place itself mattered not to him but to the French, who would pour into the threatened terrain rather than sacrifice the town at its center. There, in a topographical trap between the heights and the river, he had the means and the methods to destroy the swelling enemy army even while husbanding his own. The French would shed so much blood by holding Verdun or so much prestige by abandoning it that they would lose their ability or their will to continue the war—soon, before the following winter. They had lost, after all, so many hundreds of thousands already. Conquest there mattered less to him than *Ausblutung*—bleeding out, the mortal bleeding of the enemy in a battle of attrition that seemed to rest upon a tactical paradox—an attack upon a fortress with no design to take it—and a monstrous and sanguinary ambition. He himself fathered the improbable myth of Moloch, a Phoenician and Canaanite God appearing in the Hebrew Bible, seized upon by posterity in France and Germany alike to demonize, deride, or ponder his motives in attacking Verdun.

Ausblutung, Falkenhayn insisted in an article published in the semiofficial *Militärwochenblatt* in 1919, had been the achievement at Verdun, and *Ausblutung*, he repeated in his memoirs published the following year, had been his goal from the start. Between quotation marks, he reproduced a long memorandum he had written to the Kaiser on Christmas Eve 1915, setting forth his strategic thinking for an assault upon Verdun: "to bleed to death the French forces . . . whether we reach our goal or not."[4] After the war researchers at work on official and semi-official histories of the war in the Reichsarchiv could find no trace of the original memorandum.[5] No one ever did. Yet everyone cited it, in anguished re-appraisals of the great battle. Many criticized the thinking in the Christmas memorandum, and some denied that it ever governed the battle that followed, but few denied its existence. The Allied bombing raid that destroyed most of the archives of the Imperial German army in 1945 also disposed of any hope of finding the famous memorandum. Later some historians came to doubt the authenticity of the document that most of Falkenhayn's contemporaries declined to challenge. He might have fabricated it for his memoir. Was the thinking behind it at least genuine, even if the memorandum was not—had he resurrected his authentic thoughts in a fake form? The answers, *faute de mieux*, lie in 1915 and 1916.[6]

Falkenhayn himself died in 1922. He had offered his last word, such as it was, in the memoir, and had been scarcely more prolix about the matter when alive, dissembling his innermost designs behind irony, reserve, and unfailing courtesy. And behind protean pronouncements and dialectical drills that left his staff at OHL wondering where he stood and what he wanted—he seemed on occasion so elastic, so fickle, that a general remembered him as "more interesting than trustworthy," and an exasperated Minister of War, a friend, once called him a "dilettante."

Others called him worse. Falkenhayn's elegance of manner and sleekness of appearance could incite the envy of less magnetic rivals for office and influence. "I can hate and this man I do hate," the choleric Erich Ludendorff had written, and by the summer of 1916 one of the most gifted generals on the Western Front, Prince Rupprecht of Bavaria, had developed for his superior nothing less than a "burning hatred." Falkenhayn had enemies—at court, in the army, in the government. Were it not for the Kaiser, he would have been isolated; and an isolated man is an uncommunicative man.[7]

Like so many in the officer caste, he had been born into a family of Prussian landowners, but his military career had been anything but typical. Six years in China with the German legation had opened his eyes to political horizons beyond the parade ground or the battlefield. Successive promotions over the heads of older, more senior officers had raised eyebrows, until the day in September 1914 when he succeeded Helmuth von Moltke as chief of the General Staff, in the wake of the defeat on the Marne that had shattered any hopes of a swift German victory in the West. "He was known to some as a heartless, ambitious climber," an Austrian representative at the Kaiser's court wrote, "who stepped indifferently over corpses in pursuit of his goal."[8]

He seemed an unlikely heir to the illustrious Alfred von Schlieffen, whose sometime Plan to outflank and encircle the French already lay in ruins when the newcomer assumed his mantle though not his prestige, which still ran high at OHL. Falkenhayn's frontal assaults in the autumn of 1914 yielded little save casualties, the race to the sea, and four years of static trench warfare, and before the end of the year the bloody failure to break through the French and British lines at Ypres had brought him, here and there, the epithet of traitor. The memory of that autumn haunted him. His ill-wishers began to multiply.[9]

They included the Chancellor, Theobald von Bethmann-Hollweg, who suspected him of harboring aspirations to his own office in the Wilhelmstrasse in Berlin, and Foreign Minister Gottlieb von Jagow and others at the Foreign Ministry in the same street, who saw in the Balkans and the Middle East the crucial theaters of the war, and Crown Prince Rupprecht of Bavaria at the front, upon whose Sixth Army Falkenhayn had pinned his hopes at Ypres in the ill-fated operation of the autumn of 1914, and above all Generals Hindenburg and Ludendorff on the Eastern Front, whose local priorities and vocal appetites for annihilating Russia Falkenhayn did not share. Russia, he maintained, could be defeated at points, so weakened as to cease any offensive action for a while, but could always withdraw into her inner vastness rather than accept defeat and dishonor. He believed, too, that to deprive the Western Front of too many divisions would invite disaster there. And only *in extremis* would he concede to another enemy within, his ally and Austrian counterpart Conrad von Hötzendorf, that the Italian front deserved their most urgent attentions. Falkenhayn was a Westerner—he believed the war would be won or lost by their regiments in Flanders, in Picardie, on the Somme and, he later accepted, by their U-boats in the Atlantic. In this at least he was consistent.[10]

Time, he reminded his listeners, was not on Germany's side. This was 1915. How could Germany, lumbered with weak allies, ever outgun, outpace, or outlast two of the world's greatest land armies and its greatest fleet, with oceans and colonies behind them? To say nothing of the new army of millions that Great Britain was mobilizing as well and already shipping to the Channel ports and the Western Front? Germany had failed to defeat all three of them in 1914; she was unlikely to do so now or later. A strategic imperative began to drive Falkenhayn's ruminations: he must find a way to fracture the unity of the Entente.

Better yet would be to hive off one of its members, severing it by war and seducing it by diplomacy, and since late 1914 Russia had been his chosen candidate. He shifted his gaze eastwards dispassionately, moved by a sober ambition—to paralyze rather than annihilate the enemy. At least twice in 1915 success beyond all expectations crowned the German campaigns. But Falkenhayn struck each blow to bludgeon the belligerent Russian empire to the peace table, not to wipe her off the map. A peace of victory would follow, one whose terms others might negotiate but whose conclusion would free him to wage war on one front rather than two. On the other fronts he waited and held back. Italy entered the war in May 1915 and Austria found itself engaged on yet another mountainous front, but Falkenhayn held no illusion that the Entente could ever dissolve in the Alpine snows, even that Italy, with her capital 600 miles to the south, could ever lose the war there. In the West, between the sea and the Swiss border, he imposed on his armies an active and opportunistic defense, prudent yet strategic.[11]

The Russians would not play, however; their military calamities bred no disposition to a separate treaty, no willingness to break their word to the Entente and go their own way in return for peace. In June and again in August 1915, Czar Nicholas quashed such rumors. Just as decisively, Falkenhayn's own countrymen would not play either. Rather than make peace now, or make do with less in the east, Hindenburg and Ludendorff habitually aspired to encircle the withdrawing Russians in sweeps and wide pincers, beyond Gorlice and Tarnow, beyond Warsaw, beyond Vilna; they resented Falkenhayn's parsimony, his begrudging release of forces from the West, so much so that Hindenburg tried to have him removed from his position at OHL. From the Foreign Ministry came renewed plans for a war of annihilation against Russia and her ally Serbia. Falkenhayn retained the Kaiser's trust and stayed on. But by the end of the summer he had given up any thoughts, for now, of a separate peace with Russia.

At least Russia no longer posed any threat for quite a while, or so Falkenhayn thought. Britain did. She had connived in 1905, he believed, to inveigle his country into a war against China and Japan, and in 1911, during the second Moroccan crisis that had brought Germany to the brink of war with France, to isolate and encircle his country. England would follow her interests, Falkenhayn knew, and those interests lay with the Entente. History was repeating itself. A century earlier the same sea power had challenged a different continental hegemon, Napoleonic France; now England was once again at work, with her blockade, her diplomacy, her dispatch of expeditionary forces to the continent. This time the hegemon was Germany.

How could Falkenhayn strike back at England? Forge another European front, as Napoleon had? Several times in 1915 he talked of a league of European states, including neutrals, from the Baltic to the Aegean, a *mitteleuropäische* security and trading bloc. But Chancellor Bethmann-Hollweg, among others, showed no more enthusiasm for such projects than he did for a peace of understanding with Russia. They would not dissuade England, he objected. Wage another *guerre de course*, the kind of war once waged by privateers and corsairs against enemy shipping, with modern means? England would starve without control of the seas, but unrestricted submarine war, Falkenhayn argued to a largely hostile navy in the spring of 1915, would provoke the neutrals sooner than it would kill the prey, and Germany did not need any new enemies right now. As for defeating England on land, closer to home, he could not reach her at Dunkirk or Calais and still less force capitulation with another frontal assault on the treacherous terrain of Flanders. Then attack through Persia or on the Suez Canal, visionaries at the Foreign Ministry enjoined. Hints of blackmail came Falkenhayn's way, veiled threats to pin to his lapel yet another campaign lost, like that at Ypres in 1914, or lightly ruled out, like an all-out war in Russia the following year. Some of his closest collaborators resented the nonchalance with which he dismissed or accepted such weighty projects.[12] "All is casual!" Wild von Hohenborn, the Prussian Minister of War, complained in the autumn of 1915, after Falkenhayn had finally agreed to a German operation against Serbia—probably to please his new Bulgarian ally. "In the last analysis all in Falkenhayn is egotism—not even sacred." Placid and consistent, Falkenhayn held fast to his Western priorities, and above all to his fixation on the primal foe,

the imperial power that denied Germany her position in the world, Great
Britain. But he saw no way for now to lay her low, to detach her by a *coup
de force* from the Entente.[13]

That left France. Falkenhayn respected the country, admired its culture,
and spoke its language. Along with so many of his compatriots, he also
thought of France as a second-rate power, no military equal, a threat
chiefly as an ally of England. When the war broke out he had expected
her defeat. By 1915 this had not happened, but with Russia out of action
for now he turned his mind to finding the way.

Falkenhayn had wanted war in 1914. Nonetheless, he had not shared
the ambient optimism about its brevity. More than his compatriots, he
had taken the measure of the Entente, if not of France. Unlike Hindenburg and Ludendorff, or Jagow at the Foreign Ministry and Conrad in
Vienna, Falkenhayn in 1915 brooded over the finite realm of the possible. While they craved to annihilate and conquer, or imagined heady
imperialist vistas, he struggled to devise deliverance from the unyielding
strategic predicament of numbers and geography. Feasible victories, plausible goals—*realpolitik*, perhaps Bismarckian, attended his approach to
East and West, an abiding sense of limits, and the strategist who turned
his gaze to France and fixed it on Verdun was neither a visionary nor a
Moloch but a conservative, a realist, and above all a skeptic. In his strategic sobriety at least, the reflections Falkenhayn later claimed to have set
forth in the Christmas memorandum to the Kaiser had the consoling ring
of truth to them.[14]

"Falkenhayn is casting thoughtful glances at the west," the Minister of
War Wild von Hohenborn noted early in the summer of 1915. Falkenhayn had been casting glances all year, but at different points up and down
the front. In March and April he pondered the Somme, more especially a
line north of the river and around Amiens, where the French and British
armies met and whence he might push to the sea and sever one ally from
the other. But he soon gave that up, pressed by the operations that spring
and summer in the east and by doubts about disposing of adequate force
at the point of attack. In the summer and autumn he talked repeatedly
about Alsace, and in particular upper Alsace, the southern cornerstone of
the French front. He might expel the French from this parcel of prewar
German territory they still held on to, after Joffre's ill-fated offensive

into the province in August 1914, and from their own Belfort just to its south. Eventual peace talks might proceed more happily, he reflected. His advisors were dubious. An unsuccessful attack from the Black Forest, through the Vosges on one side and neutral Switzerland on the other, gave pause. And how could the capture of Belfort open the door to any offensive into France beyond? Falkenhayn considered the other options.[15]

Like Belfort, Verdun presented the advantages and disadvantages of a quiet sector, one enjoying the obscurity that indifference by now had come to bestow upon it. It presented no compelling strategic interest—unlike Amiens, Ypres, or the other northern nodal points of the threatening Entente coalition. Natural defenses and fixed, man-made fortifications had long deterred hostile inroads anyway. Yet Verdun could arrest the restless attentions of a high command always anxious to maximize surprise and minimize casualties. A well-executed attack there might pulverize the astonished garrison. Late in July, while still contemplating Upper Alsace, Falkenhayn began talking to his generals about Verdun and the *pays meusien*, the *Maasgebiet*, around it.[16]

"Verdun" formed a salient that protruded into the German front, held there by the Fifth Army, and from where they stood the generals could discern little more than wooded heights and the dim escarpments of forts cut into the living rock. The town itself lay hidden from their view, behind the same Côtes de Meuse and the belts of dense forest to the north that shrouded the approaches and kept invaders at bay. Beyond, to the west of the town, gentler hills, staggered in overlapping plateaus, descended slowly across Argonne and Champagne as far as the Marne valley and the wide basin that held the capital. A natural amphitheater of sorts, the survivor of the coastal cliffs and watery inlets of a distant geological age, protected Verdun, and presented from the air a tumultuous and troubled landscape, as though of some petrified inland sea.

To an attacker in 1915, the place looked as forbidding as ever, endowed with natural bulwarks that defenders had only to perfect. They had long done so. The Gauls had built a fortress, the Romans an *oppidum*, a protected village, the Bishop of Metz a chateau, the Marquis de Vauban a citadel for Louis XIV; now the military engineers of the Third Republic, led by Séré de Rivières, had buttressed the outlying hills with a curtain of concrete and armor. The largest of the new forts was also the highest, encrusted at almost 300 yards up atop the massif of Douaumont and commanding the Côtes de Meuse and the plain of Woëvre beyond. An attacker would have to advance across fire-swept plateaus or down enfiladed ravines, and fall each step of the way under the guns of defenders he might not even see, gathered behind their redoubts and within their woods. But the terrain, artfully approached, could bedevil the defenders as well. A weak and slow river, the Meuse, crossed the hollow from south to north, winding through a wide, deeply embanked bed of grassland and meadow that it flooded punctually every winter. Its sluggish but invasive presence cut the defenders' positions in two and threatened to play havoc with any elastic defense in depth. And the woods were neutral: those on the periphery, once in the hands of an attacker, could serve him just as well. Under their protective cover units could re-group, reinforcements could gather, sinister designs could germinate unseen. The ravines, too, could turn traitor. As they ran down to the Meuse they approached one another, seeming exemplars of the converging lines of attack that German tacticians had preached since the days of the elder Moltke. Verdun was not impregnable if the attacker could only find the way to turn the defender's assets into his own.[17]

During the invasion of 1914 Crown Prince Wilhelm, son and heir to the Kaiser, in command of the same Fifth Army that he would launch against Verdun in 1916, could not or would not attack the position directly. Instead, he and his generals avoided besieging the forts, stayed out of range of the forts' guns—except for one, the Fort de Troyon, which never fell and only held them up for several days—and maneuvered at a distance, hoping to envelop Verdun and mask it from the French Third Army to the south and east, heavily engaged in Lorraine. They were thinly stretched, and dangerously exposed as well after the German armies to their north and west retreated from the Marne in September. The Fifth Army pulled its pincers back from around Verdun, but still threatened it on three sides. Why not besiege the place and eliminate the salient, its commanders impatiently demanded to know that winter, led by the Crown Prince himself. Falkenhayn was tempted, and once appeared to yield. Wilhelm Groener, head of the railroads, ordered a new local line put in, just in case. In the end Falkenhayn had other priorities. Fighting for the heights north and south of the salient, at Vauquois in the Argonne and at Les Eparges on the Hauts de Meuse, continued through the spring of 1915, a savage war of mines and close-quarter combat that turned the hills into volcanoes and cost both sides more than 65,000 fatalities. Relative calm reigned inside the salient, at Verdun and within its forts.[18]

No abrupt change of heart or mind inspired Falkenhayn to reconsider Verdun late in 1915, no compelling revelation about its strategic or symbolic importance. It presented neither the weakest point on the French front, nor the gateway to the shortest route to Paris, nor the Entente's most active rail nexus, one whose seizure would choke off the movement of men and materiel.[19] French morale would suffer from its fall, but no more sharply than from losing again what they had recaptured and still held of Alsace, the emotive plot of land that Falkenhayn eyed until late in the day. He only gradually resolved to strike Verdun, and even then never stopped looking beyond it, to a renewed war of movement on the Western Front that might compel the enemy to renounce victory and seek a political settlement.

After the war, some of Falkenhayn's intimate yet distant contemporaries recalled that he had never conceived of Verdun as an end in itself, still less of the assault as a self-sufficient operation that would end the war. It was a *Teilstück*, a fragment of a longer script. Count von Schulenburg, at first a staff officer and later General Staff chief in the Fifth Army, looked back upon Falkenhayn as upon a chess master thinking several moves ahead: to defend Verdun the French would have to weaken their fronts in Aisne or Champagne, to support their allies the British would hastily improvise a relief offensive in Artois, whereupon waiting and rested German reserves would attack one enemy and counterattack the other, exploiting the exhaustion of the first and the inexperience of the second. In the mind of General Groener, the railway chief, Falkenhayn had indeed intended to take Verdun, but only in order to attack again in Artois or Champagne. Colonel von Tappen, chief of operations at OHL, agreed, and remembered as well that when Falkenhayn was still considering Upper Alsace or Belfort, in the summer and autumn of 1915, he spoke in similar terms. He would attack from the Black Forest, for example, with five or six divisions— almost as many as he would soon envision for Verdun—in order to draw off enemy forces and veil his offensive plans elsewhere on the front.

At the beginning of December, when Belfort still seemed a candidate, Falkenhayn met the Kaiser at OHL headquarters in Pless, the medieval Polish castle in Upper Silesia, and held out the prospect of ending the war in 1916 by limited offensives which would provoke the Entente into futile attacks of its own. Many years later, exiled in Holland and bereft of his crown, the Kaiser recalled the project for Verdun that Falkenhayn had presented to him ten days or so later, in his saloon carriage in a journey east to Vilna around mid-December. Its premises were much the same. They must bring the French to attack, they must expect and counterattack a British relief offensive, they must wrest the decision in the West in 1916. "The hope persisted," the Kaiser remembered, "to break up the English front." Verdun was to be a violent prelude.[20]

For weeks after the die was cast and the Kaiser had given his assent to the assault at Verdun, Falkenhayn was still talking about attacks and counterattacks elsewhere on the front, especially in the British sector. Early in the New Year of 1916 he told Hermann von Kuhl, the chief of staff of the Sixth Army that stood facing the English in Artois, to expect attacks once the operations at Verdun were under way. "Through the combination of Verdun and Artois," Kuhl recalled, "he hoped to reach a decision without a great breakthrough battle." Later that January Falkenhayn declined requests from the Fifth Army for more divisions at Verdun. They would need them for the coming offensive, the army's commanders insisted. The Sixth Army would need them soon against the British in Artois, he replied. The army command objected that the English would not attack until they were ready to do so. Falkenhayn remained obdurate. With Verdun under attack, he wrote, "the English could not in this situation leave France in the lurch." Something similar might happen in Champagne. What forces did he have to meet a French relief attack around Vitry-le-François, he asked the commander-in-chief of the Third Army, General Karl von Einem, early in February. Neither army was to move first; each was to wait. He would not hear of sending them precious reserve divisions now to seize the initiative and attack first, as the commanders and staff officers of each army preferred. The Third might do so once the danger at Verdun forced the French to weaken their front in Champagne, but not yet. Groener had no doubt: he noted on 11th February, the original eve of the attack on Verdun that was scuttled by weather the next day, that Falkenhayn thought of the operation as the first step—no more—to a decision in the West. The same day Falkenhayn again told Kuhl to expect the English to attack in the spring. "He hopes," Kuhl reported to his commanding officer, Prince Rupprecht, "that movement will return to the war as a result of the Verdun operation."[21]

At the meeting on the 11th Falkenhayn expounded his thinking about Verdun more clearly than ever before or since. He had just returned from Pless, and had summoned the chiefs of staff of every army on the Western Front, except General Konstantin Schmidt von Knobelsdorf of the Fifth, to meet him at his headquarters in Mézières. Three of them later recalled his words. He insisted that they could win only in the West, but not by some major breakthrough battle—the enemy's own experience of those was cautionary enough. They would attack Verdun with relatively modest forces. "Whether the fortress itself fell, was an open question. The essential point was to force the French to believe that a great danger threatened there." They would weaken or denude other parts of their front to defend Verdun, or they or the English would counterattack, unwilling and unprepared—in Artois, Champagne, Woëvre, or Upper Alsace. Whatever happened, the enemy would suffer heavy losses. "Then we could attack." Verdun was a preliminary operation. Nothing else can explain Falkenhayn's inveterate parsimony there, nothing else his perennial aversion to parting with his reserves before and even during the battle.[22]

Nothing, if not his belated claim to have aspired solely to bleed the French army white and spare the blood of his own. The Christmas Memorandum had little to say about the *Teilsstück*, the ancillary place of Verdun in the chain reaction of attacks and counterattacks elsewhere on the front, and much about the *Ausblutung*, the attrition that was supposed finally to consume the French army.[23] Yet he had been expansive about the first and almost silent about the second at the very time he was supposed to have composed his memorandum. As given to posterity in his memoir, the memorandum is at odds with the recollections of his contemporaries. So neat an inversion of the historical record vindicates the skeptics and the disbelievers, and begs for explanation.

Before the offensive, Groener, Kuhl, and Tappen later recalled, there had been little talk of *Ausblutung*. Tappen could not remember any discussion either of the *Saugpumpe*, the metaphorical suction pump that Falkenhayn claimed to have conceived, a diabolical device to draw the French into the hellfires of Verdun more or less at will, at variable speeds of his own choosing. He had unearthed this as well in the Christmas Memorandum, but no one could remember much about it from the time.[24]

After the war most took him at his word and some saluted his attempt to find a creative new way to end the war, even though it had come to grief on the battlefields of the Meuse. Nothing had worked for anyone in the West. In the summer of 1914 Moltke, as Chief of OHL, had failed to envelop the French armies; in the autumn Falkenhayn, as his successor, had failed to break through them; the following year the French had failed in their turn at the same, in Artois and Champagne. At Verdun, to believe Falkenhayn's own postwar account, he resolved neither to envelop nor to break through but to bleed the French army, a doctrine that struck some of the historians of the interwar years as unprecedented in military history. Yet the idea of slowly sapping the enemy's will in a war of exhaustion, an *Ermattungskrieg*, was unexceptional. In Germany alone, its potential had preoccupied Clausewitz, troubled the elder Moltke in his later years as chief of the General Staff in the 1870s and 1880s, instilled doubts in his greatest successor, von Schlieffen, about his own plan for a swift battle of encirclement and destruction. Hans Delbrück, the military historian, had scandalized the General Staff before the war by arguing that such designs had inspired the campaigns of Frederick the Great.

Attrition was a tactic, one that initially promised only to save friendly lives and spend hostile ones, but, suitably magnified, one that might aspire to the status of a strategy. At times, in the Great War, it promised to become an end as well as a means. In 1915 General Sir Henry Rawlinson, commanding officer of the Fourth British Army, had begun issuing injunctions to "bite and hold," to seize a parcel of land, no more, from the enemy, build up the defensive position, and await the response. The ploy rested on two postulates that practice more often than not would invalidate—that the enemy, once expelled, would axiomatically seek to return, and that his losses when he did so would greatly exceed those of the defenders. But after the massacres that had shut down movement and maneuver, after the abortive envelopments and failed breakthroughs, attrition seemed, if not an immediate way out of the impasse of 1915, then at least a way to turn it to one's advantage. In France, the same year, a little-known General Pétain had favored the idea as well. Why should not Falkenhayn invoke the same option as he considered Germany's prospects in the West in 1916?[25]

The elastic concept of war of exhaustion—*Ermattungskrieg* or *Erschöpfungskrieg*—drifted in and out of German deliberations about the Western Front throughout 1915. Usually it meant letting the enemy consume himself in costly yet fruitless local offensives, the same attritional calculus at play in Rawlinson's "bite and hold." It meant wearing the enemy down, as Minister of War von Hohenborn wrote his wife in the spring of that year, and making him suffer more than the Germans. Von Hohenborn hoped for more actions like that at Neuve Chapelle in March, when the British attacked the German lines and lost, so Wild believed, 700 officers. Over time such unsustainable losses could decide the war. As for the French, he approved all that they had been doing in the West until then: "We have had to stay still and let the French wear themselves out." But this was a passive strategy, suited to a season when the Germans were mounting large offensives in the East. More active variants sprang to mind, including accelerated exhaustion. When Falkenhayn met the Kaiser at Pless early in December and proposed ending the war in 1916 by partial offensives that would provoke the Entente to counterattacks, he envisioned it would "thereby bleed itself to death," the phrase that would later surface in the Christmas Memorandum he would reveal to the world in 1920. Now, at Pless, he was still thinking of Belfort. The general idea was to provoke the Entente to exhaust itself in the West with a renewed war of movement. It was no more precise than that. It might mean no more than extinguishing the enemy's faith in victory. By the middle of the month Falkenhayn had replaced Belfort with Verdun.[26]

Around the same time he changed his mind about waging a new and categorical form of *Ermattungskrieg*: unrestricted submarine war. He now favored it. Earlier in 1915, when U-boats had sent the *Lusitania* and then the *Arabic* to the bottom along with many of their passengers, he had glanced anxiously at the wavering neutrals—in the Balkans, and most especially across the Atlantic—and urged restraint upon the Navy. Now, in mid-December, he jettisoned his inhibitions. Italy had joined the Entente, Bulgaria had joined the Central Powers, and the American threat, if serious, was remote. The time had come, he argued then and again in January, to scorn the humor of the remaining neutrals and use the weapon of last resort against England. The Admirals guaranteed the success of unrestricted submarine warfare. It would break English resistance within six or eight months, they assured him.[27]

In fact, Falkenhayn had long yearned to challenge England. He had never shared the Admiralty's prewar reluctance, if only because the confrontation, in his eyes, was inevitable. He had said so in 1907 and he said so again now, just as he conceived and planned the attack on Verdun.

Whether at sea or on land, he sought to wear out the Entente and force it to the table, rather than destroy it and dictate peace terms at will, both wild hopes. And desperation at sea might provoke rashness on land. To foil the newly unleashed U-boats the English might overreach and try to capture the ports along the Belgian coast from which they set forth. The German offensive under the waves, like that in the hills around Verdun, might provoke the improvised attacks that Falkenhayn hoped to repel with such finality. They were linked in his mind—complementary components of the same strategy. "We are all agreed that England will fight until a decision," he told an emissary from Admiral Alfred von Tirpitz just as the artillery of the Fifth Army was first scheduled to bombard Verdun. "I have made up my mind in favor of the U-boat war and am counting heavily upon its prosecution. I will throw my weight behind it and I will prevail."[28]

The big guns at Verdun, like the U-boats in the Atlantic, would hasten *Ermattung* by active means. Breaking through was not possible: not on this front, in this war, and with such inferior means. With a superiority of over a million men in the West, to say nothing of materiel and munitions, the English and French had failed to break through in 1915. They had come closest in Champagne in September, when General von Einem, who received the brunt of the attack, had been on the verge of giving up and ordering his Third Army to retreat. Falkenhayn had hurriedly brought two army corps from the Eastern Front, allowing Einem to hold. Stalemate had set in again. Eighteen French attacking divisions had been unable to get beyond the first of two lines of the German defenses, held by only seven defending ones, and the General Staff chief who now committed only eight to the attack on Verdun could not expect them to open much of a breach in the enemy front there. And even if they did, how would they exploit it? Since the summer of 1914 the Germans had held the plateau that dominated Soissons, a mere 60 miles from Paris. They were still there. Would a narrow breakthrough almost 200 miles away bring them any closer?[29]

No, but the French might react in three ways to an assault on Verdun, Falkenhayn told the assembled chiefs of staff of the Western armies early in February. They might withdraw, they might resist, or they might attack elsewhere on the front. The first he thought the least desirable, as it would spare the French bloody and vain assaults to retake the town or the forts around it. The second he thought the most likely. The third he thought the most desirable, as it opened the way to the renewed war of movement and the prepared counterattacks he so ardently wished to execute.[30] Each helped, each nourished the wider hope: the French, he believed, were on the verge of exhaustion anyway. Such varied prognostications only threw sand in the eyes of the generals and staff officers around him, keeping them from grasping their superior's designs. Years later they struggled to agree upon his immediate objective at Verdun. To take the town, the chief of staff of the Fifth Army, General von Knobelsdorf, thought. To ensnare the French army, his chief of operations, Colonel von Tappen, insisted on one occasion, only to contradict himself on another. Others were not sure. Was Falkenhayn himself? He did not help matters by speaking only of "attacks in the Meuse region in the direction of Verdun." Groener finally reproached him for his inconstancy, his wishful adoption of one scenario after another. But one man's fickleness is another's respect for contingency. Falkenhayn had no sole expectation at Verdun, only preferred outcomes that would accelerate the ultimate outcome: the exhaustion of the Western allies in 1916.[31]

In the middle of December 1915 he asked the Crown Prince and Knobelsdorf to draw up plans for Operation *Gericht*, the attack at Verdun. The code name—"judgment," more or less—reflected its Delphic author, who continued to dissemble his full designs from all who might expect to share in them. On the 7th of January Falkenhayn wrote to Chancellor Bethmann-Hollweg that he had not decided to launch a major offensive in the West. But if he did, he added, no one should expect that it would end the war, only that it would shake up the scene in France. On the 22nd of February, the day after *Gericht* began, the Bavarian emissary to the Kaiser's Headquarters explained to his minister that they were not to speak of an "attack on Verdun." He did not know why. Perhaps OHL wished to head off any dismay should they fail to take Verdun, he surmised. Or perhaps Verdun was not their true objective in the first place.[32]

"I will prevail," Falkenhayn had told Tirpitz's aide. As it happened, he did not prevail: the Kaiser did not authorize unrestricted submarine warfare, the English did not attack elsewhere, and Verdun did not fall. However, the French did defend it, and at great cost. This Falkenhayn contrived to elevate after the war, most famously in the Christmas Memorandum, into his *sine quis nihil*, his overriding objective, and he enlisted in the cause figures that grossly exaggerated the ratio of French to German losses but that few could contest in 1920. Memoirists usually record more diligently their predictions made good by events than those that history invalidates, and Falkenhayn dwelt more expansively upon the single expectation that might pass for prophetic rather than delusional. Mention of *Ausblutung* had rarely passed his lips until the battle was several weeks old and none of his fondly imagined English or French counterattacks elsewhere on the front had materialized. Was *Ausblutung* a possibility or a plan? Falkenhayn's contemporaries confused the first with the second when they trusted his recollection and labored to reconcile it with their own, or discovered in it the culprit for their failure to take Verdun. The Christmas Memorandum's apologia for *Ausblutung*, appearing belatedly in memoirs composed apparently without original sources at hand, bears all the marks of contrivance and none of authenticity.[33]

Yet the full memorandum, whether it sprang from memory or imagination, recalls convincingly enough the acts and utterances of a commander who harbored no Napoleonic expectations. When Falkenhayn published it, historian Hans Delbrück attached him to the tradition personified by Pericles, Hannibal, Gustavus Adolphus, Marlborough, Eugen, Frederick, and Wellington: distinguished by patience and defined by the extended erosion of the adversary's staying power. In 1916 Falkenhayn, too, set out to suppress his enemies' will, not their existence, but Delbrück failed to notice that unlike his illustrious predecessors he pretended to precipitate rather than draw out events, to hurry an enemy whom he declined to await any longer. For all his realism, Falkenhayn shared the besetting sin of domestic rivals and foreign foes, all would-be masters of the unbridled conflict: their hubris. No battle punctured his illusions more violently, or assured his downfall more inexorably, than the battle of Verdun.[34]

Falkenhayn had tried to push the pace in the West in 1916, but so had his predecessor and so would his successors. In 1914 von Moltke had tried to envelop and destroy the French armies before Russia could fully mobilize. In 1918 Ludendorff would try to break through the front in five offensives before the Americans could overwhelm the balance. Falkenhayn was not acting so differently when, in 1916, he tried to force the issue before England became strong enough to do the same. At Verdun he hoped to damage France in some manner so irretrievably that England would give battle before she was ready, or even lose heart altogether. It marked yet another ploy by a power confident of its superiority today but anxious about its inferiority tomorrow, a sentiment of urgency and a presentiment of doom entirely consistent with the way the Wilhelmine Reich fought the war and even with the way she had entered it.

No single vision of how Verdun would develop concentrated Falkenhayn's mind. But his alternative futures there were no hazier than those that lay beyond the six weeks of the Schlieffen "plan" in the mind of its author of 1905 or its executor of 1914. Or any less distinct than those discernible in Ludendorff's words before launching Germany's last offensives of the war, Operation Michael and its increasingly desperate successors in the spring of 1918: "We will punch a hole into [their line]. For the rest, we shall see. We also did it this way in Russia!" A common compulsion to win in the West before it was too late drove such gambles, notably bereft of any center of gravity, any strategic plan. In the end the logic of the war explains more than the idiosyncrasies of the men. Falkenhayn had underestimated the French, as he later admitted. But this, too, partook of shared habit. "The English army at the moment is not capable of operating in the field," Ludendorff assured his listeners at the time of Operation Michael, only to admit after the war that he also had underestimated his adversaries.[35]

When Falkenhayn later claimed that he had intended solely at Verdun to bleed the French white, a heretical pretension that would indeed set him apart from his compatriots and that would damn him in the eyes of posterity, he sounded as implausible as Douglas Haig, commander of the British Expeditionary Force, who contended after the Somme in 1916 and after Passchendaele in 1917 that attrition had been his lone objective as well. He had a more glorious exemplar than Haig. "We engage everywhere and then we see," Napoleon had said, suggesting Falkenhayn's own game of shaking the tree at Verdun and then waiting to see where the fruit would drop. But after another occasion, after a narrowly averted disaster at Marengo in 1800, Bonaparte had also contrived to convince contemporaries and much of posterity that he had planned all there that day, including his near rout at the hands of the Austrians and his rescue in extremis by General Desaix. Falkenhayn, before and after Verdun, had been no less creative.[36]

At first, in February and early March, military specialists in the German papers could only unwittingly give vent to Falkenhayn's Byzantine ways of thinking. Perhaps the action on the Meuse was diversionary, they speculated; perhaps the high command would shortly divulge other objectives elsewhere on the front, or keep the enemy guessing—along with themselves. No one yet mentioned *Ausblutung*—not yet; enemy losses indeed exceeded their own, it seemed, but the members of the press had no motive to divine Falkenhayn's later elevation of attrition into the sole and self-sufficient raison d'être of the operation. The fort of Douaumont fell on the 25th, and others might soon, and to ascribe such dull designs to such dazzling feats would have seemed gratuitous, even contradictory.[37]

When forward movement came to a halt at Verdun, and the town and all but its most famous fort stood in French hands for all to see, the German press began to elevate French casualties into a self-sufficient goal. Even before then, the papers had envisaged that the French would incur heavy losses simply to keep the Germans away from the forts that protected Verdun. They reflected, too, that their superior German firepower would save the lives of their infantrymen. These were only collateral gains. But early in March the military specialist of the *Berliner Tageblatt* placed them more squarely at the center of informed strategy. He reminded his readers in one article that the destruction of enemy forces, as every General Staff officer knew, and not the conquest of forts constituted the object of war in itself. In another he observed as though addressing French readers that "while the blood of France flows that of England only drops." Ten days later the impasse at Verdun inspired new heights of abstraction. In the *Münchner neueste Nachrichten* General von Blume acknowledged doubts about the goal of the attack on Verdun. Had they sought a decisive outcome at all? He heard his readers ask. The goal, he answered, was not the conquest of the mighty fortified ensemble, but the "defeat of the substantial forces that the enemy has committed to its defense, and which they will unfailingly continue to reinforce." Only the word *Ausblutung* was missing, the word Falkenhayn himself would endow with such notoriety when he launched it in print immediately after the war.[38]

Meanwhile French military correspondents, still perplexed by the assault on Verdun, searched for a point of reference, for some earlier battle that might explain the eruption of this one. It was the biggest battle since Charleroi, one of them thought, even though he still hesitated to define German intentions; perhaps since the Marne, according to another one. More often, the first battle of Ypres came to their minds, when Falkenhayn, in late October and early November 1914, had attempted to break through the nascent Allied front in Flanders—they called it still the battle of the Yser, after the canal that had turned the fields into swampland when the Belgians opened its locks. They might have named this one the Battle of the Meuse. The parallel still did not explain much.[39]

In the years and decades that began during the First World War, and before and after the Second, schoolchildren as well as grown readers of popular histories read that the Germans had intended at Verdun to do away with an intolerable obstacle that had paralyzed their offensive in 1914, to sever the French armies of the east from those in the north, to secure a base for a march on Paris, to gild the reputation of the Crown Prince, to capture a whole French army by cutting it off, to deny access to the rich mining region of Briey, to capture again a proud warlike city that the Prussians had entered in 1792 and the Saxons in 1870.[40] The myth of the past that pulled, of German strategy driven by historical obsession, jostled its competitors. Their national imagination had been riveted on the place since the partition of Charlemagne's empire there in 843, a French commentator explained immediately after the war. Nothing could have inspired Falkenhayn, the Crown Prince, or Knobelsdorf less.[41]

But in 1920 French authors had picked up Falkenhayn's own version as well. No one saw anything excessive in adding another motive to all the others for the climactic assault on Verdun. That year the historian Gabriel Hanotaux, in his guide to the French battlefields, attributed every conceivable intention to the Germans at Verdun, and adopted unquestioningly that of *Ausblutung*, turned on and off at will, from Falkenhayn's article of the year before. General Malletterre, in the popular account he published in 1921, did much the same, invoking the Christmas Memorandum now that Falkenhayn had published it. In 1935 Albert Malet and Jules Isaac excised chauvinism from their remarkable school textbook and treated Verdun as a symbol of the horror of modern war, and employed Falkenhayn's sinister words to do so. The monstrosity of the German design vanished from the school texts authorized by the Vichy regime, though the theme returned durably after its demise. A kind of military vampirism became a leitmotif of Verdun, the threat the French *poilus* had foiled. In February 1966, on the occasion of the 50th anniversary, *Le Monde* published two articles by a historian of note and called the first of them "Pour saigner à blanc l'armée française" ("To Bleed White the French Army"). It used the phrase again in its own editorial; so did the

French minister of veterans.[42] Falkenhayn's confession only demonized him as the Moloch and magnified the defenders' ordeal.

Very occasionally, some challenged the leitmotiv. Pétain's memoir of 1929 challenged Falkenhayn's of 1920. The chief of the German General Staff had grander and worthier goals than bleeding the French army at Verdun, Pétain insisted, correctly. However, he wrongly imputed instead to Falkenhayn the ambition of encircling the French army at Verdun in a decisive *coup de filet*, a new Sedan, where, in 1870, the Prussians had trapped the French army as well as its emperor, Napoleon III. In time Charles de Gaulle appeared to agree with the general under whom he had served at Verdun and to whom he had dedicated *Le Fil de l'épée* (*The Edge of the Sword*) 16 years later. In his speech before the ossuary at Douaumont on Pentecost day 1966, the first president of the Fifth Republic dwelt at length upon the German objectives at Verdun. He did not mention that of bleeding the French white, *pace* the declarations of his minister of veterans three months earlier. The Germans, he said, had wished strategically to rupture the French front, tactically to use their heavy artillery, and symbolically to wreak revenge for the Marne by conquering "a spot known forever as the rampart of France." No one noted the omission. Thirty years later, during the 1990s, professional historians began to dismantle Falkenhayn's pretense among one another. A decade after that they shared their doubts. In 2008 the authors of a Franco-German history of the war, suitable for a wide and interested public, pronounced Falkenhayn's Christmas Memorandum a forgery and the goal of *Ausblutung* a transparent excuse for his failed offensive. That year school texts began to tell a different story as well. "To account for his failure," the *Manuel d'histoire franco-allemande* explained to French students in 1ère (12th grade) in 2008–2009, "[Falkenhayn] claimed to have wanted to bleed the French army white." On both sides of the border, a history closer to the truth was beginning to percolate into society.[43]

Yet, during the same autumn of 2008, a Franco-German film made two years earlier and rebroadcast on French television described Falkenhayn as a "sanguinary monster" convinced that his attack would bring him "certain victory."[44] The legend of *Ausblutung* died hard, a tale more fetching than the reality: that Verdun had germinated in his mind as a secondary affair, ancillary to the wider developments that he fondly envisaged would bring the war to an end.

3

Verdun under French Eyes

VERDUN HAD SAVED NOT ONLY FRANCE BUT ALL HUMANITY, David Lloyd George, the British Prime Minister, declared among its ruins. And years later, in 1930, a French officer who had taken part recalled February 21, 1916, as "the tomb of the hegemony that Germany sought over the universe." In such retellings Verdun had been the great existential battle of the war, perhaps of all wars. But Falkenhayn never endowed it with such standing. Nor, at first, did published opinion in his intended victim, France. Nor, more surprisingly, did Joseph Joffre, chief of the French General Staff. Verdun began and remained for him, as for his German counterpart, ancillary to his grand strategy, a secondary affair. His countrymen transfigured it, helped along by Falkenhayn's obligingly sinister rendition, and made of it in the light of legend "the most terrible battle the world has ever known."[1]

Falkenhayn's counterpart at the head of the French General Staff was as different from him as night from day. Joffre was a man of few words and fewer ideas. He pondered rather than imagined the possibilities, projected confidence rather than creativity, and set a steadfast course that banished the clutter of contingency from his presence. No maps or documents crowded his desk at the General Headquarters at Chantilly, unless photographers from the press were calling, and aides who promoted their ideas too vigorously irritated him no end. He had come from peasant origins and risen through the engineering corps, and personified the citizen-soldier, neither destined by birth nor favored by genius to wear the laurels of the land. This son of a barrel-maker cared little for protocol; when the Duke of Connaught, Governor-General of Canada and third son of Queen Victoria, came to lunch at Chantilly to bestow decorations on His Majesty's behalf, Joffre told him to sit where he liked.

47

Falkenhayn, articulate and inventive, scion of a social caste that celebrated the warrior's calling, could attribute the precocity of his promotions and the favors of the Kaiser to his talents and his origins, and
always, even when aggrieved, observed all the formality that his milieu
demanded. Joffre ate prodigiously and never allowed the alarms of war to
disrupt his appetite or interrupt his sleep, even when the Germans neared
Paris in August 1914. Or when they attacked Verdun in February 1916. At
such moments Falkenhayn, who ate little and drank moderately, would
leave the table early and work late into the night. And the two looked different: one was corpulent, the other sleek. Joffre complained bitterly one
Good Friday when meat disappeared from the lunch menu at Chantilly.
"I am a Republican general," he exclaimed, as though to bring ideology to
the rescue of gastronomy, and had the vital item reinstated.[2]

Unlike Falkenhayn, Joffre was popular, so popular that his critics could
not touch him, not for now. He was "le grand-père" ("the grandfather"),
the unruffled sexagenarian whose sangfroid had saved the country, most
obviously in September on the Marne as the Germans neared Paris, less
obviously since then but no matter: the legend, at the beginning of 1916,
still moved millions even as it piqued a few highly placed detractors. The
tributes of the humble flowed into Chantilly from all over the country—
regional delicacies, sweets, poems, offers of marriage, cigars, paintings,
national adulation that his allies in the Entente matched with displays of
deference.

No such satisfactions gladdened Falkenhayn. He had stymied all the
Allied attempts at breakthrough in the West, broken through the Russian
front in the east, overrun Serbia, but no acclaim came his way, nothing
that outshone the glow around Hindenburg and Ludendorff ever since
their overwhelming victory against the Russians at Tannenberg in 1914.
But he had the Kaiser, whose esteem mattered infinitely more to him than
the infatuations of the *profanum vulgus*. Joffre could bank on the people
of a liberal republic, Falkenhayn on the monarch of an authoritarian
empire; each rested his security upon the locus of sovereignty; and each
would see it fatally undermined by the battle of Verdun.[3]

For over a year Joffre had been waging a war of partial offensives.
During the first winter of the war, before the army could recover from
the summer and autumn carnage, he had begun a fruitless and bloody
search for local breakthroughs. Sometimes they failed altogether, as in

Artois in May and June of 1915; sometimes they overran the enemy's front lines along several miles, as in Champagne in September, only to encounter him in strength farther back and lose all forward movement once again; sometimes they took a ridge, as at Hartmannswillerkopf in Alsace in December, only to lose it the next day. "I am nibbling at them," Joffre said, but the critics began to stir. They thought the scope of the offensives too narrow, or their frequency too limited, or their execution too flawed. On the eve of Verdun voices in the press and the parliament were rising. They demanded action, innovation, an end to stagnation. Even positional warfare, the combative former Prime Minister Georges Clemenceau complained, called for imagination. Prudence was all very well, *L'Oeuvre* granted, but by now France, "the fatherland of initiative" stagnated under the sway of the aged. No one challenged the wisdom of the offensive imperative or the conventional fixation on breakthrough; no one, except General Pétain, but he as yet had little influence.[4]

Like Falkenhayn, Joffre wanted to restore mobility to the battlefields of the Western Front. And like Falkenhayn, and many of his corps and army commanders, he had concluded by the end of 1915 that no single break-through, however deep, would do so. The opposing generals had concluded that only successive or simultaneous operations would allow the strategic exploitation of tactical successes that had eluded them until now; only the progressive disintegration of the front, deliberately undertaken and methodically carried out, would bring the enemy to decisive battle in open country. But unlike Falkenhyan, set to part strategic ways from his resentful and demanding Austrian ally Conrad von Hötzendorff, Joffre viewed his war as the Entente's war and was determined to orchestrate the moves of each partner. He no longer set any store by some solitary, chimerical French victory, no longer believed the Allies could wage separate wars and launch separate offensives as they had in 1915. They must concert from afar. Since 1914 the outnumbered Germans had made the most of the interior lines that geographical cohesion bestowed, and they had freely shuttled divisions in a matter of days from quiet to active fronts, from west to east in the spring, from east to west in the autumn, wherever necessity called. This, too, had to stop. The Allies must turn the enemy's advantage against him, and attack concentrically and simultaneously on all his fronts.[5]

They agreed as much at Chantilly in December. But when and where? A wide breakthrough on the Western Front—25 miles wide, enough to resonate all along the enemy front—would require an estimated ready supply of 5 million heavy artillery shells; at the beginning of 1916 the French were making about 400,000 a month. It would also require allied offensives elsewhere before and during the action, above all on the Russian front, perhaps in the Balkans and the Alps as well. By the 18th of February Joffre and Douglas Haig, Commander of the British Expeditionary Force (BEF), had agreed to linked attacks north and south of the Somme, but not before June and July when the weather would allow what the numbers would promise—success in battle—and when the Russians would have recovered from their staggering losses of the year before. Between now and then, the British, Joffre thought, could carry out several large attritional attacks that would consume German reserves, much as Falkenhayn contemplated at the same moment using up French reserves at Verdun or elsewhere. Haig demurred at this. But, at one with Joffre in cultivating strategic patience, he also grasped that operations of the scope they envisaged demanded production, preparation, and time. So much had changed since the heady enthusiasms of August 1914.[6]

What if the Germans struck first? They might try late in that winter of 1916 to knock the Russians out of action once and for all. Then, Joffre and his staff reasoned, the Franco-British offensive would come sooner, perhaps in the second half of April. What if the enemy attacked in the West, to disrupt the Allied offensives there before they left the minds of their planners? Ponderous preparation made for poor surprise, and no offensive there, on that scale and in this war, remained secret for long. Then the German attack would come from inferior strength, and the Allies in the Entente would contain it and counterattack. "That development," Joffre told the government and his allies at the end of January, "would thus be entirely favorable to us and we can only hope it will come to pass."[7]

As though to fulfill his wishes, the German Fifth Army attacked Verdun less than a month later. Intimations of such a move had been coming in for weeks, even before Joffre issued his confident prediction. From French embassies in neutral countries, the crossroads of intelligence traffic of all sorts, came reports of impending German offensives in the West. From Bern, Bucharest, Stockholm, and Copenhagen came persistent, often contradictory rumors throughout January of German preparations for an attack—in the Verdun region, but also elsewhere, in Flanders, near Arras, perhaps. Some 75,000 Turkish soldiers had been sighted near Verdun; Bulgars as well. Meanwhile German units had left to attack the Suez Canal. Yet the Germans were determined to end the war soon, and to do so in the West, this according to an American diplomat in Berlin—what to believe, whom to heed?

At the end of January Danish intelligence services pointed to a likely offensive at Verdun in a month's time. Soon movements of troop trains suggested much the same. From early February long trains began rolling through southern Germany along axes that converged on the front in Lorraine. French prisoners working in Heidelberg watched 100 of them go by on the 4th alone, loaded with troops fresh from a successful campaign in Serbia. Ten days later the trains still rolled on.[8]

By then the French could rely upon their eyes and ears at Verdun itself. The dense forests north of the town hid the enemy's preparations, and arduous efforts at camouflage and deception, above all the absence of any attack or jumping-off trenches ahead of the first lines, deprived the waiting French of the kinds of omens that had blessed the Germans with a measure of clairvoyance about their enemy's intentions in Champagne in September. But telephone listeners brought intercepts, and soldiers in the woods could hear distant mines detonate, explosions that betrayed heavy works in progress, and observers could hardly overlook the destruction of church spires, the kind that their artillery used as reference points and range-finders. When the skies cleared and the planes got through, an occasional aerial photo revealed as well new dugout entrances and a widening arc of troops and munitions depots stretching all the way from Argonne to Woëvre. And prisoners, refugees, and deserters, the unwilling conscripts from Poland, Alsace, or other uncertain parts of the German empire, told tales—of pioneers building fortifications above ground and shelters deep below the front lines, of heavy artillery pieces unlimbered and shells and mortars piled high, of leaves canceled and mail stopped, of hospitals in Metz emptied "because," as a deserter from Lorraine warned, "something terrible is going to happen."[9]

Ever since 1914 Joffre had shown little interest in Verdun, other than to deprive it of men and materiel he wished to employ elsewhere. In 1914, as the French and British were counterattacking on the Marne, he had issued orders to leave the place to its own devices, which General

Maurice Sarrail, in command of the Third Army, had obeyed only selectively. But enough of the Third Army had pulled back from Verdun to leave the town and the surrounding forts exposed, their garrisons at the mercy of a German attack. It did not come, not in anything like its later fury, but so Verdun remained, a quiet salient on the Western Front after the Battle of the Marne, threatened on three sides by the army of Crown Prince Wilhelm. Joffre and his staff did not trouble to strengthen the defenses there. In fact, they further weakened them. In August 1914 the great fortresses at Liège and Namur in Belgium had fallen, however heroic their defense, and German howitzers had reduced much of the fort of Manonvillers in Lorraine to rubble within two days. Joffre and the "Young Turks" proclaiming their modernity around him in the Operations Section at Chantilly dismissed the forts around Verdun as obsolete hulks in the new age of trenches and heavy artillery. In August 1915 they reduced the garrisons and removed most of the guns from them, and integrated the entire "place forte," like others in France, into the armies in the field. Siege warfare was passé. They forbade any commander there to allow the enemy to trap or confine him inside the town, its old citadel, or the surrounding forts.[10]

Later that month Joffre began withdrawing infantry from the newly renamed Fortified Region of Verdun for the attack in Champagne in September. Some of them returned in October, but the defenses in the Region began to look so feeble that voices rose in alarm. By the end of 1915 most of the 1,000 artillery pieces in place at the beginning of the war had gone, and with less than 80,000 men left, only two could defend every three meters of the 75-mile perimeter. How could such thin lines, without artillery cover, resist any concentrated enemy attack? How could they even build new ones in time?[11] General Frédéric Herr, in command of the Region, protested to no avail. More dangerously for Joffre, the Chamber of Deputies began to meddle. Its Army Commission sent its own delegates to Verdun to investigate. An officer there had informed against his own army, and no ordinary officer—the right-wing Colonel Emile Driant, sitting deputy from Nancy, in command of a Brigade of Chasseurs Alpins at Verdun and son-in-law of the famed nationalist general Georges Boulanger, had bypassed his superiors to rouse the government to action. Only later did he see Joffre. The defenses left Verdun at the mercy of an *attaque brusquée*, a sudden surprise attack, Driant warned, and the parliamentary investigators agreed. Concern spread to the cabinet. "The matter is serious," Joseph Galliéni, the Minister of War, noted in his journal. A small political scandal followed. In a lordly letter Joffre pointed to measures taken and works in progress. "Nothing," he concluded, "justifies the fears you express in the name of your government," and he threatened to resign: "it does not suit me either to answer vague insinuations whose source is unknown to me." The cabinet met, and President Raymond Poincaré helped calm the waters amid official protestations of loyalty to the Généralissime. The scandal blew over, but Joffre's critics had discovered an outlet for their discontents and a byword for the passivity they discerned in the high command: Verdun.[12]

No sense of local veneration moved Herr or Driant, still less the ministers and deputies in their wake, to sound the tocsin at Verdun. They invoked no symbolic or strategic exception for the place, no uniquely sacred duty of vigilance there. In December, the anxieties they confided to their journals wandered well beyond it. Abel Ferry, one of those stirred to visit the scene by Driant and no friend of Joffre, had heard of vulnerabilities up and down the front, notably between Lunéville and Nancy—60 miles from Verdun. Galliéni worried about weak points "towards Verdun and Toul, between Berry-au-Bac and Soupir." During the December acrimony Poincaré ruminated more about Joffre's than about Driant's revelations; on New Year's Day he speculated that the Germans might strike at French public opinion through the "famous place" of Verdun, but confessed that he might be hearing the voice of his native Lorraine, so much of it lost since 1871, speaking in him. Attention kept returning there, but the enemy, not the symbol, had attracted it: in January the possibility of a German attack on Verdun hardened into a certainty.[13]

"We cannot wait until the situation has shifted against us to take necessary precautions," Herr wrote in the middle of January, an understated way of proclaiming his plight imminently irretrievable. A week later General Edouard de Castelnau, Joffre's newly named second-in-command, arrived on a hastily improvised inspection, and pronounced many of the first lines serviceable but many of the second and third ones a shambles. Two weeks after that the text of an inspirational message from Crown Prince Wilhelm fell into the hands of French intelligence officers. "My friends," he had just told his troops of the Fifth Army, "we have to take Verdun. It must all be over by the end of February, and then the Kaiser will hold a grand review on the Place d'Armes of Verdun and peace will be signed."[14]

But by then Joffre had stirred. He had already promised new measures in December, even while dismissing his critics. In January the reports from Verdun galvanized him and his staff into action. They reorganized the local command arrangements, sent in a regiment of engineers, kept two divisions there they had almost pulled out and put them to work building earthworks and organizing new defensive lines; they created a new army corps out of two other divisions and moved it to within striking distance; they moved heavy artillery in, and civilians out. By the 12th of February, when the German Fifth Army hoped to attack, French infantry were readying themselves in the front lines, new artillery batteries were setting up positions beside old ones, and engineers were placing explosive charges in the forts and under the bridges to destroy them if they could not hold them. The weather was awful. But had it not worsened and delayed the German attack by ten days, Verdun might have offered little resistance at all.[15]

When it came, on the 21st and the following days, the German progress through the pulverized French lines handed Joffre's enemies a powerful weapon, one they did not hesitate to wield once the emergency had passed. Already the issue had set one bureau at General Headquarters at Chantilly against the other. There, the first bureau handled materiel and personnel, the second intelligence, the third operations, and the fourth— also known as the Direction de l'Arrière—transport and logistics. Now Joffre's detractors reproached the "Young Turks"—so named for their arrogant identification of themselves with all that was modern in war—in the third bureau for their blindness to the evidence at Verdun and their deafness to the entreaties of their fellows in intelligence in the 2ème bureau. By impugning the judgment of the Young Turks, they aspired to topple the idol these so jealously guarded, Joffre. But the Généralissime had treated Verdun no more meanly than other strongholds on the front. Commanders at Amiens, Belfort, Nancy, and Calais had pointed just as plaintively as Herr at Verdun to lines too sparse in troops or artillery too weak in caliber, and to just as little avail. Joffre had other priorities; he was gathering his armies for the coming concentric Allied offensives on which he pinned such high hopes. And what if the enemy attacked elsewhere, in Champagne for example, where he gave intermittent but no less ominous indications of aggressive designs? Prudent as ever, Joffre kept divisions handily in reserve, close enough to the front to arrive in time to close a sudden breach or arrest a sudden surge, as 7th and 20th Corps did in February. Verdun did not fall.[16]

Why defend it at all? Even when the officers of the 3ème bureau had stopped dismissing the intelligence reports, they acknowledged the imminence but not the gravity of a German attack. They even welcomed the menace, as Joffre once had, confident of their strong hand. "It's coming, it's coming," their section head, Lieutenant-Colonel Renouard was heard to exclaim on the 20th of February, "but if the Germans attack Verdun, they'll fall flat on their face [sur quel bec de gaz vont-il tomber]!"— seeming to promise an explosive reception. Four days later, unnerved by the intensity of the offensive, befuddled by alarmist reports of 25,000 prisoners and 800 guns lost, of this position taken and that one abandoned, they envisaged withdrawal instead. Verdun was a point on a map, they now insisted, not France herself.[17] They might abandon the place and establish a new defensive front farther back, between the Meuse and the Aisne, one that would arrest the German offensive, fasten onto the rest of the French front, and protect the main rail lines linking Paris to the east. And they traced four such lines on the map, each topographically possible, the nearest between three and five miles behind Verdun, the farthest about 12, along the river Aire. On the scene, Herr, already their scapegoat, resigned himself to withdrawing from the right bank of the Meuse, driven not by their consternation but by his own. General Fernand de Langle de Cary, commander of the Groupe des Armées de l'Est and Herr's immediate superior, thought no differently. Engineers readied the forts and bridges for destruction. It was an option.[18]

Not for long: the government would not hear of it. Aristide Briand, Prime Minister and thus head of the government, traveled to Chantilly and listened to the Operations officers at a table with Joffre. He threatened to cashier the lot of them if Verdun fell, for the morale of the country was at stake. This was surprising. Briand, in office since October, a politician's politician, was not famed for courageous stands of principle. "Briand, what a chatterbox!" Galliéni had complained to his notebook in November. The Prime Minister inspired scarcely less trust in the President of the Republic—the head of state—than in the Minister of War:

"Briand," Poincaré noted at the end of December, "resembles an Oriental, a Levantine, envelops himself in the smoke of his cigarettes, dreams, and seems scarcely to act." And Galliéni returned to his diary to elaborate again in February, days before Briand came to Chantilly: "Briand, likeable, turning fact into farce, but indecisive, lazy." How odd that Briand should now wax so intransigent before the high command at Chantilly. But Poincaré also insisted that they hold Verdun, come what might. This, too, was surprising, not because Poincaré lacked conviction, but because he had scruples about interfering in operational decisions. He took umbrage at the ignorance in which the General Staff kept him, lamented the liberties it sometimes took, and chafed at his powerlessness to react; but he respected the constitution out of legal principle and Joffre out of political tact, and shrank from crossing the line that separated statesman from general in a time of war. He had no compunctions now.[19]

The dividing line supposed that in the conduct of war the government would set the political objectives, the high command the operational ones. Arcane enough in the abstract, the line sometimes disappeared altogether in practice, as Joffre acknowledged. "It is often difficult," he wrote the government in late October 1915, "to trace the frontier between the domain of pure policy and that of strategy." All the more so in a coalition war, when a military choice—to send troops to Salonika, to the Dardanelles, to the Suez Canal—could ruffle an ally or estrange a neutral; all the more so when a war of military élan, as this one had begun life, had become a war of national endurance, when the reciprocity with which military outcomes and popular morale fed each was so vital that no one questioned it and so mysterious that no one fully understood it.[20]

Most obviously, victories demanded national support, if only to sustain the flow of men and materiel to the voracious front; somewhat less obviously, national support demanded victories, and Poincaré had brooded late in 1915 over the detriment to home and hope from the year's meager gains and massive losses. Opinion polls had not yet enriched public life, but Poincaré needed none to awaken him to the symptoms of discouragement. His letters from the humble served: "Disaffection is deepening," he noted in November after hearing from another malcontent—a woman, not even a voter. So did the tides of parliamentary impatience, the reproaches of a rival like Clemenceau or of a less renowned deputy such as René Renoult of the Army Commission of the Chamber, who called on him in December to rebuke the Generals, the Ecole de Guerre, the cabinet, himself, all signs, Poincaré reflected, of "a truly general and profound malaise." So did his Minister of the Interior, Louis Malvy, who warned him that month about a small but visible pacifist movement within the labor unions. At moments he despaired of the temper of the governing class and of the *Union sacrée* that he had called for in the patriotic bloom of the first days of August 1914: "Insults, slander, violence . . . that is what has come of the *Union sacrée*." And he resented becoming the brunt of the outbursts, the outlet for the frustrations of the nation, blamed for all but responsible for nothing. Had his compatriots not read the constitutional laws? Now, two months later, officers talked of abandoning Verdun.[21]

As matters stood on the 24th of February, the French 30th Army Corps at Verdun had lost 60 percent of its men—dead, wounded, or missing—and one of its divisions, the 72nd, had almost ceased to exist. The military logic that drove Herr on the spot and that the officers at Chantilly allowed, even ordained, was a withdrawal from the right bank of the Meuse, or from Verdun altogether. Such a maneuver would rescue what was left of the troops and guns there from encirclement or destruction and establish a new defensive front: it would trade space for time. But the political logic that drove Poincaré and Briand forbade it. A defensive debacle, coming on the heels of the serial offensive setbacks of 1915, would do little to raise the spirits of a restive Chamber and a discouraged nation, and even less for their own political health. In president and prime minister alike, the politician's interest married the patriot's conscience. Neither ever contended that the issue of the war hung in the balance at Verdun. But neither ever stopped insisting, in the weeks and months that followed, that withdrawal even from the right bank alone was inconceivable.[22]

Joffre needed no convincing. In August and September 1914 he had left Verdun to fend for itself. Not this time. He gave every sign of sharing Briand's convictions in the argument at Chantilly. Perhaps he reflected as well that to abandon in haste a stronghold of the likes of Verdun would not help his own political cause, so recently threatened in the name of defensive readiness. Joffre had always been a canny political actor. He knew how to maneuver in the corridors of the Chamber—he could have been a deputy, the future Prime Minister André Tardieu said of him—and he adeptly used his prestige abroad, among neutrals as well as allies, to silence his critics at home. He could not afford to lose Verdun, not at this stage in the war. And perhaps he had grasped what Briand and Poincaré had already placed on the table: that Verdun was above all a question of prestige. A subtle transition had elevated the issue from the military to the psychological plane. Edouard de Castelnau, who was just as adamant, returned to Verdun. Joffre sent for Philippe Pétain.[23]

Still, Joffre would not allow the battle to disrupt the grand strategy of the Entente, so laboriously forged at Chantilly in December and since. Even with Verdun under the most intense artillery bombardment in history, Joffre doubted that Falkenhayn was casting his last roll of the dice or making his climactic effort of the war there. It made no strategic sense. He suspected a diversion, or a violent prelude to other operations, and on the 22nd he warned his army group commanders and his British ally that new attacks elsewhere on the front might soon follow. They did not. By March Joffre had surmised that the Germans were trying to throw off the coming Allied offensives and undermine French morale as well. He grasped even if he did not know that in the eyes of Falkenhayn Verdun was secondary. It was in his as well. He would not allow the enemy to scuttle his own strategic vision or deflect his gaze from the summer offensives and the shimmering prospect of victory. He would reinforce Verdun as needed. But no more than the dire warnings before the German attack would the alarums and emergencies on the Hauts de Meuse after it upset his strategic priorities. Verdun, in the end, was not the thing.[24]

Amid the agitation at Chantilly, he retained his Olympian calm. Visitors found him in his office, saying little, seated astride a chair and untwisting his fountain pen when willing to sign an order, twisting it shut when not. On the night of the 24th, when his second-in-command Castelnau requested permission to leave for Verdun, he found that Joffre had gone to bed at ten, as usual. And when Pétain arrived the next morning, Joffre greeted him warmly: "Well! Pétain, you know, things are not at all bad!"[25]

Meanwhile the eyes of the country turned towards Verdun with bewilderment. The journalists had the greatest of difficulty in conveying a sense to the events there. Only later did they affix the diabolical design of *Ausblutung* onto the mind of General Falkenhayn, helped along by his own retrospective embellishments; but before then they needed a national narrative of their own for the interminable battle, and soon enough they found one.

At first the inhabitants of both countries were left to unravel an unstated paradox: their newspapers, graphic yet sober-minded, seemed eager to convey the heroics of the battle yet anxious to belittle its stakes. In these early days, a surprising meeting of minds united the newspapers of both sides, at one in dismissing the strategic import of Verdun, especially to themselves. Fortresses no longer mattered much, French readers learned. They were mountains of stone without tactical value in the age of modern artillery. And what if the French had ceded ground? "What do we risk?" *L'Action* asked. "To withdraw momentarily by several hundred meters, paid for with 100,000 German corpses?" As for Verdun itself, a few papers boldly suggested that it might not matter either. It was an empty shell, whose conquest made no military sense. "They'll not have Verdun," Gustave Hervé, the one-time pacifist and revolutionary now turned nationalist, assured the readers of *La Victoire*, "but, let's not mince words, even if they do, we'll have them." In *L'Oeuvre* a general explained that the loss of Verdun would be "regrettable," but no more so than that of Soissons, Reims "or of any other sector of our lines." If Verdun fell, *L'Humanité* pointed out soberly, there would be no call to despair for France; there would be time to bar the route to the capital. And what made the Kaiser think, the *Echo de Paris* wondered, that Verdun, which it called "an obsolete defensive position" was France's largest fortress— "what then of Paris?" Somewhat inconsistently, the paper also assured its readers that Wilhelm knew that in modern war Verdun was just a name "like any other." In those early days of the battle the situation was close to desperate, although their readers did not know it, and a docile French press had little appetite for exalting a place the high command risked losing any day. Oddly, neither did the Germans. They celebrated the capture of Douaumont, and reported the advances of their infantry on the right bank of the river. But they avoided holding out promises they could not keep and prospects they could not confirm.[26]

As though in compensation, each ascribed vital stakes to the events for the other side; the objective, discretionary for oneself, became a matter of life and death for the other. If Douaumont was so unimportant to the French, the *Frankfurter Zeitung* asked, plausibly enough, why were they sending in an entire army corps to retake it? The correspondent of *Berliner Tageblatt* announced a political crisis in Paris in the wake of the military emergency at Verdun, and hinted at Sedan in 1870, when the French had lost an army, an emperor, and a regime. The French journalists outdid their German confreres. Verdun, the readers of *Le Matin* and *L'Echo de Paris* learned, had long held the German foe in a hypnotic trance—perhaps for obscure reasons of historical prestige, out of a desire to retake what an Austro-Prussian coalition had retaken from a vulnerable and revolutionary France in 1792. Dynastic anxieties deepened the compulsion: driven not by strategic interest but by herd instinct, the German Fifth Army charged blindly at the meaningless objective, led by a Crown Prince in search of laurels and unleashed by a Kaiser bent on saving the prestige of the Hohenzollerns. To cap it all, a political imperative forced the imperial hand: the German empire desperately needed victory of some kind, to galvanize the sagging morale of its subjects and salvage its reputation of invincibility abroad. In short, each side pronounced the prestige of the other at stake, and each denied the preposterous assertion: "Verdun was the trump card on which Germany gambled its destiny," *Le Journal* announced. "What nonsense!" said the *Frankfurter Zeitung*.[27]

"The news from Verdun is better," a Canadian war volunteer noted in her diary on the 28th of February, "and the Paris newspapers sound more satisfied and hopeful." By then French reinforcements were arriving in strength and the German advance had stalled; emergency passed for one side, opportunity for the other. Only then did the events of the preceding days begin to acquire for the French the transfiguring character of legend, and to impose upon the Germans the convenient but troubling explanation of attrition.[28]

Enough idle speculation, the papers began to grumble early in March. The fate of France hung in the balance. The Germans had so decided. Why worry about motives or strategic objectives when the lonely stoicism of the French *poilu* was holding the Germanic masses at the gates of France? In one way or another, over the course of ten days, Verdun had become a struggle between right and might, individualism and collectivism, French civilization and German barbarism. By the middle of the month, three weeks after the German attack, the existential narrative of German invasion and French resistance had dissolved all doubts about origins or stakes. Who worried about them anymore? In February they had spoken more often than not of Ypres and the Yser. A more ancient and heroic historical parallel lay at hand: Thermopylae.[29]

Like the Spartans facing the Persians in 480 BCE, the outnumbered French were dying today in defiles and ravines to keep the alien hordes from the heartland. In 1792, with the Prussians already in Verdun and the wooded hills of the Argonne before them, General Charles Dumouriez wrote to the Minister of War that the passes there were "*les Thermopyles* de la France." But, he added, "I'll end up better off than Leonidas," referring to the Spartan leader. Goethe, who had been there with the Prussian army, invoked the image in his recollections, seeing the French re-enacting an ancient stand. On the 25th of February 1916, four days into the battle of Verdun, *L'Echo de Paris* resurrected it anew: the army of the Crown Prince, it recalled, had vainly tried in 1914 to break through the Argonne, "les *Thermopyles* de la France." The next day, in the same paper, Maurice Barrès expanded the terrain—"The Argonne and Verdun seem always the Thermopylae of France"—and *Le Matin* quickly followed suit. Antiquity now resurfaced east, not west, of Verdun, and in the middle of March General Pétain turned Dumouriez's allusion into his own. "Monsieur le Ministre," he told an official visitor from neutral and much courted Greece, "we have our own Thermopylae—in Vaux." Unlike Douaumont, the fort of Vaux had so far resisted every assault. And he too added, "we won't be crushed like Leonidas."[30]

The image took, even while the battle lasted. "Here is the defile of centuries and of Europe/The Atlantic Thermopylae of the West . . . ," André Suarès, the poet and essayist, was writing in June, in a poetic prayer of 33 stanzas for the dead at Verdun. This was a war between the *esprit de patrie* and the *esprit d'empire*, a lecturer at the Collège de France explained in December 1916, and he alluded pointedly to the imperial ambitions of the Persian Xerxes. Before the war ended, one of the first published chronicles of the Battle of Verdun repeated Barrès verbatim, and just after the war the historian and veteran of the battle Louis Madelin began his own account by explaining that the ravines of the Côtes de Meuse were France's own "Thermopylae," the heights where the German wave would break. In the years that followed, school textbooks and popular histories rarely injected the historical antecedent into their renderings. Many, however, especially in the early postwar years, appropriated its linked and timeless images: the would-be conqueror, the emblematic plot of home turf, the valor that compensated for material insufficiency. "Thanks to their sublime valor, France was saved!" And, not incidentally, a new Persia was undone. "It was at Verdun that . . . France broke the will to hegemony of the Germanic Empire," the Minister of Veterans declared when he visited the town in February 1966 to mark the 50th anniversary of the battle. "We fought this battle by ourselves and won it by ourselves."[31]

When it ventured to define German objectives at Verdun more precisely, postwar pedagogy unintentionally undermined the existential legend of Thermopylae. It repeated some of the speculation of the first days of the battle and added more of its own, without pausing to note the seeming inconsistency between the varied pursuit of lesser ambitions on the part of the Germans and their supposed insatiable thirst for conquest. The legend of *Ausblutung*, in which the French would bleed to death by repeated attempts to expel the German invader from the crests above Verdun, matched poorly with that of Thermopylae, in which valiant defenders denied entry to an adversary superior in numbers and richer in treasure. For both to work, waves of Spartans would have had to break themselves in useless attacks against Persian invaders waiting behind their newly conquered heights. And a calibrated design to bleed the French white was not easily reconcilable with an obsessive drive to conquer Verdun. Yet for 80 years and more the canonical French accounts married the two. One legend operated at the level of strategic and tactical design, the other at the level of national epic; each left the other intact. Besides, Falkenhayn's confession of sanguinary aspirations only demonized him and magnified the defenders' ordeal. *Ausblutung* supported the existential legend, but only if the faithful did not scrutinize it too closely.

Like the inspiring model of Thermopylae, the self-serving distortion of *Ausblutung* appeared in the early days and weeks of the great battle, and resisted demystification for long decades afterward. Launched by the Germans as a preliminary affair, and reluctantly accepted by the French as a secondary one, the Battle of Verdun became the emblem of cold-bloodedness on one side and of selfless resolve on the other.

And, seen from a distance, the controlled response of the French reflects a sober appreciation of the exigencies of the hour. The nation's morale alone demanded that they hold the salient, but beyond political necessity lay a tacit strategy of persistence. They could tie the enemy down on the Meuse in the spring while preparing with their ally for the Battle of the Somme in the summer. Without saying so, they would play for time, and even though Joffre had insisted that victory would have to come in 1916, their war now began to invert the logic of their enemy's: weak today, France would be stronger tomorrow. "I am waiting," Pétain would say, "for tanks and the Americans."

Such truths vanished in the afterglow of victory. Instead the legends of Moloch and Thermopylae traveled the decades, taking wing even as the great battle began, and assured of life by endless and somber retellings.

4

The Offensive Trap

IN 1916 NO ONE EVER ACHIEVED A DECISIVE BREAKTHROUGH, envelopment, or flank attack at Verdun. Local offensive operations sometimes carried the day and pushed the enemy back, and fanfares sounded in Paris or Berlin as though to celebrate historic feats of arms, but nowhere did maneuver or surprise or frontal assault ever decide the issue. Verdun resembles a *reductio ad absurdum* of the war in the West, all too symptomatic of the syndrome that dragged it out for so long: the temptation and the treachery of the offensive.

"You see," Falkenhayn told the generals on the 23rd of February, "that I was right again with this attack." He had provided eight new and rested divisions for an attack on the right bank of the Meuse. The Crown Prince and his chief of staff, General von Knobelsdorf, had requested ten in addition to those they already had, if not to attack on both banks, then at least to provide impetus and élan and a ready reserve at hand just behind the divisions already in line. Falkenhayn demurred, just as he had when the Sixth and Third Armies requested more divisions for new operations that he was unwilling to approve elsewhere on the Western Front. He had no desire, he had replied, to find himself in another Champagne battle, when, surprised by the force of the French attack in September 1915, he had only restored the situation *in extremis* by rushing in two corps from the Eastern Front. He had now given the Fifth Army at Verdun eight of the 25 divisions he held in reserve. The others he would keep for now, not for the Meuse but for the entire Western Front, to be deployed where the opportunity arose and when the moment struck. "Our challenge," he had explained, "is to inflict heavy losses on the enemy at decisive points with a relatively modest outlay of our own." As for Verdun, the infantry were to feel their way forward, rather than surge blindly ahead, once the artillery had devastated the enemy's positions. If they still encountered stiff resistance they were to wait. Economy was the key.[1]

And all was going according to plan, noted Colonel von Tappen, the Operations Chief at OHL, with satisfaction on the 23rd. Unevenly but inexorably, six German divisions had pushed forward along an arc of about five miles that stretched from one blasted wood to another, from the village of Bois d'Haumont almost due north of Verdun to the Bois de Ville to its northeast. Every nightfall the arc tightened a little more: it had moved a little over a mile by the night of the 22nd, and another by the night of the 24th. That day the village of Samogneux disappeared from the map, its dwellings reduced to rubble by German artillery, its bunkers emptied by flamethrowers, its garrison killed or taken prisoner. The next day another army corps attacked westward from the plain of Woëvre farther south. When Fort Douaumont fell the same day, all of the first and most of the second French lines were in German hands. They were now six miles from Verdun. Only a weak line of forts, Belleville, St.-Michel, and Souville, poorly organized and barely equipped, stood between the deserted, smoking town and its attackers. Confidence reigned. Assured of its momentum, 7th Reserve Corps made plans to cross the Meuse at Regnéville on the morning of the 27th. At last, one of its machine gunners reflected, they had recovered what they had ardently wanted—a war of movement.[2]

By then the French had evacuated the villages of Brabant and Ornes. During the night of the 24th they began to evacuate the exposed salient of Woëvre as well, rather than run the risk of seeing their forces in the open plain cut off by the German 5th Reserve Corps that had just begun its attack there. They readied explosive charges in the forts and under the bridges, and began pulling some artillery back to the right bank. "So I'll pack up bag and baggage and go be a prisoner in Hunland [Bochie]," a quartermaster informed an ambulance driver early in the morning of the 26th, when he broke the news that Douaumont had fallen. All night the driver had watched, bemused, as artillery fire illuminated the hilltops of the Côtes de Meuse and the snow-covered fields below. The engineers would blow up the bridges, he assumed, and leave them all to their fate on the doomed right bank of the river. The next day they blew up a 240 mm gun on its rails in Cumières rather than allow it to fall into German hands.[3]

The Germans never reached Cumières. On the 28th their advance ground to a halt. French resistance on the right bank and artillery fire from the left bank had been intensifying steadily. Many of the German regiments, now badly exposed, came under flanking fire from French guns on the hilltops of the Côte de Marre and le Mort-Homme on the left bank. Around Fort Douaumont attacks and counterattacks answered each other as the French tried to retake the Fort, unsuccessfully, but crippled German forward motion. The village of Douaumont, less than a half-mile from the Fort, kept changing hands. It finally fell on the 4th of March to the Germans, after eight days of savage fighting that left nothing standing.

Verdun was Douaumont writ large. Equilibrium was setting in, made of local attacks and counterattacks, house-to-house fighting, and incessant shellfire that stopped German infantry in their tracks or confined them to shelters hastily excavated in the frozen ground. In the fields of Woëvre southeast of Verdun they could get no farther than the foothills of the Côtes de Meuse, which rose steeply from the plain and left them para- lyzed by the French artillery lodged on the crests above. Farther north the Brandenburger officers of 3rd Army Corps realized, even if their Fifth Army command did not, that they could do no more. "From now on it's over," a French priest in uniform reflected on the 29th. "The enemy is persuaded of our strength; they'll leave us alone. The road to Verdun is closed, at least for now, as far as we're concerned."[4]

Most worrisome of all, German losses by the end of February were no lighter than those of the French—some 25,000 dead, wounded, or missing. A commonality of suffering had not figured into their plans or tempered their optimisms—"we are in movement, the enemy on the run."[5] Why had the German assault columns broken on the inner line of French resistance, why had such momentum given way to such immobility?

Their breakthrough at Gorlice-Tarnow against the Russians in Galicia in the spring of 1915 and the loss of their own front lines to the French in Champagne in September of the same year had confirmed in the German military mind the *sine qua non* of any infantry offensive: artillery prep- aration. However sharply the commanders of the Fifth Army and the general staff at OHL might have differed at first over the scope of the infantry attack at Verdun, army and high command were at one in placing high hopes on the deluge of large-caliber artillery shells that would precede it. Untroubled by any enemy counter-battery fire—their own heavy guns were out of range—they would pulverize the obstacles that stood in the way of their infantry. What better way to exploit their superiority in heavy artillery—almost five times that of the French at Verdun as the attack began—than to economize their own infantry losses? "Gentlemen," artillery officers assured an infantry captain, "there will be no offensive for you, only a promenade!"[6]

At Verdun, as well, their local air force, built up in the weeks beforehand, allowed German artillery observers to identify French targets whenever the weather allowed. With 168 planes, 14 balloons, and four Zeppelins, the Fifth Army had managed to keep the skies over Verdun largely free of French aircraft in the days before the attack, and enjoyed for the moment something close to aerial supremacy. On February 20th, when the weather cleared briefly, 14 German planes, black crosses emblazoned on their fuselage, took off for general reconnaissance, shortly followed by four others for artillery surveillance. A French squadron finally rose to meet them. At dawn the next day, the 21st, more German planes took to the skies over Verdun, this time unchallenged.[7]

It was partly because of such air cover, partly because it enjoyed such free rein that morning, that the German shelling could exceed in intensity anything the French or anyone else had ever endured.[8] This was Champagne multiplied ten times over, but with a difference in kind as well: the German artillerists were blanketing entire zones with their shells. They directed their fire not merely onto positions they wished to take or onto lines they wished to obliterate, but into all that nature had grown and that man had erected as well, making up in density for what they lacked in precision. That day they saturated successive zones within a 25-mile arc between Avocourt on the left bank and Etain on the right bank of the Meuse—the northern front of the Région Fortifiée de Verdun—with a million high-explosive shells of the heaviest caliber known to man, 280, 305, 380, even 420 millimeters wide, and with lesser shells bearing toxic gases as well. Method rather than rage, the system of the power hammer rather than the obstinacy of the battering ram, drove the destruction. The morbid calculus presaged the carpet bombing of later wars that would raze entire cities and ignite entire landscapes, but for now the thought was purely tactical: to devastate, so that the infantry could infiltrate.[9]

And infiltrate the infantry did: the solace of safety attended their steps, for the moment. To their west the waters of the Meuse and to their east the escarpments of the Côtes de Meuse protected them against flank attacks from enemy infantry on either side and artillery fire from one, the eastern. In front of them the providential big guns had destroyed trenches and blockhouses, neutralized artillery, cut communications, interdicted the traffic of supplies, disrupted the enemy's command chain all the way into Verdun itself—how deeply and for how long they could not know, but for now the silence beckoned. In leaps and bounds, some of them advanced several miles in the first few days. Only firepower—the artillery—had allowed them to do so.

Firepower, and the defenders as well. The French may have known of the attack, but not of its timing. By shelling zones instead of targets the German artillery had dispensed with adjusting its fire beforehand, and the infantry had attacked at dusk from their habitual trenches and not from the specially dug jumping-off points ahead of them: neither gunners nor infantrymen had quite given their timing away, as the French and everyone else had in their offensives of the year before. And in any case, surprised or not, the French were not ready. They had been working feverishly for ten days, but still too many points were undermanned, too many trenches unfinished and poorly connected, too few heavy guns in place. Four divisions had arrived in February and two more were disembarking that day at stations nearby, but still the French could oppose only 130,000 men in the entire Region Fortifiée de Verdun, between Argonne in the north and St. Mihiel in the south, to the 250,000 assembled by the German Fifth Army. When four German divisions, the Saxons of 7th Reserve Corps and the Hessians of 18th Army Corps, began pouring south into the Bois d'Haumont and the Bois des Caures, a single French infantry division, the 72nd, was there to meet them. In the adjoining woods north of Fort Douaumont and Fort Vaux, another solitary division, the 51st, received the brunt of two divisions of Brandenburgers. There were too few of them, too few to counterattack as soon as the first German reconnaissance groups appeared in the woods, to say nothing of the waves of attacking infantry that would follow during the next 48 hours. The survivors of the heavy bombardment and *Trommelfeuer* of the 21st emerged in the late afternoon from their shattered dugouts, stunned or dazed or blinded by tear gas, to find themselves quickly outnumbered.

And how could reinforcements reach them? The first and second lines, still discontinuous and only occasionally connected by communication trenches, inhibited lateral or vertical movement even before the heavy shells reduced them to chaos.[10]

And for much of that first day of Verdun the French artillery watched. Since February 10th the Region had received 85 more heavy guns, but the heaviest was a single 305 mm, while the Germans were sending massive 380 mm and 420 mm shells their way. Inferior in number as well as caliber, uncertainly supplied with munitions by a rail line from Ste-Ménehoulde on the left bank that German guns had now cut, enveloped on their narrow front by a wide arc of incoming fire, the French guns effectively abandoned the infantry. They could only direct occasional fire onto the distant forests of Spincourt and Haut-Fourneau, where the fireworks display, the incessant flashes from the mouthpieces of giant barrels, betrayed the emplacements of German heavy artillery.[11]

The nadir of passivity came on the 25th when the fort of Douaumont fell without firing a shot. The high command had deemed such concrete behemoths indefensible, no more capable of withstanding the projectiles of long range heavy guns than their fellows at Liège or Namur in Belgium or Manonvillers in France during the battle of the frontiers in August and September 1914. The following year Przemysl, a Galician fortress system almost as imposing as Verdun, had fallen in its turn, seeming to confirm the newfound uselessness of forts in the age of heavy artillery. As defensive organizations, trenches were both more primitive and more modern than forts, once the self-sufficient bulwarks against the invader and now so many mere links in a continuous chain of armies in the field. In August 1915 the high command not only abolished the forts as *places fortes* and integrated them into local army commands,[12] but more rashly, it bequeathed almost all their ordnance to the field artillery. They kept only some smaller pieces installed in turrets, unusable elsewhere, and no garrisons or supplies to speak of. On the afternoon of the 25th, a company of Brandenburgers glimpsed the grey silhouette of Douaumont through the swirls of snow and the chaotic fountains of smoke and fume from exploding shells. The fort was eerily silent. Only occasional 155 mm shells left its turrets for points unknown. They climbed into the outer ditch, now half filled with rubble, and over the escarpment and entered the inner labyrinth of the fort through an open door. Inside, at the end of dank passages dimly lit by oil lamps, they found some 65 Territorials commanded by a retired noncommissioned officer and armed with 1874-model Gras rifles. Active infantry units had never received clear orders to defend Douaumont or any other fort; new orders to re-occupy it had gone astray in the confusion. And no one had time to detonate the explosive charges already in place. The incredulous Brandenburgers had at first suspected a trap. But incompetence rather than cunning had handed them the mightiest fort in France. As even the German generals recognized after the war, Douaumont had fallen by accident.[13]

Douaumont could have held, if only enough men and machine guns had arrived to hold it. In September 1914 Maubeuge, under siege by the German Second Army, could have held out as well, perhaps not forever, but certainly for longer. Its fall released two German divisions for the race to the sea that autumn. The static war on the Western Front was like that: only a conspiracy of circumstance, preparation, and error made for any significant movement. The art and the preparation of one side had to encounter the ineptitude or the improvidence of the other for positions to fall or lines to fracture; the attackers, however canny their timing or massive their means, depended on the cooperation of the defenders to penetrate, let alone rupture, the front. Even then they could not move far. Reinforcements of all kinds filled the breach, and the defensive powers of modern weaponry quickly reclaimed their primacy, just as fatigue and strategic consumption slowed and disabled the intruders. They might break in, but they could not break through. Even before Douaumont fell, the French were recovering and the Germans flagging.[14]

In Champagne in September 1915, the French infantry had overrun the German first lines, largely thanks to their artillery, only to find the second lines impregnable. An artillerist, still there when the Germans attacked Verdun in February, shared a sense of *déja vu* with his uncle. "The boches seem very active around Verdun and their furious attack seems to have partly succeeded," he wrote him on the 26th. "It's highly likely though that they won't succeed in breaking through our second line of defense and that they'll stop, just like us in Champagne." He was not far wrong. The German infantry did breach some second lines, and took Douaumont, but even an element of surprise, an artillery deluge to drown all others, and a comfortable weight of numbers could not bring them much farther.[15]

Try as they might, the German gunners could neither penetrate every recess nor destroy every obstacle with their heavy shells. Tunnels and dugouts, if they lay deep enough and escaped direct hits, shook but survived. Not even the most violent bombardment could bring down fort walls recently reinforced with ten feet and more of concrete and earth, even if turrets, barracks, pipes, and water cisterns cracked from the impacts and the vibrations made for human misery within.

And the artillerists, firing onto zones, could not see every redoubt: they might have destroyed much of the first and second lines, but they had missed the intermediary positions set up on the far side of the ravine in the Bois des Caures after Castelnau's hurried inspection in January. Aerial observation of enemy targets gave little help to the German gunners because pilots were ordered to concentrate on interdicting air space to the enemy instead—a slowly losing battle, even as it deprived their ground forces of reconnaissance and observation. Even when pilots did try to identify French batteries, the fire on both sides soon became so intense that they could not communicate with their own bases.[16]

Unpleasant surprises awaited the German infantry. Once into the woods, they came under fire from isolated but intact machine gun nests whose existence they had never suspected. In the open and in the clearings, as early as the evening of the 21st, they fell under flanking artillery fire from 75 mm and 155 mm guns, ensconced on the hills of the left bank or concealed in positions on the right bank, or left in forts that had not been disarmed, such as the Fort de Marre on the left bank and the Fort de Moulainville on the right—from French field pieces that went into action as though to atone for the silence of their heavier fellows. In the Bois d'Haumont some of the Saxons of 7th Reserve Corps took cover in the woods, only to encounter chaos as troops amassed, officers lost their men, uprooted trees blocked forward movement, and unseen machine guns began firing at them. Nearby in the Bois des Caures the Hessian patrols abandoned by night some of the trenches they had occupied by day. Too many of the chasseurs of Colonel Driant—the same Driant who had sounded the alarm over the defenses at Verdun in December—had emerged amid the wreckage to greet them once the artillery lifted its fire. Three days later thousands of such spectral survivors had fallen in the woods all around or disappeared into captivity. They had fought a rearguard action, often at a heavy cost: of Driant's 1,200 chasseurs, only a few hundred, many wounded, broke out and back to Vacherauville by the evening of the 22nd, and he was not among them; by the next night the division to which they belonged, the 72nd, had effectively ceased to exist.

However, with life and limb, they and the others had bought time for the relievers: that night of the 22nd the troops of 20th Army Corps began moving into line among their dead and their debris. The next night three fresh brigades arrived in relief in the same sector, the 20th Army Corps was disembarking, and another corps, the 7th, was soon at hand in reserve. Too few to stop the enemy, but just enough to slow him, the guns on the left bank and the survivors on the right bank had caused enough mayhem among the assailants to snatch the breathing space their army needed. Once again on the Western Front the defenders had reinforced their lines before the attackers could get through.[17]

The reinforcements had come by road. Most had no other way. In December 1915, when Driant was sounding alarms about defenses in Lorraine, an obscure and retired battalion commander was warning of an impending logistical disaster there. The defenders, he feared, would be starved of sustenance for want of any rails to carry it. For their part the Germans had 11 rail lines with normal gauges converging on points behind Verdun. Joffre and his general staff already knew it. Earlier in 1915 they had pondered ways to assure survival and even success there—oddly, for in August they disarmed the forts. That measure, nonetheless, demonstrated a conviction that the defense of Verdun, should it come to that, would fall to armies in the field rather than to antique battlements of stone.

A single small rail line, a glorified tramway by the name of *Le Petit Meusien*, ran from Bar-le-Duc in the south and brought 400 tons of supplies and munitions into Verdun a day; an army in the field there would demand ten times that, to say nothing of the 15–20,000 men a day in relief and reinforcement as well. Another rail line from Ste-Ménehoulde, east of Verdun in the Argonne, came so close to enemy guns in the bend at Aubréville that it could easily be cut—as indeed it was, in the early hours of February 21st. In 1915 the General Staff considered deflecting the line beyond the range of the threatening guns, then abandoned the idea on the sensible grounds that the enemy, in an offensive, might move forward. They considered as well building an entirely new line that would bisect the salient to Verdun, but soon abandoned that too, on the less sensible grounds that the urgency of the threat hardly justified the scope of the project. In the autumn they decided to widen *Le Petit Meusien* to an eventual capacity of about 1500 tons a day. But that would take time, and would still fall far short unless they opened a different artery between Verdun and the vital heartland: the road.[18]

During the French offensive in Champagne in September, long lines of trucks had brought men and munitions every night to the Fourth Army. As vehicles, they could reach the lines in ways that trains could not, for their roads ended almost where the trenches began. But the frustrations of getting there, the bottlenecks and breakdowns, had revealed an endemic indiscipline that had nearly undone the blessings of a technology still in its infancy. At Verdun the *service des transports automobiles* began imposing its will even before the battle began. On the afternoon of the 19th, as the first trucks of a fleet soon to number 9,000 vehicles began to gather in Bar-le-Duc, a general from the *Direction de l'arrière*—logistics—assembled the nucleus of a staff in a lycée near the station. By midnight on the 22nd they had requisitioned the 50-mile road from the station of Badonvilliers outside Bar to the faubourg Glorieux outside Verdun, closed it to all but automotive military vehicles, policed each 10-mile stretch of it, regulated the departures of convoys on it, and assigned 20 maintenance workers and troops for each mile of it. And the traffic began to flow. From elsewhere, along the valley of the Ornain that crossed it, came horse-drawn artillery and materiel, and along the *Petit Meusien* railroad that ran alongside it came rations, but up the road from Bar came men—in time 6,000 trucks and cars every 24 hours, one every 14 seconds, bringing 90,000 uniformed soldiers a week. The men had traveled by train to stations along the way and climbed into waiting trucks for the journey to Verdun, the night march, and the front lines. On the 29th of February, in Dombasle, near Nancy, a chaplain wondered at the interminable convoys going by. They were evacuating the town. "That's nothing," an officer told him, "next to the traffic on the road from Bar. I was there the other evening, and thought I was on the Avenue de l'Opéra." The "route de Bar" had not yet assumed the second identity that the nationalist writer Maurice Barrès would bestow upon it: the *Voie Sacrée*, the Sacred Way.[19]

Three days earlier, February 26th, Philippe Pétain had arrived at the town hall of Souilly to assume command. He had come from Chantilly, where

Joffre had given him command of the Second Army and the defense of Verdun. All on the snowy route suggested disorder and even panic, from the somber expressions and bitter words among the officers around Joffre to the disarray on the road to the chateau at Dugny that General Herr, until yesterday the commander of the fortified region, had used as his headquarters. Columns of troops and vehicles slid off the frozen ground, horses fell, traffic stopped. They crawled along at two miles an hour. "A mad house," one of Pétain's aides thought the chateau, where de Langle de Cary, in command of the central Army group, and other senior officers awaited them. The news from Verdun was uniformly bad. "Everyone was talking and gesticulating at once." They arrived at Souilly at midnight and spent the night in a notary's house without a working fireplace. Pétain had double pneumonia. They moved into the town hall the next morning.[20]

By then, in the ambient gloom, the situation was already stabilizing. Herr and de Langle considered the right bank lost, a receptacle for enemy shells from which they ought to extricate French forces or face losing them altogether. But the Germans could not advance much farther, the French reserves were arriving, the road from Bar was teeming. On the 25th Joffre had issued his order from Chantilly to defend Verdun at all costs, and Castelnau, his second-in-command, put a stop to any talk of withdrawing from the right bank with a telegram sent even before he had arrived on the scene: "We will defend the Meuse on the right bank. There is no alternative to stopping the enemy on that bank, alone." Pétain aspired now not to invent resistance—it had already sprung to life, blessed by the political and military hierarchy—but to impose method upon it: to make a virtue of necessity, and transform a stand into a system.[21]

Pétain was a man of method rather than élan, friendlier to small-scale attritional warfare than to the *offensives à outrance* (all-out offensives) that had cost the French so heavily throughout 1915. In practice this made him something of a black sheep. Few saw him that way. He was 60, a recent general, little known because not easy to know, and perhaps popular for that reason. In December 1915 some cabinet ministers and deputies urged him upon the government for the position at Joffre's right hand at the General Staff at Chantilly that soon went to Castelnau instead. They endowed Pétain with miraculous qualities, Poincaré reflected, only because they had heard little about him. They knew that his 33rd Corps had briefly broken through enemy lines in Artois in May that year. Perhaps they did not know that he had resisted orders for further attacks there, regarding them as futile, nor that after the offensive in Champagne in September he had quickly concluded that no attacker in this war could break through the enemy's second lines without a massive superiority in men as well as an exhaustive artillery preparation. Rather than "think of renewing attacks as costly as those of September," he had declared then, "it seems we should proceed methodically to the attrition of the enemy." Impatient as they were for results, his well-wishers might not then have smiled so easily upon him.[22]

On the 26th he added an order of his own from Souilly to those that Joffre and Castelnau had already issued from Chantilly: "Shut down at any cost the effort the enemy is making on the Verdun front. Any parcel of terrain the enemy snatches will give rise to an immediate counter-attack." To hold terrain at all costs, to contest every trench and shell-hole, the defenders needed firepower, which meant more reserves, and these Joffre agreed to send: 30th Corps had been withdrawn in shreds, but 20th Corps had arrived on the right bank, 2nd and 7th Corps on the left; two other corps were in reserve, and two more on the way. Fire-power also meant heavy artillery pieces, which the Second now lacked more acutely than any other French army on the Western Front, and these Pétain removed at once from the corps commanders, much to their dismay, and placed under his command, for use when and where they were most needed. The defenders also needed more obstacles to place in the path of their assailants, which meant more dugouts, redoubts, block-houses, all the architecture of defensive warfare that the French had been trying to complete and the Germans to destroy, and this the engineers and the Territorials now set about building or rebuilding inside and outside the forts, even under enemy fire. Rationalize and centralize: local com-manders found their sectors designated now by impersonal letters of the alphabet, the equivalence of which suggested a sameness of task and purpose that only the Second Army could impose. And the very move to the modest town hall in Souilly, more removed from the din of the front than Herr's old headquarters in Senator Charles Humbert's château in Dugny, conveyed a managerial simplicity redolent of planning and pro-duction goals. A system was taking shape.[23]

Meanwhile Pétain watched the left bank of the Meuse for any sign of a German infantry attack there. An advance of even a mile or two southward from the positions they held might silence the artillery that was wreaking such havoc among the Germans on the right bank, use up the reserves, bring supply lines and the bridges over the river within range of the German field artillery—might, one way or another, isolate the French divisions on the right bank. But the attack did not come, not for now.[24]

Had the Germans blundered? Falkenhayn's critics, German or French, always thought so. His reluctance to attack at once on the left bank, they reflected, betrayed a timidity already manifest in his unwillingness to risk more divisions on the right bank. The road to Verdun was open, the Crown Prince complained, and he could have marched in with his Fifth Army had Falkenhayn only given him the men he needed. And both he and Knobelsdorf, his chief of staff, had wanted to attack on both banks, as they later recalled for the sake of history. So had General Groener, head of the railroads, and Colonel Bauer at the Operations section of OHL; both also accused Falkenhayn of wishful thinking and a fatal fondness for half-measures. Besides, he had placed too much store by the heavy artillery, others added. And when Falkenhayn pretended that the single design of *Ausblutung* had driven him, he handed his detractors yet another weapon. Varied in their complaints, the critics united in blaming the failure to take Verdun on human agency, and more precisely on human error.[25]

Oftener than not their reproaches reflected the wisdom of hindsight and overlooked their momentary enthusiasms. Neither Knobelsdorf nor the Crown Prince cared to recall their heady optimism at the time of the attack, limited as it was. "Very well, then take everything today!" Knobelsdorf happily told 7th Reserve Corps on the 21st as the artillery lifted. Neither he nor the Crown Prince had requested more reserves on the eve of the attack or during the next few days, even when the advance slowed. And later, somewhat inconsistently, the Crown Prince blamed not the numbers but the "rascals" who had deserted and betrayed them, and the weather, the snow and fog that had given the French nine more days in which to prepare for the open secret, the German attack. Perhaps they might take the right bank, perhaps the entire fortress system, perhaps luck would create its own opportunities, Groener reflected ten days before the attack, in a fine example of the idle "hopes and wishes" he later imputed to Falkenhayn. "I think the affair looks good!" the Prussian Minister of War, von Hoheborn exclaimed just before the attack began. Merely two weeks later he was identifying errors in planning. There had been doubters, such as Bauer, but few naysayers and no Cassandras.[26]

They were still learning. Before 1914 the army had tried storming Verdun in several exercises, always from the north, sometimes on one bank, sometimes on both. No one yet knew that the artillery would leave enough of the enemy intact to bedevil the infantry, that his forts would resist and the mightiest only fall through ineptitude, that he would resupply himself quickly and massively by road. No one knew how to employ their fledgling air power or their lumbering long-range artillery to close down a 50-mile roadway or destroy the bridges across the Meuse. Shells landed on the road, and trucks were hit, but the 380 mm guns were inadequate in number and range to interdict such intense traffic on such a long stretch. Along its ditches over 8,000 men worked day and night to maintain it. German airships and fighter squadrons bombed the stations and cut the rail line and damaged the roads out of Verdun. But visibility was too poor and the loss rate too high to deflect them from the primary tasks of reconnaissance, artillery observation, and control of the air, and to allow the nascent science of strategic bombing to take flight. Of the 34 bridges over the Meuse, not one fell to bombs from the air. No one yet knew, in short, how to attack the enemy's logistics instead of his defenses.

However, Falkenhayn did know what Pétain also knew: that massive infantry attacks on a wide front cost heavily and never succeeded fully, and he knew as well that they had less blood to spill than their enemies. He would strike a first blow at Verdun in one way or another while anxiously watching the rest of the front, but to minimize his own losses and maximize the enemy's he would attack on a small front with intense artillery and limited infantry. He even briefly withdrew two divisions, rather than squander them on the Meuse.[27]

In short, Falkenhayn did not pine to take the place at any cost. Would it have been worth it? Groener, for one, doubted that the conquest of the place would greatly alter the operational picture in the West.[28] Probably, as the critics lamented, the right bank or Verdun itself would have fallen by the end of the first week or two had the Fifth Army expended more forces on both banks of the river. The French would have withdrawn from the empty town, handing the Germans a moral victory and a handsome cache of materiel, but the lines would have reformed several miles back, reasserting this war's law of defensive supremacy that Falkenhan had so tried to test with deliberate economy on the 21st of February. He had foreseen the French resolve to defend Verdun and misjudged the rest, especially the losses. Their own were high. And the closer they came to Verdun, the farther away it seemed.

At the end of the first week of the battle a pause set in. Both sides found themselves digging trenches and dugouts under the ceaseless artillery fire of the other. The war of movement, so dear to the hearts and minds of the attackers, had lasted for a few days, only to end in paralysis. Something akin to a siege began, with attackers and defenders resorting to desperate sorties and raids in quest of an advantage, and finding each time what the first week had already confirmed. Attacks were cursed from the outset unless minutely prepared, massively endowed with artillery and infantry and attended by the ever-elusive coordination between the two, and, lastly, blessed by demoralized or derelict defenders. Even then the gains were modest. The lines moved a bit and reformed.

On March 6th the Germans finally attacked in strength on the left bank. They continued intermittently for the next six months, though never managed to get beyond the Côte 304 and le Mort-Homme, the hills five or six miles northwest of Verdun. The poorly manned outer woods a couple of miles farther north fell quickly, but the well-defended hills became the scene of some of the most savage and inconclusive fighting of the Great War. With intense artillery and furious infantry assaults the Germans might capture some terrain—a quarter of a mile of French trenches on a slope of le Mort-Homme on April 9th and 10th, a few hundred yards more, a trench here and there on 304 in May. Using the same methods, the French soon drove them off. When their 75 mm field artillery did not stifle the infantry attack as soon as it began, immediate counterattacks by their own waiting infantry soon did the rest. The 32nd Corps counterattacked 15 times this way on le Mort-Homme, and 12 times they succeeded.

The crest became a zone of flux, as infantry from slopes and reverse slopes ebbed and flowed and defenders and attackers kept changing roles and places. A ridge or hilltop, in this war, assured little of the security it might in earlier ones. "The battle is won!" Napoleon suddenly exclaimed during the battle of Wagram against the Austrians in 1809. He had caught sight of Marshal Davout's regiments atop the strategic heights of Neusiedl, turning the enemy's left. Now, the temporary masters of such heights sat exposed to artillery fire from the reverse slope or from longer range guns on distant hills. Before their attack on May 29th, the Germans concentrated the fire of 25 batteries onto the hapless defenders of le Mort-Homme. By December the Germans were holding onto it and Côte 304. What had they gained? Half a dozen more hills rose between them and Verdun, bristling with fully prepared French defenders. Nine months of shelling had piled up the corpses and destroyed the topography—the deforested hills, now smoking like dormant volcanoes, were a dozen feet shorter, forever—but left the tactical situation unchanged.[29]

On June 23rd, almost exactly four months after the opening bombardment, the Germans launched a new general offensive on the right bank. Once again they began with a massive artillery preparation, now including 100,000 poison gas shells launched the day before. Once again they broke in, this time overrunning the French lines by more than a mile, all the way to the fort which stood at the tip of a promontory from which it took its name, Froideterre, only three miles from Verdun. And once again the defensive means of modern weaponry, artfully exercised, asserted themselves. Even deprived of most of its heavy ordnance by official orders, and of most of its outer and inner walls by large-caliber German shells, a fort could still repel attackers as long as the defenders within its ruins retained the will and the means to keep them at bay. Units of the 1st and 2nd Bavarian Infantry Divisions approached Froideterre casually, as though visiting an undefended heap of rubble, only to be driven from the inner court by machine guns and from the roof and glacis—the slopes descending from the parapets—within seconds, by 75 mm guns firing by the hundred *boîtes à mitraille*, lethal new projectiles that no longer exploded into a few jagged pieces of steel but instead drenched the assailants with shrapnel. Soon French infantry counterattacked. The same blood-soaked routine followed on July 12th, when the Bavarian Leibregiment, the nucleus of the elite Alpenkorps, stormed nearby Souville, technically not a fort but close enough, after a nocturnal bombardment that turned the superstructure into an amorphous mass of brick and concrete. This time a hail of grenades decimated the confident assailants as they scaled the escarpment. It was the closest—2.5 miles—they ever got to Verdun during the war.

General Ewald von Lochow, in command of the army group on the east bank of the river, had doubted the wisdom of such costly pushes ever since mid-May. He had called instead for incremental improvements to their existing positions. Later, in August, he called a renewed plan to take Souville pointless. It would require, he feared, weeks of heavy fighting, and would leave the enemy in possession of good artillery observation posts even if it did fall. It would be as difficult, he assured his listeners, who included the commanders of the Fifth Army and Falkenhayn himself, as taking Fort Vaux—which had indeed fallen on 7th June, but only after three months of blood and toil. As with Douaumont, German success owed much to French negligence. Disarmed by order of the high command since August 1915, slated for destruction on February 26th but saved by the inability of the agents to carry out the order in the chaos of the German attack, Vaux provided little more than lodging for troops in transit during the battle, its garrison unconcerned with the obsolete arts of defending a military fortification. It had even opened the northeastern and northwestern corners onto the Bois de la Caillette outside, as though inviting the enemy in. Because of circulation problems Pétain's order to rearm the fort remained a dead letter, and the 75 mm guns and *boîtes à mitraille* that had saved Souville were absent or unusable here. Even so the defenders held off the Germans skillfully and tenaciously and only gave out during the final assault in the first days of June because their army failed to supply or relieve them: thirst, rather than the flamethrowers, explosives, and poison gas of the German Pioneers, cost the French the Fort de Vaux.[30]

And when the French resolved to recapture their fallen strongholds they too fell prey to this war's unyielding hostility to the offensive. One of them, General Charles Mangin, tried to retake Douaumont on 22 May with his 5th Infantry Division. Known to some of the men as a "mangeur d'hommes"—"devourer of men," a pun on his name, but meaning "the butcher"—he was as temperamentally suited to the offensive as Pétain was to the defensive. In the event, his assault on Douaumont failed. The artillery preparation, enough to damage the fort but not to put its German guns out of action, left the infantry exposed to artillery fire as they approached, swept by machine gun fire from turrets, casemates, and the windows and doors of barracks once they reached the fort's rooftop and its inner courtyards. Too weak with just a single division to absorb such heavy losses, they soon ran out of reserves and whole battalions were shredded or cut off. Liaisons with their own artillery were nonexistent, one of the regimental commanders complained, and the departure zone was primitive, its communication trench impassable, its jumping-off trenches unfinished: the Territorials had not had enough time. Mangin's reach had exceeded his grasp, the devourer devoured.[31]

Pétain had never been enthusiastic about the venture. But he was gone from the Second Army headquarters at Souilly, still in command but more remotely: on May 1 Joffre had sent him to Bar-le-Duc, farther south, to command of the Central Army Group, in which the Second Army, the army of Verdun, as it came to be called, only joined its neighbors. The Généralissime handed the vacant command of the Second Army to General Robert Nivelle, who shared Mangin's offensive fervor and wasted no opportunity to indulge it. After the German attack on Souville on July 11th and 12th he ordered Mangin to clear the approaches to the fort and retake the ruined village of Fleury-devant-Douaumont. The attack failed, not for lack of infantry but for the now-familiar inadequacies of the artillery preparation beforehand. Untouched German machine-gunners, dispersed in shell-holes, swept the terrain, and when the 3rd Zouaves advanced on Fleury most of the regiment's officers were killed or wounded. The story repeated itself in the following days.[32]

In October Nivelle and Mangin tried again to retake Douaumont. This time they left nothing to chance; a frontal assault across open terrain was always dangerous. They sent in three divisions on a front wide enough to envelop the fort, assured themselves of air superiority, prepared the attack with three days of artillery shelling, intense training for the troops, and an elaborate organizing of the departure zone. The troops went in methodically, equipped with compasses and a sure knowledge of the terrain and preceded by a creeping artillery barrage that kept pace ahead of them by calibrated clockwork. The fort fell in several hours.

As it turned out, the Germans had already abandoned it—not, as their propaganda and the Wolff news agency and wire service in Berlin later claimed, because they no longer wished to keep it, but because they had panicked. They had feared a violent incineration of the entire garrison the day before, when fires set off by the bombardment threatened to detonate munitions vaults and ignite rooms packed with flammable rocketry. They withdrew under cover of darkness to more secure positions, not far from those they had occupied before their assault in February. At three o'clock the next afternoon the battalions of the Régiment Colonial du Maroc—the Marsouins—spilled over the ruined parapets and into deserted lodgings and acrid passages, into almost as desolate an edifice as the forlorn behemoth the Germans had wandered into on a snowy day eight months earlier.[33]

On the 2nd of November the French recaptured Fort Vaux in much the same way. When two officers and a sapper emerged through the machine gun openings of the southwestern casement that evening they entered caverns and galleries lit by lingering fires, resounding with grenades and rifle cartridges set off by smoking debris, and littered with four machine guns, several hundred thousand cartridges, a thousand bottles of mineral water, and 3,000 cans of food and rations—the vestiges of occupants who had decamped in a hurry. The intruders also found instructions for the defense of the fort, written by German officers who had expected their attack. Instead the besieged had given up the ghost. For all his offensive method, Nivelle had conquered an absent foe.[34]

So many still believed, in 1916, that movement held the key to victory in war. And still prized the offensive, because of the choice it allowed and the surprise it created. At Verdun, Nivelle, Mangin, and Knobelsdorf, among others, still revered such canons, as ancient as war itself; so, farther away, did Joffre and Haig, and, farther still, Ludendorff and Brussilow and Conrad von Hötzendorff on the wide open fronts of the East. Yet Verdun proclaimed that breakthrough only happened against an enemy already broken.

Once, logistics had restricted the mobility and the size of armies; moving and supplying an army required more ingenuity than assembling it. When an army could move no more than 10 or 15 miles a day, when convoys and baggage trains struggled to supply it with food and fodder even more than with ammunition, a few hours gained followed by a cunning descent by a detached corps upon an unsuspecting enemy might decide the outcome of a battle or even of an entire campaign. To steal a march, to surprise an already engaged foe when help was too far to arrive in time—the quest for such moments had inspired Napoleonic and Frederician ambition. Now, in one day, massive armies could cover 20 times the distance by rail their smaller and lighter ancestors could on foot. Long trains sped armies of millions to front lines on distant borders, and kept them supplied there every day with all they needed and more, even with the tonnage in materiel and munitions now dwarfing that in food.

Ironically enough, however, the machines of the age of speed immobilized the armies of the day at the point of contact. They could move them swiftly to the front but no farther, least of all into enemy territory, where advance on foot was all that technology could offer the infantry and where like vehicles would rush in enough defenders to meet them. It had taken the German General Staff four days to move as many divisions from the Eastern Front to Champagne in September 1915, just the time it took for the French attackers to run out of steam and come to a halt on the German second lines. And at Verdun the trucks were moving up the road from Bar-le-Duc within 24 hours. But once near the front lines they too could travel no farther. Logistics no longer favored the bold.[35]

Once, firepower had worked only at close range and presented solutions and obstacles to attackers and defenders alike. Its progress had led attacking generals to resort to movements on the wings or outflanking movements—at Sadowa in 1866, at Sedan in 1870, in Manchuria in 1904 and 1905. By 1916 artillery and machine guns multiplied range and firepower many times over, but, like locomotion, had the perverse effect of shutting down movement in battle. The new rapid-fire killing machines, the guns that laid down impassable barrages at 3,000 yards or scattered the terrain with their projectiles at 8,000 or 10,000, and that did so not at random with "tirs de fantaisie"—"shots in the dark"—but onto targets identified by aerial observation and communicated by wireless—these machines kept the infantry away, rendered attacks less frequent and more costly, put off the close-quarter shock that had once provided the be-all and end-all of battle. Employed as counter-battery, they more easily nullified the enemy's offensive than his defensive capability; they usually neutralized rather than destroyed the artillery on the other side.

There the men would take cover in earthworks and dugouts that had been growing daily in strength and sophistication since the start of the war, until the bombardment lifted and they emerged to find enough of their pieces still intact to rain grief upon the best laid plans of hostile infantry. And the guns themselves, prisoners of their hunger for industry's munitions, could not travel far from their base during an offensive across the cratered surface and blasted earth, moving up quickly and leaving their source of supply far behind them. The guns at Verdun that thwarted so many attempts at breakthrough never assured a single one themselves.[36]

Once, when armies were modest, supply lines constrained, and fire-power limited, battlefields were small—a few miles wide in Napoleon's day. They allowed what frontal firepower incited, outflanking movements. Now they were immense, sometimes tens of miles wide, saturated with firepower, and as inhospitable to movement around their wings as the Western Front itself, contained by the sea at one end and the mountains at the other. At Verdun the Germans tried to attack their foe from the wings, from Argonne on their right to Woëvre on their left, and found him as solidly entrenched as in front of them. And where did the center end and the flanks begin? Spatially as well as temporally, battles on the Western Front never ended; they petered out, or faded into troubled obscurity. An offensive had little to gain from an attack on a flank so distant that it lost all connection to the center.[37]

Still, in 1916, the old faith died hard. Before each new push on the Somme Haig assembled masses of cavalry for the breakthrough and the pursuit far beyond that never came. And Nivelle thought he had found the way at Verdun. He had found, he believed, swift and sure methods of concentrating fire on narrow zones and pushing through there, seeming to echo the optimistic predictions of the Germans in February. In the middle of December, on the eve of another local offensive that would bring the French back almost to their lines of February and eloquently confirm the demoralized state of their enemy yet leave him in impreg-nable positions only a little farther back, Nivelle preened himself on dis-covering the recipe to rupture the front and win the war. "So, d'Alençon!," he told one of his trusted staff officers, "we now have the formula, we'll beat the enemy with it." In February 1916 Falkenhayn had piqued himself no less warmly: "I was right again." Now Falkenhayn was gone. And five months later Nivelle was, too, in the wake of his disastrous offensive at the Chemin des Dames.[38]

Verdun, from a distance, resembles a succession of offensives doomed by the nature of modern warfare. Neither Falkenhayn nor Nivelle nor Joffre nor many others close enough to know better wanted to admit that. Nor, *a fortiori*, did most of their compatriots then or later on.

"Nothing there resembles a proper battle," the military analyst of *Le Petit Journal* wrote with gloomy resignation in April, "the same game can last forever [. . .] and it might not ever be possible to put an end to the battle of Verdun." Seemingly he had understood. But more often the French chroniclers labored to find in the nation's long military past a source of familiarity if not of inspiration.[39] When the news was bad they reminded their readers of Marengo, lost to the Austrians at three o'clock only to be retaken at four, or of Bonaparte at Rivoli, waiting to send in the reserves until the locus of the principal Austrian attack became clear, or of the river at Friedland or the cemetery of Eylau. Such historical parallels made little sense in February and early March 1916, and none at all when the hopes of a sudden and shining victory dissolved in the mud and the impasse that even the most sanguine narrators could not dispel. Eylau, fought in 1807, had involved 75,000 French soldiers, cost them 22,000 in total losses, and lasted two days. Verdun was not Eylau.[40]

Less glorious parallels came to their minds, especially sieges from the Crimean war of six decades earlier or the Russo-Japanese war in Manchuria of one decade earlier. Verdun was Sebastopol, Verdun was Port Arthur, but where was the garrison at Verdun, defending the walls of the port city? The analogy did not hold.[41]

Unable, like their French counterparts, to explain what was happening at Verdun, the German newspapers yet resisted, unlike them, any temptation to call in their own history to the rescue. They declined to invoke inspiring precedents, including the most beckoning of them, the encirclement of the French army at nearby Sedan in 1870 that ended the Second Empire if not the Franco-Prussian war. When movement came to a halt at Verdun but the battle did not, the German war correspondents proposed analyses that in the end mirrored those of their adversaries. Why so long, they asked. Sometimes they buried their own enthusiasms over the sudden conquest of Douaumont to answer gravely and inconsistently that pause and preparation preceded advance in modern warfare, and anticipated the inverse volte-face that their French colleagues would perform when their own turn to triumph came in the autumn. More often they echoed the attritional refrain, inverting the losses but armed with the same assurance that no contradiction could undo them. The losses of the French were twice their own, thanks to slow and meticulous preparation; the more the French had spent themselves at Verdun, the more the Germans had approached their own goal, which consisted not in the site "but in the systematic attrition (*Zermürbung*, yet another variant of *Ausblutung*) of the French army."[42]

As for the offensive trap, this was too technical to hold anyone's interest, too uninspiring to enthuse, on either side of the border. Instead posterity came to exalt the defensive spirit of the one and the offensive will of the other, in ways that salvaged their pride but missed the infernal dynamic of their encounter.

Between poetry and popular song during the battle itself and the schoolbooks and novels that kept its memory alive long after it had ended, the theme of "ils ne passeront pas!"—"they shall not pass!"— defined the French epic version.[43] In disparate media the *poilu* fending off the Teutonic attacker appeared and re-appeared like a choral response. Music-hall songs sang of Driant as of Roland in the defile at Ronces- valles in the eighth century, of the humble and just *poilus* now guarding the heavens lest the Teuton should seek to enter there too;[44] poems and novels depicted human chest against inhuman steel;[45] histories for chil- dren and adults alike celebrated the *poilu* as the sole force that had filled the void left by material and mechanical deficiency and saved the country. This, in their eyes, was what had happened at Verdun.[46]

By contrast the Germans, when they came to celebrate their own at Verdun, elevated the offensive spirit of the common soldier above his other virtues. Their heroes there were also victims. The German leadership at Verdun, unlike the French, provoked lasting controversy and bitter reproach. The battle had lasted so long, in their eyes, because Falken- hayn and his staff had failed to win it. There was no Pétain here, nor any Mangin or Nivelle, only the tragic *Feldgrau*, betrayed by his command and even, by extension, his country.[47] In some of the most popular novels of the interwar years he is melancholy and abandoned, robbed of his victory in February and again in June by the "gambler" Falkenhayn, and victim of the bitter law by which "victory always slips from the German hand at the last moment."[48]

The French solemnized the endurance of their *poilus*, the Germans the initiative of their *Feldgrauen*. The myth of the "storming" of Douaumont on one side of the Rhine answered the even more chimerical legend of the "trench of the bayonets" on the other—the apocryphal but much visited site where the infantrymen of the French 137th Infantry Regiment were supposed to have stood stoically at their posts, as the trench caved in on them, leaving only the points of their fixed bayonets in view above the soil, the everlasting vestiges of the French will to resist.[49]

As it happened, both *poilu* and *Feldgrau* fought offensively as well as defensively at Verdun, depending on where and when they stood, as valiant in one posture as in the other. In the turmoil of movements that neutralized each other and finally brought both sides back to the starting points, any student of military science could recognize one of its most ancient laws: that equivalence of force, even rough equivalence, favors the defender.[50]

5

The Prestige Trap

VERDUN HAD GIVEN THE GERMANS NOTHING TO CELEBRATE, once Douaumont had fallen and their advances of the first few heady days had come to a halt. By the early spring of 1916 little that Falkenhayn or his generals had hoped for had come to pass. The French had defended Verdun, as he had hoped and expected, but neither they nor their English allies had counterattacked elsewhere to relieve the pressure there. On March 21st, one month to the day after the attack on Verdun had begun, OHL acknowledged as much. But Falkenhayn refused to change course— refused to launch instead offensives against the French in Champagne or the English in Artois, in spite of urgent entreaties from some of the generals there. Falkenhayn no longer believed in frontal breakthroughs, and he still feared English or French attacks elsewhere, even an English landing or amphibious assault behind the German front. So nothing happened. The Western Front remained as static as ever.[1]

To cap it all, the Navy did not lift its restrictions on the submarine war against the English, as Falkenhayn had been urging since December 1915. Kaiser Wilhelm and Chancellor Bethmann-Hollweg were surprised to hear from Falkenhayn late in April that he had only sent his divisions against the French in February on the understanding that the Navy would wage a "ruthless" submarine war against Great Britain. He would not, he claimed with some exaggeration, and much to the skepticism of Bethmann-Hollweg and Admiral Georg von Müller, Chief of the Kaiser's Naval Cabinet, have undertaken one without the other. On the first of May the Kaiser finally declined to resume unrestricted submarine war. Falkenhayn offered his resignation. He had not been consulted, he complained. Soon he changed his mind. Perhaps, as Müller uncharitably suspected, he had contrived a temporary scapegoat for his own failures at Verdun. Perhaps, as he himself later claimed, he had swallowed his pride and kept his office to avoid conveying an impression of disarray at the summit to Germany's enemies in the Entente. But one more fissure had undermined his edifice of assumptions, and still he did not call off offensive operations on the Meuse.[2]

With success so elusive and failure so costly, reason might dictate that the Germans suspend their initiative, or the French moderate their response. Why ten months and more of debilitating attacks and counter-attacks, why the losses that irreparably weakened each national protag-onist, just to return each side to its original lines?

After the war Falkenhayn's contemporaries, already perplexed by his words in the Christmas Memorandum, took him to task for his acts as well—for persisting at Verdun so long with so little and for so little. He should have risked more forces to take Verdun, the Crown Prince wrote in his memoirs, or called off the enterprise within weeks once the attack on the left bank had failed to neutralize French artillery. Count von Schulen-burg, who replaced Knobelsdorf as chief of staff of the Fifth Army at the end of August, said much the same. A cold look at the general situation by early April at the latest, he said after the war, dictated a withdrawal to the original lines to build up more reserves. By June the imminence of a Franco-British offensive on the Somme and the reality of a Russian one in Galicia added an even more compelling argument for withdrawing to their original lines, holding there defensively, and releasing the divisions on the Meuse for their beleaguered fellows and allies elsewhere. In his own retrospective account of the battle, Pétain, usually unstinting in his respect for his German adversaries, said much the same. Falkenhayn, he wrote, should have saved his regiments at Verdun to fight another day, in another place.[3]

Generals do not readily abandon their own enterprises, and once before, at Ypres in November 1914, Falkenhayn had resisted calling off a costly and ultimately futile offensive. But on several occasions, he had considered drawing a line under his "operation in the Meuse region in the direction of Verdun." A week into the battle he refused to send in any new division there without withdrawing an old one. When the subject of breaking off the offensive came up, he did not rule it out. At the end of March he himself raised the prospect with the Minister of War, and again with the commanders of the Fifth Army. In May, and again in July, and again in August shortly before his dismissal, Falkenhayn weighed the merits of consigning Operation *Gericht* to oblivion.[4]

He was not alone. Ever since the 21st of February the French had periodically asked themselves what sacrifices Verdun justified and what, if anything, they should give up there. For long months they denied the aggressors the wretched spoils—the ruins and the blasted earth on both banks of the Meuse—until the battle reversed itself and they recaptured in the autumn most of what they had lost in the previous winter. Stasis alone might vindicate their defense, less perplexing in its tenacity than the obstinacy of the attackers, but still they contemplated withdrawal now and again, asking themselves less urgently but just as pertinently as the Germans whether it was all worth it.

Pétain came from a long line of Picard peasants, and differed in his origins as much from his counterpart Crown Prince Wilhelm as Joffre did from Falkenhayn. But like the Crown Prince, he mentioned withdrawal as an option, even threatened it on occasion, only to yield to the inflexible refusals of his hierarchical superiors.

He had arrived at Souilly on the evening of the 25th of February armed with an unequivocal order from Joffre: "Yesterday the 24th I ordered that we hold on the right bank north of Verdun. Any commander ordering a retreat will be court-martialed." Nevertheless, that day local generals had already set tactical withdrawals from the right bank in motion, and Pétain had approved of them. The withdrawal from the plain of Woëvre made sense to him—why waste forces there when they lacked them so cruelly closer to Verdun? Forward lines need not be held at all costs, in his eyes, a leitmotiv he would invoke again during another emergency in 1918, when, as chief of the General Staff, he enjoyed the authority to apply it. Within 24 hours he and his staff had drawn a line of inner forts to which they might withdraw on the right bank, one that ran north of the city, close to the river, through the forts of Belleville, Saint-Michel, Souville, Tavannes, and Moulainville, an inner "ligne de la panique," the panic line. Similar contingency plans soon appeared for another such line on the left bank, this one running from the crest of le Mort-Homme around Verdun and down to Dugny on the Meuse. The would-be line of resistance leaked out, giving rise to the rumor that Pétain planned to withdraw to the left bank. He did not, though the thought did not unnerve him, however loyally he set about carrying out the order that sanctified every inch of the land. Late in June, when the enemy briefly took the village of Fleury and the post of Thiaumont and held the fort of Froideterre in his grasp, Pétain told Joffre that he would withdraw to the left bank if, as seemed imminent, the *ligne de la panique* on the right bank fell.[5]

Every time the dark horse of renunciation, even partial renunciation, crept into German or French councils of war, it suffered the same fate. The advocates of persistence prevailed, one way or another, and ambition rather than abnegation carried the day.

Inside the high command of the Fifth Army, a pattern set in. Every few weeks a council of war weighed calling off the offensive, and every few weeks the martial option won out: whatever they did at Verdun, they would not give up fighting. The Crown Prince soon tired of partial attacks and limited objectives, and urged that the offensive be significantly strengthened or summarily suspended. Chief of Staff Knobelsdorf vigorously advocated such efforts until he was relieved late in August. Sometimes, as in mid-May, when he lost faith but quickly changed his mind, much to the bewilderment of the Crown Prince, Knobelsdorf resigned himself to suspending the action, but never to calling it off once and for all. Below them the Fifth Army's group commanders and chiefs of staff were divided. Most proclaimed their willingness to continue as long as reinforcements arrived. He could not do so otherwise, the chief of staff of the Eastern Army Group, Major Wetzell, announced in mid-May. In August one general of the Eastern Army Group, Hermann von François, insisted on continuing the offensive; another, Ewald von Lochow, thought it pointless. In the end all that mattered was the opinion of Falkenhayn, and each time, overcoming his skepticism and his hesitations, he heeded Knobelsdorf's exhortations more than Crown Prince Wilhelm's warnings. He opted to continue. It cost him his job. When Hindenburg and Ludendorff took over at the summit of the General Staff, they cut the Gordian knot within three days of his departure. "The attack on Verdun," they decreed on the 2nd of September, "is to be suspended; the line attained is to be built into a long-term position." Whatever this meant—respite or renunciation—no more than Falkenhayn could they bring themselves to break off the battle altogether, even if they did not renew the attacks of its first six months. It went on.[6]

Joffre would not hear of withdrawal either. He even wished for a more aggressive defense on the Meuse, and sent Pétain upstairs, to the command of the Central Army Group in Bar-le-Duc. The Group encompassed the Second Army in Verdun, but the more aggressive General Nivelle now took over its command in Pétain's stead. As it happened, the move from Souilly to the headquarters of the Central Army Group in Bar-le-Duc did nothing to silence the irksome Pétain, who kept demanding more reinforcements for his army at Verdun. During the crisis on the *ligne de la panique* in June, when Pétain threatened to evacuate the right bank unless he received them, Joffre hastily sent three more divisions. He would not hear of withdrawal. "I must make clear to you," he wrote back, "that you must continue with a stubborn resistance on the right bank of the Meuse...."[7]

Why was withdrawal, even tactical withdrawal, so unpalatable to men for whom Verdun remained a secondary battle, a piece of a wider puzzle?

Was it perhaps the thirst for fame or glory, or the play of personalities? Graveyards teem with generals who persisted for personal reasons— vanity, ambition, politics—long after they should have desisted for military ones.

The unspoken commands of deference may have induced Falkenhayn to heed the enthusiasms of Knobelsdorf over the misgivings of the Crown Prince. Knobelsdorf, though subordinate to Falkenhayn, was older in years and senior in service, and had preceded him as commander of the 4th Guards Regiment before the war. And Knobelsdorf's own direct superior, Wilhelm, the Kaiser's son and heir, did not have the ear of his distant father, who granted him no more access than anyone else in the chain of command, and much less than that accorded to his favored counselor, Falkenhayn—his only counselor, as some would have it. The Crown Prince, though a Hohenzollern, was strangely isolated, and Falkenhayn could disregard his views without risk of imperial wrath. The play of persons at the summit of the Fifth Army, compounded by the fear of a shaming admission of a strategic error, might have kept Falkenhayn from abandoning his project at Verdun. But had a thirst for glory alone sustained his obstinacy, he would logically have committed far more of his forces there than he did. Vanity was not all.[8]

Among the French an undeclared war for renown emerged among the generals on the scene. For long the face of the providential savior appeared uncertain, until Pétain's profile came lastingly to dominate the battle of Verdun. Generals came and went and enjoyed passing glory. "The glorious defender of Verdun," wrote Gustave Téry of *L'Oeuvre* of General Humbert, commander of the neighboring Third Army during the early days of the battle, the ephemeral savior who carried a notebook full of Napoleon's sayings with him—the way, he told an admiring Téry, to beat the Germans. He soon vanished from the papers. Castelnau, by contrast, already was a name, that of the savior of Nancy in 1914 and of Joffre's new second-in-command, and when he galvanized the wilting local commanders into action he seemed set to attach it to the salvation of Verdun. Standing on the steps of the modest *mairie* of Souilly, he inspired the reverential war correspondents "with his calm, his sangfroid, his smiling presence of mind." But he soon left the scene and went back to General Staff headquarters at Chantilly.

For months Robert Nivelle dominated the news from Verdun, especially at the end of the year when his successful counteroffensives earned him the sobriquet of "the victor of Verdun." For a while the papers spread his fame, mistakenly assuming him to be the architect of new defensive tactics in July and of breakthrough in December. Nivelle craved the adulation. Asked how he had retaken the old French positions in the damp wintry terrain, and how in a sea of mud his men had moved up, he replied "If I ask them to do it, they'll do it." His reputation elevated him to Chantilly and the high command, until his failed offensive on the Chemin des Dames in the Aisne in April 1917 ended his hour in the sun and with it his dubious claim to have saved Verdun from the Teutons.

Lesser lights shone briefly as well. Sometimes a photo of General Mangin, whose 5th Infantry Division had briefly sojourned on the outworks of Douaumont in May and retaken the fort for good in October, appeared alongside that of Nivelle in the newspapers. His celebrity, too, fell victim to his enthusiasms on the Chemin des Dames, and Mangin took his place among the mounting ephemera of the war.[9]

Pétain, who succeeded Castelnau on the steps at Souilly on the 26th of February and left them for the command of the Central Army Group in Bar-le-Duc on 1 May, never openly cultivated the fame that some of his predecessors and contemporaries did. "The newspapers exasperate me," he wrote to his future wife, Eugénie-Annie Hardon. "I requested that silence about me be imposed." In March only instant photos, surreptitiously taken and poorly reproduced against his will in daily papers, betrayed his face to an unknowing public. Twenty-five years later it would adorn the hall of every public building in the land, as the head of a French state who had appealed to the German invaders for an armistice and entered upon a path of "collaboration." But for now he affected not to care for such celebrity, and tirelessly proclaimed to Eugénie-Annie his profound indifference to the gallery. Even the flood of marriage proposals that this eligible yet sexagenarian bachelor now received in his morning post washed over him harmlessly. "I was subjected this week to a veritable matrimonial assault [...] I need as much tenacity to loosen the embrace of these ladies as to resist the Hun."[10]

He reaped the most durable renown nonetheless. Even from Bar, where Joffre, exasperated by his stubbornness and his seeming tactical passivity, had hoped to put him out to pasture, he continued to importune the high command with his incessant demands for troops and above all guns for the interminable battle, and with Nivelle in eclipse Pétain's image came to suffuse forever the ordeal of Verdun. At first it was Napoleonic, the persona required to lift him from relative obscurity into the light of national fame. The reporters introduced him as the general whose speed, decisiveness, and offensive spirit had carried the day in his sectors at Arras and in Champagne the year before. He was "a leader, a real leader." Whether the battle did not suit the allusion or he clearly conveyed little of Bonaparte, the papers soon exalted his serenity over his dash, his "moral ascendancy" over his aggressiveness. They praised his realism and his simplicity, his common sense: they praised the *poilu* in him.[11]

During the German occupation 25 years later discretion reigned about the Battle of Verdun, both in published word and official commemoration. Pétain had saved France then as now, the public learned, and his name symbolized all those of the "300,000 French buried there in their glory." He had asked to be buried with them. After the liberation in 1944, discretion reigned instead about him—at the 30th commemoration of 1946 General de Lattre de Tassigny did not mention him at all, preferring to remember Mangin, and later de Gaulle alluded to him but not by name. Eventually, by the 1960s, he recovered his place in the history books and the secular liturgy of state ceremonies, and the laureate of Verdun re-emerged from behind the pariah of Vichy.[12]

Pétain's counterpart, the Crown Prince, neither sought nor reaped the same attention. Even in the early days of the battle, when fortune seemed to favor German arms, he appeared only modestly, praised by the Wolff wire service or a major daily but hardly apotheosized. The only German commander who captured renown comparable to Pétain's during and after the war was Paul von Hindenburg, whose renown sprang from the Eastern Front and who had little to do with Verdun. Much more than their German confrères, the French newsmen attempted to link Verdun to a face or a name. Only rarely did they pierce the veil of secrecy that shrouded the calculations of their subjects. Pétain, like the others, might have savored the esteem that came with holding Verdun, and feared the stain on his honor should he ever lose it, but no more than Falkenhayn did he act out of amour propre alone. Fame beckoned. Nonetheless both men had to justify themselves to doubters and superiors, and even to themselves, and when they did so they spoke the language not of affect but of soulless calculation.[13]

Whenever Falkenhayn began to invoke the goal of *Ausblutung*, of slowly bleeding the French to death at little cost to themselves, whenever it rather than his original designs became his leitmotiv for continuing his offensive at Verdun, it rested not on fact or evidence but on faith.

At first, though, it was Crown Prince Wilhelm who shone with optimism about the impact of their attack, and Falkenhayn who injected the note of doubt. The Crown Prince confidently assured Falkenhayn in a written report that the French offensive strength was broken, that they had too few divisions left to mount anything other than small local attacks elsewhere on the front, that with adequate reinforcements he could decide the fate of the French army at Verdun. "Alas not!" Falkenhayn scribbled in the margin, and replied with all the skepticism of which he was capable. The enemy, he riposted—and he meant the British as well as the French—could do much more than the Crown Prince imagined.[14]

Soon Falkenhayn adopted the same optimistic note, even as the Crown Prince began to drop it. The longer the battle, the deeper grew the discord between the two, and the stronger the meeting of minds between Falkenhayn and Knobelsdorf. Both came to invoke the one remaining premise that might now justify the daily slaughter on the Meuse: they were wearing the French out, inflicting many more casualties than they were taking.

One week into the offensive, with equilibrium setting in and the initiative slipping from their grasp, the generals of the Fifth Army told Falkenhayn that if their losses ever exceeded or even equaled those of the French, they should break off the attack. Falkenhayn did not disagree, but remained optimistic. On occasion he inverted the proposition: as long as they were losing less than the French, he pointed out, the virtues of Verdun became self-evident. The French would slowly exhaust themselves there, he predicted, and when in July the Kaiser requested a *tour d'horizon*, Falkenhayn replied as confidently as ever about Verdun. They had resolved, he repeated, to bring France to her senses through *Blutabzapfung* ("bloodletting"). And Knobelsdorf, the Crown Prince complained, espoused the stratagem even more volubly than Falkenhayn.[15]

Whenever the wisdom of protracting the inconclusive battle came into question, Falkenhayn renewed the same sanguine and sanguinary rationale for pursuing it. Early in April he told the chief of staff of the Third Army that the French had already taken 200,000 casualties at Verdun. In August he told the Kaiser that the French had lost 250,000 more men than the Germans. He had aimed, he reminded his sovereign in a lengthy telegram, to bleed the French army or exhaust the French nation at Verdun, and he asked rhetorically where they would be if the French had found the forces to attack in strength on the Somme or the German reserves he had husbanded had not been on hand to defend there. The French had lost more than three times as many as the Germans, he claimed anew in 1919, in his first public attempt at self-justification, and in his memoirs the following year he returned to the charge—only this time he set the ratio at 2.5 to 1.[16]

Neither he nor anyone else had any basis for so optimistic a postmortem or so macabre a calculus. He had no reliable way of knowing that the French losses by early April amounted to about 100,000, which they did, still less for claiming they were twice that. Neither during nor after the war did any statistics allow him to stretch the gap between French and German losses so mightily—over the course of the battle they came to approximate each other. He knew on the basis of his own army's reports that German losses were high, but on this he did not dwell in his reports. And he contradicted his own numbers, and betrayed confusion if not bad faith. German losses were 30,000 a month, or about 100,000 in all, he had told Bethmann-Hollweg at the end of May. But a week earlier he had placed them at 134,000, as the Chancellor did not fail to note. Falkenhayn, like Knobelsdorf, chose to believe what he could not know, and called in numbers that no one yet could question, data that no one could verify and no one could falsify, the invaluable instruments of wishful thinking and special pleading.[17]

They sprang from semi-submerged habits of the mind. The French were on the verge of exhaustion, they would fall, the German high command insisted, and the paragons of such overconfidence brooked no skepticism. When the Crown Prince, at the end of March, had fallen prey to the contagion of temerity and pronounced the French army broken, Falkenhayn had raised the skeptical eyebrow, and recalled him, as the commander of the Fifth Army, to his senses. But he, too, never lost faith in French weakness for long. In July he told the Kaiser that the French could not hold out for another winter. And the Kaiser himself, cheered by such assurances, repeated them to his entourage. The French might give up soon at Verdun, he told them in April—two deserters had said so. And did not Verdun tie the enemy down, did not its urgency condemn him to passivity elsewhere? The French participation in the Somme offensive in July strongly suggested otherwise, but the surprised German high command quickly inverted the logic and recovered its conviction, so deep-seated was the premise: they must persevere at Verdun, if only to restrain more French forces from fighting on the Somme.[18]

Meanwhile Pétain also had come to see Verdun as a battle of attrition—an essential battle, without any doubt, but limited in its promise. To spare his army high losses and inflict them on the enemy he required infantry divisions and heavy artillery, a logic that linked threats of partial withdrawal to demands for adequate force. The German *attaque brusquée* of February 21, he argued in May, had succeeded thanks to the poverty of the French defense. The enemy's next attacks, on the left bank in early March and again in early April, had broken with "enormous losses" on the lines of the armed and waiting French at le Mort-Homme and elsewhere. This was the battle he wished to fight. But now, in May, with concentrated attacks and heavy artillery on narrow sectors, the enemy was grinding the French down at Verdun once again. Pétain no longer needed one new division every two days; he needed two every three. He no longer needed heavy- and medium-artillery to narrow the gap, but instead to prevent it from widening. No longer could the fresh combat troops come from *la noria* ("the waterwheel"), his system of rapidly rotating divisions from the Central Army Group and the Second Army in and out of the front lines. They must come from elsewhere on the front.

He demanded as well, more pressingly every day, equally attritional relief operations elsewhere on the Western Front. He had heard about the coming offensive on the Somme and disliked what he had heard. The massive frontal assault would gain little ground, cost "thousands" of lives, and do little to deter the Germans at Verdun, he argued in May. Better to keep them under constant threat at various points on the front than launch one all-out offensive which would exhaust the assailants—their English allies, mostly—after a few days. "Better," as he put it, "a threat of eruption than an extinct volcano facing the Germans." Better to adopt German methods, apply sustained pressure and use them up as they were slowly using up the French Second Army on the Meuse—better to mount smaller Verduns in reverse, he proposed in effect. Verdun, if only Joffre would send him the forces he needed and if only the British would quickly mount lasting relief operations elsewhere, would at least wear the enemy down, "since we cannot aspire to do anything else for the moment."[19]

Actually, Joffre did aspire to something else at that moment. He acceded to Pétain's demands with the same parsimony that his counterpart Falkenhayn displayed, not because he feared new attacks elsewhere, but because he was planning one of his own. Verdun, in his reckoning, would allow the Entente to win on several fronts in the summer, and above all on the Somme. The longer Verdun lasted, the more it would impair the German defense on the Somme. It must not fall, but it must not starve grand strategy either by an immoderate appetite for resources. So Joffre would provide enough to hold there and no more—a tenuous calculus that nearly snapped during the crisis on the *ligne de la panique* in June, when Pétain threatened to evacuate the right bank and Joffre hastily sent him three more divisions. He nonetheless would not hear of withdrawal. He wished for a more aggressive defense on the Meuse, even as he begrudged Pétain his incessant demands for reinforcements and his stubborn skepticism about the coming Somme offensive. Sending him away to command the Central Group solved little. The move from Souilly to Bar-le-Duc silenced neither Pétain nor the squabbles over what was needed at Verdun and why.[20]

Joffre's will to defend yet deprive Verdun, his spirit of mean commitment, bedeviled him. To justify the French response to the Germans at Verdun he gave himself over, in the manner of Falkenhayn, to reassuring fictions about relative losses. On March 10th he told his British counterpart Sir William Robertson, Chief of the Imperial General Staff, that French losses at Verdun amounted to 30,000, the Germans' to twice that. Robertson soon grew skeptical. In May he expressed doubts to Prime Minister Herbert Asquith that the French had lost as few and the Germans as many as Joffre claimed. But to hurry the British along Joffre goaded them just as ardently with warnings of imminent French exhaustion. In April he asked Premier Briand and President Poincaré to impress upon Asquith when he visited Paris that victory in the long term was no solution; they had to win quickly, or face a war of economic exhaustion. "France," they should tell him, "which has spared herself no effort until now, is reaching the limit of her strength [. . . and] will emerge from this sort of war more or less ruined." Optimistic in one breath, pessimistic the next, Joffre urged resolution in their habits and moderation in their demands upon the defenders of Verdun, and kept his eyes fixed on the locus of his expectations, the Somme.[21]

When the infantry went over the top there on 1 July—for the British army, the bloodiest single day in its history—had Verdun weakened the German defenders or the Allied attackers more? The battle of the distant apologists, ably led by Joffre and Falkenhayn, proved as inconclusive as that of the soldiers on the scene. Whatever hopes Falkenhayn might have had of preempting his enemy's Somme offensive lay buried with the German dead on the crest of le Mort-Homme or in the ditches around Souville, and after the Maasmühle, the mill on the Meuse, had decimated the reserves available to OHL he could field only five divisions against the 14 British and five French that attacked that first of July. Still, the French had envisaged sending 40 divisions to the Somme, and Verdun cut their contribution to 14. Perhaps the forces entombed or still committed on the Meuse could have allowed the French to push more deeply or the Germans to resist more vigorously that day. Verdun assured neither deliverance nor disaster to either, and the measurable contribution of one stalemate to the other remained forever shrouded in ambiguity.[22]

Neither Joffre nor Pétain could comfortably indict the other once the Somme offensive had run its course by November. Pétain's naysaying proved less than clairvoyant: the battle lasted over four months, forced the Germans to divert heavy forces from Verdun, and culminated, along with Alexei Brussilow's offensive in Galicia and Rumania's entry into the war, in the deepest crisis in German military fortunes since the Battle of the Marne. But it never vindicated Joffre's optimism either. His frugality on the Meuse yielded few riches on the Somme. At Verdun, where Joffre provided the minimum and Pétain demanded the maximum, they did not think alike either. They argued over the wisdom of withholding forces from Verdun for yet another frontal assault on the Western Front, and of waging offensive warfare on the Meuse or anywhere else. Joffre, unlike Pétain, had never fully renounced the goal of victory by breakthrough. Nor had Nivelle when he succeeded Joffre in December 1916. Pétain had, but only once he succeeded Nivelle after the disastrous offensive on the Chemin des Dames in April 1917 could he bring his strategy of limits to the French high command, by then as much a matter of necessity as of choice.

In the end the calculus of competitive loss, of weakening one's enemy more than oneself, rested on shaky, conjectural foundations, whether articulated as loss figures or as relative force on the Somme after the blood-letting on the Meuse. Such hopeful computations vindicated holding on at Verdun less frivolously than ambition or vainglory, but both betrayed self-delusion as well as self-doubt, discernible in recurrent justifications to themselves of the wisdom of the endless battle. Both sides' refusal to withdraw sprang more deeply from a fixation that expressed itself in different ways and yet required little explanation because it was so widely shared—from a kind of collective vanity that went, oftener than not, by the name of prestige.

The Latin *praestigium*, meaning artifice or illusion, lay at the root of the early French word *prestige*, suggesting a magician's legerdemain—prestidigitation. By the eighteenth century the word acquired its modern sense, suggesting reputation rather than sorcery. The German inherited the French term, in turn signifying, by the late nineteenth century, *Ansehen*, the esteem that a visible subject might come to command. Still it insinuated appearance, contrived or not, the kind that might spring, at Verdun, from persistence or renunciation.[23]

As long as the murky stalemate there permitted an occasional glimmer of hope, failure was unthinkable. To call off the engagement and pull back after all they had sacrificed, conveying signals of weakness and irresolution to the enemy abroad and the people at home, might save manpower only to wreck willpower. The battle that no one on either side expected to decide the issue of the war became the battle of prestige that no one on either side ever dared to give up.

Among the German generals no one, not even the increasingly disillusioned Crown Prince, contemplated avowing a defeat they had not yet suffered. Pessimists of his ilk would suspend the attacks but still retain German gains, and repel the enemy with an active, tenacious defense. A compulsion to save face, to show the world they had not lost and would not desist, gripped the warriors, and inspired an aversion to renunciation behind many a costly attack or counterattack during the long summer of 1916.

Such inclinations bent Falkenhayn's mind as well. In July, one week after the British and French infantry attacked on the Somme, Knobelsdorf urged the attack on Souville: that or retreat, he argued, and his thinking traveled to the Kaiser's headquarters and from there to the corners of the empire. They must attack Souville, the Bavarian military delegate reported to his war minister, just to show the world that they were strong enough "not to let go of the enemy at Verdun." Falkenhayn hesitated. The attacks had failed, they were now to remain strictly on the defensive, he told the commanders of the Fifth Army at its headquarters in Stenay. "Then give us the order in writing," the Crown Prince's new chief of staff, Schulenburg, said. But the order never came. "Hold, hold, it's only a question of that," Falkenhayn repeated over the phone five days later, but he lacked the courage of his convictions, and allowed local attacks to continue on the right bank late in July and early in August. They had, he insisted, to convince the enemy of their offensive intent, and hold him at Verdun, away from the Somme.[24]

Two weeks later, in the middle of August, the argument took up again and ended again in much the same way. The bad weather would soon be upon them, Falkenhayn reminded his generals. They needed to conserve men and munitions, other fronts beckoned. Should they continue offensive operations at Verdun? No, the Crown Prince replied vehemently: he could not send their last fresh forces on such a narrow front into such concentrated enemy fire for such a doubtful outcome. Yes, General von François, in command of the attack groups on the east bank, replied: to advertise their failing confidence, to concede a French success, to withdraw after so many months into defensive passivity, would proclaim weakness. It would only incite the enemy to attack, and the Allies to recover their faith in victory. The Germans must display aggressive intent, tie down the French forces—"that alone is valuable." Perception, for him, was all. Von Lochow, in command of the east bank, sided with the Crown Prince; Knobelsdorf argued for renewed attacks on Fleury and Souville. The Kaiser intervened. The attacks must cease, he said.

Even then Falkenhayn contrived to save his battle. They must hold the line, he told the commanders of the Fifth Army, dig in and build positions they could hold through the winter, but also give every sign to the enemy of pursuing the offensive. He was trying to square the circle and marry defensive prudence to offensive show. This was no order at all, the Crown Prince objected. What sense was he or Knobelsdorf to make of it? Nonetheless a kind of logic was in play: whatever they did, and even if they suspended their attacks, they must not signal weakness to the enemy.[25]

More to the point, they must not signal weakness to their own people. This, the two countries' leaders in their own ways sought to assure. Falkenhayn lost his position at the summit of OHL because of the failures at Verdun, but no well-informed official, let alone any reader of the German press, might have suspected as much. The ostensible cause of his demise, the occasion that emboldened a widening circle of conspirators that included the Chancellor and most of the Foreign Ministry, was the entry of Rumania into the war on the side of Germany's enemies. Falkenhayn saw "no imminent danger" he told Bethmann-Hollweg on August 18th, of Rumania's entry, and it was this desperate optimism, rather than that betrayed by his cryptic description two days later of the situation at Verdun as "not unconditionally unfavorable," that handed his enemies their official excuse to overcome the Kaiser's lingering attachment to his favorite general.[26]

Two years earlier, the demise of Falkenhayn's predecessor von Moltke at the summit of OHL remained shrouded in secrecy from the German public, lest it divine the reason: their country's defeat on the Marne. Now, as Hindenburg and Ludendorff took over, they fell prey to the same anxieties. They fretted about discouraging their publics even as they imposed a strategic sea-change: they would stand pat on all positions on the Western, Italian, Eastern, and Macedonian fronts until the defeat of Rumania, and then turn to the destruction of Russia while still holding defensively in the West. But they could not bring themselves to break off the battle of Verdun and allow the French to reap the harvest of a German default. Pride forbade what prudence counseled, and the new masters of OHL declined to surrender land so painfully acquired to save troops so sparingly counted, and sacrifice the cultivation of glory to the economy of force. Hindenburg feared his people. The soldier might give up most of the ground taken at Verdun since February, and hold behind a shortened defensive line, but the warlord might not. He dared not tell a nation surviving on the bread of adversity in the expectation of feasts to come that all, at Verdun, had been in vain.

So they held, but at a fearsome cost—their munitions limited, half of their heavy artillery gone to the Somme, or to Rumania, or to Russia, their troops exposed in the cratered and fire-swept terrain, laboring hopelessly to build the *Dauerstellung*, the lasting line of Hindenburg's and Ludendorff's wishes. Now, in the autumn rains, their losses exceeded those of their adversaries, and when the French counterattacked in October and December they easily took back their old positions from a weakened and demoralized foe soon bereft, as General Karl von Einem complained, of his forward lines as well as his "prestige."[27]

Prestige, for the French, meant not ceding any more terrain after the last week in February. Then the government, quickly endorsed by Joffre and Castelnau, had prevailed upon the wilting staff officers at Chantilly to defend every village, hill, and fort, and Pétain had arrived in the town hall of Souilly to set up his headquarters and take command of the Second Army, thenceforth the army of Verdun.

Whatever their differences over priorities and ends and means, Pétain and Joffre never differed over the task at Verdun: to frustrate German ambitions there. An obscure sense of primordial principle, perhaps prestige itself, united them, untouched by chronic strife over strategy and tactics. Mirroring the anxieties that even German skeptics such as von Einem or Rupprecht voiced over the loss of reputation that German arms would suffer if the high command gave up the operation on the Meuse, French expectations rested on the defense of the place that Pétain later called "le boulevard moral de la France."[28] At Chantilly, in February, Joffre had understood as much. Though faced with the disruption of his fondest offensive projects, he had not argued when Briand and others had elevated Verdun into a moral and political imperative. From the outset Poincaré had understood as much. He looked to Pétain for bold ripostes so hopefully that he greeted even the hypothesis of withdrawing onto the left bank of the Meuse with the disdain that political necessity reserved for military contingency. "Don't even think of it, General," he told Pétain at Souilly in March, "it would be a parliamentary catastrophe." In the trenches officers had understood as much. Under bombardment in the Fort St. Michel in the spring, an artillery lieutenant listened as his colonel regretted the French failure to order a tactical withdrawal. Here they were, with their backs to the river and the enemy in a semicircle around laying down concentric fire upon them. But, the lieutenant reflected, "in terms of morale, evacuating the place would be impossible."[29]

In a negative way, the critics of Joffre promoted the same transcendental stature of Verdun when they tried to nail the early losses there to his own negligence. Since the honor of the country itself rested on the shoulders of the men at Verdun, how could the high command have left them so defenseless at the start? The vilification of Joffre required the beatification of Verdun. What better way to indict his conduct of the war than to suggest that the sons of the country were paying the price under the walls of Verdun?

On June 16 the Chamber of Deputies, much against the wishes of Briand and of Joffre, met in secret session to debate Verdun. At once André Maginot, deputy from the Meuse, proclaimed that the events there had opened their eyes to the blundering ways of the high command. The passivity, the negligence, the makeshift improvisation—all now came to light in the lamentable defensive works of Verdun, which had forced the men to withstand German shellfire not in shelters, trenches, or block-houses but in shell-holes and open country. The deputy's hyperbole, like that of his fellows, did not carry the day; the Chamber overwhelmingly voted its confidence in the government. Joffre stayed on. And the newspapers observed absolute discretion about the deputies' cloistered indignation, just as a silence escorted Falkenhayn's departure in August, lest the nation appear to lose face at Verdun.[30]

Such stakes were not at once apparent to the citizens at home, who could make little of the enigmatic pedagogy that came their way in the early days of the battle. A vain search for Napoleonic precedents in the columns of the mass dailies soon gave way to myopic narrations of minor movement. Readers could derive no inkling of the tides of battle until the first clear French success, the retaking of the fortress of Douaumont, eight long months into it. Rumors of the fall of the fort in February drove crowds to besiege newsstands and editorial buildings in the vain hope of making sense of the sibylline communiqués from the high command in Chantilly. What were they to make of the communiqué issued at 11 p.m. on the 27th, two days after the fall of the fort, that "our troops are closely surrounding the enemy units that have managed to gain a foot-hold"? Alarm vied with aplomb; people fought for papers, tried to read between the lines, exchanged contradictory intelligence, whispered that intercepted radio telegrams spoke of the loss of the fort. In a bank a man withdrew his savings and announced he was leaving; a dozen employees—young women and aging men—remonstrated with him. Under a porte cochère a woman with no sons at the front predicted German victory and an older man bearing the rosette of the Legion d' Honneur protested indignantly. Plays were canceled, theater halls emptied. Even when the fright passed, along with the short-lived hints from the authorities and the experts that Verdun might not matter, only a toponymist or a lifelong resident of the Côtes de Meuse could decipher the maps that appeared on the front pages of the national dailies. In Germany the *Frankfurter Zeitung* discerned a ploy to hide German successes behind a blizzard of place names. Pierre Renaudel, the Socialist deputy, complained as well. He asked politely that the military communiqués explain what the maps might mean. Months went by.[31]

Prestige filled the void left by strategic enigma. Once mentioned, it became a self-fulfilling prophecy, an utterance that transformed a local into a national affair and rendered renunciation unthinkable.

At first, when the stakes appeared obscure and the outcome doubtful, especially for the French, the adversaries imputed anxieties over pres-tige exclusively to the other. This abstraction was what drove the enemy, explained the ferocity of his attack or the desperation of his defense. Such condescending analyses had become commonplace by now on all sides. Britain trembled for her prestige in the Orient, the German press had been declaring at the end of December 1915, in the wake of the debacle in the Dardanelles. In February and March each side applied the diag-nosis to Verdun. It assumed varied overlapping formulations. The French discerned national, dynastic, or political insecurities in German behavior, and even personal ones as well, notably those of the Crown Prince. In March General Berthaut assured his readers in *Le Petit Journal* that the Reich urgently sought at Verdun to raise the morale of its people and burnish its tarnished reputation of invincibility among nations near and far. The Germans insisted in return that Verdun mattered most to their enemy, that its name alone inspired his losses there.

Less tendentious analyses appeared as well, conceding at least implicitly that the prestige of their own country lay at stake as well. At the end of March the *Frankfurter Zeitung* asked openly whether Verdun was a battle between two nations in any traditional sense at all. Without at first discriminating between its national protagonists, the paper pronounced the battle a contest over "military honor and political prestige." In April the same General Berthaut looked just as dispassionately at the furious fighting for the villages of Malancourt and Vaux, at either end of the front. Whole or intact, they had no strategic or tactical significance, he mused. But they meant all to morale, because by now people recognized their names and heard in them the sounds of battle. Prestige had invented itself.[32]

The message had inspirational uses. Encouraged by the censors and conveyed by the press, it promised to move the readers and inculcate the noble ways of endurance. Better to take heart from the fortitude and staying power of the *poilus* than fright at their losses. Once abroad in the land, the message relied on personification to catch fire: it identified Nivelle and still more Pétain with the sufferings of the *poilu* and the aspirations of the country. To do so it resorted to the simple expedient of ventriloquism. Popular adages issued from the lips of the fêted commanders as though they had coined them. "Ils ne passeront pas," some of the soldiers had said in March at Verdun; "halte-là, on ne passe pas" ("stop there, no entry"), the popular song proclaimed. When Nivelle uttered the words he affixed his name to the battle. And when Pétain congratulated his army for repulsing the "furious assaults of the Crown Prince's soldiers" atop le Mort-Homme in April, he sent his message to the papers, which published it together with the words that assured his own place in the sun: "Honneur à tous! [. . .] Courage! on les aura." The papers did not explain, because they did not need to, that the phrase was not his. A year earlier the intensely chauvinistic musical revue *1915*, the work of Louis

Verneuil and his fellow-playwright Rip (Georges-Gabriel Thenon), had opened at the Palais-Royal. In it the star Vilbert sang "On les aura," which, along with the most famous popular wartime song "La Madelon," quickly enthused the Parisians as well as the soldiers at the front, when it reached them. Long after the revue closed, in November of 1915, Vilbert went on singing it—247 times, by his own count, at charities, in the provinces, in Paris, and libretti and gramophone records sold by the thousands. But by then "On les aura" had become Pétain's phrase, even though he had at first recoiled at the colloquialism, and so it would remain.[33]

In both France and Germany the myth of martyrdom, of human ramparts here and a materially superior foe there, enjoyed an almost preternatural longevity. But in France international celebrity, of a sort that never rewarded their enemies, sustained it as well.

In the version that lasted, the *poilus* saved France and elevated her name all over the world. The early treatments of prestige, preoccupied more with deriding the enemy's craving for it than with celebrating one's own, never vanished altogether. Early in 1917 Castelnau, visiting Petrograd, informed the press that German prestige had suffered mightily from their inability to take Verdun in spite of huge losses. And the battle of Verdun was now over, he added. But the messianic variant took hold more durably, both at home and abroad. Poincaré expressed it most forcefully well before the battle ended, when he visited the town in September 1916 and explained to the assembled foreign dignitaries in the cathedral of Verdun the meaning of what had happened there. "Gentlemen," he said, "here are the walls on which the high hopes of Imperial Germany shattered." Somewhat confusingly, he described German designs, ripening over 15 months, to forestall the coming allied offensives by means of a theatrical coup that would seize a spot "whose historic name would gild its military importance for the German people." And he went on to insist that the German play for prestige had only exalted that of France: "And observe, Gentlemen, the fairness of things. The name of Verdun, to which Germany in its intense dream had attributed symbolic importance [. . .] now signifies among the neutrals, as among our allies, the most beautiful, the most pure, the best there is in the French soul. The town had saved the world, he told his listeners, and its name would resound for centuries in every corner of the globe.[34]

As though in response, the Allied representatives decorated Verdun with their most solemn tokens of monarchical good will—the Cross of St. George from Russia, the Military Cross from Great Britain, the Cross of Leopold I from Belgium, the Gold Medal of Military Valor from Italy, medals from Serbia and Montenegro—to add to the Légion d'Honneur and the Croix de Guerre that Poincaré had already bestowed on behalf of the only Republic in the coalition.

Encomiums came in from private well-wishers far from the fighting: "The manner in which you have undone the barbarians at Verdun was hailed here with the greatest joy," a professor at the University of Glasgow wrote in January 1917 to a friend serving in the Army of Verdun. Universal renown descended upon the little garrison town, conveyed by commentators down the decades. Almost unthinkingly, they presented Verdun as the point at which the world had stopped to watch France and its persecutor, "a kind of duel before the universe, a singular, almost symbolic struggle in a closed terrain," as a radio commentator put it in 1966. Or the point from which resistance to brute force might inspire any and all defenders of freedom: "'Ils ne passeront pas' . . . a fait le tour du monde"— the phrase had traveled the world, as a historian said on television in 1996. "The Spanish republicans adopted it at Guadalajara as they faced the Italian armored divisions. . . ."[35]

Such was the message that posterity naturally retained and that eclipsed the lackluster military realities—the incomplete yet almost adequate defenses, the de facto equilibrium, the defensive and offensive tactics on all sides, the impasse, the mental confines, the battle that went on because no one could break it off. In a scene in *La Grande Illusion*, filmed 22 years later, Jean Renoir showed a country anxiously following the news of Fort Douaumont lost, retaken, lost again, in a seemingly infinite sequence of monotonous feats of arms. He was intimating that prestige had dignified futility, and kept the endless battle going.

6

The Attritional Trap

ONCE GRANDER OUTCOMES FAILED to crown their undertakings, generals on the Western Front habitually aspired to inflict heavier casualties than they suffered. "I am nibbling at them," Joffre had declared in 1915, unable to claim much more for his offensives in Artois and Champagne. Douglas Haig, steeped like Joffre in traditions of decisive battle, retrospectively discerned more incremental and less Napoleonic ambitions in his goals on the Somme. He had inflicted, he told his government, such heavy losses that in "another six weeks, the enemy should be hard put to it to find men." And Falkenhayn, famously, wished posterity to believe that he had intended only to "out-kill" the French army at Verdun. But attrition happened more than it was chosen, rationalize it how the commanders might. It took the form of a war of materiel, as different as night from day from the war of August 1914, and aimed to save lives as well as to take them.[1]

"One does not fight materiel with men": the axiom that the French army set forth in its instruction of January 1916 expressed the lessons it had learned since August 1914, when the defensive powers of modern weaponry, epitomized by the machine gun, had inflicted carnage on attacking infantry. In 1815 a battalion with 1000 flintlock muskets could fire about two shots per minute at a range of 1,000 yards at each soldier of a comparable battalion advancing at them. Now, armed with magazine rifles and four machine guns, the same battalion could fire about 200. Its firepower had increased a hundredfold in a hundred years.[2]

The axiom of January 1916 thus carried an unspoken corollary, that one fought materiel with materiel, announcing both the reality and the paradox of the coming battle at Verdun. Firepower saved lives, if it neutralized that of the enemy. But it never did so for long enough to assure any kind of lasting decision. As a result the reliance on materiel prolonged the battle, multiplying with one hand the casualties that it had economized with the other.

In 1914 no such paradox troubled French military doctrine. Maneuver over fire, infantry over artillery, men over materiel—all stemmed from the conviction that the offensive was the only arm of victory, that the war would be short, mobile, and violent, that massed foot soldiers would decide its outcome. The artillery was ancillary. "Artillery no longer prepares attacks, it supports them," the army regulation of 1913 had decreed, and the French possessed for such purposes the ideal weapon— the 75 mm field gun, the best of its kind in the world. With a range of about five miles, highly mobile, firing rapidly and indirectly—at invisible targets, if necessary from a covered position—along a straight trajectory, it sufficed, the experts thought, for almost any demand that its master, the advancing or onrushing infantry, might make of it. And it could do so in modest quantities—a single battery of four 75 mm guns, they thought, would suffice along a 700-foot-wide front to hit any moving corps of enemy soldiers. Successive echelons of batteries were useless. So was longer-range heavy artillery. It was inaccurate and lumbering, suited to little more than the outmoded ways of siege warfare. Why worry about distant fixed targets when the enemy infantry was the thing? Arguments challenged but failed to overturn the conventional wisdom, and in August 1914 the French went confidently to war with an adequate complement of light field guns and almost no heavy ones.[3]

The Germans imagined the coming war much as the French had, but appreciated firepower more keenly. Heavy artillery in particular concentrated some minds. They would, after all, have to overcome some mighty fortresses in their march through Belgium and northern France. They entered the war with 2,000 heavy pieces against 308 French, and discovered new uses for them even before the war of movement had ended in the autumn. Out of range of the enemy's guns, they could fire with impunity onto French 75 mm field guns, troop concentrations, communications networks, and defensive organizations. They did not bring victory in 1914, but once the front stabilized and the trenches appeared, they threatened to pulverize the enemy's offensive organizations or render his defensive lines suitable for assault, *sturmreif*, when the moment came.[4]

German factories continued to mass produce the weapons that had served the army best. In 1915 and early 1916 they more than quintupled their production of heavy artillery, favoring in particular the 150 mm howitzer that had repeatedly proven its worth: by early 1916 their stock of these had risen to about 3,000, from 416 in August 1914. Just as ominously for the defenders at Verdun, they doubled their production of the giant, long-range siege guns, including the 305s and the gamma-420s that had broken down the walls of Liège and Namur, the lonely behemoths that gave Falkenhayn such confidence and announced the primacy that he, as much as anyone, wished to accord materiel over men. Twenty-six of them stood waiting in the woods north of Verdun before the 21st of February.[5]

By then the French had long been scrambling to keep up. Ever since the war of movement had revealed their vulnerability in heavy artillery so unequivocally, they had been making, improvising, or contriving long-range heavy guns in any way they could—stripping them from warships and coastal defenses, removing them from forts along the frontiers, turning them out in the foundries and factories of a militarized hinterland. By February 1916 they had some 3,500 of them, and they kept striving to narrow the gap, kept setting new production goals to endow their armies with the heavy guns that fulfilled the necessary if not the sufficient condition of victory. But between putting pen to program and rolling out the great guns on road or rail months or even years might elapse. At the end of May, in the midst of the battle of Verdun, Joffre launched a new program to give every infantry division in the French army two groups of 155 mm guns, every army corps its own heavy long-range artillery regiment with four groups of guns, and the high command disposition over the heaviest pieces of all. By the armistice of November 1918 the French had almost as many heavy as light guns—over 5,300—but factories were still struggling to meet the goals of the May program two years earlier. The French never did attain parity with the Germans.[6]

Nowhere, not even in Champagne in September 1915, had artillery so saturated the ground as at Verdun. From the opening moments German shells of at least 100 mm in caliber began falling on targets two and three miles behind the French front lines, on roads, intersections, installations, and forts. Whenever they attacked again in the next months, on the plateaus of Douaumont or Vaux, the hilltops of le Mort-Homme, or the approaches to the fort of Souville, the Germans applied the same tactics, designed to pulverize the enemy so as to spare their own. Heavy, long-range artillery *à tir courbe* (arcs) preceded a cautious reconnaissance and eventually an infantry attack in thin groups or open formation, some-times now carried out by assault units specially trained in new infiltration tactics. They expended shells to save men.

And the French generals never stopped clamoring for heavy artillery. Looking back over their defense of le Mort-Homme in March and April, the general in command of the sector, Henri Berthelot, reflected that more of it would have spared them many a mishap—they could have pounded enemy organizations in depth even before their own 75 mm field guns entered into action against enemy infantry. It might, he implied, have spared them having to retake their own lines so often, at such high cost. Berthelot added that whether to defend terrain or to retake it they needed one heavy piece for every 350 feet of terrain. Pétain needed no convincing. "The artillery struggle before Verdun is becoming harder every day," he complained to Joffre at the end of May, and the figures he compiled showed a German superiority of 1,730 heavy artillery pieces to 548. Such was the disparity at Verdun that they could mount no major offensives until the autumn, when the German superiority vanished as they withdrew materiel to other fronts. Until then the French had enough heavy guns to contain but not to push back their adversaries.[7]

If only, General Herr complained later, they could have preempted rather than reacted to the German attacks. That would have required the heavy guns they did not yet have. In the meantime they enjoyed rough parity in the light artillery—the invaluable 75 mm and the other pieces with calibers between 65 mm and 90 mm—and machine guns, the defensive weapons that shredded the ranks of the attackers and left the hillsides, ravines, and embankments littered with German corpses. They saved the day.

All too often unable, because of their inferiority in long-range artillery, to silence the heavy German guns, the French would sit out the bombardment as best they could, waiting for it to lift or lengthen and for the German attackers to leave their trenches. Often the German preparation spared the French front lines, too vague and thinly occupied to be visible, and left many of the French light artillery pieces untouched, so that when the German infantry moved out they fell prey to machine guns and rapid-firing 75 mm artillery pieces. On le Mort-Homme on the 22nd of April they suffered 1000 casualties this way, and the attempt to take Souville in late June ended in slaughter as well. So too did a German attack southeast of Douaumont in mid-April, one of many. That day, General Mangin reported, they had fired 26,000 75 mm shells at their German attackers. Such quantities would have beggared the imagination of the French high command and the Ecole de Guerre on the eve of the war. Then they had anticipated needing 13,600 rounds of 75 mm ammunition every day for all the French armies in the field; by the summer of 1916 they needed 77,000—not to mention 24,000 heavy shells, which they had hardly expected to need at all. Exigencies kept climbing, in a spectacle of appetites aroused but never appeased, a spiral of voracity and consumption on permanent display in the natural amphitheater of Verdun.[8]

To magnify effective firepower—to project it over ever greater distance—generals now turned to the third dimension. Before the war Foch had proclaimed airpower a weapon without a future—"All this, you see," he had told a journalist, "is mere sport, and for the army it's nothing." In 1914 it had provided valuable reconnaissance during the battle of the Marne, little more. Now, at Verdun, Pétain understood that without air superiority he could not hope to prevail. "Rose, sweep the sky for me! I'm blind!" he told Commandant Charles Tricornot de Rose, two days after arriving at Souilly. Rose, once a cavalryman, now the pilot who had grasped the offensive capabilities of fighter planes and who would die not by enemy fire but by accident in May, had grasped the tactical support that machine guns in the air could provide infantry on the ground.

By identifying and locating targets for long-range artillery or dropping bombs of its own, airpower was already extending the effective range of ground-based guns. Both sides strove to deny such powers to each other, to master the skies over Verdun by filling them with their own aircraft: the Germans from the first day, the French once they stemmed the German tide and eventually flowed back over most of what they had lost. Unable to rely on an overtaxed domestic aircraft production, the Second Army borrowed when it could from its neighbors, but thanks to such expedients its massed squadrons controlled the air when the infantry retook Douaumont in October. Formed into *escadrilles*, usually of eight planes each, they carried out with impunity most of the newly conceived missions that modern war entrusted to airpower, including artillery observation, counter-battery, and tactical support as well as reconnaissance. They guided their long-range artillery, destroyed some of the Germans', and disrupted with their machine guns columns of reservists trying to reach the front lines. At Verdun airpower came of age, not as a remote contest between celestial warriors but as the spatial extension of terrestrial firepower. "If we're chased from the skies," Pétain said, "then it's simple, Verdun is lost."[9]

If Verdun was not lost, the country had its factories as much as its soldiers to thank—the production lines that during the first five months of the battle almost doubled their daily output of powder and increased their monthly production of 75 mm guns by a third, and doubled the number of fighters at the front over the course of the year. And it had its scientists and technologists to thank—specialists who extended the range of the few heavy guns they did have in the absence of enough new ones, brought phosgene gas shells to the army of Verdun, and developed synchronized machine guns in flight in imitation of their adversaries. Verdun marked the watershed in which productive capacities determined military possibilities, and the armies demanded of machines what they could no longer ask of men. "Ever longer ranges, ever larger calibers, ever faster firing rates, ever more guns in line," General Herr wrote, "that is the lesson of Verdun."

Mechanization exacted rationalization: so much materiel, so much reorganization. In 1915 a quickening flow of rules and regulations portended innovation, but in the year of Verdun the structures of French arms began to evolve in ways that would make the army of the armistice unrecognizable to a visitor alighting from the mobilization of August 1914. Artillery and aviation units began to absorb more and more men, infantry less, cavalry infinitely less. Among the shrinking infantry, which lost almost half its men between 1916 and 1918, the ratio of materiel to men soared. In June 1916 the General Staff eliminated one of four companies of each core combat unit, the battalion, reducing its effective size from 1,000 to 750 men, and of the remaining three companies one consisted solely of machine gunners. Regiments that had six machine guns in 1914 now had 24. In the other two companies new weapons proliferated—grenade-launchers, trench mortars, *canons de 37*, light machine guns, automatic rifles, figments of science fiction to succeed the omnipresent infantryman of 1914, clad in red leggings and armed only with a Lebel 1886 model rifle, a bayonet, and incurable optimism.[10]

And to accompany them went a drastically revised offensive doctrine, issued in January 1916 in three *Instructions* that jettisoned the old catechism. Expressions from its quixotic lexicon—"take at all costs" and "take at any price"—had disappeared, replaced by injunctions never to attack without adequate artillery and by an order of precedence that announced the coming ascendancy of materiel: "artillery devastates, infantry submerges." Eight days after the *Instruction* of January 1916 that warned of pitting men against machines came a new one, warning against offensive objectives that exceeded the depth possible to the artillery. The mindless élan that bore infantrymen beyond the range of their own artillery and only recently passed for empyrean valor now roused deep apprehensions. "For infantry in combat," the *Instruction* of January 26 decreed, "order takes precedence over speed."

Offensive battle now consisted not of a single frontal action, but of successive advances from position to position, with intervals between to bring up the guns that would shell the next objective before the advance resumed. The methodical rupture of the enemy's front, minutely prepared and deliberately executed, had taken the place of maneuver, war in the open country, and dramatic breakthrough. Surprise and relentless pressure remained talismanic articles of faith that no commander could abjure, but how, under the new dogma, was he to realize them? The *Instructions* did not say. In November Pétain set forth the uses of airpower in modern battle, in the wake of its contributions to the retaking of Douaumont. It must, he said, be massed, command mastery of the air, and destroy the enemy's powers of observation as well as elements of his long-range artillery; and he looked forward to the day when aviation would restore mobility to the battlefield.

That lay in the future, for at present armed prudence was the order of the day. Even Castelnau, the epitome of Napoleonic decisiveness, had suspended his old faith in *l'offensive à outrance*. At Nancy in 1914, a stretcher-bearer at Verdun recalled, Castelnau had ordered them to attack everywhere, and in depth; now, at Verdun, he told them to resist everywhere, "whatever the cost."[11]

Terrain mattered not for its sacredness but for the advantages its crests, reverse slopes, and promontories might confer upon firepower.

Douaumont recommended itself as an unrivalled observatory; le Mort-Homme and Côte 304 as flanking heights from which artillery could sweep the positions below; the peninsula of Froideterre and the nearby fort of Belleville as strongholds before which Verdun itself was defenseless. Terrain served materiel; each village, each wood, each fort promised access to some yet more advantageous position, keenly coveted and jealously guarded. After February defenders might lose positions, never concede them, as assailants took precarious possession and the besiegers exchanged places with the besieged.

In the ceaseless contest the old forts around Verdun acquired uses that neither their designers nor their detractors had ever imagined. Conceived in the decades after 1871 to withstand siege and encirclement for long months, they were supposed to deflect and channel the invader into the open gap that stretched for 50 miles south to Toul. There armies in the field could engage and destroy him. Then Joffre and his staff dismissed siege as history and forts as relics, unable to withstand the heavy guns of the new age. But at Verdun they did; the great German guns could damage but not destroy the fixed fortifications. Shells of all calibers fell on Douaumont, but the ramparts, casemates, and turrets of the fort that the Germans took in February and that the French retook in October endured; they fell by default, their defenders absent or cut off or inept. The forts of Verdun provided supports for firepower and protection from the enemy, housing guns and sheltering infantry from the infernal environs. Far from diverting the enemy, or from surviving as museums of obsolete warfare, they became adjuncts in the battle of materiel, gaining in tactical what they had lost in strategic significance, serving to save lives within and extinguish them without: emblems of attrition.[12]

Did attrition save lives?

At Verdun the French and German armies lost fewer men than they had in the war of movement of the late summer and early autumn of 1914. At Verdun approximately 375,000 men on each side were killed or wounded or went missing over ten months of battle.[13] Four months of the war of movement, between August and November 1914, had cost the French about 850,000[14] and the Germans about 670,000[15] losses—though among all their armies engaged on the Western Front. Loss rates—the incidence of casualties for a given number of men engaged over a given period—make for more meaningful comparisons, and they convey the message more reliably: at Verdun the French and German armies were losing men at a slower rate than in battles they had undertaken not with attrition but with rupture or breakthrough or even encirclement in mind. The German Fifth Army at Verdun suffered a lower average loss rate than the Ninth Army during its offensive in Poland between October and December 1914, or the Eleventh Army during its offensive in Galicia and southern Poland between May and August 1915.[16] The French Second Army suffered a lower average loss rate at Verdun over ten months in 1916 than the armies over three weeks in September and October 1915 in the Champagne offensive, which had never been envisaged as a battle of attrition.[17] When breakthroughs tempted and Verdun resembled earlier battles in intensity as well as futility—in February and early March, in late May, again in late June and early July—losses peaked among attackers

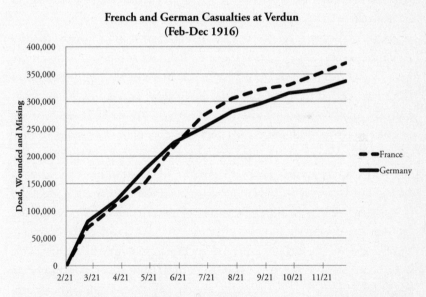

Figure 1.1 **Stalemate in the Abstract:** This chart shows how closely French and German cumulative losses at Verdun track each other. They would probably be even closer, if German losses, based here on the ten-day reports of the 5th Army, were revised upward to take full account of the lightly wounded (see Appendix on Sources: Losses). *Sources:* Hermann Wendt, *Verdun 1916. Die Angriffe Falkenhayns im Maasgebiet mit Richtung auf Verdun als strategisches Problem* (Berlin, 1931), 242–43; SHD, 7N 552 (*Etat numérique des pertes*); Ministère de la guerre, *Les Armées françaises dans la grande guerre* (Paris, 1926), tome IV, vol. 3, *appendices.*

and defenders alike.[18] But these paroxysms concealed the commonplace: attrition, over time, reduced loss rates.

Just as strikingly, French and German loss rates, for the first time in the war, tended to approximate each other at Verdun. Throughout the war the ratio of losses suffered to losses inflicted had favored the Germans. They killed and wounded more than they lost, whatever the front, whoever the enemy, whichever the engagement; they fought more effectively than their adversaries. On the Western Front, however, the disparity declined over the course of the war. Against the French the ratio had risen as high as 2.2:1 during the spring offensives of 1915: for every soldier the Germans lost the French lost two and sometimes more. At Verdun the ratio fell to almost 1:1 over the ten months of the battle, perhaps slightly in German favor, and hovered there during some of the French offensives of the summer of 1917, even though it remained in German favor for the entire Western Front for the duration of the war. Verdun appears as a watershed, the point when the protagonists suffered as much as they inflicted and the casualties became more balanced as well as less Carthaginian or devouring.[19]

In spite of a war supposed to doom the attackers in futile over-the-top assaults, no correlation between loss rates and offensive or defensive actions at Verdun withstands scrutiny. French losses actually rose when they defended in the spring and fell when they attacked in the autumn; German losses rose and fell whether they attacked or defended. A measure of doctrinal drift, both cause and effect of the recalcitrant casualty counts, emerged. General Herr thought artillery most effective on the offensive, served by a plan rather than reacting to a surprise; General Mangin thought offensives more effective than counterattacks; Pétain thought the reverse. No weight of numbers, either, helped the French overcome the late superiority of their German adversary and match their killing powers to his own: the Second and Fifth Armies faced each other in the field with equivalent hosts of several hundred thousand men each at most moments of the long battle. The Germans, by 1916, had lost some of their best commissioned and noncommissioned officers, in the massacres of 1914 and the unstaunched bloodletting ever since; but so had the French, even more so. Seen through numerical grids more precise than those available to the commanders of the day, the countervailing carnage still perplexes.[20]

"One does not fight materiel with men," but one did fight with materiel against men—to kill more on the far side of no man's land but also to save more on the near side. The greater the density of artillery deployed, the lesser the loss of one's men—such was the enduring lesson of the first 18 months of the war, learned most painfully and now applied most consistently by the pupils who had sacrificed the most, the French. From year to year, as their guns increased, their losses fell, in absolute numbers and as a percentage of men mobilized, and the connection appeared strongest in 1916, when the rate of their fatalities fell by a third as the number of their batteries rose by a quarter. In Champagne in the previous autumn, where they had suffered an average of 4,000 casualties for each infantry division, they had deployed an average of 13 artillery batteries on each half-mile of their front. During 1916, with 17 batteries per half-mile at Verdun in May, when they were fighting defensively, and 19 per half-mile on the Somme in July, when they were fighting offensively, their losses per division fell to about 3000 on each front. Even at the costly Chemin des Dames offensive in April of the following year, with 25 batteries per half-mile, their average divisional losses fell to 2,600. The correlation held until 1918, when the scope of the German offensives and Allied counteroffensives exceeded the limits that materiel had recently been able to impose upon human losses. But where the French could commit enough mechanical weaponry—including the new tank—as at the second battle of the Marne in July, when their losses per division fell to 2,000, the message held: firepower saved manpower.[21]

From the moment when the first German 380 mm shell tore off a corner of the cathedral at Verdun, the guns all around never stopped proclaiming the elemental intensity of the modern message. Sixty million more shells landed during the next ten months. A year and a half later, in August 1917, when the French finally assaulted and recaptured le Mort-Homme and the Côte 304 for the last time, they began with an artillery preparation that dwarfed in its torrent of steel—six tons for every yard of their front—any bombardment or curtain of fire that they or their adversaries had laid down at Verdun the year before. They put in play a local superiority in materiel, as they had before Douaumont the previous October, the only way to gain or regain terrain. In its absence, rough material parity, at least, could limit casualties. Like means made for like losses, over time, and if the loss ratio for the Western Front in 1916 still favored the Germans, they did not have Verdun to thank for it, but the quieter sectors of the front, where their adversary would not or could not apply the methods that he had learned to respect on the banks of the Meuse.[22]

Nonetheless Verdun also unveiled the poisoned chalice of the new attrition: it was indecisive. Light artillery could shut down an enemy offensive, and heavy artillery neutralize his defenses temporarily, but neither could annihilate the reciprocal threat from all his guns. Temporary local superiorities in materiel might allow the pursuit of limited objectives, the most that the new realities could offer the offensively-minded; but limited objectives made for unlimited duration. Among equals, the materiel that prolonged lives also deferred decisive outcomes, and the artillery that protected its infantrymen also yielded the impasse that slowly killed them. Attrition in its modern guise, a French officer wrote on the eve of the battle, meant consumption of time more than consumption of men: "that is why modern battles last so long."

Month after month the battle went on, as time, the real victor of Verdun, exacted the blood on both sides that materiel had aspired to preserve on each, until by December some 160,000 French and 140,000 Germans had died there. "I'm beginning the eighth week of battle," Pétain wrote in the middle of April to Annie-Eugénie Hardon. "If anyone had told me it would be this long!"[23]

In its slow sapping of life, it resembled no other battle that France had fought. If 2.4 million Frenchmen had taken part at Verdun from February 21 until December 31, 1916, many of them more than once, and if 378,000 of these had been killed, wounded, or taken prisoner, the effective loss rate there came to about 16 percent.[24] In victory and defeat alike it had often been higher, far higher, in the past—perhaps 50 percent at Blenheim in 1704, almost 60 percent at Waterloo in 1815, 34 percent at Borodino in 1812, 29 percent at Wörth in 1870. Even at Austerlitz, where they gave up no prisoners, the French lost about 15 percent of their troops in dead and wounded. But all these battles lasted a day or less, Verdun 300 and more, and the size of the army dwarfed those in the others.[25]

On a few dark days entire divisions in some of the woods and ravines at Verdun might suffer the calamitous loss rates of their ancestors. Between February 21 and 26 the 72nd Infantry Division lost 9,747 men, over half its effective strength in the Bois des Caures, where Driant fell as his chasseurs held up the German advance; the 51st Division nearby in the Bois de Ville and the Bois d' Herbebois lost 6,296, over a third of its men, in the same way. Loss rates never reached such heights again, but they threatened to at moments, as in late May when Mangin's 5th Infantry Division lost 5,602 men in its failed attempt to retake Douaumont, or early July when the 128th Infantry Division lost 2,248 in the fierce fighting around Souville and Fleury.[26] Entire regiments might disappear, and a few violent days might leave as many dead, wounded, and missing as some epic daylong encounter of the past, but Waterloo lasted ten hours, Verdun ten months, and comparing part of one battle to the sum of another would yield a meaningless finding.

Perhaps the long Russian campaign of 1812, with its army of almost 700,000, offers some sense of historical kinship. However, in its long agony, from June to December, it killed many more Frenchmen and allied soldiers than Verdun did, inverting the roles between invaders and invaded, and ending badly besides. To ignore differences of scope and etch behind Verdun a long perspective of defensive stands on French soil out of the wars of the turn of the seventeenth century, the War of the Spanish Succession at the turn of the eighteenth, or the Revolutionary and Napoleonic wars at the turn of the nineteenth makes no sense either. They were cross-bred with civil wars and often found illustrious Frenchmen among the ranks of the invaders.[27]

Not even the most credulous of newspaper readers, in any case, could confidently state the French losses in this singular affair. They were high, but the enemy's were higher, of course. How much higher? They were "enormous," "extraordinary," "immense," the papers wrote. L'Eclair put them at 100,000 on March 6, Le Matin at 300,000 a week later, when Le Journal predicted that to take Verdun the Germans would have to sacrifice 800,000 men. Late in May Le Matin still put them at 300,000, and added that French losses were serious but not comparable. Joffre endeavored to put out a more precise estimate. For every 12 men the French lost at Verdun, he told L'Indépendant des Pyrénées orientales at the end of May, the Germans lost 30: "At this rate I won't be the one to break off the battle." Joffre was from Rivesaltes, where the paper originated, and perhaps he thought to give it a wartime scoop. Instead the Minister of War reproached the censors for the article's indiscretions—not about the losses at Verdun, but about the coming offensive on the Somme. Everyone knew of the continuous carnage at Verdun but no one knew much more. The numbers remained obscure. In Paris a midinette (seamstress) told a customer that the Germans could have Verdun as far as she was concerned: "The Kaiser! I would certainly give him Verdun for three hundred thousand Germans!"[28]

Out of such darkness grew a tenacious habit of inflating the losses at Verdun. The black-out on reliable information gave free rein to the most macabre imaginings, and the myth of the human holocaust at Verdun lived long into the postwar era. In the autumn of 1918 the film director Abel Gance was in the Midi, finishing the film the public watched the following year, *J'accuse*, his silent epic mixing romance, betrayal, and the horror of war. He was making the most famous scene, in which the swarming specters of dead soldiers, risen from an unnamed battlefield, return to trouble the consciences of living civilians in an unnamed village. Local military authorities, blind to the potentially subversive dimensions of the script, released for the purpose some 2,000 soldiers, who milled about in open air camps on eight-day leaves from their sector at the front—Verdun. Gance had them play the dead, but in his eyes they were already dead, as he later put it: "Those 2000 soldiers who knew they would never survive that hell. . . . In a few weeks or months eighty percent of them would disappear. I knew it and so did they. . . ."[29]

The hyperbole could serve pacific protest. Only four months into the battle, Alphonse Merrheim, a revolutionary socialist, assured his listeners that 350,000 French had already died there. The habit grew. As a German school manual of 1927 had it, "Verdun became the bloodiest battlefield the war ever saw" and figures of 500,000, of 800,000, even a million dead appeared in the press. A million had died there in all, Ernst Glaeser, the German journalist and author, assured his readers the same year. A French primary school book repeated the figure in 1935, but planted in its young readers' minds the notion that it applied to the dead of each side. But triumphalism had its hand in the exaggeration as well. To dramatize the futility of the German assault French authors took to conveying some sense of the scale of their losses and remained silent about their own: the Germans had uselessly lost 500,000 at Verdun, a popular author recorded in 1918, only to increase the figure to 700,000 in a new book the following year. The half-million figure for German dead seemed to catch on, perhaps because it was easy to retain: another popular author repeated it in 1919, followed by schoolbooks in 1923 and again in 1926.[30]

A generation of schoolchildren grew up believing that Verdun had indeed been the most terrible battle of all, that it was, in Glaeser's words, the "capital of death." After the Second World War the media followed suit. An early television newscast, in 1956, spoke of 400,000 French and 600,000 German dead—the round million, again.

Later newscasts habitually elevated Verdun into the "the most murderous battlefield of the war." In 1984 one of them informed viewers that 700,000 men had faced each other and that 700,000 had died. This suggested a death rate of 100 percent. How the victims had since written memoirs and resurfaced at commemorations and appeared in front of the same program's cameras appeared not to preoccupy the producers.[31]

At least once a veteran of Verdun came close to such hyperbolic estimates himself. As he and his unit went up to Verdun, he told his radio listeners in 1966, "We knew beforehand that we would only be relieved once we had lost 75 percent of our men. That would be the fare and in fact that was the fare," and once in the citadel they encountered others: "they too weren't ignorant of the fare, a 75 percent loss rate." The number was no more accurate than any of the others. He was closer to describing an hour at Waterloo than a month at Verdun.[32]

The spectacle of attrition, of lives steadily lost in a tide of materiel, perplexed the military specialists in the papers. Already at a loss to explain the stakes of the battle, they hesitated to specify its nature. Verdun marked a return to the war of movement in open country, *Excelsior* affirmed, on the bizarre grounds that all the fighting there was offensive, and the paper advised the combatants to jettison the habits that 18 months of positional warfare had instilled. *Le Journal* sprang to the defense of those who had disparaged the forts, explaining cryptically that the positions might matter, but not the edifices. It was the strangest of battles, Commandant de Civrieux acknowledged humbly in *Le Matin* as the sixth week began— in war battles grew in intensity as the conclusion neared, but this one had proceeded by fragmentation, by the dispersion in time and space of mediocre attacks. Soon commentators here and there took to defining the monotony as well as the novelty of attrition and methodical battle, and to revealing a bleak and modern vision of victory. "We must wear out Germany," *Le Petit Parisien* explained, "kill as many of its men as possible, oblige it to expend as many shells as possible. In a word exhaust it by all means, to force it one day to give up, beaten." Gustave Hervé in *La Victoire* conjured up not the sun of Austerlitz breaking through the clouds but the desolation of Armageddon. "When the enemy has no more men to be massacred, he will stop." In fact Verdun was not strange in the least, *Le Rappel* concluded; it was the same attritional struggle they were waging everywhere else. And in July *Le Matin* undertook to explain methodical battle to its readers. In an unsigned article it explained how four months of Verdun had shattered the illusions of breakthrough and taught the army to construct its offensives "step by step, but confidently" that would slowly drive the enemy back over days, weeks, or months, "a patient and methodical application which saves men and expends materiel."

Nonetheless the dash of the past never lost its hold. In the middle of October *Le Matin* explained again that maneuver was dead, along with short, fluid battle. Ten days later it attributed the swift recapture of Douaumont to speed and surprise and the "magnificent élan" of the French infantry. It made for more inspiring reading.[33]

By then the German war correspondents had long ceased trying to make much sense of the developments on the Meuse. They had gone from exalting the "old Prussian élan" of the Brandenburgers who took Douaumont in February to dwelling on French loss rates in March. After that there was little else to write about. Attrition made poor news copy.[34]

On the 15th of June 1940, as he stood at Fort Douaumont addressing his troops on the occasion of the fall of Verdun that day, General Weisenberger recalled that in 1916 he had thrice been engaged as a young officer in "the greatest battle of attrition of all times" without ever getting close enough to Verdun to set eyes on it. Why had they failed then with so many losses over so many months and succeeded now with so few in a single day?—because the spirit of National Socialism, born amid the *Frontgeist* and blood-camaraderie of Verdun, had not yet permeated the German people then, "while today the dynamic of the National Socialist Reich drives our army forward and into the citadel and town of Verdun."[35]

So this was what attrition now meant—the triumph of spirit over materiel. On both sides of the Rhine a compelling urge to vindicate the human element left its mark on screen and in print, on the pages of schoolbooks and, in France, upon the walls of war memorials as well. Meanwhile the sober and dispassionate intuitions of military minds unlike Weisenberger's, seeing in the strange and sanguinary happenings on the Meuse not the triumph of spirit over materiel but the reverse, withdrew behind closed doors and later vanished from the view of public history.

Weisenberger's paean was only the latest in an exaltation of the common man at Verdun that had begun during the battle itself. Machines, French newspaper readers learned in the spring of 1916, only rendered moral character more important than in the past, and machines, Groener, the German railway head, reflected, only made the human spirit more vital, more transcendent than ever. Pétain said no less in April, when he colloquially rescued the human element—the "we"—from the impersonal carnage: "Courage, on les aura!"[36]

In France the "we" braving the industrial onslaught meant the peasant as well as the *poilu*. Lieutenant Péricard, one of the best known survivors of Verdun, happily identified one with the other, against the city-dweller. The "holy peasants of war" of André Suarès' contemporary poem were the saviors not only of France but of rural civilization: "they are man against the demon and his machines/the heart against the device/the seed that lives against the gold/that kills and the paper that deceives."[37]

The peasant-soldiers in uniform, muddied and resolute, lingered long into the postwar celebrations of the battle. They became the first victims as well as the first heroes in Léon Poirier's 1929 film; they peopled the pages of novels; and they inspired reiterated tributes from Pétain, himself a son of the land, whose vindication of the traditional against the modern dimensions of the battle prefigured the cult that defeat would foster in 1940 and the return to the land that much of his Vichy regime's propaganda and some of its legislation would so ardently promote.[38]

The anxious creed affirming the human element continued to echo across the Rhine as well. Towards the end of the 1920s, proliferating novels of the front began to make of the *materialschlacht* there the crucible of a new kind of human community. In 1930 both Franz Schauwecker and Werner Beumelburg made of daily death in the immediate vicinity of Verdun the midwife of unconditional altruism, one quite distinct from the selfishness of the home and the rear and promising a radically new postwar fatherland. The next year Paul Coelestin Ettighoffer's *Gespenster am Toten Mann* (Ghosts on Le Mort-Homme), that took its title from one of its longer constituent episodes on le Mort-Homme at Verdun, set *frontka-meradschaft* against the sordid politics of the home front. Hans Zöberlein, whose endless novel *Der Glaube an Deutschland* [Belief in Germany] appeared the same year, exhausted his readers with the recitation of ten battles—grinding and repetitive, Verdun the longest by far, conveying the untiring quality of the men who had mastered the new nature of war. "That," he wrote, "is the unrivalled marvel of the German soldier."[39]

In the deepening crisis that polarized the country and threw up pacifist and militarist literature alike, the dead, the willing and patriotic dead, became consensual and almost totemic figures of esteem. In Ettighoffer's account of the battle in 1936, the survivors withdraw in December past the corpses of their fellows, gazing at them and the distant homeland and forming the words: "Don't forget us, the soldiers of Verdun!"[40]

The Nazis quickly picked up the call, electing Beumelburg to the Senate, publishing 42 editions of Zöberlein's opus, that concluded after 900 pages with the incantatory coda: "The war is over/The struggle for Germany continues!/To the front, volunteers!" They seized, too, on earlier novels about Verdun, crowning authors who had not unanimously embraced their ideals in the past but who accepted their laurels now. The *Feldgrau* of Verdun, they wished to convey, was a National Socialist before the letter. In 1935 Ernst Kabisch, another specialist of the battle of Verdun, discerned among the *Frontkämpfer* of Verdun the nascent *Volksgemeinschaft* (national community) dear to Nazi hearts, and Ettighoffer, who had not explicitly espoused Nazism in his earlier evocations of Verdun, imagined, in a radio play, the dead at Douaumont awakening and clambering back into the trenches, assured that National Socialism had made their country whole again.[41]

The day that general Weisenberger addressed his troops in Verdun, on June 15th 1940, the Nazi paper *Völkische Beobachter* announced that "the sacrifice of the 400,000" who had given their lives at Verdun in the Great War had finally been fulfilled. The longest battle, it seemed to say, had only just ended. And the redemptive power of race now tried cohabiting with that of the land in a bizarre mythological accommodation between Hitler's Germany and Pétain's France.[42]

Meanwhile, on both sides of the Rhine, the military specialists trying to understand the longevity of the battle had resisted such conceits, and the hallucinatory visions of rusticity or racial regeneration. Not surprisingly, the French and German analysts drew diametrically different conclusions from the great attritional battle; more surprisingly, both were right.

Contrary to a tenacious legend, Verdun did not inspire among French military planners of the interwar years a faith in some Wall of China that would protect them when Germany recovered its strength, as it surely would. Verdun never hypnotized them, never instilled in them an obtuse fixation upon defensive strategy; it never lulled them into some siege mentality that led as though giving Nemesis her dues to the Maginot line and the disaster of 1940. Yet the long battle mattered.[43]

They did not need it to resurrect the principle of the inviolability of the territory, at least as old as Vauban's "pré carré de la France," the homeland protected by his forts around the borders. It resurfaced now not because Verdun had shown that it might be, but because the invasion and occupation of the country's richest mining and industrial zones had shown that it must be. But how?[44] Consensus finally emerged in the early 1930s around some kind of defensive-offensive strategy, holding near the frontiers or beyond in order to strike back eventually. The national strategy, mixing necessity with wishful thinking, emerged painfully from a tangle of diplomatic, financial, political, and structural constraints that appeared to render a purely offensive doctrine—seizing the initiative at the start of hostilities, as in 1914—progressively unthinkable.[45]

In these discussions the long attritional battle, distant from the eventual Maginot line some 20 years in time and 40 miles in space, surfaced only intermittently and inconsistently. The staunchest advocates of fixed fortifications pointed to their resilience on the Meuse, at the 120,000 shells that had fallen on Douaumont and inflicted only minor damage. But Verdun had held just as much because of the war-hardened armies around the forts, the echeloned artillery behind them, the planes and balloons above them. Among the military planners of the interwar years the fitful remembrance of 1916 only helped dignify projects driven by other, more urgent compulsions. Forced by the gains of the peace settlement to defend a longer border with Germany, uncertain of their Italian one, unable to count on the military presence of Britain or the United States, convinced that only a professional army could wage a truly offensive war and compelled to rely upon a mass of short-term conscripts, and fearful by the mid-1930s that an unduly offensive posture would ignite civil strife at home, they turned to secure instruments that precedent suggested might work. Their defensive plans spurred their recollections, rather than the reverse.[46]

By contrast the offensive lessons first learned at Verdun and mightily confirmed by the allied offensives of 1918 suffused their primordial thinking about war itself. Offensives required superior force, and materiel, and method, and above all time. In the interim, the everlasting interim,

defensive firepower, fortifications of some sort, and limited counterattacks could keep the enemy at bay. Verdun became the first of the cru-
cibles that fused the elements of a new doctrine: *guerre longue, bataille
conduite*, long war and methodical battle, the symmetrical inversion of the
military doctrine of 1914.

Between the wars the Ecole de Guerre rarely strayed from it, imposing
upon officers the scrutiny of its victorious applications in the summer and
autumn of 1918, and bending the new instruments of war, notably the
tank, to its dictates rather than fitting theory to fact: doctrine became
dogma. A citizen-army, the only kind the country was willing to offer,
richly endowed with will if not with skill, could fight such a war; the
poilus had already done so. The endurance that the laymen depicted to
schoolchildren and cinema-goers allowed the method that the specialists
preached to officer cadets and ministers, and the legend of Verdun joined
its lesson in the national strategy that generals, politicians, and citizens at
last managed to agree upon for the next war.[47]

Most German military analysts after the war concluded that Verdun, in
conception and execution, had been a mistake. They took Falkenhayn at
his word, believed his pretended goal of attrition misguided, and turned
once again to the strategies of encirclement that his great predecessor von
Schlieffen had preached before 1914.[48] For now they closed the door on
the lengthy frontal assaults of the sort that had come to grief on the banks
of the Meuse. The doctrine of a short and mobile war, the schematic
opposite of the French, developed as the answer to Germany's interwar
predicament. Unlike the French, the German officers of the postwar had
the movement in the East to inspire them as well as the impasse in the
West to admonish them. New manuals appeared preaching envelopment
if possible and breakthrough if not, ambitions that required the cultivation of initiative, improvisation, and flexible command among the
officer corps—the very virtues discouraged by the rigid and centralized
tenets of methodical battle across the Rhine.

Heinz Guderian, who had fought at Verdun and sought in the 1930s
to restore mobility to the battlefield with independent armored columns,
called on his colleagues in the general staff to jettison the failed concep-
tions of positional warfare. The last war had revealed their bankruptcy,
and he warned that if they clung to the "old solutions of 1916," they would
"entrench themselves in the dead end of a war of position, and forever

bury all hope of winning a swift decision." Guderian and like-minded reformers aspired to move faster than before and to remain in movement in the face of enemy fire. And they derided the virtues of patience in the attack that Verdun and all that followed had imposed. "At no price," he wrote, "will we agree to waste our time in long preparations and endanger the principle of surprise under the pretext of heeding the doctrine that 'only firepower allows subsequent movement.'" They believed, he insisted, precisely the opposite.[49]

The paths that led from Verdun and the battles of 1917 and 1918 to the French long war and the German short one were twisted, determined more by accident and circumstance than by willpower. But in much the same way that French doctrine recruited the popular legend of the stoical *poilu*, the German blitzkrieg that swept all before it between 1939 and 1941 exalted the spirit of the German soldier, the *Geist* that a sterile command had betrayed on the Meuse in 1916 and to which the "November criminals"—all those who had conspired to accept surrender in 1918—had delivered the *coup de grâce*. "There is what can help me!" Hitler exclaimed to Guderian in 1933 as he observed the tanks in motion at Kummersdorf in 1933, "there is what I need!," and six years later the Third Reich, fusing military innovation with the myth of redemption, presented the world with a seemingly revolutionary way of war.[50]

The campaigns that began in 1939 appeared at first to vindicate the rejection of all that Verdun had come to symbolize. But the Germans' short offensive wars gave way to a long one, the sort that 1914–1918 had taught them they could not win, and their eventual annihilation came at the hands of industrial powers whose habits—slow, methodical, overwhelming—strangely bore more resemblance to the *guerre longue* and *bataille conduite* that had emerged from the First World War than to the blitzkrieg that had introduced the Second.

Neither Pétain nor De Gaulle had predicted anything less. The path to victory lay in the exhaustion of the enemy and his nation, Pétain said in 1933, thanks to "a prudent and methodical tactic, conforming to the problems of massive deployment of materiel." Just so, de Gaulle said in his appeal of June 18th 1940 as France fell: "struck down today by mechanical power, we can win in the future by superior mechanical power. There lies the destiny of the world." The cunning of history came late for France, but Verdun returned to haunt her enemies. "Stalingrad is beginning to play a role like that of Verdun," the diplomat Ulrich von Hassell noted in his diary in September 1942, and two months later Hitler, speaking at the beer hall in Munich on the anniversary of his failed putsch 19 years earlier, drew the same ominous comparison: "I do not want to have a second Verdun there," he said, to explain why the siege of Stalingrad was taking so long.[51]

In 1936 Ettighoffer, who had fought at Verdun, might elevate the will of the infantry over the power of materiel in his nonfiction account of the battle: "The war of materiel aims to nip the infantry assault [*Sturmangriff*] in the bud," he declared categorically, "but the will to win is stronger." But when *Storm of Steel* author Ernst Jünger, who had not fought at Verdun, spoke there in 1980, he did so to repudiate his youthful enthusiasms on the Somme: "In those days, as we crowded together in the shell-holes, we still believed that man was stronger than materiel. That proved to be a mistake."[52]

In this way history reaffirmed the industrial method that legend disdained, and dethroned the manly ideals that it elevated. The two parted ways, even though the men of the legend ardently wanted the machines, which saved their lives and took those of their enemies. History and legend seemed not to notice each other. "Things are simple," one of the men had written at Verdun. "Positions are crushed beneath huge projectiles. Infantry are ordered to stay in place. They stay, and wear down. Our artillery fires a lot, but its range is inadequate." He was a cavalryman by training, thrown into an utterly new kind of war, easy to understand but difficult to accept. "The facts of the problem are elementary. They contain realities that are horrible for some. Nobody can grasp this without having seen it. But that's enough, let's leave it." And legend did, by making the battle of materiel the battle of the *poilu*.[53]

7

The Nightmare

By 1916 THE WAR THAT HAD CONCENTRATED and rationalized mass armies as never before had also scattered the combatants who composed them. Its unprecedented violence had deprived them of the esprit de corps that drill had instilled and that closed formations had assured in earlier days, and etched figures onto an empty battlefield. At Verdun some of the men, under the bursting of the ties that bound them, found that the place sentenced them not just to death but to isolation as well. To them it seemed a hell all its own; to an outsider, it seems a hell no doubt, but whether it was a unique one, unlike any other in the Great War or all wars, is another question.[1]

During the German assaults on the crests of le Mort-Homme and Côte 304 and on the ruined village of Bethincourt on 9 April, Falkenhayn observed the proceedings from a battle stand some three miles away, across the river in the woods of Consenvoye. Even this proximity was unusual, suggesting a keen interest in Fifth Army's local effort to gain the tactical edge on the left bank of the Meuse. He usually contemplated the armies up and down the Western Front from the Olympian heights of OHL headquarters to the north, in Charleville-Mézières.

General von Gallwitz, whose attack group was in action that day, commanded the operation from even farther away to the northeast than Consenvoye, from Romagne. He reflected there upon the modern commander who sits by the phone with a map and a colored pencil, waiting, pondering, issuing orders, and never seeing his men live or die.[2]

"The larger the battlefield," Alfred von Schlieffen had written in a fanciful yet premonitory article seven years earlier, "the less it offers to the eye. There is nothing to see in the great wasteland." No Napoleon on horseback took in the scene with an eyeglass from some commanding hilltop. Instead, far away, the modern Alexander pored over a colossal table map that bristled with red pins. Automobiles and motorcycles came and left in haste, officers rushed in, coded messages arrived by telegraph, by telephone, from airplanes and airships in the skies. But he changed no plans, granted no urgent requests for reinforcements from the army and corps commanders in the field. Long before, he had told them which roads and paths and directions to follow, which daily objectives to meet. All Schlieffen's imaginary warlord could do now was plot their progress on the great map that lay spread out before him.[3]

At Charleville-Mézières the Bavarian military representative managed to find the hills south of le Mort-Homme on a map drawn to an obsolete scale of 1:80,000—too grand to allow much detail, the vestige of a day when maps encompassed the distances that armies were supposed to cover. Why dwell on topographic trivia they would sweep past? A crude reproduction sufficed. But a war of a thousand discrete spaces and myopic aspirations set in, a war of ants, and with it came new maps luxuriant in detail and microscopic in scale—1:20,000, even 1:10,000. At the headquarters of the French General Staff in Chantilly, on the third floor, the cartographers obediently rolled up their old vistas and began instead to render the terrain meter by meter. A thicket, a rivulet now captured their attentions, along with a communications trench or a machine gun emplacement, and they labored loyally with their pens to turn the latest intelligence into the newest image, for the terrain, unlike the position, never remained unchanged for long. It was Penelope's labor, the artistry that gave staff officers and generals on both sides of the border their bearings. In Charleville-Mézières the Bavarian attaché soon laid hands on a map of 1:25,000.[4]

But out there, on the ground, even the mapmakers' latest and most scrupulous artifacts often seemed detached from reality, insultingly so to men quick to resent the ways of a remote hierarchy. At times they felt duped. Arriving at Vaux in the night of the 28th of February, a lieutenant found none of the defensive works the map had promised, no shelters, no machine guns, only a little barbed wire, and he and his company found the same *terra incognita* at Douaumont. On Côte 344 near the ruined village of Samogneux in April, the officers' maps were useless and they had no time to reconnoiter the terrain before coming under heavy fire. Another

Erich von Falkenhayn, Chief of the German General Staff from 1914 to 1916. He left contemporaries and historians guessing about his intentions at Verdun. (Library of Congress, LC-USZ62-85081)

Kaiser Wilhelm II and his six sons. Crown Prince Wilhelm, heir to the throne, is to his left. The strait-laced emperor deplored his son and heir's womanizing. (Library of Congress, LC-B2- 3195-12 [P&P])

Generalleutnant Crown Prince Wilhelm of Prussia, Commander of the German 5th Army at Verdun, visiting his troops. He came to regard the battle of Verdun as pointless, but Falkenhayn paid little attention to him. (Bibliothèque nationale de France, image # btv1b6933384b.f1)

General Joseph Joffre, Chief of the French General Staff from 1911 to 1916. He was famed for the robustness of his appetite and the tenacity of his habits. (Library of Congress, LC-B2- 3239-13 [P&P])

General Philippe Petain, commander of the French 2nd Army in 1916. His career seemed almost over in 1914, when at the age of fifty-eight he was an elderly colonel in command of a regiment, but gained fame at Verdun in the First World War—and at Vichy in the Second. (Library of Congress, LC-B2- 4848-4 [P&P])

General Petain on the steps, President Raymond Poincaré off to the left, and Joffre a commanding presence in the center: tale of three men whose rapports were never easy. (Library of Congress, LC-B2- 3798-6 [P&P])

French soldiers entering Fort Vaux. In November they had recaptured the fort—but it was empty of Germans. (Library of Congress, LC-USZ62-55898)

"Ready to attack," as the caption released to this photo taken at Verdun in 1916 would have its viewers believe. Such fairy tales in the press disgusted the men at the front. (Bibliothèque nationale de France, image # btv1b90444802.fl)

Soldiers of the 164th infantry regiment, at rest in a front-line trench. (Bibliothèque nationale de France, image # btv1b6951876f.f1)

A French *poilu*—"hairy one"—at rest. In popular parlance the term designated "brave one" as well, and in fact beards were fast disappearing from the French army, thanks to the gas masks with which they interfered. (Bibliothèque nationale de France, image # btv1b9044484q.f1)

Verdun in 1916.

Verdun in 1919, before all the ruins were cleared and the town was rebuilt. (Library of Congress, Image # 2007663165)

Troops carry the remains of the nameless dead to a yet unfinished ossuary in 1927. (Bibliothèque nationale de France, image # btv1b9039257d.f1)

A mountain of bones, doubtless assembled here for interment in the ossuary that was inaugurated in 1932. It contains the remains of about 130,000 French and German soldiers who died at Verdun. (Library of Congress, LC-USZ62-62659)

August 1932; 3,000 schoolchildren on the steps of the monument to the "Victory of Verdun." (Bibliothèque nationale de France, image # btvb9035081.f1)

The German delegation at Verdun in July 1936, in a ceremony "for the peace of the world." Four months earlier the Third Reich had remilitarized the Rhineland and would soon send its Condor Legion to Spain. (Bibliothèque nationale de France, image #btvb9045969.f1)

The cemetery outside the ossuary, containing the remains of another 16,000 soldiers. (Photograph by Jean-Pol Grandmont)

officer recalled the trench in his sector near Bezonvaux that appeared on the official map but not on the ground, a Platonic trench, so peremptorily had the Corps headquarters demanded that the men perform the impossible and dig it at once in the frozen ground, so anxiously had they pretended to comply.[5]

Between the notional and the real terrain lay the gulf between war imagined and war experienced. Even an army with its numbered corps, divisions, and regiments became an abstraction when modern weaponry worked its singular ways upon the men. Schlieffen, like others, had grasped before the war that the new range and rapidity of defensive firepower would disperse the vulnerable attackers and drive them to move and fight as individuals. It had become a war of captains, Joffre remarked, demonstrating by misquoting that he at least had read the prescient officer, Ardant du Picq, who even before the Franco-Prussian war had seen what was coming. Fixated on the already enormous battlefields of his day, Ardant had worried about the minds and the morale of the men. "The soldiers lose their leaders, the leaders lose their soldiers," he had said, ". . . and one can rightly say that battles today more than ever are battles of soldiers, of captains."[6]

In any given moment between half and three-quarters of a million men might fill the battlegrounds of Verdun and its environs. Yet how many there knew only emptiness and solitude, and came to represent it, drawing on their sensations and their reactions there, as unlike any other battle, as uniquely otherworldly!

To the French approaching from the south, up the *Voie Sacrée*, the villages, hollows, hillsides, and woods seemed to teem with men and beasts, like giant fairgrounds, and enclosures once full of cattle now held piles of artillery shells and rows of trucks. Barracks, tents, and makeshift shelters sprang like undergrowth from the soil.

Part of the road ran along heights that dominated a landscape resembling a simmering and troubled sea. In spring and summer its greenish and sickly yellow waves rolled as far as the horizon, where they gave off smoke and an incandescent glow, and where the high forts of Douaumont and Vaux suggested ridges of foam.[7]

In February and early March, when snow and ice covered the land, the men huddled in the trucks amid equipment, rifles, and water bottles, and passed refugees from villages ruined by shells intended for the long road itself. And, whatever the season, they encountered an unceasing counterflow of revenants from the distant fires. Through the coarse canvas that covered the trucks and flew open in the wind they glimpsed uniformed figures pressed together like themselves, but yellow with mud and inert as corpses. They met as well bizarre convoys bearing wrecked artillery pieces, 75s or 155s, sinister silhouettes that brought consternation to some of their faces.[8]

Of the five senses fixing the impressions that men consigned to paper, no single one predominated. Many heard the sounds before they saw the sights. In early March in Ligny-en-Barrois, 25 miles south of Verdun as the crow flies, they heard "a muffled, distant rumbling, rising, fading, rising again." Upon arriving in the sector a young recruit wrote his uncle of the "unholy din" that greeted him. "What a concert! What a rumble from all sides!" But probably still more of them blended visual with aural impressions in a kind of synaesthesia, and naturally rejected any factitious separation of the two. With the crimson sky came the earthbound drumroll. From Dieue, six miles to the south of Verdun on the *Voie Sacrée*, the distant hills seemed enveloped by a menacing pall, but Jacques Péricard, the officer who would later fill columns of text with the recollections of others, saw the horizon as a "circle of thunder"—a cognitive confusion only to the literal-minded, for why should they distinguish the concert from the film, the novel spectacle that never paused and filled the atmosphere the closer they came?[9]

Some passed President Poincaré's old house at Sampigny on the Meuse, some 25 miles south of Verdun. The Germans had shelled it in 1914, and pillaged a chateau at Pierrefitte farther north, leaving its furniture, piano, and *objets d'art* in pieces. Verdun itself first came into view at night, usually, from around the hills that had obscured it. In the early weeks it flickered from a distance with small crimson fires, and when the trucks entered its deserted streets they drove through rubble, wooden beams, tiles, broken glass, and telephone cables that dangled sadly between houses or stretched in tangled heaps across the ground. Beds, cupboards, and armchairs lay scattered among the ruins, and misshapen iron girders, twisted by the flames, rose pointlessly among them. In houses that retained their silhouettes the curtains flapped in the empty window frames "like flags on a parade day."[10]

The town decomposed progressively, not all at once, and the passing soldiers who found neighborhoods damaged in the winter might return to find them destroyed in the summer. From the first days a chaplain recalled only the ruins of a college gallery, a collapsed façade, the shell casing in the garden by the cathedral. In August, from a little over a mile, a pilot still made out the streets, squares, and intersections of an urban being, but from 500 feet he looked down upon its skeleton, upon decapitated or eviscerated houses and, especially to the north and along the river, upon neighborhoods reduced to heaps of stones, tiles, slates and rubble. "Verdun is dead, truly dead. . . ."[11]

Above and beyond Verdun, the shells echoed in the ravines, and men often found themselves deaf to each other at a meter or two. In the forest of Hesse, bivouacking in huts made of branches and mud, a newly arrived enlisted man and his fellows found the din of their own batteries all around infernal. No painting could portray the inhuman fracas, insisted a Territorial lieutenant, himself an art historian, a scholar of the visual, now voiceless from shouting. A disembodied battle of sounds raged, of "whistling, roaring, rumbling, grinding, tearing, all the barking of machine-gun fire," and even the dark and silent silhouettes of the French and German airships and dirigibles, gently inclined in the heavens, suggested to an artillery officer some "celestial musical score," as though their apparition could only portend some new symphonic outburst.[12]

From here the fray was still invisible, at least on the ground. Trenches disappeared in the dull dun landscape and clouds of smoke drifted across the horizon. "Where then are the wondrous armies killing each other?" a chaplain wondered, gazing out from the Fort de Tavannes toward unseen front lines. The sky was a different matter. By day the glowing halos from the artillery paled, and the shells sent up columns of smoke and earth so thick they eclipsed the sun itself. But by night sudden yellows and oranges flashed from the big guns, and greens, whites and dark reds quivered like shooting stars, the signal rockets fired by infantry officers somewhere, out there. The streaks of light cast hallucinatory, infinitely variable shadows that danced in the forest. In March a second lieutenant watched from Verdun as the nocturnal fires of burning villages several miles distant, Bras and Charny to the north, Fleury to the east, spread an immense fan of light across the snow between them. Was he experiencing, he asked himself guiltily, "Nero's spasm, delighted in unhappiness as long as it has beauty?"[13]

The French traveled there from afar, oftener than not up the *Voie Sacrée* and through the town or its outskirts. They came to relieve those already in line, in a regular rotation that imposed the same journey into desolation upon two million and more of them at one time or another. Many more of their adversaries had traveled to the place weeks and months before the destructions even began, ignorant of the why or the wherefore, through less ominous landscapes and into less threatening habitats. The Crown Prince's army, unlike Pétain's, had long been on the scene. Its men had occupied the villages, toiled or rested in the distant woods, watched as artillery pieces, machine gun companies, troop transports, and long trains moved past them towards points ever closer still to the city and the river, to 32 unloading sidings where they disgorged still more munitions and men. Instead of artillery fire the newly arrived heard the incessant shuffle of boots on muddy roads, the neighing of horses, and the grinding and spinning of wheels. Rainwater and melting snow came through the beams and the blankets below ground and lay ankle deep in the trenches above ground, and in February, when the men learned the point of their presence and waited as the weather delayed their attack from day to day, the steady drip sounded like the ticking of a death-watch. Even after the 21st and during the long months of battle that followed, relief units and reinforcements came by rail in less frequent rotations, through quieter parts of the front, and sometimes from the other side of Europe, in a journey that lacked the premonitory sights and sounds that topography and logistics visited upon their ceaselessly renewed French adversaries.[14]

All the more powerful the shock when they came upon the scene—and quickly Verdun leveled its attackers and defenders, and the poverty of human expressive means made for a crude identity of reactions. From Chaumont, some six miles from the front lines, a lieutenant in the elite Bavarian Leibregiment contemplated the scene he would penetrate with his unit that night. The noise dwelt in his memory, but no more than the French then or later could he neatly separate sight from sound. A muffled roaring filled the landscape, he recalled, a "perpetual, subterranean, boiling rumble like that of a mighty volcano," and shells from the Fort de Marre flew overhead with a vibrating rush that ended seconds later in a deafening impact and that every soldier had long come to recognize—for this was late June. He might as well have quoted the French, their impressions of "gurglings, lappings, whisperings, a thousand rustlings" as their own shells traveled, so closely did his visual and aural register reproduce their own, and the closer the combatants came to the front lines and to each other the more they shared the same wretchedness of condition and of prospect.[15]

In May, outside Douaumont, two officers, one French and the other German, watched the same shell fire illuminate the night "like yellow flowers blooming on a dark meadow," and listened to the same detonations howl in the valley. Later they would publish their accounts in works that answered each other like choral responses.[16] Outside Douaumont in February a German student, now in uniform, contemplated the same scene of destruction and desolation that provoked a French officer to exclaim later on that he found it "impossible to imagine a more appalling corner of the earth."[17] Moonlight bathed the same landscape outside Fort Vaux in May that German artillery had illuminated in March, littered with twisted corpses, the same that a German had described as "ghostly" and that a French conscript called "the most horribly wrecked corner of the front."[18]

And very quickly, on the way up to the line, they set eyes upon the wounded, walking or prone, and climbed over them in forts and shelters, and heard them in the night. Arriving in the environs of Verdun on the 27th of February with his surgical team, the future author Georges Duhamel encountered them crowding the roads in dog-carts, in wagons pulled by horses giving off mists of sweat, in vans, escorted by exhausted medical assistants and stretcher-bearers; but troops now converging from points near and far always enjoyed the right of way.[19] On the road from Landrécourt a *poilu* crossed paths with several companies of wounded men, the skeletal remains of their regiments, staggering by as though drunk, morose, and muddy, led by an officer leaning on a cane. "It's no longer an army! It's only corpses!" a Territorial muttered as he watched them move by. The wounded lay in command posts waiting to be evacuated, they stood or lay in the snow outside the hospital at Baleycourt waiting to be let in, they waited for treatment or transport in the subterranean galleries of Douaumont and Vaux as troops struggled by them or sat where they could.[20] A Bavarian chaplain noted the sights of the wounded in his journal, bloodied men dragging themselves back from the front lines, leaning on canes, in the incessant rain. Others retained the sounds. Nocturnal cries of "Medics! Help! Mother!" rang in the ears of

German survivors long afterward, and outside Douaumont one of them listened to the wounded, to the moans of bloody figures on tarpaulins carried in columns through the darkness by bowed silhouettes; and sometimes they fell silent.[21]

Relief operations happened under cover of night, and the nocturnal journey into the front lines was a descent into the land of the dead, who greeted the living and even flung themselves at them as they approached. "The shells rip open and disinter the dead and send them past your face in shreds," one of the men wrote home, but often they encountered their first corpses underfoot before they ever set eyes upon them. Beyond the faubourg Pavé, a French major later recalled of their trek up to the line from the suburb on the right bank, past the farm of the Cabaret rouge and up onto the hillsides, they began walking over the first corpses— runners or men sent for food, killed on the way.[22] Or the dead betrayed their unseen presence by odors—odors that made even some asphyxiating gases bearable to one well-traveled French captain, as he and his men stumbled with their shovels on long-buried bodies near Douaumont; odors that swept over a Bavarian lieutenant as he neared the makeshift morgues in the ruined houses of Chaumont, reeking of chloride and lime, that pervaded the soup of a German gunner near Louvemont, that arose from the spilled blood of the newly killed and attracted swarms of blue and green flies.[23] Soon the dead came into view, by the roadside in the Bois des Caures, some covered by blankets, in the Bois d'Haumont, slowly disappearing beneath the falling snow, at the bottom of shell-holes and trench fragments. First the odor, then the sight of the greatcoats in the shell-holes, an artillery mechanic noted of his climb from the Casernes Marceau on the edge of the town up to the lines around Fort Souville. In his trench near Fort Vaux a *poilu* awoke one day to find a corpse on the parapet staring at him, too dangerous, too exposed, for him to move. It might soon be him, he reflected.[24]

They could not easily bury them all. In June the general in command of the 1st Bavarian Infantry Division, which had taken heavy losses in the attack on Thiaumont, complained that too many corpses and body parts lay scattered about, menacing the health and the morale of his troops. All, and not just the health services, he said pointedly, were to help remove the dead and bury them in mass graves with plenty of lime chloride to disinfect them. He warned against individual graves, likely to be thrown up by artillery fire. And they were: coming up the line and in position the men watched as shell fire violently exhumed the lifeless remains of their fellows and their foes and tossed body parts and shreds of uniforms, like rag dolls without their stuffing, into the air. "The jackals even kill the dead," complained a second lieutenant in the colonial infantry, who had buried a comrade the day before only to see him flung up and cut in two by a shell the next. "It's to die twice."[25]

The teeming necropolis of Verdun engulfed the newcomers, who soon acquired the ways of passive resistance to its insults. Under the rhythms of mass artillery fire they could only cling to life with sharpened senses, bent like larvae into the hollows of trench walls and the sides of craters, as the earth rose and fell and shell splinters and stones rained down. They listened to the incoming projectiles with the practiced ears of the cognoscenti, and distinguished the trench mortars that droned as they pirouetted to earth, the quiet rush of the tear gas shells, the yelping of the 75s, and the richly varied music of the heavier calibers. When shells of 100 millimeters and more landed nearby the men watched flames shoot up, jet-black clouds of soil and smoke ascend, and tree trunks, beams, sandbags, and mess tins fly before their eyes. But the shells landed as deliverance, for they had spared the listeners. To hear their fracas was to escape their fury. Then they waited for the next one. And they knew them by sight as well, so well that they graced them with sobriquets, "pelos," "gros pépères," "gros noirs," "gros jaunes," "gros verts," "marmites" in French, and "Brocken," "Grosse Kiste," "Ostereier," "Zuckerhut" in German. With even greater detachment, they might observe them from afar, like bystanders at a visual feast. In June a French artillery officer on Côte 304 looked on the glow of German guns firing from Montfaucon some three and a half miles away, and on pincer-like beams from projectors sweeping the sky, red tracer shells, green, white and red rockets, flashes of anti-aircraft fire, a display of fireworks unlike any he had seen before. It mesmerized him and three of his fellow spectators.[26]

Below ground the spectacle darkened. In the Tunnel de Tavannes, dug through the Côtes de Meuse in peacetime for the rail line between Verdun and Etain but now usurped by the exigencies of war, a subterranean camp hosted a population of transients. Two or three thousand troops, prisoners, invalids, and corpses cohabited there with horses and mules, and with their carcasses, in the murky and fetid air, with little sanitation, shaken by the shells that hammered the entrance and the exit. Newcomers from the ravine outside found the sights and scents nauseating.

The forts at least could open their vents, as long as poison gas did not find its way through them. But the underground galleries of the most exposed among them served the same ends and took on the same aspect as the Tunnel de Tavannes, dark and foul, saturated with the refuse of battle. The passageways of Douaumont reeked with every odor of the front, a German lieutenant found in July as he came through with his company on the way to Fleury and Souville. "It reeked of chlorine and sweat, of wet clothes, of powder and latrines, of singed bandages and carbolic acid, of damp mortar and charred wood." In Fort Vaux, by the smoking light of kerosene lamps, a French chaplain looked onto recumbent bodies on top of each other, and a *poilu* smelled the odor of blood on the stairs and in the corridors where the wounded lay. Everywhere, in every fort, the walls ran with rivulets of damp that collected on the ground and sometimes turned it into mud that rose ankle-deep.[27]

And even if the detonations above ground sounded distant and muffled under the vaulted masonry of the galleries, shells hitting the superstructure sent violent tremors down to the huddled refugees below. Deep inside Vaux, the 1100-pound shells that fell on the fort and sent blocks of cement four or five meters square into the ditches also shook the French occupants with the vibrations of a giant jackhammer. The concrete sang, trap doors rose and fell on their hinges, dust and debris filled the air. Douaumont, hit by French 280 mms, trembled from its turrets to its foundations, and the Germans within inhaled clouds of cement and limestone particles as lights went out and soldiers trying to move through halted in their tracks. The structures kept the men of the catacombs alive, at least, but left them vulnerable to the threat that their fellows in the trenches and shell-holes above had some prospect of escaping: fire.[28]

In May, during the French bombardment two days before their failed attempt to retake Douaumont, a shell ignited a grenade depot in the fort and set off a holocaust that annihilated an entire German battalion, some 800 men. In October, when another French shell set off another grenade dump and flames spread to an adjoining room full of rockets and munitions, a panic inspired by memory, a *sauve-qui-peut* in the shadows, swept the entire garrison, and when the French Marsouins arrived the next day they found the fort almost empty. Easier to flee a fort than a tunnel: in

September, when yet another tinderbox—grenades or rockets—exploded in the Tunnel de Tavannes, fire raged through the makeshift wooden partitions and chased the victims it had not yet consumed towards the exit, where German shell fire awaited them. Four hundred died. Days later the tunnel was still smoking. In October, the same day that fire drove the Germans from Douaumont, a French lieutenant entering the Tunnel de Tavannes found that catastrophe had bred reconstruction, an urban renewal of sorts, with electric lights, medical posts, sanitary installations at regular intervals, bunks raised along the walls, so that traffic passed below the reclining figures instead of over them—but still the subterranean city shook as though from seismic shocks, and still the doctors operating with rolled up sleeves by the light of lamps darkened by flies could not send the wounded on as quickly as they came in.[29]

The chronic physical torments that plagued the men above and below ground, in the front lines and farther back, by night and by day, lent a baneful consistency to their sojourn. "Ever the rain, the fog, the mud...." Especially the mud, that encrusted the men in the front lines from their boots to their helmets and turned their greatcoats yellow, a distinctive, glutinous mud that clotted their hair and stealthily gripped their joints, not liquid enough to wash off but just solid enough to cling to their heels at every step, to engulf their huts at the rear, to swallow them up in brimming shell-holes. Rainfall varied its depth and its consistency, and so did the labors of men, whose movements, bombardments, and excavations set off landslides and inundations, but no one escaped it and sometimes its noxious presence eclipsed even brutal reminders of mortality: "What most struck me at Verdun . . . the mud," a centenarian, a Zouave lieutenant sent there four times, recalled in 1996. "To get killed in war is common . . . but to live in mud is atrocious."[30]

They had company: they heard the rats nibble, jump, tumble from beam to beam, feebly shriek behind the corrugated iron roofing of the dugouts, they watched them feed on corpses and carcasses, felt them scurry across their faces at night. They named them, as they had the inanimate shells—"gaspards" for the French, "Verdunratten" for the Germans, who elevated the local rodents into the fatted chosen of the species. Blankets and clothing crawled with lice, the pullulating, devouring lice, and they named them too—"totos" most often in French, "Nachtenbummler" (night loiterers), "Schnellaüfer" (sprinter), "Fremdenverkehr" (tourist traffic), "Kostgänger" (boarders), "Mitesser" (dining companion) and a string of other German cognomens, the surest sign of ubiquity. In the trenches, shell-holes, and forts the men lived among the rats, lice, fleas, and insects, creatures that only persecuted them, far from the draught animals on whose existence they depended so heavily for supplies of all sorts; but at times they heard the strange, almost human cries that issued from the depths of the woods, the protests of wounded horses and mules.[31]

Hunger occasionally threatened them, when their rations ran out and they found themselves cut off from the mobile kitchens that kept them fed in the front lines, or when *corvées à soupe* sent under cover of night to fetch the victuals never returned. Often food arrived cold, or shot full of holes, or eaten by rats. But there, under fire or isolated like troglodytes, they craved water above all. Thirst stalked and sometimes subdued them. It forced them to surrender in Fort Vaux, where every night volunteers had been carrying in cans and gourds from the Tunnel de Tavannes and the Bois Fumin, enough for the men to drink out of for thirty seconds every three hours, until the German noose closed, the cisterns cracked, and fever swept the fort with incoherent babble, hallucinations, and dreams of water springing from rocks at home. No sources supplied the left bank of the river, and those that watered the right bank fell prey to artillerists who divined their presence even if they could not see them. Bullets and shrapnel pierced the cans and pails that bent and bowed men carried in twos through the night. In mid-June, at Fleury and Souville, the men were dying of thirst, under constant fire in the scorching heat. Some drank out of ponds poisoned by rotting corpses. Horse-drawn wagons loaded with barrels scattered under German fire, and when men came through on foot bearing basins and buckets chaos broke out and discipline collapsed amid cries of "Drink! Drink!"[32]

Earthly metaphors soon proved their poverty in the preternatural setting of Verdun. Sometimes images of extinct volcanoes or storms at sea suggested themselves to authors at a loss for words to record their impressions. A French chaplain felt violently seasick from the intense shell fire on the crest of Haudromont in March, as though he were clinging to a wave-tossed raft in the aftermath of some shipwreck. A German lieutenant at Fleury in June saw an angry sea around him, the earth rising and falling with an oceanic swell.[33] But the scribes of battle more often conjured up realms of the otherworldly when they put pen to paper and summoned up the will to depict if not to comprehend their surroundings. The underground shadows in Tavannes—"the tunnel, what a vision from Dante"—and the nightly gloom and flashes outside the fort of Froideterre—"the antechamber of Hell . . . imagined by Dante"—required no great literary artifice to become in the eyes of their beholders the Inferno made real.[34] "Hell," a German general called it on the left bank; "hell," a German machine-gunner called it on the right. They left their shell-holes one February dawn, a French chaplain said, "like the damned leaving Hell." The figure of speech seemed to come naturally to their lips; in June the French postal censors noticed its recurrence in the lexicon of letter writers throughout the Second Army. And they noticed as well a competitor, "nightmare." Among French and Germans alike, a dream-world pervaded the underworld, peopled by spectral apparitions and lit by hallucinatory flares. Had he been watching a specter?, a lieutenant in the woods of Avocourt asked, as the dark reds, yellows, and greens that had streaked the sky all night paled in the dawn and the noise abated. In the chaotic terrain between Chaumont and Ornes a German lieutenant sensed an evil fantasy, and he insisted elsewhere that any memory of Verdun dissolved into a violent and indistinct dream. His countrymen in particular encountered spirits who transfigured the land and its creatures into a murmuring spirit-world. Ghosts walked abroad, in the ruined church spire in Mogeville, the moonlit path through the blasted woods, the exploding munitions depot at Azannes; and in the chalk-white faces of men who crawled out of collapsed trenches, or made their way back from the Bois des Caures as inert and expressionless as the walking dead, or sat silhouetted like the damned in the catacombs of Fort Douaumont. Like their French adversaries the Germans expressed the travelers' awe rather than the soldiers' vainglory, and discovered at Verdun an accursed province—not a battle, but a world.[35]

Spectators of their own spectacle, the men reacted to the *enfer* or the *Hölle* as though in it but not of it, and displayed a detachment akin to alienation.

Newcomers once addled by romantic renditions of war and its nobility quickly and bitterly shed their illusions. In May, on the crest of le Mort-Homme that the French had taken in April and still held, a second lieutenant lamented the wretched lot of his fellow-infantrymen. This war had abased them, he reflected, from warrior caste to dispensable medi-ocrities destined to disappear as the man-servants of heavy materiel, without heroism, without firing up the imagination or the esteem of the nation. Flashes of fanfare or pageantry, the vestiges of period ceremonial, appeared quaintly obsolete to the trench-wise and the blasé. In February, as the Brandenburgers of the 3rd Army Corps moved up to the line, the band struck up the *Preussens Gloria* and the *Yorkschen March*. A pioneer found the display comical, complete with corpulent *Musikmeister* who wore two pistols and who minutes later returned with his band to the rear as the *Sturmtruppen* and their men went up to the lines. No matter that in its heyday the chivalric ideal was already hard to reconcile with the ignoble realities of medieval campaigns; the infantile visions of vivid *chevauchées* that had escorted him to the front, a French captain noted in his journal, did not long survive the sight of the filthily clad men cringing below the parapets: "it can't be repeated often enough. This war has destroyed the romance of war."[36]

An impression of fighting an unrecognizable war, one bearing little resemblance to that of 1914 and none at all to any earlier, took hold of the men of Verdun, sometimes even before they arrived. *Poilus* marched in helmets and horizon blue greatcoats through Champagne towards the banks of the Meuse in 1916, past faded red kepis that hung on wooden crosses by the roadside. They were all that was left from the battles of September 1914, sartorial relics of a heroic age, *memento mori* from a bygone war in the sun. And what had become of the Napoleonic lore of their upbringing? The timely charge, the pregnant moment that school-books had celebrated and that journalists still lamely invoked? "Over there, you'd music, you'd the works, here you've nothing," a corporal said, recalling the retreat from Sarrebourg in 1914. "You saw the flag. For a long time we haven't seen it, the flag. No point in saying the flag, you die for it." War turned into toil, cavaliers into commoners. A cavalry lieutenant from a moribund squadron found himself running messages across the shell-holes at Verdun, placed in some kind of command over a hundred other converted horsemen. They, too, had dismounted and gone about their lowly runners' errands out of sight, out of earshot, alone—just as exposed to danger but remote now from the encouraging chorus of equestrian war, exemplars instead of more solitary and obscure varieties of human resolve.[37]

Despair, whether disguised as indifference, fatalism, or a nihilism that Louis-Ferdinand Céline would later convey in a great novel, or proclaimed by way of response to the daily assault on the senses—despair provided a semblance of distance from the scene. A French stretcher-bearer watched porters fill up their cauldrons and sacks with food and water from a rolling kitchen and walk three miles across moonlit snow back to the front lines, silently, listlessly.

In front of Souville a French lieutenant, an art historian, a man of thought and of words, took refuge from the sights and especially the sounds of artillery fire behind a carapace of imbecility. "In the end we're overcome with weariness," he noted. "We're capable of passing thought, but any extended meditation is impossible. . . ." The stultifying shredding of his faculties left another art historian diminished and lethargic, as though he had somehow shed his soul; but perhaps the descent into mindlessness preserved him from more violent disorders of the spirit. And the sentiment of passively participating in a violent game of chance, a lottery in which everyone's name had been entered, plunged some of them into an intellectual stupor that kept the darkest thoughts at bay: "Empty of any thought, man stays without horror in these ravines of hell. How can he think of death, when he cannot think of anything?"[38]

Fear, anguish, and horror still penetrated such defenses. No mental torpor could stifle fears as trenchant as the novel instruments of death. Which unnerved the most? Gas, insidious, unannounced, bringing "the death to fear above all others?" That arrived, as a Bavarian sergeant reported in May, as a hissing, fist-sized bluish fireball, hit the trench wall or parapet, and spread out into a 35-foot-wide toxic cloud. Or mines, and the sinister subterranean tapping in no man's land, that suddenly stopped and signified to the listeners and patrols above that the enemy sappers' work was done, the detonation only a matter of time.

Gas and mines dealt death less widely than shells and bullets, yet boasted a terror all their own. That of artillery fire was cumulative. It grew louder, faster, nearer; nerves gave out; fevers set in. It passed, along with the horror it might have provoked if any body parts had flown and any blood had rained. But for some able to compare, it was the most shattering ordeal of all. An airman, exposed in a slow and lumbering French Farman, a *cage aux poules* (chicken coops), to the guns and speed of a German Fokker, still found the celestial dogfight nothing like his subjection to a terrestrial *marmitage*. It was swifter, kept him mentally occupied, never drained his will or his hope of prevailing. Death always stalked the airmen, but it came suddenly and brusquely: "We die a lot, we suffer little." The anguish of a sustained *barrage* or *tir de destruction* was unknown in the skies.[39]

But of all the mental states induced by their besieged senses, none manifested itself more chronically than solitude. Solidarity with their fellows scarcely tempered their awareness of severance from the known world, proximate or remote, and their recurrent apprehensions of abandonment and oblivion.

Forebodings began even before they moved in to relieve the units in line. The worst, a lieutenant recalled many years later, worse than battle itself, was the slow Calvary of the climb to the lines, with all its premonitory fears. Merely finding the unknown reaches of the front could tax the surest navigational sense. They moved by night, to hide from enemy shells, in Indian file, section by section, through labyrinthine ways and tangled, blasted woods. "Verdun means first of all the nocturnal climb of men bent beneath the weight of pack and munitions, stumbling in the shell holes," President René Coty remembered, and to lose sight of the men ahead, to wander into the wrong communication trench, to disperse amid sudden bursts of shell fire might set off hours, even days of anxious searching. The men, fixed on the single shadow in front of them, lost the officers ahead— the quarter-mile that separated them might as well have been ten. And the officers lost the men. "Pass the word ahead. They're not following," rose the nocturnal complaint, and officers would circle back, like sheepdogs tending a straggling flock. He had been given false directions, a lieutenant suspected as he tried to find his battalion one night, seeking bearings from anyone able to give them, and he reflected that all the Germans had to do was to disguise themselves as *poilus* to sow utter confusion, so tenuous was the lifeline that linked them, so fragile the order in procession.[40]

Once in line, the recollection of the impassible pathways and mangled communication trenches down which they had struggled only deepened their sense of isolation from the world they had left behind. No one could reach them, no one could reinforce them. From the heights of headquarters the problem appeared technical. Ground conditions and enemy artillery had made communications so poor, the staffs of Bavarian infantry divisions concluded in August, that regimental orders took hours to reach battalions in line, even when distances were minimal. Neighboring regiments ignored each other's objectives, and infantry and artillery, deprived of any telephone communications, could not coordinate their timing. Carrier pigeons alone assured any kind of liaison, the 1st Bavarian Army Corps concluded bleakly in June. He had to memorize his orders, a German lieutenant recalled, because once inside the flaming wasteland he and his men knew that no communication with their own was likely—not with the high command, not with the artillery, not by light signals, not by wireless telegraphy, and only rarely, uncertainly, by runners.[41]

For them, as for the French, the reality was psychological. "Many complain of the anguish a troop feels when it believes itself abandoned by the rear," General Chrétien wrote of the troops of 30th Corps as they faced the German onslaught, "leading sometimes to a general depression that can end up paralyzing all action." By the 26th of February, the day after Fort Douaumont fell, a German lieutenant listened to the echoes of infantry firing in the woods of Hardaumont and suddenly grasped that their airmen were blind and their artillerists silent, that he and his fellows were left to their own devices to advance unaided from tree to tree, that they were fighting their own war. Desolation could blacken their waking hours, a conviction that all, commanders, reservists, artillerists, pilots, had deserted them. They shrank to fragmentary figures in a limitless landscape. The lunar look, the empty battlefield, sprang from both the psychological and the physical ravages of modern gunnery, which imposed distance between armies and estrangement between men. "Each of us," one such recalled after scaling a hillside crowned by a ring of fire, "is alone, isolated on this erupting earth."[42]

He was speaking, like Schlieffen before and Joffre after him, of combat. But even behind the relative security of the trench wall, or at rest in barracks and encampments further back, or on their nocturnal relief journeys up to the lines, nothing betrayed the men's sense of solitude in life more eloquently than their fear of physical disappearance in death. An officer lamented the loss of the ritual observances that saw off the deceased in the mortuaries and chapels of civilian society—"here, a man disappears without anyone noticing." His words unwittingly captured as well a deeper dread of pulverization and extinction, of consumption, likelier than not, by the explosion of a mine or a 305 mm or a 380 mm or a

420 mm, a prospect that attended the men daily and that haunted some of them more than death itself. One night a chaplain feared the void, the prospect of physical annihilation from shell fire, more keenly than he had feared a banal end that morning from rifle or machine-gun fire.

To die alone in the darkness of a dugout or crater held its terrors, whatever the instruments of extinction. In a shelter on the Côte de Froide-terre a second lieutenant reflected on the gulf between death in daylight and death in obscurity, one seen and applauded, the other unseen and ignored, and on how courage demanded its audience, played to its gallery. Later, left alone on le Mort-Homme during a relief operation, the same fear of vanishing from human company and human memory gripped him. And at the base of the Ravin de la Dame another lieutenant contemplated a stream, dammed by dislodged earth, overflowing into the shell-holes along its banks and filling them with *glaise*, the famous Verdun *glaise*, and he imagined slowly sinking into one of them, alone, his cries drowned by the sounds of battle, to end only as "missing."[43]

To listen to some of the men there, and still more to some who were not, Verdun stood apart, even transcended history itself. Two weeks before he was killed there, a second lieutenant spoke of Verdun as though of Armageddon or mass suicide. "Peoples [nations] are gripped by a mania for death and destruction," he wrote after an attack on the Ravin de la Mort, near Fort Vaux, in which his commanding officer was killed. "Yes, humanity is mad!"[44]

It was worse, some of the soldiers at Verdun insisted, than anything they had seen yet. Worse than the Marne, because of the German heavy guns, an artillery lieutenant reflected in May on Côte 304; worse than Champagne or Artois, he had reflected in March near Fleury, for much the same reason. During the shelling of Fort Douaumont just before its ignominious fall in February, some *tirailleurs marocains* gave Lieutenant Péricard, the supposed author of the cry "Debout les Morts!" ("Arise, O dead!") to know that Champagne had been a "joke" next to this. The word spread among the neighboring battalions: "you know, Champagne was small beer next to this, the *tirailleurs* said so!" It was the worst ever, a munitions driver complained in May, stuck with his battery between the Fort St. Michel and the Tunnel de Tavannes as the French tried to retake Douaumont: "what an artillery fight. I've never heard anything like it, it's appalling!!!"

In almost identical terms, German transplants to Verdun from other fronts proclaimed the peerless horrors of their new environment. "I've already seen a lot," a lieutenant wrote his parents, "but I've never known the war to take on such an indescribably horrifying aspect." This was the worst, they said in so many words—the side of le Mort-Homme the worst spot anywhere, an infantryman wrote, the artillery battle the worst ever, a driver on his hospital bed said: "there has never been, in any theater of operations, an artillery fight like it. . . ."[45]

Their claims fell on friendly ears, on sympathetic bystanders willing to accept without much scrutiny that Verdun surpassed any violence that war had yet invented. In the rainy autumn of 1916 some Austrian officers visited General von Zwehl and his 7th Reserve Corps, dug in on the Côte de Talou and the Côte du Poivre some six miles north of Verdun. They had traveled from the Isonzo in the Alps, one of the most fearsome fronts of any, but they assured their ally that even their positional warfare at 3000 feet paled beside his, waged down muddy trenches on fire-swept hillsides. The press did not dwell on the horrors of the place; it had instructions not to; but how could their civilian readers not apprehend the distant reality, when letters arrived to tell them about it, followed by the letter-writers themselves? In March, men in the Second Army wrote to their friends and relatives at home that the bombardment was worse than anything in Artois or Champagne; in July, that any sector would be "paradise" next to Verdun, save perhaps the Somme, newly raging—but in August even that seemed preferable to a Zouave contemplating his return to the lines at Verdun. "Since I went to war, I've never seen a massacre like it," went the constant refrain, presenting the postal censors with repeated exercises in comparative horror: "where we are it's overheating, a real hell, [I've] never seen anything like it since the war started, a real furnace." In October 1917, long after the very worst was over—at least at Verdun—they were still saying the same: "but we'll never come across a sector as terrible."

No surprise, then, that civilians should come to think of Verdun the way its temporary occupants did, especially when accounts such as Péricard's were published long before the war even ended. In a small town away from the scene some workers billeted an artillery officer, the same who had reflected on the macabre distinctions of Verdun. His hosts needed no persuading. They received letters from a brother, a medical aide in a field hospital there, and they uttered the town's name as though wielding a byword for massacre and butchery.[46]

Yet the novelties at Verdun were no longer novel. Long before they arrived there, men had lamented the eclipse of splendors they had known or imagined by indignities they had suffered but accepted. "Where are the fair [honnêtes] battles of yesterday? Bouvines, Austerlitz, today it's treachery, a soul-sickening struggle in a pit," a seminarian asked—in Neuville St. Vaast, in June 1915, ten months before he set foot at Verdun. Where were the sky-blue tunics, the blue shakos with white borders, the half-belts braided with copper and all that set the warriors apart from the rest in 1914? They all looked like infantry now, one of their number complained in Argonne in December 1915, all save the horses. "There it is, the scientific war of the 20th century, stripped of all that lent beauty, élan, enthusiasm, the ideal, sweeping manoeuvers, heroic charges," a noncommissioned infantry officer noted at Main-de-Massiges, in Champagne, six months before he arrived at Verdun and seven before he was killed there. "We're waging a war of miners."

For some even the company of corpses had long lost its grisliness. Late in life an infantryman, already 21 years old and a veteran of almost 30 months when he arrived at Verdun in 1917, recalled how body parts there shone in the dark like glowworms. But the odor of their decomposition, the feel of their presence underfoot, had proved especially edifying two years earlier, when he and other newcomers to the war had first dug trenches near Santerre in the upper Somme. By mid-September 1914, near the forest of Champenoux outside Nancy, a future captain at Verdun had already overcome his nausea at the ubiquitous dead, and when he stepped on them at night during marches he no longer even noticed.[47]

In one respect at least the afflictions of battle had even moderated by the time of Verdun. Medical services, overwhelmed during the battles of the frontiers and the war of movement of 1914, and poorly equipped to adapt to the positional warfare of the following year, were changing their ways. No preparation among the French could treat the wounded as quickly as they poured in during the first days of the attack in February; the Bavarian medical personnel, understaffed and deprived of forward treatment posts, could only issue unanswered calls for more stretcher-bearers when reports came in of whole battalions decimated during the attacks around Thiaumont in May and June; systems failed before such carnage. But in other ways they displayed a resilience that numbers sometimes confirmed. No longer did the French services evacuate all their wounded by rail to distant treatment centers, as they had the year before during their offensives in Artois and Champagne. Some they now treated close to the lines, others much farther back, in a new chain of treatment graduated according to a revealing neologism—"emergency traumatology"—and resembling one already in use among their adversaries. Never had so many wounded passed through the system so continuously—on average, 1,400 French every day, during the first 100 days of Verdun—and the unremitting sequence of injury and treatment hid a corollary: that the numbers in the "killed" and "missing" columns of the after-action reports and loss tables might have risen much higher.[48]

Halfway through the Great War, Verdun introduced few torments not already invented, and even attenuated some of them with tactics and innovations that at least reduced statistical loss rates. And in its day no one could demonstrate that it outdid in violence or grotesquerie contemporary battles in the East or the West. In any given day the impressions and sense data from the Somme might as well have come from the Meuse. There Robert Graves, who would leave a war memoir as famous as his *I, Claudius* novels, had walked among the bloated corpses in the wreckage of Mametz Wood, and earlier in the war had barely been able to distinguish a violent thunderstorm from an artillery bombardment; there, one of Graves' fellow-officers, Sidney Rogerson, had vomited with his men as they dug trenches and unearthed bodies at every yard; and there, the economic historian R. H. Tawney had known injury and the intense sense of isolation that came with combat and no man's land. In September the French soldiers on the Somme began to speak of it as though of Verdun, the censors noted, and the familiar words now issued from their pens too—"horror, furnace, butchery." The Somme was larger, Verdun was longer, but rain-soaked trenches collapsed and buried their occupants along one river as easily as along the other, and few survivors of the two great battles of the Western Front in 1916 gave themselves to the foolhardy exercise of competitive misery.[49]

Rogerson struggled through mud he called "unique even for the Somme," and descriptions of a "unique mud"—the infamous *glaise*—punctuated letters from Verdun. A sense of experiencing the unexampled gripped the men, even when they acknowledged the toll of earlier ordeals:

"Verdun is terrible, but not more than Arras or the Yser in 1914," a second lieutenant in the colonial infantry conceded in the Tunnel de Tavannes. But he went on to shed his ancillary reserve and pronounce the battle terrible in every sense, leaving men alone in the open emptiness, cold, hungry, sleepless, and helpless against modern materiel.

And it was true: they had never seen the ghostly necropolis of Verdun, with its ravines and fortresses and relentless self-perpetuation, nor felt the same isolation from the world behind them. Such mental states did not lend themselves to learned comparisons in recent or distant military history; they were never meant to compete with others or weigh in some balance of bloodiness, any more than Ernst Jünger's own allusions on the Somme to Dante—*lasciate ogni speranza!*—and to the sickly scent of corpses in the ruins or on the road there betrayed any willful claim to local exceptionalism. Subjectively singular but objectively plural, such experiences resisted comparison at any level other than statistical, a task emotionally meaningless and intellectually impossible for the men who endured them.[50]

Posterity mistook the subjective imaginings of the men for the objective realities of the war, and conferred upon Verdun a mantle of singularity in suffering that other sites of the war might justifiably contest.

Verdun sat as though by tacit accommodation atop the pinnacle of horror. No one sought overtly to dislodge it, but on occasion alert officialdom awoke to the implied slight to the others. Already in May 1916, at the height of the battle, President Poincaré had taken care not to elevate it about the others, not to make of it a national place of memory before its time. Greeting the refugees from Lorraine, he spoke of "the heroes of the Marne, the Yser, and Verdun," and of Nancy, which some of them had fled, as a "martyred city." In 1936 a Senegalese deputy, Galandou Diouf, proposed striking a medal to commemorate the 20th anniversary of the battle. "For us, the French," he argued, the Battle of Verdun evoked the "climactic Calvary of our poor and admirable soldiers," whose torments amply justified the epithet already in vogue for the place: "hell." But the Ministry of Defense demurred. The operations of 1914–1918, it pointed out tactfully, "form a whole in which the numerous episodes deserve equally for various reasons to be glorified." A medal for Verdun, by the Ministry's lights, would require the creation of many others, and the more they struck, the less each would mean. Diouf's project died.

But still "*l'enfer* de Verdun" tightened its hold, among the most varied of raconteurs.[51]

Its length, twice that of the closest contender, the Somme, etched familiarity into millions of bystanders even as it compounded the carnage. Should they exalt or condemn the suffering? The sustained violence of Verdun fixed the minds of patriots and pacifists alike, and as so often, remembrance began not after but during the event.

Why were so few members coming to meetings, a socialist complained in Paris in May 1916, when they should be fired up by "massacres of men like that at Verdun." Another wrote from Verdun the following month urging the resumption of relations between socialist parties across enemy lines to bring peace and an end to "the atrocious butchery of Verdun." In June a reader of Sebastien Faure's "Ce qu'il faut dire (What Must Be said)," a paper that did not hide its anarchist and revolutionary sympathies, found himself stationed in the trenches on the Somme, a fortnight before the great Allied offensive there. At least he was not at Verdun, he wrote to a friend, and lived by the hope he never would be. "How much this simple word evokes. What sufferings, what crimes, what atrocities it unveils. Is it possible that the minds of certain men conceived such monstrous destruction?"

However, the slaughter there could just as easily inspire patriotic and even bellicose exhortations. Even on the far Left, it served on occasion to dampen the ardors of social protest. "You are wrong to complain," a union leader in Toulouse told two munitions workers who had interrupted him to complain about working conditions, "because if you think you're unfortunate you should think of those at Verdun." And amid waves of applause he appealed for unity and effort. He might as well have spoken in the secret session of the Chamber of Deputies two months later, in June, when the foes of Joffre, some on the Right, lamented the carnage at Verdun not to vent any anti-militarist passions but to urge renewed vigor in the war and a renewed high command to prosecute it.[52]

Ever since, the human experience of combat at Verdun has provoked celebration and rage and much else in-between. In 1930 a German Communist magazine, AJZ, published an angry article about the recovery of bone fragments on the battlefield. Workers were earning a few Deutschmarks a day to recover the remains of the "million who fell as victims of the murderous Imperialism at Verdun." Macabre photos with even more macabre captions accompanied the text.[53] That year the Verdun veteran and author Beumelburg's highly successful novel *Grüppe Bösemüller* made the ordeal of the German soldier at Verdun into the crucible of national regeneration, the rekindling of altruism among the people. The following year his fellow-author Hans Zöberlein did no less in *Der Glaube an Deutschland* [Faith in Germany] in a more overtly National Socialist vein.

On both sides of the Rhine "Verdun" resounded as an inspiring as well as an invidious utterance. The "high-point of French heroism" in the words of France Inter radio in 1960 became six years later "one of the greatest military genocides in history" in the words of *Le Monde*, which found in the barbed wire of the battlefield the thread connecting the *poilu* of the First World War to the deportee of the Second. Among such discordant commentators, Verdun acquired its preeminence not because the experiences there stood apart from others in the war, but because they resembled them.[54]

For the French in particular, the infernal yet monotonous repetitions of the battle captured the war on the Western Front with all the power of a grim and macabre parody. Most of the French in uniform spent the war on French soil, not in Gallipoli or Salonika or at sea, and almost two-thirds served at some time at Verdun as well. They would fight too many different battles in too many theatres in the next war for any one engagement to speak for the rest. But in this one the longest battle provided the strongest memento. In 1932 Céline, in *Voyage au Bout de la Nuit*—*The Journey to the End of the Night* is the most common translation—provided few place names in his antihero's sojourns in the mad international slaughterhouse of the front—vague allusions to the Ardennes, the Nord, the villages burning on the Meuse. But Drieu la Rochelle, in *Gilles*, made Verdun the symbol—of the other half-world when his own hero gazed at the fine trees in the Bois de Boulogne—of breakdown when his own life seemed in crisis: "It was Verdun again, the moment when an overwhelmed human being can no longer hold up the vault of the sky and lets it come down in a gibbering chaos."

For the French, Verdun offered all the torments of the other battles but lasted so much longer that it killed more than any one of them—lasted so much longer that, as Paul Valéry said when he welcomed Pétain to the Académie Française in 1931, it had amounted to a kind of war within the war. "Let them not speak to us of the heroes of antiquity, nor even of the great soldiers of the Emperor," he also said—they had fought visible enemies in the open, for only a few hours, without gas, or shrapnel, or flamethrowers, or blindingly bright nights, and as he honored Pétain the distinction between Verdun and the Great War vanished in the air under the Coupole.[55]

More Germans died on the Somme than at Verdun in 1916, and in five months instead of ten; many of the victims at Verdun had arrived from distant fronts in the Balkans or Russia, and many of the survivors would leave to return there, to a different war with other ordeals, other crimes; the battle on the Meuse could not monopolize the iconic niche in Germany as effortlessly as in France. Eighteen months before, the myth-makers of the Reich had already invented the sacrifice of Germany's singing youth at Langemarck and the consummation of Teutonic revenge on Slavdom at Tannenberg. Yet unlike them, and as in France, Verdun lived on as the place name that signified protracted human suffering. "Stalingrad is hell on earth," a German soldier wrote home in September 1942. "It is Verdun, bloody Verdun, with new weapons."[56] On its own, such a doleful association would not have assured immortality to the battle. But the myth of selfless and squandered valor did the rest. Watching his shredded battalion straggle back, frustrated and abandoned, from the ruined village of Douaumont, a Prussian major saw in its sacrifice some miniature likeness of his country's desperate struggle.[57] In German novels, films, and even in scrupulous retellings, the motif rose to a dirge or elegy on the lost war that no defensive success like the Somme, no puzzling retreat like the Marne, could attain and that naturally stamped Verdun with the tragic seal of noble failure. The same connection might have driven General Karl-Heinrich von Stülpnagel to return in July 1944 to the banks of the Meuse, where he had fought in 1916, and attempt suicide after conspiring in the failed plot on Hitler.

Winners and losers, critics and apologists, patriots and pacifists and many others who were both or neither or somewhere in-between invoked the interminable miseries of Verdun to tell their stories and assure the place of its macabre popularity. It served them. They gave Verdun its surpassing reputation for grimness, mixing well-documented human experience with poorly documented loss figures and implicit but illusory comparisons. They transformed the truth of the participants—"we'll never find a sector as terrible as this one, it's impossible"—into the fiction of posterity, "the most appalling battle of the Great War," confused the subjective with the objective, and recast human experience as historical parable.[58]

8

Rancor

"I CAN'T WAIT FOR THIS MISERABLE WAR (*vile guerre*) to end"—the words, always the same, kept recurring in the mail from Verdun, a postal censor complained on Bastille Day 1916. The men felt that it would have to end, because if it did not the world would. Or they would lose their will to carry on, or kill themselves.[1]

Revolt was the nightmare that had pursued the high commands since 1914, and that—in spite of its infrequency in the French army until 1917 and the German until 1918—still preoccupied them during the year of Verdun. For a century resistance to military service had declined dramatically: in the French army desertion rates had fallen from over 50 percent during the Consulate and the Empire to about one percent at the turn of the twentieth century. The war had done nothing to reverse the trend. And Verdun was no exception. This was fortunate for the high commands. With armies so vast and men so dispersed on the empty battlefield, with old regime social distinctions between officers and men so attenuated in the intimacy of the trenches, the harsh and increasingly obsolete weapons of fear and duress hardly sufficed to maintain discipline and keep the men at war.[2]

Many wonder what did. Hatred of the enemy, love of country, habit, a culture of war? Some other force that supplanted mere physical constraint? Before any answers emerge from Verdun, the pattern of obedience and of the morale supposed to sustain it invites renewed scrutiny.

Indeed, few of the men revolted, however much they disliked the war and Verdun. Yet sometimes grumbling crossed the line into insubordination, in ways that varied as greatly as temperaments and the provocations that tested them. Far more consequential breakdowns on both sides in 1917 and 1918 eclipsed those at Verdun, which have long been dismissed as the aberrations of misfits among the resolute. But to look again is to see their outbursts as flashes illuminating a gloomy landscape, symptoms of a mentality that history did not record and that legend could not acknowledge.[3]

Late in August an infantry captain returned from leave to his company in the hills north of Verdun. On the beams of the dugouts graffiti had appeared. A few verged on defeatism: "Down with war, we need peace!" A few were bellicose: "the grenadiers of the 10th regiment never desert their posts, whatever happens!" Most were sardonic: "Villa des Totos"— House of Lice; "charming location for immediate sale or lease."[4]

Such uneven levels of enthusiasm appeared elsewhere. A photographer in a Brandenburger regiment wondered in February as he neared the Hermitage Woods why they had not yet reached Verdun. The commander of a neighboring company, eager to test his men's seasoned siege skills on looming Fort Douaumont, wondered the same. Keenness, the manifestation of excellent morale, was natural among well-fed, well-trained, and above all successful military units. Yet others in the same regiment were more sluggish, content to settle into the captured French dugouts, mull the red wine they found, and help themselves to tinned meat. They would let the artillery do the heavy work, or so they thought, and then take Douaumont when it was ready to be taken, perhaps in a day or two. Motivation and morale might vary from company to company, like waves, for no apparent reason.[5]

Interrogators of prisoners observed in the enemy the same varying signs. Some of the French prisoners the Bavarians took around Fleury and Souville in June and July seemed war-weary and open to desertion. Others, even those who had suffered greatly under German shelling, especially the officers, made an excellent impression, confident of victory and of the mounting German losses. Yet a doctor among them asked whether and when he would be exchanged and sent back. "It's a dirty trick," he complained to a fellow-prisoner, on learning he would be sent back in a month. He had hoped for several months of restful captivity before resuming his labors.[6]

Motivation is individual, morale collective. But they intersect ceaselessly, since contagion can stimulate or stifle the first and imitation can raise or lower the second. This only renders the variations more random, their causes more elusive. The interrogators who went to such lengths to plumb the depths of the enemy's morale—an undertaking unimaginable only a generation earlier—might as fruitfully have pondered the inconsistencies of their own.[7]

They did not, of course, have the benefit of the rich literature on morale and combat motivation that social scientists, historians, and military personnel have generated since the Second World War.[8] Greed, idealism, desperation, hatred, fear, peer pressure, and seemingly infinite permutations of such compulsions can help explain the willingness of men to fight in conflicts of the remote or recent past, and morale, as a collective state of mind, reflects almost as protean a mix of determinants. Its intricate chemistry resolves itself into recognizable general levels—high, low, or middling—but obscures local patterns. Food, drink, leaves, weaponry, comfort, rest, training, leadership, the courage of conviction and the smell of victory: how often and how consistently, in a battle that resembled a war, could all the ingredients lift all spirits? So many physical elements varied the mix, so many changed from month to month, or place to place, or unit to unit, that morale became as mercurial as the weather, the supplies, or the compassion of the command.

Ludendorff, not known for his empathy, but aware of the axioms of more celebrated strategists including Napoleon, acknowledged the importance of food to military outcomes. "The efforts of the Army in the field," he wrote in his memoirs, "depend to a high degree on their rations. That, next to leave, has the most decisive effect on the *morale* of the troops." Of all the matters that the French military censors scrutinized in the rivers of letters that flowed to and from the soldiers of the Second Army, none surfaced in their reports more urgently and consistently than creature comforts in general and food and drink in particular.[9]

Sometimes, when their rations ran out and shell fire cut them off from convoys, field kitchens, and water tanks for days, the men understood that there was no one to blame but the enemy. But farther back, during quieter moments, they blamed their own. "We're shamefully fed"—there was too much canned beef, the *singe* (literally, "monkey") that had entered military life at the turn of the century and now would not leave it, or rice and canned fish, not enough potatoes or vegetables or water or wine. The culprits, anonymous but obvious, were the supply services, the *Direction de l'arrière*, the General Staff—the "they" of the rear. More than shortage, the monotony rankled; the Germans lamented a "marmalade war," so oppressive had the staple item become in their daily diet. Such privations sapped the spirit as much as they deprived the body. "They always give you the same grub, it wears you down in the end." And occasionally the men themselves established a link between their diet and their willingness to fight: "we don't give a damn about the Boches," or krauts, one of them wrote, using the now common diminutive of the derogatory *alboche*, for German and *caboche*, or cabbage, "but at least give us something to drink if we are to 'get' them." At such moments the anxieties of the command about morale in the trenches and in the rear appeared anything but inflated.[10]

Even when the food was varied and savory, the weather might ruin it. This was a major issue for the personnel—officers, doctors, or priests—who scrutinized the moods of the men. In his diary an alarmed Catholic chaplain in one of the Bavarian regiments drew a direct link between rain, mud, and mental depression in the ranks. Day of rain, day of gloom, among the French—exposed to the elements for weeks on end in one of the coldest and dampest parts of the country, or protected at best by makeshift dugouts or cabins, the men wrote almost obsessively about the weather and above all the rain. It drenched them and the paper they wrote on, flowed in the trenches and filled the shell-holes, made the ground so treacherous that shelters collapsed and they stopped digging them. Sometimes, when it stopped, they had no other uniforms to wear. They hated the rain more than the cold, even more than the shelling: "As for the shelling, we're used to it, but our worst enemy is the bad weather, the raging rain. . . ." Like food, the weather mattered more than physically. It demoralized, sometimes deeply: "Never have I been so sick and tired of it all."[11]

When the weather relented—during the battle in May and June, for in July and August the heat became oppressive and in the autumn the rains returned—and the food improved, life could become bearable. "Sun has killed our gloom!" one of the soldiers exclaimed at the start of May. This might have fostered the Robinson Crusoe syndrome—the practice of turning the terrain and its hastily dug habitats into a home, with a modicum of space and comfort, a place to write letters, play cards, sculpt trench art out of shell casings, a place so familiar that they resented leaving it even for the secure barracks of the rear. But the Crusoe syndrome left few traces at Verdun in 1916. It had surfaced in the sector before; both the anthropologist Robert Hertz and the novelist Maurice Genevoix described something like it, a preoccupation with comfort rather than death and the transformation of the makeshift shanties of the autumn of 1914 into the safer and warmer dwellings of 1915. It lasted until the heavy fighting came back. At Verdun, with the enemy forced on to the defensive and a suitably subterranean cave claimed by a suitably small group of dwellers, tables, chairs, and creature comforts might sometimes provide a refuge that approximated a home. More often, however, the incessant shelling destroyed all semblance of domesticity in the front lines, and the constant rotation of troops ruptured any sense of permanence the troops could enjoy even in the rest- and training-camps of the rear.[12]

Shelter might miraculously restore the spirits and the determination of men coming in from the elements, the Bavarian chaplain noted with wonder at the end of March. But early in May, even as the cold relented, he returned to lament their acute demoralization. All had contrived to wreck the men in body and soul, he reflected—the exhaustion, the super-human striving, the lack of water, and the paltry rations reaching them in the front lines, the incessant rain that had turned the earth to mud and filled the trenches with water. He had stopped marveling at their mental resilience. "The division," he exclaimed five days later, "needs rest!" And in July the French censors compared the "lassitude" they read in French letters to those in captured German ones. There was no difference, they concluded. It was palpable in both.[13]

The men wanted to escape, even to some other part of the front, convinced as some of them were that any sector promised an improvement over this one. "I indeed want to leave for anywhere at all." Frustrations about leave darkened their letters and their mood. "If only they gave us some leave! It lasts so long, so long!" They waited impatiently for their "tour de 'perm'," and complained when it was canceled, especially if hopes had run high; and when leave came and they returned from six or eight days away, their letters betrayed the same depression, the same gloom that the food or the weather might induce. It was circular: postponement deepened the dejection that had already set off the craving for leave.[14]

They made little pretense of altruism, but the hardships of others could dishearten them as surely as their own. The soldier-historian Louis Madelin, poring over some 1,000 letters written to or by dead or captured

German soldiers at Verdun, discerned a note of reciprocal and occasionally competitive misery between front and home. Even as the battle raged, he published his findings with tendentious, undisguised satisfaction but with extracts that stood the test of time. Letters from home told of price-gouging and shortages, of demonstrations in Berlin and dairies sacked in Geestemünde and Lehe, of imminent civil strife in Crefeld and Cassel. From Strassburg, in Prussia, came plaintive words from rivals in misery, just as deprived, just as hungry, as their correspondents at the front.

Echoes of lamentations had uncertain effects on morale at the front—tales of packed pantries might have worked more dangerously on the willingness of the men to endure their privations—but hardships imposed on civilians could embitter their relatives in uniform. In France, when prices rose and shortages threatened, when the government imposed meatless days and closed the shops early, some of the men fretted for their families and seemed in the watchful eyes of the censors to lose faith in the nation's leaders. They could not understand, one *poilu* wrote, that he was suffering to avoid suffering for his own. Then let them make peace, a German wrote to his hungry parents in March, if there was nothing left to eat. When another German, a gunner, returned to his village in the Wesertal on leave, he soon saw through his family's simulation of well-being. Basic foodstuffs appeared but hunger threatened, and he did not know whether to envy them their joyless lives. Too many, unlike him, had not returned. A pall of melancholy had settled over the land. How could such moods not affect his own when he returned to his regiment at Verdun?[15]

The sufferings of family only intensified the pains of separation. To some these were the hardest of all to bear. Absence bred anxiety—over the hay, the harvest, the women at work, and over temptation, which led some of the men to urge fidelity upon their wives where others might have remained silent:

> you above all, be very good, my little wife, think of nothing, think of me, of what I am enduring; that way you'll be strong in the face of temptation. . . . Above all do not receive any soldiers at home, not for any reason, not for anything.

A longing to return expressed itself temporally as well, as nostalgia emerged from separation and the distant home came to embody the receding years of peace. In July censors noticed a spreading longing for the prewar among farmers from the Sarthe and the Mayenne trapped, as they saw it, in the "hellhole" of Verdun: "We were so happy before."[16]

Ultimately, obviously, such sentiments could only end with the war itself. But in the meantime the civilian and military authorities could relieve some hardship and mitigate some resentment. By late June, when the *Direction de l'arrière* had made a determined effort to improve the quantities and varieties of food and drink, the men complained less and enthused more over the meals they were eating and the wine they were drinking. They wrote of enough bread, and sardines, and cheese, and jam, and three-quarters of a bottle of wine a day; and a month later of four courses with every meal and a liter of wine a day. They were twice as well fed as before, one of them wrote, and when the weather turned and the cold came back the culinary complaints did not.

The powers in place could do little about the weather. The theorem needed no demonstration: "morale," one of the censors noted, "tends to rise and fall with the barometer." Nonetheless, they strove to supplement their men's natural defenses against the elements by sending more clothes and more blankets. These improved, too, along with the cuisine. When new galoshes—*galoches*—arrived, and gloves lined with rabbit fur, and woolen sweaters, and sheepskin for their overcoats, the men acknowledged the manna, and in the rare moments when all their creature comforts seemed assured they could wax almost dithyrambic: "nothing wants, we're like princes." Still, lined up in a trench with no roof between them and the elements, it was not long before their thoughts turned cold again.[17]

The authorities could deploy only two remedies for the psychological pains of separation: letters and leaves. The will to carry on might flag in the absence of any word, any sign, any parcel from home. Even when the news was bad, when the mail brought word of grief or melancholy in the family, it filled the silence with dialogue of a kind—"the letter, sole consolation." Writing letters mattered as much as receiving them; among ten men at rest, an artillery lieutenant noticed, one would be reading and three writing letters; and mostly, the censors observed again and again, the men wrote not about the war but about the personal and mundane preoccupations that had traveled with them to the front and still pervaded their thoughts. The farmers among them worried constantly about the women in the fields. "Have you harvested the hay? Is the wheat good?"

More than letters, leaves bridged the gap. They became the subject of constant hope and repeated disillusionment. The high command kept adjusting them, canceling them in the spring only to reinstate them late in May, much to the joy of the men, or announcing in July that five percent would be eligible—just enough, one of the men complained, to raise hopes and then dash them. In October, when a new regimen promised leave every four months, some of the men thought it too good to be true. To the watchful censors, such reactions typified the mercurial shifts in spirits that the granting or withholding of leaves could provoke. In May, as Pétain left the command of the Second Army for that of its parent Groupe d'Armées du Centre, he worried too about the amenities of leave, such as having the itinerant soldiers met in the stations and provided with proper clothes for their brief excursion into civilian life. No matter how tolerable their dugout or edible their meals, even at rest in the rear, the *poilus* at Verdun, like those anywhere else, fell prey to the gloom that came with sequestration without end. "We want to see children, women, civilians, buy something. Instead nothing, nothing, nothing."[18]

A conviction of superiority, stemming from numbers, or weaponry, or recent victory, could inspire hopes as surely as the revelation of the enemy's own strengths could dash them. An assurance of success could lift morale, disillusionment could depress it; and Verdun saw both, almost on a daily basis.

In February, before and during the initial bombardment, German soldiers waiting in the woods exhaled airs of confidence and optimism. Already well fed and well rested, the infantrymen believed the infallibility of their heavy artillery would make for a "promenade" when the time came for them to cross the lines of an enemy who had given few signs of life. They held this, a lieutenant recalled, from Corps staff officers themselves. This would be no charge into enemy machine guns as at Mons in 1914, no Champagne or Gorlice even, a major in a Brandenburger grenadier regiment came to believe as he arrived on the scene, fresh from the Eastern Front, and he sensed that the men knew it. "The mood of the men? Brilliant." Some looked forward to an end to the monotony, and some, even, to an end to the war. Whatever Falkenhayn intended, they believed themselves about to assault and conquer the cornerstone of the French defensive system on the Western Front. Here was the surest sign any troop could give of sterling morale—an eagerness to attack.[19]

The loftier the expectation, the deeper the disenchantment. At first, when progress seemed to restore the promise of a swift and victorious war of movement, the optimism of the eve held up. When groups of French surrendered in Haumont woods, they gave shape to the promise of a walk in the park and rekindled the enthusiasms of the advance Brandenburger units. Behind them came their comrades, buoyed by the news and confident of the same.

A week later the elation had vanished, the anticipation had died. "A bitter headwind now whispered to us that the days of our advance were numbered." They had been fighting without pause, suffering "massacres" in the face of machine guns, as they told their French captors, who found them in states of depression they had never yet observed among their German opponents. Further east prisoners taken during the fierce fighting around Douaumont village made a similar impression. One of them told French interrogators of the message they had read before the offensive, assuring them that they would take Verdun, "the heart of France." Now their superiors told them of a "momentary halt."

Even before the losses mounted, a lieutenant later recalled, distress began to multiply among his men, manifesting itself as an urgent desire to be relieved. Several weeks later some Bavarians told of a steep and steady drop in morale in their regiments. They had come from the East, from Serbia, expecting to make short work of their next adversaries, the French. So confident were they of their own superiority that they patronized their fellow-Bavarians already entrenched in the static war of the West. Almost at once, under the avalanche of shells, they began losing their collective nerve, and their morale sank below that of the compatriots they had derided. The same forcible disillusionment had sapped the will of other Bavarian regiments, they told their captors. The descent from the clouds had been abrupt and violent.[20]

It prefigured many others among French and Germans alike. Verdun, for all its bleak and quotidian repetition, was made of great expectations routinely dashed by meager results. Its highs and lows were mental rather than tactical or territorial, made of hopes that faded and dejections that lifted. Whatever vistas the French attempt to retake Fort Douaumont in May had floated before the eyes of participants and nonparticipants alike, its failure left some of them even more disconsolate than before. A captain found the men in the Tunnel de Tavannes listless, slumped over, pervaded by a sense of the insurmountable strength of the enemy. In October they recaptured the fort, along with a rich harvest of German prisoners: an incontestable success, one that lifted spirits all over the Second Army. Those in the six to eight divisions that had taken part displayed a heady spirit in their letters, and even those who had not participated reacted to the news with enthusiasm if not rejoicing—it intimated that victory was possible, even within reach, and lifted men out of the *cafard*—literally, a cockroach, and a word for depression—that so many had displayed in recent weeks and that the censors had not failed to notice in their letters. Their own losses had been light, the German prisoners filed past, Fort Vaux also fell a week later, without any fight at all. A kind of resurrection seemed under way, and one of the officers reported happily that morale had not reached such heights since 1914.

The renaissance did not last. Within weeks depression had reclaimed its sinister hold over hearts and minds. The onset of winter, the realization that the end was hardly at hand, the resumption of a monotonous and wearisome life—gloom had returned, even though, as one of the censors pointed out, the men seemed to recognize that the government had done much to improve food, clothes, and leaves. No matter; in January omens of discontent, muttered reproaches about the conduct of the war, ushered in the new year of 1917, the year of mutinies.[21]

Perhaps, as restless generals and strategists affected to believe, an endless and static defensive battle undermined wills as surely as a failed offensive one. Joffre certainly thought so. When Poincaré visited the Somme shortly after the offensive opened there in July, he remarked to Joffre on how spirited the men seemed, how their confidence shone by comparison with the lassitude he had seen at Verdun. Discipline seemed loose, and some of the men seemed slightly drunk to the strait-laced head of state. Joffre thought he had just measured how tonic was the offensive in one place and how toxic the defensive in the other. Hindenburg thought the same. When he took over the reins from Falkenhayn in the late summer of 1916, both Verdun and the Somme left him with a painful sense of the thanklessness of forced defensive positions. They both wasted and starved nervous energies, he thought, and he discerned in officers and men alike an aspiration to a new kind of offensive war. The self-serving dimension of such diagnoses eclipsed whatever ray of truth they might have cast: each generalissimo would pin his hopes of victory on massive and largely fruitless offensives. The swings between optimism and pessimism and everything in-between varied too frequently and too widely for the simple panacea of offensive war to master them.[22]

They moved with the weather, the general health, the prospects, the successes and failures, the fleeting illusions of a technological edge—in February the appearance of new steel helmets, new flamethrowers, and storm troopers trained in some new tactics drove confidence among the waiting Germans to new heights, and in July, as his unit prepared for the doomed attack on Souville, a German lieutenant looked with some warmth upon the new *grünkreuz* gas shells stacked high in the woods. They would clear the way, he thought. The pendulum also swung with rest and the recovery of comfort: the Catholic chaplain of the 11th Bavarian Infantry Division noted how mental as well as physical health had returned to the troops after two weeks of rest. They could now, he observed, look with equanimity upon their coming transfer to the Eastern Front, once again. But how often did the troops rest? The German rotations, irregular and infrequent next to those of the French, often left troops in line, reinforcing them as needed, until mental or physical exhaustion left them unable to continue. In April, on the left bank, five German divisions faced three French. But the French kept replacing theirs, usually every three weeks: since March the same five German divisions had stayed in place, while ten French had come and gone. Raw newcomers, unknown and distrusted, only deepened the Germans' distress and weakened their cohesion. Officers held them back rather than risk them in local attacks. "Regular troop rotation . . .—that is the challenge!" the Prussian Minister of War noted in May. "The French do it!"[23]

Many who kept journals tried to account for the vicissitudes of collective sentiment, discerning historical shifts over the long months they spent on the banks of the Meuse. Once at rest after the early days of combat at Verdun, a mobilized Jesuit priest wrote, enthusiasm gave way here and there to "l'esprit de carotte" (a habit of ruse or of shirking). Even the most courageous soldiers in the trenches, he added, were finding ways to evade duties and exercises.

The challenge of identifying the elusive, unstable, and volatile matter known as "morale" of the armies of the Western Front, still more of plotting its movements, in the end defeated the censors and the analysts, who sometimes retreated into the haven of meaningless pronouncements:

"There is nothing worrisome in the reports, which does not mean that there is nothing to worry about." Or occasionally they might summon up the courage to return the riddle to their superiors. It all depended on circumstances, one of them wrote in July from Verdun, as he studied the mail; men in combat differed from those behind the front, men engaged at Thiaumont and Fleury that week differed in their outlook from their more optimistic fellows on the left bank; and the truth, he realized, was that there was no such thing as an *état d'esprit* of the whole army of Verdun.[24]

Officers at all levels of command tried to create one, though they did not easily succeed. The fear of losing control over the men, the fear that had so afflicted every captain in the centuries when the dregs of society filled the soldiery and when desertion rates were high, still beset the army of the educated, of subjects and citizens acculturated to the modern state, because men still disobeyed, deserted, mutinied; and they still did so at Verdun.

Disobedience, more versatile in its expressions than obedience, ranges from a slovenly disregard of etiquette to full-fledged revolt against commanding officers, from insolence to insubordination, from returning a few hours late from leave to not returning at all. Verdun bred license as naturally as any other site on the front, and every month men here and there received light punishments for drunkenness, theft, unkempt uniforms, picking berries or vegetables from orchards or gardens, for sleeping on sentry duty, for disorderly conduct. From the French command, here as elsewhere, came captious complaints of men frequenting inns and taverns after hours, of failing to salute cars flying generals' pennants or streamers as they drove by, of raucous revelry in village streets. From the German command came complaints of drunkenness and disrespect. The spirit of insubordination, a Bavarian general complained to his divisional chaplain, was "a sin against the 4th commandment." Regrettably widespread, it was vital to extirpate it. He seemed to fear informality and the disrespect that life at such close quarters with the junior officers bred among the men. It must stop, he insisted.

Such abandon, in French or German, implicitly scorned the prudery of authority, but signified no conscious defiance of local superiors whose indulgence or benign indifference may have allowed it, as higher commanders were fond of pointing out. Such acts reflected no planning, no thought, no anger, only the appearance in wartime of habits and dispositions as likely to flourish in peacetime as well, infringing other codes, ignoring other prohibitions.[25]

Reproach, even poorly articulated, marked a more menacing level of insubordination, hinting at overt opposition rather than unruliness. Murmurs of dissatisfaction and dissent stopped well short of rebellion yet revealed a recurrent and semi-submerged presupposition among the men: that they inhabited one world, their leaders another.

One week into the attack on Verdun, a German machine-gunner sensed the unspoken thoughts stirring among his fellows—about senseless sacrifice and the failings of their commanders. A mordant irony might spring to the lips of men at the mention of their illustrious generals, whose utterances might come back to haunt them. The men collected and swapped with one another choice morsels of official wisdom, the comments of generals near and far. "Say! Joffre really is 'nibbling' at them!" the wounded men in the snow outside the hospital at Baleycourt in February joked. "We've had a visit from M. Joffre," one of the men wrote in the December gloom. "Probably he'll bring us no good. When these gentlemen bestir themselves, they want something" (*c'est pas pour des prunes*).

The enthusiasms of General Mangin, who attacked Douaumont unsuccessfully in May and successfully in October, earned him the esteem of his superior Nivelle but the sobriquet among the men of devourer, "le mangeur d'hommes." Exasperation at the entire military and political leadership might erupt on occasion, as when a noncommissioned officer received orders to defend Fort Tavannes to the last man when Fort Vaux nearby had just fallen: "No more trenches between Tavannes and Vaux. Not that there ever were any. And the Chamber [of Deputies]! And Herr and Pétain! Maurras, too. What windbags and stooges!"[26]

Irrelevant or inept orders might provoke sarcasm at the distant officialdom that had issued them—"famous instructions for gas" that protected no one, idiotic instructions about the use of light signals, orders to counterattack that arrived too late, "as usual." The sense of isolation that gripped so many units in the front lines at Verdun only heightened their impression of engaging in a dialogue of the deaf with their distant regimental or divisional commanders. Complain as they might, a decorated noncommissioned officer wrote, they could not change anything, "and that precisely is what makes our 'good fellows' grumble: we bury their demands by crying out with all available means in service: Aren't they admirable! Then we don't listen to them." By extension their plight might fade into oblivion as it grew in distance from those hearing faint rumors of it. Men crowding through the subterranean galleries of Fort Vaux might rail against men strolling the carpeted corridors of power, and charge that those who had made this war had no idea what it was like.[27]

More than political anger or social resentment, such outbursts reflected the gulf between men at the front and those farther back, between the war of the soldiers and the war of the staffers. The distance rankled, as much among the officers as among the men under their command, even more so, considering their intermittent exasperation with the mental straitjackets they discerned in communications emanating from headquarters and in the generals who occasionally visited them in their trenches, elegant and eloquent but deaf to their entreaties.[28]

Only the high command had been surprised by the German attack on Verdun, a lieutenant later recalled, and he remembered too how he blamed the arrogant *brevetés* (officers from the Ecole militaire, the Parisian center for higher military education for career officers) of the 3ème bureau, the operations bureau, at Chantilly, who refused to listen to the reports of the 2ème bureau, the warnings of Driant, the alarms of Herr. Joffre had not listened either, he went on. And they persevered in their ways, first refusing to acknowledge the German assault, then lying about it in their communiqués. Joffre himself, along with others, should be court-martialed for the lamentable defenses at Verdun, a divisional general there confided to his diary. After 1914 the généralissime became the living incarnation of Colonel Louis de Grandmaison's prewar doctrines of *l'offensive à outrance* ("all-out offensive," come to grief in 1914 and 1915), an officer noted in his journal. He cited General Lanrezac's judgment about Joffre—"for the whole war Joffre will always be one idea behind"—and added an equally tepid judgment of his own—"Joffre is an organizer, not an imaginer." How imagination could have won this war he did not explain, but his implicit protest against the dominion of darkness resonated among fellow-officers who consigned their frustrations to paper, and probably among many who did not. The blind, they complained in their various idioms, were leading the sighted. In April 1916 a captain in Champagne, soon to find himself at Verdun, called on a general in his chateau set in a verdant park. "We can understand," he added afterwards, "how so many generals understood the war so poorly." His arrival at Verdun did little to moderate his asperities. He also blamed the command for the poor state of the defenses. How, he wondered, could the lowly face firing squads and Herr go free?[29]

Tactical as well as strategic obtuseness angered those doing the fighting. On both sides a recurrent grievance emerged in the reports that officers sent back to divisional or army headquarters or in the thoughts they jotted down on paper: absence bred ignorance. The command issued mindless instructions, conceived in darkness and pitifully mismatching means to ends, grasping no limits to the possible, because it did not understand the conditions at Verdun. It was not there.

The reports of two Bavarian infantry regiments—the King's and the Crown Prince's, no less—from Verdun in late August resemble indictments of the divisional or corps command with only the names of the accused left out. Orders and objectives arrived too late, and remained opaque or unknown to noncommissioned officers and the men under their command, or to neighboring regiments who in consequence had no idea what the other was up to. Maps were unreliable, given to credulous troops without photos or aerial reconnaissance. Why could the equipment that the few storm battalions enjoyed not be made available to the others? Why had so few received any training in siege tactics? And why, why were they not given time to prepare for the offensives asked of them? The plaintive litanies seemed to swell to a dirge on the very day that Falkenhayn was relieved as chief of the General Staff. He had not kept Romania from entering the war, people said. But the insiders knew that the serial mishaps of Verdun had impeached his judgment more than any diplomatic reversals in the Balkans.[30]

Falkenhayn had company: neither the Crown Prince nor his chief of staff, Knobelsdorf, escaped accusations from soldiers serving in their army that they had attacked Verdun with inadequate means on the right bank, held it back during the early days, exposed it cruelly to the ravages of French guns from the left bank instead of attacking there as well. The critics in the ranks had no wind of the debates that raged within the command of the Fifth Army and the General Staff, and could only guess at the principal architect of the bloody impasse in which they found themselves. Some, perhaps many, looked with indulgence on the Crown

Prince, who showered them with cigarettes when he went by and who wished ardently, they had heard, to put a stop to the folly on the Meuse. In their eyes Knobelsdorf was the true instigator, clinging, as an officer wrote his wife, to his preconceptions with almost criminal stubbornness.

But whoever the culprit, however illustrious the scapegoat, the presumption of error in high places could madden men who felt pushed either too far or not enough. "A mad rage gripped me," a colonel recalled of the night of the 21st of February, when his infantry regiment was held back at Samogneux instead of pushing ahead to Vacherauville, "[as] the entire outcome of the war could have been decided here." His message was unambiguous: his commanding generals had snatched defeat from the jaws of victory.[31]

The officer dreaded his own command more than the attack itself, a French major wrote in a blunt indictment of the tactical mind of the French high command. "He is suspicious of it, thinks it capable of throwing the troops unthinkingly into murderous fights; he has lost confidence...." He was writing at Souilly, the headquarters of the Second Army, at the end of May, penciling his thoughts down in a long document. They would shock, he said. But he went on. The distrust extended not to the officers fighting by their sides, the regimental colonel or even the nearby brigade general, but to the divisional generals and beyond. They had ordered his battalion in recent months to hold tight to a spot that just happened to concentrate much of the enemy's artillery in the sector, to support at great risk a regiment near the Tunnel de Tavannes that had never requested any help in the first place, to cross two miles of unfamiliar territory without maps, under intense artillery, in order to occupy a plateau in full view of the enemy guns in Fort Douaumont—engaging a brigade or a battalion under such conditions, he mused, would have won its commanding officer a good mark in a war game before 1914, or a promotion during the war of movement in the autumn of that year, but at Verdun it marked a heresy that could only end in bloody failure.

Worse, such orders reflected not only an ignorance of tactics but an indifference to the unstaunched bleeding of the infantry, "the most precious of arms." And the men blamed the command for housekeeping failings that endangered them almost as gravely—for the absence of trenches or communications routes or shelters. Officers and men clamored for disciplinary revenge, and the gulf between the command and the men only continued to widen. And far from combat, in training camps at the rear, men still resented the instruction that came their way. They learned nothing, one of them complained, when all they needed was to rest.[32]

Praise for the captains who shone by their compassion and mental sobriety only damned the others by comparison. "He's the only one of the top commanders who likes the men," an infantry officer at Verdun said of Pétain. He recalled how impersonally General de Langle de Cary had reviewed his regiment in the Argonne, announcing curtly "now you are to parade before me." Pétain had emerged from his command post in the old town hall at Souilly to bid farewell from its steps to the troops as they left. And Pétain, he added, had understood before anyone that artillery, not infantry charges, held the key to this war. So common was the misconception that Pétain alone understood the imperative of saving lives that an otherwise well-informed infantry captain misattributed to him the axiom that the General Staff had issued in January: "one does not fight with men against materiel." To extol the virtues of one commander was usually to deride the pretentions of another. The same captain adulated Galliéni as the savior of Paris and even of France in 1914, only to pass over Joffre, the chief of the General Staff and titular victor of the Battle of the Marne, in silence. Any encomium could be tainted by such unspoken yet live reproaches aimed at the anonymous upper crust. An officer in the 74th Infantry Division found that the men around him trusted their divisional commander, General de Lardemelle, not to get them killed "out of stupidity, weakness, or ambition"—as though another would. Elsewhere such dark suppositions enjoyed just as much currency. When an artilleryman left Verdun for the Somme in August he added there to his compendium of official inanities the heartfelt injunction of another divisional commander, informed of the exhaustion of his troops: "They can all croak, as long as they take Tahure."

Nonetheless, Verdun captured a distinctive sense of abandonment and sequestration among the officers and men on the scene, one they might temper with realism and equanimity but that was never very far from their minds. "They criticize their commanders," an infantryman reported of his fellows in the summer of 1916, "[they] find them too distant in any case. But they add: 'It's true that if they get themselves killed as in the beginning, none would remain; already we have to add a gold stripe to a corporal to have a lieutenant.'"[33]

Officers could interpret orders creatively, heeding the spirit rather than the letter. A lieutenant in Champagne, shortly before bringing his experience to Verdun, had saved his men's lives by evacuating his trench and reoccupying it only when the German bombardment had lifted, in a creative reading of the general orders not to abandon a single inch of land. Officers could argue, sometimes *in extremis*. During General Mangin's attack on Douaumont in May he insisted on a reckless patrol in the Bois de la Caillette against an enemy machine-gun nest, and only desisted when the battalion commander handed all his official and personal papers to his quartermaster and prepared to undertake the suicidal mission himself rather than sacrifice the lives of his men. Or officers could ignore orders altogether. On the eve of his next attack on Douaumont, in October, Mangin could scarcely contain his impatience. "Taïaut! Taïaut" (from "swords up!" and roughly equivalent to "charge!")—they should push forward that night, he told three divisions, but not one of them did so. To strike out into the darkness, to risk a rout, perhaps a massacre, all because some distant general believed the enemy "confused" and vulnerable was lunacy. The next morning reconnaissance patrols found the same supposedly exposed enemy alert and lying in wait, at close quarters. They had learned by now to carry out only orders that might work, an officer in one of the divisions recalled. Too many others had been tried and found wanting. "War teaches us the right way to disobey," the author and critic Norton Cru later wrote. "If all orders had always been obeyed, to the letter, we would have massacred the entire French army before August 1915."[34]

As for the wrong way—revolt or rebellion—it more typically pitted enlisted men against their company commanders on the spot, in rare and precipitate outbursts that passed like local squalls. They never threatened the integrity of either army at Verdun. They did, however, raise the specter of a loss of control over the men, and with it the besetting nightmare of any high command, the disintegration of an army through mutinies, mass desertions, or surrenders.

"You're kind to court-martial me." These were the words of a chauffeur who had refused his captain's order to stand at attention. They were not yet words of mutiny, which would have required the collusion of at least three others, according to Article 217 of the French Code of Military Justice. "I've been seeking it for a year," the chauffeur went on as his captain listened. "At the court martial you'll be dirt on my shoes. You're nothing but a bastard." He was a solitary rebel, like others whose outbursts or impulsive refusals of military discipline challenged their commanders but hardly engaged their fellows. *Bande de salauds* ("bunch of bastards") directed at officers might express frustration, drunkenness, the animus against hectoring sergeants or second lieutenants, a factious disposition or a latent indiscipline fated to erupt sooner or later, but it did not rise to a collective act of insubordination. "There's your cigarette," a soldier, already in trouble with the civilian courts, and convicted once of desertion, told his lieutenant as he flung it at his feet. The officer had reprimanded him for smoking while taking part in a group exercise. "Neither you nor someone with five stripes can make me." He had no sympathizers in his company.

Yet contagion always threatened, in the eyes of the officers, if an insult or provocation went unpunished. They could always court-martial the transgressor, which might bring him months or years in a military prison, especially if he had added physical threats to the insult. Or they might improvise, and affirm their authority without setting the regimental judicial machinery in motion. When one of his men refused an order to leave the communications trench, a French lieutenant in the Bois d'Haumont in March promptly threatened him with a court-martial and a firing squad, driven by his awareness that all had witnessed the challenge to his authority. He soon jettisoned the idea and sent him instead to a listening post in no man's land for 12 long hours. There a German sniper spotted and killed him.[35]

Such incidental confrontations defied the fictions of national character. They erupted and subsided in both armies at Verdun. Ordered to clean out a trench by a junior officer, a Bavarian soldier flatly refused and proclaimed that he would keep refusing, that he had stood before a military tribunal once before and could do so again. "You are shaming yourself before your comrades!" the officer cried, only to hear him retort that he knew no parties and knew no comrades—manifesting clearly enough the kind of anarchic individualism that no army could tolerate. Unruly behavior threatened order regardless of its intended victim. A Bavarian who had drunkenly insulted an officer and behaved incorrectly toward a Frenchwoman in the village had to answer to his regimental colonel for both infractions.

At a glance, the judicial traces of such acts of defiance hint at a roughly equivalent incidence in the rival armies. During eight weeks at Verdun between May and July, the 1st and 2nd Bavarian Infantry Divisions sentenced about five or six men each for offences against their superiors; during four weeks of equally heavy fighting the French 14th Infantry Division sentenced some four men for "offences to a superior": small numbers, comparable in scope, signifying only the ubiquity as well as the infrequency of such episodes.[36]

Just as impulsively, a soldier might leave the scene and wander, sometimes far and wide. He would do so just when his unit was moving into line or already under fire, saving his own life perhaps but exposing himself to the direst of penalties for "abandoning his post in presence of the enemy." Typically, the deserter would disappear under cover of darkness and claim later that he had been separated from his unit in the hail of shell fire or the confusion of group movement, and had never managed to find it again. The truth was not always clear.

Repeat offenders, the serial deserters, the recidivists who cursed their captors or their officers as they headed to confinement made matters easier for the authorities. And solitary deserters who disappeared from the rear under no enemy threat had little choice but to plead emotional *force majeure*, a matter in their eyes of nominal guilt and moral innocence. Bad news from home, a long separation made longer by leaves canceled or denied, a personal crisis might coax forbearance from a military tribunal more easily than cowardice under fire, but when the call of home—a father dying in Munich for a Bavarian deserter, a family affair in Meaux for a French one—coincided with an imminent move into the front lines, matters became more obscure. Judges might believe one motive rather than the other, but the two might easily unite. "It's depression that got me," as one of the hapless deserters lamely explained. Where, between spinelessness and homesickness, was the inconsistency?[37]

Studies of desertion elsewhere on the Western Front suggest the same multiplicity of motives, the same absence of pattern, in the acts of desertion that military tribunals inevitably had to judge. So unclear is the pattern, if one even exists, that one study of the German army suggests that weather, more than the intensity of the fighting, might have driven desertion. There, desertion may have ranked high in the order of offenses committed, but as a percentage of men in uniform, deserters were infinitesimal: 0.5 percent for 1916, the year of Verdun and the Somme. Another study suggests that about 100,000 may have deserted from the German army during the war; not many, out of the 13 million who served. At Verdun scattered evidence from both armies confirms the low incidence. Quite logically, as historians have noted, desertion was easiest in the quiet and passive sectors, or in those closest to borders with neutrals— not at Verdun. Engaged in some of the most intense combat of the entire battle, around Fleury and Souville between May and July, desertion in the 2nd Bavarian Infantry Division and an equivalent number of French regiments appears to have hovered at only 0.2 percent.[38]

Such impersonal statistics merely reflect the limited dimensions of the transgression—circumstantial but not systemic, a miscellany of individual flights on the margins of a mass army engaged in a seemingly endless war. They could not, in any case, concentrate the mind of the high command as powerfully as did the greater menace: collective acts.

9

Warning Signals

THE SOLITARY MUTINEER IS A CONTRADICTION IN TERMS, a legal nonentity. But when men in groups begin to mock their commanding officers or flout their orders, the danger to the cohesion of the unit and ultimately of the army rises, as though past the first level of closely observed flood warnings. During the long battle at Verdun these raised the specter of a loss of control over the men, and with it the besetting nightmare of any high command: the disintegration of an army through mutinies, mass desertions, or surrenders.

At some point in most of the armies of the Great War, fears became realities. For the Allies that point came in 1917. In late April 1917, days after General Nivelle's costly offensive at the Chemin des Dames in the Aisne had come to a halt, mutinies and unrest began to shake French divisions in the region. In May the agitation spread, reaching a peak in early June. Perhaps 35–40,000 soldiers had taken part, but the magnetic field had touched many more before the high command was able to neutralize it with a mix of repression, executions, and concessions. The "halo" was widening just as "trench Bolshevism" was spreading in the Russian army, along with mutinies and mass desertion, three months after the revolution of February overthrew the Tsar and only a few more months before that of October, which soon took the country out of the war. In November, during their collapse at Caporetto, some 30,000 Italians were killed or wounded, while 300,000 surrendered and as many deserted. In 1918 demoralization durably changed sides. During the summer the German army in the West began in its turn to disintegrate from within, as the desertion and still more the surrender of perhaps a million troops, prompted not by revolution at home but by failure at the front, so frightened the high command that in the autumn it sought armistice terms.[1]

Understandably enough, much historical work on sedition in the armies of the Great War has concentrated on the extensive outbreaks in the last 18 months of the conflict. A succession of studies of the French mutinies of 1917 and of their repression began with the pioneering work of the French historian Guy Pédroncini in 1967. He concluded that the mutineers, provoked by massive and failed frontal assaults, were limited in number, patriotic in spirit, and restrained in grievances. Later Leonard Smith, an American historian specialized in the experience of French soldiers in the First World War, traced the history of a single French infantry division throughout the war and discerned in its men an insistence upon negotiation with their superiors and upon making gains proportional to sacrifices: both inspired them to withhold their obedience in the spring of 1917. Stéphane Audoin-Rouzeau and Annette Becker, in *14–18: Understanding the Great War*, their seminal work of 2000, ignited a controversy over a "culture of war." They tended to marginalize the mutinies; like their predecessors and some of their contemporaries, they downplayed the agency of any widespread antiwar animus, even among the mutineers themselves. Most recently another French historian, André Loez, following paths opened before him by Nicolas Offenstadt, re-examined the entire question in *14–18. Living and Dying in the Trenches*, a thoroughgoing study that by its title intended to answer Audoin-Rouzeau's and Becker's earlier work. He placed the mutinies on a continuum of social behavior that was indeed deeply hostile to the war without necessarily being "pacifist."

The discussion is no less lively among German historians seeking to explain the collapse of 1918. For Wilhelm Deist, a specialist in late nineteenth- and twentieth-century German military history, German soldiers had by then acquired the arts of evasion and learned the mass tactic of the clandestine strike; for Wolfgang Kruse, a wide-ranging historian of modern France and Germany, deep-seated social divisions between officers and men finally boiled over; for Benjamin Ziemann, a German social and cultural historian, and a specialist in relations between the front and the homeland in Germany during the First World War, conditions by 1918 allowed for a quantum leap in the level of desertion among soldiers who had long been disillusioned anyway.[2]

Such arguments implicitly or explicitly ponder why such revolts did not shake the armies sooner—or, to ask the same question, why the men held out as long as they did. At Verdun the question is inescapable, but answers must await a re-examination of the premise, which presupposes a binary choice between consent in one year and refusal in another. The humor of the men did not often lend itself to such absolutes. Even if outright mutiny was rare in both armies in 1916, the anxieties of the high commands ran high at moments, and nowhere more so than at Verdun. These were not hallucinatory flashes, but well-grounded fears, even if the "brass hats" misunderstood the causes of the malaise. For anyone caring to look closely enough, Verdun displays unmistakable precursor signs of the events of 1917 and 1918.

In early May the Prussian Minister of War acknowledged in his diary that German soldiers in the trenches outside Fort Vaux were refusing to leave them. Others declined again in June, preferring the protection of their earthbound shelters to the uncertain glories of storming well-defended French positions. The telltale presence of armed patrols just behind the front lines betrayed the apprehensions of the officers who gave the orders about those supposed to carry them out. Officers acknowledged to their French captors that to persuade young conscripts to leave the trenches they had drawn their revolvers.

Similar anxieties could grip their adversaries. During the savage fighting around Fleury in late June a French cavalry officer, transferred like so many of his fellows to the infantry, faced the thankless task of breaking the news to an exhausted battalion that it was to return to the front lines. Would they obey? Would discipline break down? He did not know. The fear of mutiny, "every officer's worst nightmare," proved illusory—this time.[3]

At the beginning of June parts of a Bavarian infantry regiment awaiting orders in a supply park began behaving "boorishly," as one of their lieutenants put it. They tore down the fences, littered the ground with empty beer bottles, and disrupted the flow of men and traffic. Worse, once handed their equipment and their grenades, they refused to leave. They laughed at the noncommissioned officers who ordered them to move on out; they derided the lieutenant; they even lay on the grass and blocked the exit. Their ringleader, a corporal named Mändl, had a history, a recent history, for a week earlier he had strayed from his unit, fallen into the arms of another one, and vainly resisted return in the hope, he explained, of remaining in captivity at least until his company had returned from combat in the front lines. Now he was forced into a different stratagem to save his skin, less rusé, more public. Since October 1914 he had fought well and given no trouble. But Georg Mändl had clearly had enough of fighting. And he succeeded: two soldiers, pioneers from the supply park, led him away, and he spent two years and ten months safely in prison—long enough for the war to end and then some. The incident passed.[4]

Others did not. On the night of the 26th of May, as a French battalion in column was leaving its rest camp near Mourmelon in the Marne for the train station, Ste-Ménehoulde, and the trenches of Verdun beyond, shots were fired, punctuated by shouted insults to the officers. Men from different companies had gathered as though by pre-arrangement and vanished into the woods or regrouped at the rear of the column. Seven at least had coalesced into a clique of conspirators, bent on never making the journey to Verdun. "They banded together to make trouble," a corporal later said. One of them, later executed for "group revolt under arms," made no excuses and showed no remorse for his seemingly suicidal misdeeds. They won't get me with bullets and shells," he wrote in a letter seized in his prison cell, "I've suffered too much, better death from twelve of our bullets than to start these torments all over. I'm sick of it all." He summed it all up at his trial. "I was down in the dumps," he told his judges.[5]

Two weeks earlier, at the depot at Haudainville, some three miles south of Verdun, a gentler but graver mutiny had rippled through the ranks of two entire companies. Late in the afternoon of the 14th of May some 50 men of the 140th Infantry Regiment failed to appear at an assembly. Once again the disappearing act coincided with an imminent departure for the front lines. But this time it took the form of a loosely concerted response, complete with instigators and agitators. Men emerging from their barracks and huts found others milling about in the street and spreading the word. "Don't pack your kits, we're not going up there!" the leaders called out, and for good measure the two most avid even cut the leather straps off some knapsacks. If enough men joined in, they reasoned, the entire battalion might refuse to leave for the lines. They began to drift in small groups towards the river banks and the barges on the canal. Night fell. Powerless officers sent word to the regiment not to count any longer on the 2nd Battalion. "It's mutiny by folded arms," one of the lieutenants reported. "We can feel discipline disintegrating."

That morning the battalion had come down from the trenches near the Tunnel de Tavannes. The men were exhausted. They had spent two months in the sector and had just withstood day after day of intense shelling. Almost at once an order came to move out that night for the trenches near Fort Vaux, no quieter than those of Tavannes and considerably farther away, across treacherous fire-swept terrain. Why us, the men began to ask, and not the 3rd Battalion nearby, which had just enjoyed two days of rest? And why not have left for Vaux from Tavannes, a mere mile or so away, instead of the seven that now stretched before them from Haudainville? "I sincerely confess," one of the leaders later said, "that I would have enjoyed a bit of rest." Fatigue ignited the revolt, contagion spread it. So many were turning their backs on the front lines, one of the mutineers later explained, that he shrank from being the only one to obey orders. So he fraternized, he followed. Late that night, strolling by the river, they began to notice other companies of the battalion leaving for the trenches. Now contagion ran the other way. They began to drift back, brought to their senses by the spectacle of duty in motion and perhaps by some dim presentiment of ostracism. Some returned in time to leave with the other units that night, others left with the 3rd Battalion the next day. The military police did not come for them until days later.

The tribunals sentenced one to death and the others to prison terms ranging from two months to five years—lenient indeed, considering that this army, like others, could place exemplary over punitive justice, and shoot men *pour encourager les autres*. Their commanding officers and even the divisional general displayed forbearance and restraint, and at their hearings lieutenants and captains often praised the delinquent accused as courageous soldiers gone astray. A tinge of *tout comprendre, tout pardonner* pervaded their testimony, for the good reason that the order to leave for the front lines again so soon after reaching their rest station had made no sense, none at all. General Lebrun, who had issued it, commanded a sector made up of six divisions and appeared, in the words of one of their commanders, "manifestly not up to the situation he faced." The general insisted on enforcing his aberrant order in spite of protests from the officers carrying it out, and their clemency in the face of the men's affront to their authority spoke volumes. Unwittingly, they had added their voice to that of the embittered major at Souilly, who wrote as the mutineers faced their judges about the gulf that separated the officers in the trenches from the generals at the rear, and warned, almost, of the kinds of breakdown that Lebrun's order had just provoked in the depot at Haudainville.[6]

Lebrun was nervous. At the end of May, two weeks after the trouble at Haudainville and just as the shots rang out at Mourmelon, he vented his anxieties to his subordinates. He had heard, he told them, that officers were warning here and there that their exhausted men, told to hold on another 24 hours for relief, "might end up ordering their own relief." The life of the *Patrie*, he reminded them, was at stake, and he threatened to court-martial any officer who failed to strike down such insubordination. He seemed not to understand any more than he had at Haudainville.[7]

His superiors at Souilly and Chantilly were worrying as well, less about mutinies, which were rare, than about desertions in small groups, which were less so. The Germans were beginning their final drives to take Fleury and Souville and perhaps Verdun itself before the Allied offensive opened on the Somme, and a few of the French units had so alarmed the high command by the disappearance of some of their members that it dissolved them.

A deserter might vanish not on a solitary whim but in tandem with a partner or under the sway of a friendly persuader. Here the specters haunting the authorities began to multiply, from the flight of one to the scheme of several and, worst of all, to the secession of many. "Organized desertion"—*desertion avec complot*—according to article 240 of the Code of Military Justice, took place when two or more deserters acted in concert. Like impulsive individual acts, however, this was not always easy to establish. One night two men disappeared from their company, which had just taken up front line positions near the Fontaine de Tavannes. One of them, a trucker from St. Denis, traveled west, sleeping in fields by night. The other, a vineyard laborer, found his way to his mother's closer by in Epernay. Days later they gave themselves up. The shelling had driven them mad, they said. Had they acted in concert? It was difficult to say.[8]

At other times there could be no doubt. On the same day, at almost the same time, four others had abandoned their company at Haudainville as it set out for the front lines. The night before three had conferred atop one of the barges on the canal, away from their fellows on board below, and when the four deserted they left their arms and equipment behind. They soon split up and made their way to Paris, where they were arrested a few days later, one coming out of a cinema, the other wandering down the Boulevard de la Chapelle. With collusion so manifest and magnanimity out of the question, their judges dismissed their denials that they had acted in concert or known of the imminent departure for the front lines. They handed down two long prison sentences and two death sentences that were later commuted. One deserter was a pariah, several were a menace.[9]

In March, during the German attacks on the left bank to the north of Verdun, group desertions in the Bois d'Avocourt and the Bois de Malancourt began to thin the ranks of the 29th Infantry Division. It was losing the woods to the enemy. Reports began to come in that an officer had deserted with three or four men, a sergeant with 15. The numbers were vague, the reports late. Nonetheless, there could be little doubt, an inquiry later concluded: the division's reserves were reinforcing the right flank or counterattacking in support of the neighboring 67th, and no one remained to relieve the men in the woods. "A regrettable state of morale," the report concluded, was the result. Two officers reported that collective desertions had begun as early as the 10th of March, only two days after the German assault.[10]

Now, in June, incidents of this sort began to repeat themselves on the right bank, as intense combat brought the Germans ever closer to Verdun. While several German divisions reduced the farm and the defensive works of Thiaumont to ruins, small but serial desertions depleted the ranks of the defenders, so much so that Joffre dissolved one of the most impaired regiments, the 347th. Late in the month several companies panicked in the same sector after artillerymen abandoned their batteries without any order to do so.

Near Brabant, troubles erupted among two colonial regiments. Seven Zouaves and 21 *tirailleurs* disappeared as their units left the barracks for the front lines. The two regiments, the commanding colonels later explained, had given their all for two months and some of their men had balked at the prospect of returning to one of the deadliest sectors of the front—especially as the Moslem *tirailleurs* in particular had expected to rest during Ramadan. These were special circumstances. But Joffre warned the government that a wave of "lassitude" and "discouragement" bordered at moments on open indiscipline, just as Pétain, without openly warning about morale, was threatening to withdraw to the the left bank if he did not receive reinforcements.[11]

Such scares, however unsettling, were local, and passed when relief, reinforcements, or rotations mollified the men or eased the emergencies. No consciousness of shared cause, spread by symbols, spoken or written words, petitions, songs, or gestures as yet politicized the resentments and spread commotion or sedition across whole regiments and divisions; no mass mutinies or desertions threatened either army at Verdun. It was a matter of rest, not of indiscipline, one of the company captains had said of one of the malcontents who had wandered down to the barges instead of forming up at the depot at Haudainville in May. His fellow-officers said much the same of the other errant sheep in their flock. They saw the black sheep as drunkards or delinquents, recidivist offenders who all too often had come from other units to reform their ways and had only abused the misspent clemency that had come their way.

Dissipation, if it spread, could pose a threat of its own. In June 1915 half of the men sentenced in the 29th Infantry Division, the same that would later suffer serial desertions in the woods north of Verdun, had committed their assorted misdeeds under the influence of alcohol. But waywardness was not dissent; it carried none of the implied menace of an articulated challenge to the unit, the army, or the war itself. "I've had enough of fighting for capitalists," a factory worker shouted late in May. "If peace isn't signed in two months then I'll sign it." He was inciting his fellows to disobey, and so, probably, was a schoolteacher in the same division the same month: "Don't march! They're trying to do you in. Let them at least tell us where we're going." The tribunals rewarded their enthusiasms with five-year prison sentences. But it was the only reaction they provoked: no one had followed their examples. At Verdun, in 1916, discipline occasionally broke down not because ideas fused individuals in revolt but because frustrations drove them apart, in outbursts driven not by solidarity but by self-preservation.[12]

The high command believed otherwise. The greater their distance from the front, the stronger grew the commanders' belief in ideologically inspired subversion. Even as a soldier was writing from Verdun that "when we had to come up here for the fourth time, the men wanted no more of it, we've been here on the Verdun front for too long," Joffre was complaining that the attacks on him leaking out in the press at home were poisoning spirits at the front. That month the Chamber was meeting in secret session to listen to his critics among the deputies impeach his foresight at Verdun. The press repeated none of the philippics, and nothing in the military postal censors' own reports revealed echoes in the trenches of Verdun either. "Nobody speaks of the Chamber's secret committee," they recorded of the Second Army in June, "and no one says anything about governmental or administrative matters."

And by the account of Joffre's investigative services, revolutionary sentiment scarcely moved the insubordinate that spring. Troubled by the "serious incidents" at Mourmelon on the night in May, when a battalion faced the open revolt of a few as it left for Verdun, military justice officials asked the postal censors to sift the regiment's correspondence for any signs of pacifist or revolutionary ferment—as though worried that even if the mutineers had manifested no such fever, they might yet have been contaminated by its effects. A corporal, the postal censors found, had been requesting anarchist leaflets from a correspondent in Paris, a soldier had written of hopes of deserting to the enemy with two others, perhaps, and a few others had written of purely imaginary happenings—the murder of a major, the revolt of entire battalions. But the handful of motley authors appeared not to know each other. One was perpetually drunk. And they almost faded from view among thousands of letter writers in the regiment who displayed no such sentiments and who once in a while condemned those who did.

Thoughts of revolution, anarchist or other, had not triggered the shots at Mourmelon on the night of the 26th of May. But aspirations to profound change might yet be latent in a unit, even if absent from the antics of its most unruly members. Not without reason the high command continued to fret as the year wore on.[13]

Fret as they might about revolutionary agitation, the gravest peril both commands faced at Verdun was neither mutiny nor desertion but mass surrender—not insubordination but demoralization. Submission to the other side threatened collapse more persistently than defiance of one's own. Usually it happened on the defensive, in the face of a sudden and overwhelming attack. In February, as enemy infantry began spreading through the blasted woods north of Verdun, whole companies of French soldiers or their remnants surrendered, enveloped on their flanks, dazed by the shelling or the new flamethrowers, or addled by the passing illusion of German infallibility. On the 24th, 200 men surrendered to an enemy field kitchen near the Chambrettes farm. To believe their captors, some of the French prisoners seemed almost buoyant—chatting, smiling, smoking. "The war's over for you," a German gunner called out to a column of blue-coated French prisoners in the village of Jametz. "Ah, oui, oui!" came the scattered rejoinders, relieved or resigned, in a dialogue suggesting the captor's envy of his captive.

In March some of the soldiers who abandoned the 29th Infantry Division in Malancourt and Avocourt woods not only deserted, but went over to the enemy, according to one inquiry, as the Germans launched a determined offensive against the hastily improvised French defenses on the left bank. A German regimental history later confirmed that in some of the French units the men had surrendered in droves. In April, as the Germans attacked yet again on the left bank, General Nivelle was worried enough about reports of groups surrounded and captured to rail against such acts of abandon and remind his divisions and regiments that morale was all and the men must not doubt their own superiority. Never let the men forget, he told their leaders, that the enemy was as exhausted, as spent, as ready to give up as they were.[14]

And so he was, when on the receiving end of similar assaults. In mid-September Nivelle's anxieties emerged from the lips of a German divisional commander, as though by mimesis. The troops of the 192nd Division no longer displayed the sense of superiority they had in the Avocourt woods, he complained. "The high number of missing is eloquent proof," he went on, and he pressed his officers to elevate the confidence levels of their men. If goodwill failed to motivate them, he added, ruthless discipline would. The French had observed such local crises among their adversaries before. In June the German infantrymen they engaged seemed to have lost much of their fighting spirit. They shrunk from moving out unless the artillery preparation had been so devastating that the enemy gave no signs of life; they returned to their trenches as soon as shells began falling on them; and in the absence of their officers they might now give themselves up, and utter their greeting of surrender: "Kamerad!" Their will, in the absence of energetic leadership and effective artillery, seemed drained.[15]

At the end of the year the German high command itself was saying much the same. By then the most alarming mass surrenders of the battle of Verdun had taken place—the harvest, for the French, of their autumn counteroffensives. Six thousand Germans had laid down their arms when the French retook the forts of Douaumont and Vaux in October and November, another 3,000 when they retook Bezonvaux and its environs in December. A German gunner, almost buried alive by shell fire and surrounded with his fellows in his wrecked dugout, had little choice but to surrender on December 15. By then they had endured nine days of French shelling, he later recalled, and many were contemplating the *heimatschuss*—the self-inflicted wound promising hospital or home. Only the fear of permanent damage restrained them. He had never known such despair in his unit, and matters had not been helped by the fresh arrival from Germany of a company commander who understood nothing about the world of Verdun.

On Christmas day, at the other end of the hierarchy atop OHL, Hindenburg drew the conclusion that morale had collapsed at Verdun. Once again the unmistakable symptom was surrender—without much resistance, and in numbers that perturbed him now even more than the aspect of the Western Front had early in the autumn. Then, as the newly arrived chief of the General Staff, he had begun to fret over the impact of a prolonged and static defensive war on morale, the famous morale of the German infantry. Verdun now confirmed his worst fears.[16]

By the end of 1916, as German historians have revealed, the high command became so anxious about the general morale of the German army that it began systematically molding the content of the trench papers that the units in the field had been putting out since the beginning of the war in August 1914. Remarkably frank, even insolent, the soldierly newssheets had complained about food, about inequities, about the conduct of their officers, even; in the summer of 1916, as the last German offensive efforts at Verdun spent themselves and the Allied onslaught on the Somme began, the OHL established first a *Feldpressestelle* (field press office) and then a *Vaterländischer Unterricht* (Patriotic Education) service to inject optimism and resolve and expel the virus of cynicism from the ailing organism. Now, in the autumn of that indecisive year, Hindenburg and his quartermaster general, Erich Ludendorff, looked anew at the army they had recently taken over.[17]

Could the German infantry ever recover its old spirit, so that serial capitulations such as those at Verdun did not repeat themselves?

Hindenburg thought so, or at least said so: attention to training, indoctrination, due solicitude for the men and their food, their comfort, their
leaves, a proper rotation between combat and rest—all the familiar ingredients of the mysterious potion called "morale"—must now weigh as
much on the minds of officers as tactics themselves, he proclaimed.

Others were not so sure. The "warning signal of Verdun" as a report
later called it, had convinced them that morale had failed because of
natural reasons. Even the German soldier was not indefatigable. They had
reached the conclusion that most connoisseurs of Verdun had, that circumstances could eventually poison the will, that men and units reached
breaking points, that weapons of the spirit would not decide the *Materialschlacht* on the Western Front; and perhaps Hindenburg and Ludendorff, for all their pontificating about motivation, had as well, as they
pressed ever more urgently in that winter of 1916–1917 for the quantum
leap, the resumption of unrestricted submarine warfare.[18]

The men hated Verdun as they had hated no other place in this war. In
his heavily censored account of 1917, Lieutenant Péricard recorded the
comments of the *poilus* as they neared the depot at Haudainville and the
brown fog that even in the sun enveloped the hills beyond. "Crappy job,"
they muttered, "I'd rather take a bullet." The mutiny on the way to the
station at Ste-Ménehoulde in May had erupted when rumors of their des-
tination spread among the men: the infernal Verdun. The word met with
a visceral revulsion, a machine-gunner noted on being sent back there in
the summer of 1917, in all including himself. Deserters invoked the prospect as though to justify their own *cafard*. Returning to Verdun late in
July, even acknowledging that the fighting seemed to have let up some, a
soldier arriving from the heavy fighting on the Somme still loathed it as
abidingly as ever.[19]

Did they also hate the men who had put them there? Indeed some
of them did, to judge by their comments. "How could the minds of
some men conceive of such horrible destructions?" the revenant from
the Somme, a reader of Sebastien Faure's anarchist *Ce qu'il faut dire*,
wrote. They were perhaps more inclined to redirect their animosities
from the places onto the authors of their misery. In April, at a meeting
of the Socialist Party in Paris, a soldier on leave from Verdun railed at
the horrors he had seen there—the bodies that lay strewn in heaps on the

hillsides of Vacherauville, Douaumont, and the Bois des Corbeaux. Was there, he asked, any greater crime than the extinction of so many for so little? And what had France done—its Republic, its diplomats, even its socialists—to put a stop to it? Nothing. He no longer believed in this war.

Disenchantment, however, spread as well to others less predisposed to turn against the enterprise itself. To believe his recollections, General Berthold von Deimling was consumed with rage at his own command. He found himself immobilized for weeks with his Reserve Corps in the Woëvre plains, soaked by rain, raked by fire from French guns atop the Côtes de Meuse. By night, in the abandoned factory he used as head-quarters, he paced his room and cursed the bloody game of numbers, the game of attrition. OHL and the Fifth Army had condemned him to play functionary rather than commander. And he swore that if he survived he would turn against war itself. He was the only German general to turn pacifist once the war was over.[20]

Nonetheless, Deimling never mutinied at Verdun. His epiphany did not require that he renounce his calling just yet. And the men who blamed their predicament on official imbeciles were rarely the ones who turned on their superiors or deserted their units or gave them-selves up to the enemy. Those who did—the unhinged, the exasperated, the demoralized—never joined their visceral resentment to the others' articulated cause. Not yet.

When they did, in French armies in 1917 and in German ones in 1918, events near and far had expanded the limits of the possible, inciting mutiny in one army and mass surrender in the other. A failed offensive six weeks earlier and an apparent crisis in the high command, revolution in Russia and strikes at home, talk of a Stockholm conference, rumors of peace, a sense that disorder was spreading, that anything was possible: the French mutineers who agitated, took over trains, threatened their officers, marched on Paris, signed petitions and shouted antiwar slogans believed for a heady fortnight in late May and early June 1917 that an end was pos-sible, if only the powers would listen to them.

During the summer and autumn of 1918 the Germans, less politicized but far more numerous, agitated on troop trains or, exhausted and apa-thetic, surrendered in droves in the front lines. Only then did earlier spo-radic incidents of indiscipline take on the character of a mass movement. Ludendorff acknowledged then and later that something had changed.

He was right: the men had given up hope of winning the war, and succumbed, like the French mutineers of 1917, to subversive yearnings to end it another way.[21]

Verdun had given the high commands a foretaste of such hankerings, enough to alarm them. More than once they misdiagnosed the yearnings as symptoms of indoctrination or corruption by politics, ideas, or newspapers, or even by misguided talk of peace. In mid-December, as the Kaiser and Chancellor Theobald Bethmann-Hollweg launched a diplomatic initiative, General von Einem, in command of the Third Army in Champagne, warned that raising and then shattering hopes of peace would only debilitate the men, and days later he and his staff discerned in the surrenders at Verdun the confirmation of their fears. Joffre blamed the "lassitude" and the right bank panics of June on campaigns of criticism at home. In 1917 and 1918 their successors, confronting far more advanced signs of decomposition, spoke much the same language.

They all erred. The spirit of the German army, Ludendorff argued, was still strong in December 1916; shortly before the Armistice he found it so poor that he practically laid defeat at its door. Something had indeed changed, and it was more than the men's reading habits. Demoralization sprang not from pamphlets but from experience, and circumstances more than ideas conspired to turn minds from resignation to rejection. At Verdun no one could believe for long that the war might shortly end, and that collective strategies of mutiny or surrender might hasten deliverance from its hated grip. The armies mostly held.[22]

Their cohesion inspired inane distortions, then and later, that would lead historians to discern either consent or constraint behind such a massive acceptance of the military ordeal. The men obeyed because they wished to, even ardently: such was the legend of the trench of the bayonets,[23] of the storming of Douaumont, of cheerful sacrifice sung to the music-hall audience: "One year, two years (and even three)/We'll hold as long as we have to/what does suffering matter to us?/Death to us! But *vive la France!*" Such too was the legend of official and semi-official histories of the battle, especially in German versions in which "tragedy" unfolded as the men strained at the leash and commanders held them back. A few of the men themselves wrote that way, in accounts that stretched credulity. According to a second lieutenant in the Zouaves, his men atop Côte 304 in May laughed or sang as they took up positions, joked about the corpses they passed, took orders with good cheer; he himself even welcomed the prospect of some restorative sleep. On Côte 304, on the 11th of May 1916? And the author Henry Bordeaux, chronicler of the army's exploits, described infantry advancing on Thiaumont in July hurling grenades and crying "on les aura!" But then he had also likened the calls for help from Fort Vaux in June to Roland's horn at Roncesvaux and the retaking of the fort in November to Charlemagne's revenge.[24]

A few did sing on the way to battle, much as warriors had since antiquity and possibly before. Neither the deafening din of industrial war nor the vast emptiness of its battlefields fully silenced the human voice, however faint and archaic it might sound. In Champagne in 1915 a junior officer heard, he said, the hymn of the Girondins who had taken revolutionary France to war with it in 1792 and who celebrated in its lyrics the shedding of blood and still more the beauty of dying for one's country. *Dulce et decorum est*—and the next day, before the great offensive, he heard again the quatrains of revolutionary song, this time the more celebrated *Chant du Depart*, in which a mother offers her son to the fatherland and which became the official anthem of Napoleon's empire. At Verdun, during the retaking of le Mort-Homme on April 9, a second lieutenant heard soldiers singing the *Marseillaise*; his account of reading poetry to his men during a bombardment would cast a shadow of doubt over his aural testimony, had two other witnesses not heard the same strains. A month later, on the nearby Côte 304, an artillery officer watched as 150 mm shells suddenly landed, red rockets rose, a cry of "Barrage!" went up, and his fellow officers made for their batteries while singing the *Marseillaise*. So many stupid stories had been told about them, he worried, no one would believe this one.[25]

Verdun found its way into the music-halls, suitably amplified: "The boys of Mangin/of Nivelle and of Pétain/are now all of France/From Bezonvaux to Louvemont/yelling the *Marseillaise*/they redressed our front with one leap/Verdun! Verdun! You'll stay French!" And Jules Romains concluded his novel about Verdun with the sounds of the *Marseillaise* on le Mort-Homme on April 9.

Facts are facts. But these were exceptional, even extraordinary. In both armies men sang for recreation when at rest, or for cadence when marching at a good distance from the front lines, but closer to them and to the enemy vocal accompaniment would have been suicidal as well as superfluous. Voices competed poorly with shell fire for audibility. And the sudden enthusiasms they suggested to novelists, even novelists as scrupulous as Romains, squared unevenly with the endless outpourings of weariness and disgust that their letters conveyed to the postal censors reading them.[26]

Did they then obey, as a competing legend had it, because they had to—coerced neither by love of their country nor hatred of their enemy but by fear of their leaders? Shunned by official commemoration, which favored the legend of the hero, the legend of the victim found its way more discreetly into literary renditions and recollections of the battle. "In the shell fire of Verdun, the men hold," the veteran and writer Jean Giono wrote in an essay in 1939. "I know the place, and we hold up because the MPs prevent us from leaving it. They station them even in the middle of the battle, in communication trenches, above the Tunnel de Tavannes. To get out of there you need an exit ticket. . . ." This, too, raises eyebrows. Few others recall such a profusion of enforcers in the front lines, and the gendarmerie never acquired the ubiquity that Giono's logic would have required: "We can indeed say that if we remained on the battlefield it was because great pains were taken to prevent us from leaving it." He was a pacifist, appalled at the imminent prospect of another war.

The author and socialist activist René Naegelen, whose fiction probably hewed more closely to his own experiences at Verdun than Giono's nonfiction did, had his autobiographical hero on the *Voie Sacrée* hope for the wound that would send him home, and weigh the merits of shooting himself in the arm or leg in the trenches outside Fort Vaux. The German author and pacifist Arnold Zweig, who had served at Verdun in 1916, had the hero of his novel rebel against the military machine there, in the name of justice rather than self-preservation, and reject in his enlightenment the coercive monster that had enslaved him. Zweig meant capitalism and imperialism as well. Such works, like *All Quiet on the Western Front*, burned with missionary zeal as well as with the odium with which Céline wrote of "the torture of the regiment" in *Journey to the End of the Night*.[27]

There was coercion; crises of authority occur in most battles. But repression came lightly now for all but the most serious offences, such as mutiny or going over to the enemy. What could the eighteenth-century discipline of Frederick the Great, conceived to keep men not only from deserting but also from thinking, signify in a mass army of mostly literate men, familiar with notions of rights and of justice? A recent study of the German army finds it comparatively lenient in matters of desertion, and even mutiny; in the French army, one could find forbearance in its judges. The revolt at Haudainville in May brought out not only the sword but also the scales of justice. No repressive system on its own could compel several hundred thousand uniformly recalcitrant men to risk their lives every day. Very few of them claimed it did. "Constraint" had also to come from elsewhere—from within.[28]

In French popular culture refusal or half-heartedness never tainted the name of Verdun. Songs about the battle invariably celebrated the unshakeable readiness of the *poilus* there to defend the country—their "fierce endurance," in the ode of Théodore Botrel—bard to the armies—to Pétain of April 1916, their resounding "Halte-là, on ne passe pas!"—"you're not going anywhere!"—in another popular song that year, summed up their sacrifice, which Michel Sardou's 1979 song sought to preserve from oblivion and which the emotive host of a radio program in 1996 attached for all eternity to the two syllables "Verdun."

If any syllables hinted at recalcitrance, they were those of the mutinies linked to the Chemin des Dames in 1917. There, in 1998, Prime Minister Lionel Jospin had sought to "reintegrate" the mutineers, although he did not use the word, into the national memory. The local connection was thought to be more obvious than "Verdun." This was unjust, for the casualty rate while the French offensive lasted at the Chemin des Dames approximated that at Verdun, and the mutinies did not erupt until weeks after Nivelle's ill-conceived offensive there had stalled. No matter: a song of rebellion has forever transfigured the name of the battle and its plateau de Craonne—the small town between Reims and Soissons that disappeared in the shell fire—distilling into short stanzas a surfeit of suffering and a refusal to countenance any more: *C'est bien fini, on en a assez/ personne ne veut plus marcher* ["It's all over, we've had enough/no one wants to go along any more"] and *nous sommes les sacrifiés* ["we are the sacrificed"].

Verdun escaped such associations not by any caprice of cultural memory but because no mass mutinies ever darkened its name during its endless months. But the words of the song later dubbed the "Chanson de Craonne" already escaped the lips of some of the *poilus* at Verdun, whether they sang them or not: "I see that we're the sacrificed ones of the war," one of them wrote in July 1916, nine months before the men fell on the Plateau de Craonne. "It's always the same ones. . . ." And the mere absence of mass insubordination hardly validates the myth of inspired self-sacrifice.[29]

Later on, as the French invented a zenith of their troops' morale at Verdun and a nadir at the Chemin des Dames, Germans performed a parallel operation. They bemoaned in their failed offensive at Verdun the abyss, the point where the men parted ways with their leaders; they celebrated in their successful but costly defense on the Somme the acme of collective resolve, when "officers and men grew ever closer together in the struggle," as a German military study of 1936 wished it. These were fairy tales. At Verdun, on the Somme, at the Chemin des Dames, morale on either side was neither high enough to carry the day nor low enough to lose it. It was uncertain and uneven, it was functional. It was adequate.[30]

Between combat accepted in song and rejected in anger lay the vast *terra incognita* of glum cooperation. Pierre Mac Orlan—prompted like his fellow-novelist Naegelen to write about Verdun upon returning there after the war—recalled the men as phantoms without personality, bearing no resemblance to their official apotheoses, practically indifferent to whether they were winning or losing. He remembered some silly songs from Artois, none from here. Humanity, for him, had left the scene. Still, the men at Verdun were human enough to despise the war and yet human enough to keep on fighting it, as though driven by some automatism or collective habit that Mac Orlan divined but could not name. They wanted their war to end, they did not want to end the war; a wish had not become a cause, not yet. They carried on.[31]

IO

Enemies

"THE GREAT BATTLE OPENS," Pierre Renouvin, the great historian of war and international relations wrote of Verdun in his general history of the First World War, published in 1934. "It will . . . demand of the troops an unprecedented effort, demand of their heroism the hardest sacrifices. . . . Nowhere is the initiative of junior officers, their nerves, their courage, more severely tested. Nowhere must the soldier display more tenacity and self-denial."[1]

Heroism, courage, initiative, tenacity, abnegation—Renouvin did not ask about the mainsprings, the why, of such valor among his countrymen at Verdun, or about its constancy, or about its universality. Perhaps he considered the question irrelevant or the answer self-evident. The war veteran that he was—he had lost an arm at the Chemin des Dames in April 1917—might have answered, but the historian that he had become did not ask. He did not ask either about the valor of the enemy. What drove them, the Germans as well as the French, to fight rather than flee, to hold out rather than give up?

Resenting their subjection at one level while accepting it at another, the men kept on—so runs the most consensual rendition not only of the men at Verdun but also of most of the others for much of the Great War. Historians, especially recently, argue not over the subjection but over the acceptance, not over the sufferings of the men but over their willingness to bear them. They argue over the levels of conviction, coercion, or conformism that might explain such seemingly selfless behavior, and over the social and circumstantial forces that made for acquiescence or resistance. French, German, and British historians have tried to explain the endurance of the men by invoking institutional, social, or cultural factors—the regimental system, propaganda, a model of class relations in civil society, a religion of patriotism—coupled with coercion and military socialization.[2]

In France more recently the argument, exploring once again the motivation of the warrior and his kind, turns on whether the men who endured such conditions could have done so without a cultural fervor kindled before the war and stoked in its opening weeks, and on whether the crusade that so enthused the population at home did not also command the ardors of the civilians in uniform at the front.[3]

Like so many quarrels among historians, this one erupts from false opposites: most obviously, pacifism vs. patriotism, but also consent vs. constraint, chivalry vs. cruelty, obedience vs. disobedience, fraternization vs. demonization, pugnacity vs. passivity. At one time or another, all the combatants displayed symptoms of these and more, in manifestations too recurrent to stem from circumstance alone and yet too fragile, too episodic, to compose a "culture." Neither contingency nor character alone can explain why no large-scale mutiny erupted at Verdun, nor why German morale there very nearly collapsed by the end of 1916. The key to such collective mysteries lies not in some theory of combat motivation but in the range of reactions available to men at war.

At the heart of the matter lies the enemy. Seen as a point in time, "the butchery of Verdun" marked the high point of national fervor, the linear descendant of the patriotic poet—and veteran of the Franco-Prussian war—Paul Déroulède. His lines of 1881:

I know some who say that hatred dies
But no! Oblivion has no place in our hearts. . . .

Whether the enemy alone inspired the primordial call of self-preservation and the acquiescence of the many to the orders of the few he did not say. Besides, did the enemy present so compelling an aspect, so unchanging an essence? Historians, including Renouvin, did not often ask; yet the answer is not at all self-evident.[4]

Most often, the enemies exposed themselves to scrutiny as prisoners or corpses. As close as they came to each other, in moments of combat and inactivity alike, visual contemplation for anyone other than a sniper rarely recommended itself. It had long been that way. "Take a good look at them," soldiers told a new sergeant when he first set eyes on German prisoners on his way to the front in the Meuse, "you won't see that many in the trenches." The French infantry who wrote of their experiences might describe debris, and animal carcasses, and corpses in a ravine, and burning villages, but rarely the Germans, even only 50 yards distant. In close combat they might show their faces, suddenly appearing on a nearby hilltop, but sometimes, even then, they remained invisible. They were there, all around them yet indiscernible in the mêlées and disorderly combat that had taken the place of the ruined trenches.[5]

Unseen but omnipresent, the foe inspired varied animosities, undisciplined by knowledge or experience. In its abstract form these owed much to the cultural productions of civil society. During the Franco-Prussian war of 1870, which had yielded no insulting nicknames—no Boche—for the German, respect had initially tempered hostility, but defeat, siege, occupation, and annexations had inculcated a durably warlike image of Germania, armed with an Imperial sword and a shield often emblazoned with a menacing bird of prey. In contrast stood Marianne, feminine symbol of the Republic and the people, elegant even when warlike, the same contrast that Barrès drew when he juxtaposed the architectural heaviness of the annexed Strasbourg and Metz with the grace of French Nancy, the same that the two Alsatian caricaturists—Hansi (Jean-Jacques Waltz) and Henri Zislin—drew when at the turn of the century they began sketching bulldogs in spiked helmets—the German *Pickelhaube*—and infantry goose-stepping through peaceful village squares in a display of savage discipline and unholy pomposity.[6]

Now, when the German became the instigator of the Great War and the author of its atrocities, they spun the same fable, in language tailored to every age and intellect, to every level of sophistication, ceaselessly renewed: the enemy was real and the enemy was vile.

As Verdun began, the Opéra Comique in Paris was presenting by way of *Cadeaux de Noël* the story of four children in a burned-out farm, orphans of parents whom the invaders had savagely murdered and whose benevolent neighbor, Père Jean, hands them the instrument of vengeance, his rifle. As the battle ended in December 1916, the same theater was putting on four *tableaux* from the life of a peasant—his wedding, the harvest, the war, and companionship with a soldier from Alsace, whose martyred province was still prey to the rapacious Teuton.

More often than "heroism" or "victory," and much more often than "peace," *Le Matin* used the word "enemy" in its front page headlines—60 times a month, on average, throughout 1916. In May readers of the highbrow *Revue des Deux Mondes* learned that the misdeeds of Germany's soldiers, far from betraying the ideas of her philosophers, aptly embodied them. Leibniz and Kant and Hegel, not to mention Goethe and Beethoven, lent themselves easily to an evolution in which universal consciousness became German consciousness, Providence found its vehicle in the Prussian state, and *das Ganze*, the All, helped along by salutary violence, ousted the decrepit individualism of the humanistic and Greco-Latin enemy. No, there were not two Germanys, one welcomed by the French academy before the war, another defined by its army today. They were one and the same.[7]

The hostile stereotypes, as stereotypes of all sorts often do, sometimes contradicted each other.[8] In the French press the enemy was above all the barbarian at the gate. Repeated allusions to "Germanic masses," to hordes hurled against the ramparts of thinking humanity, to an army devoid of strategy but given to charging ahead, "heads lowered, like a herd of buffalo" and to a habit of massacre that dishonored war itself. Deliberately or not, such imagery conjured up woodland confrontations between civilization and its assailants around the *oppidum* of Verdun 1,700 years earlier.[9]

Even the weapons provoked the military commentators to familiar cultural comparisons. In the dull feral roar of the heavy German guns and the cheerful whistle of the lighter French 75s they heard the difference between the primal "they" and the refined "us."[10] Sometimes they forgot themselves. When they evoked the enemy's mechanical ways and industrial might they did not stop to reflect how oddly this sat with the German tribal motif. Nor did they ponder the lineage of so many of their countrymen, descendants of the self-same Franks and others whose hereditary habits they saw at work from the Hohenzollerns on down to each *Feldgrau* outside the walls of Verdun.

They did not need to. Echoes of such pronouncements came from the least warlike and the most thoughtful of listeners. Reading the news from Verdun in May 1916 and listening to renewed tales of atrocities from Belgian refugees, a Canadian relief worker in Paris regurgitated the litany of national determinisms. She despaired of any decent future for this unredeemable race of brutes. As for Teutonic savagery, so for Teutonic method. In October the same year André Gide, who had little to say in his journal about the enemy, recycled the myth of German machine-like efficiency into a gentle reflection—that the Germans at war were demonstrating the axiom of Maurras that no virtue could succeed without method.[11]

The men in uniform absorbed the ambient certitudes and the contradictory stereotypes as well. On leave they sat among the audiences in the theaters and music halls, and at the front they read the same mass dailies as their civilian compatriots. Many would already have taken in the ample condemnations of the other across the Rhine in the years before the war, in histories that damned and caricatures that ridiculed. They had no need for newly apposite stereotypes; they could draw on an existing repertoire. A Jesuit priest at Verdun fell back on the images of peacetime: "I see before me the face[s] of officers popularized by the caricatures of Zislin and Hansi and can hardly contain myself. . . ."[12]

The prewar motifs of savagery and efficiency, no more easily compatible now than they were then, crept into soldierly locutions at all levels. The high command was careful not to deride the enemy's military prowess, even as it denied him any ethical conscience or civilized restraint. Pétain tended to allude neutrally to "German military strength," disdaining more emotive epithets. Joffre found the enemy capable of any transgression, even of hypnotizing a captured French intelligence officer.

The images clashed. In the comparative calm two years before the Germans attacked, a captain in the Verdun sector praised the order, even the courage, of the same "evil race," the "rabble and company," that his men derided. From the same sector, the ethnographer Robert Hertz was exchanging letters that autumn with his wife about German machines of war and their worship of the *Kolossal*, their spirit of organization so suited to the requirements of mass production; but he also wrote of them as a pestilential horde, driven by a "savage dream." Eighteen months later, during the battle, an airman saw the barbarian at work in the craters he left on the ground, in the bombs he dropped from the air before turning tail—"a real Parthian tactic," he found, alluding to the ancient warriors— foes of the Romans—supposed to have shot their arrows while retreating. "And they were barbarians too," he added. And yet he deeply admired the downed yet intact aircraft he examined. He envied the motor, the fuselage, the luxurious leather interior, the prodigious machine guns with their 500-cartridge belts. Could barbarians produce such technological marvels and remain barbarians?[13]

A providential epithet lay at hand to reconcile the irreconcilables: the Germans were militarists, a "race of predators," to quote the preface to a book about the Vosges front that yet went on to extol the neatness of their trenches and the perfection of their cemeteries. "Heavy and methodical brutes," the ethnographer had called them in October 1914, when he learned of the shelling of the cathedral in Reims. He was killed in April, in the fields of Woëvre.

Around the same sector, during the battle of Verdun the following year, the same idea appeared in journals and notebooks. The great genius of the German people, an infantryman reflected just before they attacked, was militarism, their *force colossale*. This was the same Germany that had started the war, in the eyes of the literary historian Daniel Mornet; the same whose atrocities, for a captain with legal training, only embodied the lawless military doctrines of the Prussian general and military theorist, Friedrich von Bernhardi; the same whose ways of war, a Capuchin monk in uniform wrote, sprang not from the Gospel but from Nietzsche, "the philosopher of hatred and bloated pride."[14]

A literary historian, a jurist, or a monk had the intellectual means to dignify their animosities, however cavalierly they invoked earlier authorities. But half-learned stereotypes still attached themselves to less literate recriminations, fixing on the invader and on what was most German about him.

The spectacle of abandoned fields and flaming villages around Verdun could inspire anger in the most docile of French souls. They knew that was why they were fighting, an officer wrote of his men in 1915, even before the worst began; and their initial indignation, he thought, quickly turned to scorn, as though for mad dogs. The following year men on the way to Verdun drove or walked through the ruined valleys of the Ornain and the Aire, wrote home of the "Boche swine" who had devastated the land, and vowed vengeance. All the more so, as the intuitions of officers suggested and the curiosities of postal censors confirmed, if they had left families behind in the occupied regions of the northeast. Whole regiments could consist of such militarized refugees, who wrote of vengeance in the heart.

And if the aggrieved recruit putting pen to paper had been wounded, or subjected to shell fire or some other assault on his senses, his thirst for retribution could be stronger still: "for this," one of them wrote, twice wounded in three days at Verdun, "they will have to pay." In one way or another, the "bastards," "Fritz," "barbarians," and "good-for-nothings," had torn them from their families, laid waste their land, and tormented them in their trenches. The provocations sufficed unto themselves. Oddly enough, the rare whiff of success could induce the same unbridled Germanophobia, expressed in the tired epithets of a spent lexicon— barbarians, carrion, swine, dirty Boches—as though detestation fed on even temporary victories.[15]

Often the spirit of vengeance demanded more substantial ideology or imagery to brand an enemy whose presence was more felt than seen. In the spring of 1915 a corporal entered a village in Artois recently evacuated by the Germans. It stood intact. But the thought of them drunk with triumph in its streets now rankled. Later, as a sergeant at Verdun, he read through the interrogations and letters of hapless prisoners with vindictive joy, as though to slake the thirst first aroused in Artois. At Christmas 1915 a chaplain passed through Haucourt-Malancourt, north of Verdun and once a thriving industrial town, now a field of rubble. From its ruined church a great crucifix rose, like some witness, he thought, to the crimes of *Kultur*. Another chaplain at Verdun employed the same idea, but more to express the contrast between French *bravoure* and the German way of war. It suggested, in some way, the primitive and the crude, and expressed outrage in the language of national difference.[16]

Resentment of the tedium of positional and attritional war spoke in the same idiom. The foe was mechanical as well as hereditary, and as an artillery officer watched the ascending columns of smoke and earth merge into a cloud and drift toward his lines, and recalled how the Germans timed their attacks to coincide with wind direction, he discerned the modern face of a primeval menace: "This method, this minute organization in their massacres! What an appalling race!" He as well had unwittingly married the two most prevalent stereotypes at hand.[17]

Pushed to its logical extremes, cultural determinism could bring despair. A sense of helplessness attended the conviction that the adversary's superiority was ingrained, a gift at birth rather than a transient advantage. During the deluge of shells in February, with his compatriots unable to react in kind, a French ambulance driver imagined the German artillerists, calm, methodical, comfortable, as precise as automatons, and he predicted gloomily that the French would suffer the same fate as the Russians and the Serbs. Even poison gas somehow emanated from the mists of Teutonic antiquity. A cavalry lieutenant, already out of his element in the war of materiel, insisted that the French could never use gas the way the Germans did; at best they could only imitate an enemy who would always outdo them. "It's in their nature and forms so to speak their goal in life— dominate, crush, be *über alles* by any means, even the most ignoble ones." And it was true that the Germans had consistently kept a step ahead of the French, and all their other enemies, in this particular arms race. But the possibility that they might have their chemical industry to thank, rather than some sinister side of *Deutschtum*, seemed not to arise.[18]

Rumor could complete the task that more immediate sensory perceptions had begun. From occupied Lille and Roubaix, in August, came word of more crimes, of women and children—all of them—taken away, bringing renewed threats of vengeance from letter writers in the trenches of Verdun. From Vienna, in November 1916, came word of the death of the Austrian Emperor Franz-Joseph I, greeted mostly with indifference but also with regret that all the "austro boches" had not accompanied the aged emperor into the hereafter.

With the coming of the third winter of the war came murmurs of despair and calls for ethno-racial annihilation. *Race*, in the minds of all but a very few specialists of the day, had no very precise meaning that set it apart from nation or people or ethnos, and when French soldiers affixed the badge of infamy to their enemy they attributed his crimes to his origins, define them how they might. They took up the typology their age had handed them, and condemned the identity of the German even more than his actions: "accursed race, we should exterminate it."[19]

Yet the recurrent stereotypes, so compelling and so serviceable, could prove unstable, even dispensable. Thoughtful men might question them as soon as the evidence of their senses undermined them. The enemy was not always callous or ferocious, and the spectacle of his humanity could soften the hardened and the hostile. The same sad spectacle of German prisoners that could elicit a "dirty race!" from a sergeant might tempt others to jettison the mental baggage they had brought to the front and to Verdun. He would pity the German prisoners, miserable as they were, a French soldier wrote, if only they were not German. He had resisted the humane temptation.

Others succumbed. Yes, the Germans were disciplined, methodical, and taciturn, in the eyes of a Territorial lieutenant observing them in a camp in Souilly; but were they the race he had read about in Arthur de Gobineau's *Essay on the Inequality of the Human Races*, one of the founding texts of racial demography, their height and blond hair and blue eyes bespeaking their original superiority? He thought not—they differed physically among themselves, and the modern city had subverted ethnic differences as thoroughly in Prussia as anywhere else. "Might there, by chance, not be a German race? We might think so," he concluded, and undermined an essential ingredient of the pervasive construct.[20]

At times German collective behavior seemed distinctly unwarlike. Striking, a captain in the sector had already reflected in December 1914, how *les Boches* had for some time seemed to want to leave the French alone and expected the same of them. A month later, in the same sector, another officer wondered why the Germans whom he had earlier recognized as courageous and able warriors showed such little combative ardor. Perhaps they were unwilling Polish subjects, he surmised, as if to salvage the aggressive identity of the German from such aberrant behavior. Occasional declarations of affinity or even kinship with the enemy went further and affirmed a common humanity seemingly at odds with his demonic attributes. "They're men like us," an officer overheard the men say, in one way or another. And these men were not newcomers: they were chatting outside a barn, at rest after a stint in the front lines. Robert Hertz, the ethnographer, overheard the men saying much the same: "The Boches are like us. They'd rather be home."[21]

Respect in battle could and did escort the human compassion that might stir during more tranquil moments and months. Cut off in Fort Vaux on June 1, his men threatened by thirst within and the enemy without, Commandant Sylvain-Eugène Raynal yet found the words to esteem "le Boche" as a formidable soldier. The enemy's mania for method, so often the object of loathing, could command professional admiration as well, the "quelle méthode!" of a captain and former history teacher as the Germans began digging trenches and sending in reinforcements as soon as they took a position. Self-deprecatory asides might follow. The same officer, when he marveled at the science and precision of the enemy's artillery, also deplored the inertia of his own. Or pride by association surfaced, evident in the words of another captain: "a soldier like ours . . . is the best in the world, along with the Boche." Far from assimilating the enemy to the barbarian, such tributes recognized a peer, even a nonpareil.[22]

An unofficial enemy vied with the official one. Occasionally French soldiers at Verdun rejected the German depicted in the national newspapers. When they published the high command's communiqués about the German disregard for the lives of their men, a captain scoffed, for he knew better, and when they ridiculed the enemy a lieutenant protested. Their abusive depictions would only diminish the French victory. The journalists were "idiots," he thought. And when the papers asserted confidently that the Germans were demoralized or malnourished, some of the men only grumbled that they were, too. At Verdun and elsewhere, they did not always oblige by seeing the enemy as officialdom and its mouthpieces wished them to. Or as the music-hall performers rendered him: they did not readily sing the songwriter Botrel's bloodthirsty anthems performed for music-hall audiences at home, his ode to the bayonet in "Rosalie," a song that lovingly depicted its lacerations of the German, or to the machine gun in "Ma mitrailleuse," that turned the newly popular weapon into an ever-faithful spouse or mistress—"ma petite Mimi." Bloodthirsty and xenophobic songs did not often catch on among the men only meters away from the German. "May they suffer from hunger," the great actress and chanteuse Sarah Bernhardt sang, "redouble for them the pain we've suffered/strike them Lord with an untiring hand/until the day when for the deliverance of humanity/your just vengeance in its pure equity will abolish their race forever."

Soldiers were skeptical, one of the singers who toured the front recalled, and quick to suspect brain-washing. Conscious perhaps of their heterodoxy, men given to indulgent utterances took care not to commit them to letters that military censors might open. Their words survived in conversations overheard and remembered, in journals kept, in memoirs written; but not in the extensive records kept by the postal censors of the Second Army. The writers may have all supposed that their correspondents at home had no use for such thoughts from them, their defenders at the front. Whatever their apprehensions, expressions of compassion or respect for the enemy carried a mildly *risqué* dimension. They surfaced discretely nonetheless.[23]

They did not, however, surface in any predictable way. From the evidence, neither class nor ideology nor rank defined dispositions towards the enemy; no social or intellectual barrier separated the virulent from the benign or the belligerent from the pacific. Anyone might express hostility one day and indulgence the next, and in fact many did: the dividing line ran not between but within the men. Treated as political theory, Hertz's ruminations on the Germans are a salad of contradictions, mixing cultural slurs with dispassionate analysis, but as reflections of states of mind they are entirely coherent, damning the race one minute and hoping for reconciliation with it the next. Lieutenant Péricard prayed en route to Verdun that he might hate the Germans ever more, but 15 years later remembered the prisoners he saw heading from the front as identical in aspect to the French—emaciated, caked in mud, staring vacantly, and asked, "how can we hate beings so akin to ourselves in their suffering?"

Perhaps time had worked its magic on Péricard: between the bigot and the humanitarian 15 years had elapsed. But efforts at reconciling such conflicting views at the time only revealed their stubborn coexistence. Hertz compared the quiet days of 1915 in the Meuse to life in the barracks or on maneuvers, and he absorbed the ambient indifference to the enemy until he fixed his gaze on the distant German mills of Longwy, smoking away and jolting him from his torpor. When Commandant Raynal finally surrendered Fort Vaux after amply exceeding the limits of normal human endurance, he labored mentally to attribute his captors' civilities to a subterfuge or a pretense, admire them how he might. The mercurial humors of enmity fluctuated too uncertainly for any single profile of the German to dominate.[24]

German views of the French, unsurprisingly, proved just as alterable, if not as intense. The German newspapers depicted a less menacing enemy than their French counterparts; a conviction of their natural superiority almost required it. The French were weak: their plight was desperate, their government torn, their English ally perfidious, however adroitly their leaders might deceive them. The French were sordid: in the Bois d'Haumont a reporter for the *Frankfurter Zeitung* found the captured French lines dirty and disorderly, strewn about with weapons, grenades, empty tins, shell casings, blue greatcoats, and letters. Such a contrast to the immaculate German trenches! The French were emotional: they despised the Germans immoderately, thought of them in the light of the lies of a hysterical press as barbarians, and hankered obsessively for revenge in the long wake of 1871. The Germans were calmer, better educated, possessed of a deeper and less capricious temperament. One week into the battle *Münchner neueste Nachrichten* reminded its readers that Germany was superior to all its foes in every way. If the French would not recognize the dictates of German reason they would absorb them through the language of the cannon.[25]

Much of this was merely the mirror-image of the stereotypes the French had devised of them. If they, the Germans, were militarists, then the French were poor soldiers, even cowards. In April 1916 the war correspondent of the *Frankfurter Zeitung* baldly explained that in close-quarter trench combat the French would rather surrender than fight. If they, the Germans, were machines, human automatons, then the French were impulsive, the antithesis of method. The French were inferior, the unstated condition of their own superiority.[26]

Yet on occasion they spoke highly of the French as well. Their military commentators acknowledged the newfound quality of French arms—superior, one of them thought, to those of their forefathers in 1870—and even wondered now and again why the two adversaries should needlessly spill such amounts of each other's blood. Less than three weeks after the attack on Verdun, the social democratic newspaper *Vorwärts*, for one, paid tribute to the *Opfermut*, the will to sacrifice, of their enemy.

The Germans were at war on several major fronts against several major adversaries, and their newspapers displayed little of the single-minded, undiluted odium of their French counterparts. If anything they regarded England as the truly mortal enemy, one that instead of coveting some lost province conspired to eliminate Germany's global presence and quite possibly the Reich itself. France, by contrast, was only a second-rate power.[27]

Falkenhayn, for one, did not despise the French. The archenemy, in any case, was England. But he underestimated them, as did many others in the high command, repeatedly. The French had surprised them on the Marne in 1914, and on the Meuse in 1916, and again on the Somme in the summer of the same year, when few thought them capable of mounting yet another major offensive. Two weeks into the Battle of Verdun, the Prussian Minister of war, Hohenborn, thought the offensive a simple matter of softening up the French so that England might fall. A few weeks earlier Karl von Einem, in command of the adjacent Third Army to the

north, had thought the French incapable even of mounting counterattacks. These too were mirror-judgments, for the French high command
in general and Pétain in particular had never committed the same error—
that of underestimating their adversary.[28]

Among the troops of the Fifth German Army at Verdun hatred of the
French could blossom without the helping hand of chauvinism. A compelling urge to avenge a wound, a fallen comrade, or a stretcher bearer or
medic under fire could arise as easily as among the French of the Second
Army, even in the absence of the added outrage of a country invaded or
a province occupied. "Hatred," a young soldier from Hamburg told an
officer who remembered it in his memoirs, "comes entirely on its own
among men who see that their comrades are dying."[29]

Nonetheless, prejudice dignified rancor. Officers and men alike
expressed a self-serving disdain for the French trenches they entered, as
though to indulge the cultural priggishness that newspapers occasionally
dispensed to their compatriots at home. "A museum of the French
soldier's mentality," a captain in the Prussian grenadiers called the dugout
he and his men were trying to clean up in the Hermitage Woods a few
days into the attack in February. For 18 months the occupants had buried
their rubbish to soften the soil on which they slept, and now their successors disinterred the silted up residues—old chicken bones, cigarette
boxes, canned foods, old newspapers and correspondence, the tatters of
decayed clothes, contraceptives stuck to pornographic postcards. That
night the captain and his battalion slept on cold, hard ground. When, as
in February, the French departed in haste, the German newcomers might
delight in the morsels they found left behind, in the white bread, chocolates, tuna, and wine; but not in the disorder.[30]

Yet words of respect tempered such condescension, echoing the
measured magnanimity of the civilian press. These, too, issued from military authorities at all levels. In October 1914, praise from General Karl
von Bülow, who had commanded the Second Army during the battles
of the frontiers and the Battle of the Marne, reached the ears of a French
infantryman who would later find himself at Verdun. The French were
gallant, Bülow was reported to have told a German newspaper, too gallant;
they had the best artillery in the world, and if their infantry could only
learn to hide and deceive, to elude the enemy's view, they might well win.
In January 1916, just before the offensive at Verdun, some German officers

captured the previous month during the French attack at Hartmanswiller-skopf, a small peak in the Vosges mountains, told their interrogators that everyone recognized the new strengths of the French army in positional warfare. Previous prisoners had said much the same. And these officers added that they did not blame France for the war. England had inveigled her into it, they explained, and spoke, to their captors' astonishment, of the "pitié" they felt for France. Even during endless Verdun they let slip expressions of grudging respect or even complaisance for their French enemies. "I like the French as much as the Prussians," a Bavarian wrote home from the battle in May, reflecting perhaps with some hyperbole the regional animosities of another Bavarian, a civilian in Munich, who wrote to her correspondent in the Fifth Army at Verdun the same month inveighing not against the French but against the Prussians in Berlin, the instigators, she thought, of the entire war.

Mostly, if the Germans at Verdun spoke of the French as a people at all, it was of their "monstrously stubborn" resistance. The infantry feared the omnipresence of their artillery fire on the ground, and the pilots envied the superiority of their Nieuports over their own Fokkers in the air, in exclamations whose hint of desperation carried little of the patronizing or disdainful tone reserved for a declining power.[31]

In the last analysis, on both sides, hatred of the enemy required no educated understanding of his ways or his wiles; it sprang from the existential threat to self and to kith and kin posed by his presence. Reciprocal threat defined the predicament of both armies at Verdun, and most of the men there had little more experience of the other side than that. Even the learned might jettison their learning. It seemed childish, Hertz wrote his wife three weeks before he was killed on the Meuse, to ask about the why and the wherefore: "[The Germans] are the enemy who wishes death upon our women, our children, our fatherland." And men who knew nothing of the enemy, who had spent their lives across the sea, might now react to them as violently as Frenchmen who had grown up under their shadow. In May, in the woods of Nixéville, a corporal admired some Algerians and Moroccans at rest in the woods. Fine and solid soldiers, he reflected, whose hatred of the enemy was perhaps even more intense than his own. In October an African work crew came upon four German prisoners at the Caserne Marceau in Verdun and began threatening them with knives. Only with the greatest difficulty did a stretcher-bearer explain that the prisoners were helping recover the French wounded. The Africans were not convinced. It was the same behavior that an educated lieutenant had noticed among the *tirailleurs sénégalais* in Champagne the previous autumn, so intense that it had to be restrained—the manifestation, he thought, of a primal aggression that only civilization and religion could contain. The Africans had done less than his French compatriots to start this war. What could drive their animosity, if not the situation?[32]

Such hostility, the consequence rather than the cause of enmity, was intrinsic to war itself. And this war that swept up whole populations of able-bodied males and forced them to fight and cohabit with their enemies for long months and years without moving—this war bred other, more transient sentiments as well. They ranged from commiseration to genocidal fury, according to season and circumstance and the passions of the moment, and according to whether the belligerents saw each other as human or inhuman. This too was not new; comradely respect had often accompanied the sordid side of war, and chivalry and atrocity had once made inseparable bedfellows. But the longer this war went on, and the more voracious its consumption and indiscriminate its destruction, the more officialdom tried to implant an impersonal, demonic construct of the enemy in the minds of soldiers and subjects. The war required such rationales, deforming and affixing a single national trait to the face of the other. "They made us detest Germany," a veteran of the battle recalled, 60 years later.

Propaganda nevertheless could not trump experience. Apart from a few "mystics," Pierre Mac Orlan later recalled, few succumbed to Germanophobia. The French surrendered easily, the *Frankfurter Zeitung* had assured its readers; but the regimental diary of the 5th Jäger Battalion recorded its men's respect for an enemy "which . . . did everything to avoid captivity." And the veteran Paul Ettighoffer, for his part, denied that the "whipped up" press had corrupted him or his fellows in any way. The longer this war, the more threatening became talk that humanized the official enemy and absolved him, even momentarily, of guilt for all the privation and suffering he had caused.[33]

Whether the men hated the enemy, respected the soldier, or commiserated with the human being on the other side of no man's land mattered greatly to political, military, and even cultural authorities. The challenge, for them, lay in meddling with the mix, and encouraging the first at the expense of the other two, because the deeds as well as the words of the men at Verdun stubbornly displayed all three.

Ordered to sit out French artillery fire in the ruins of Fleury, a German lieutenant overcame his sense of isolation by turning his mind onto the enemy. If they all could only break out and go for the enemy's throat—he could scarcely wait for the providential moment to come.[34]

Hours of bombardment, a French battalion commander at Verdun recalled soon after being taken prisoner, could leave men's nerves so disordered that the élan of an assault, a departure from the trench at last, might come as a relief: "It's almost a relief when at last, mad with exasperation, we can leave the trench to fly ahead, to kill!"[35]

The approaching prospect of killing the enemy could promise release to men trapped by him in a passive hell. Others might delight in the act or the spectacle itself, sometimes with a guilty conscience, sometimes not. "What pleasure we took in watching the Boches fall as they advanced in serried columns," one of them wrote home in March, after enduring three weeks of ceaseless shelling. Sanguinary elation could rise in them after impulsive acts of violence, and even mobilized men of the cloth learned to cope with it. In August, a seminarian who had killed a German soldier shoveling away beyond the trench in Artois anguished over the fierce and unknown joy that had come over him. But at Verdun in April, under a fierce bombardment on Côte 304, his satisfaction left him untroubled: "I myself am happy to have come here. I had wanted it for a long time. Have killed or wounded three Boches Saturday, at 150 meters." His fellow clergymen had marveled too at their ability to overcome the same scruples. One Capuchin threw more grenades and fired more mortars at Les Eparges in November than anyone else, and was even amused to stay awake at night by tossing grenades at the silhouettes of spiked helmets. "I don't recognize myself anymore," he acknowledged. "You kill a man like a dog and, far from worrying over it, you laugh to your heart's content. Frightening, how each of us hides something of Cain within!"[36]

The line between real and imagined threat, and between killing by necessity and killing by choice, might easily vanish, as in all military combat, in a fog of reflexive fear. At a fork in the road below the Bois des Caures at the end of February a German gunner found assorted corpses. Most were French. They lay face down, facing south, as though cut down while fleeing out of the woods.[37] And surrender, always risky in war, was no safer than flight. The enemy might think it a ruse or a dangerous distraction from the killing at hand. When two Germans jumped unarmed into a French trench on le Mort-Homme during the intense fighting there in May, they were taken prisoner. Their fellows who followed were not as lucky. They fell to the mood or the nerves of their French adversaries, as a chasseur on the scene put it. "As for me," he added, "I've always started from the premise that in war you have above all to put men out of action." Others were more forthright. When they tried to retake Fort Douaumont in May, a battalion commander recalled, they killed the defenders whether they were resisting or not: "Sometimes taking prisoners takes too long. You see red. It's normal . . . it has to be that way." He composed the words, ironically enough, in the tranquility of a German prisoner of war camp after he and his men, cut off and encircled, had themselves surrendered.

In the proverbial fog of war it was not always obvious whether groups trying to surrender were as unarmed as they pretended. In September an artillery maintenance man watched as droves of Germans came down the hillside towards the French lines, unarmed, only to come under fire at once. They lay down and took cover, but when one of their number tried again that night to give himself up and bring his war to an end, the reception was no warmer. Rifle shots greeted him. The situation did not lend itself to trust.[38]

Often hostilities could not desist long enough for the adversaries to collect their wounded, as they still had during the Franco-Prussian war. A German surgeon operating in the casemates of Douaumont recalled the men bearing a Red Cross flag at the head of a convoy of stretcher-bearers only redoubling the enemy's fire. Seen from the other side, restraint required reciprocity, and medical truces could last only as long as the enemy's good faith. From time to time, the artillery mechanic noted, French and Germans allowed medical personnel waving the Red Cross to traverse the terrain unmolested by man or bullet; but the fragile armistice never held for long.

The war had started that way. In the autumn of 1914 a captain of dragoons, who later commanded an infantry battalion on the Côte 304, bade farewell to the protocol of the past. Near Brinvillers they took three Germans prisoner—orderlies waving the Red Cross and searching for their wounded: "No parleys are possible. . . . Sad that in the 20th century war should foster such mercilessly hard habits." And the same chronic suspicion, the same visions of subterfuge and deceit, greeted medics. "Do the Boche[s] fire on ambulances?" an American driver was asked at Verdun in August 1917. "Certainly!" he answered. On his way to the trenches on the Croupe d'Haudromont, a mobilized priest gazed with contempt upon the corpse of a German stretcher-bearer, whom he saw as an impostor because of the rifle by his side and the revolver in his pocket. Twenty-five thousand other French priests had been called up in this war, and only a fraction served as chaplains. Now priests bore arms, medics aroused suspicion, and even the dead incurred malevolence.[39]

How many sought, and how many found, the satisfactions of physical combat and close-quarter killing—the province of bayonets, knives, and revolvers? Or, perhaps more frequently in German hands, clubs, rifle butts, and sharpened shovels? Killing on the ground at medium or long range was the rule in this war, more so than in the next. Perhaps for that reason, the Western Front between 1914 and 1918 has proved infertile soil for historians and social scientists searching for the experience of close-quarter killing in war—in spite of all the dying that went on. In the French army wounds from shell, shrapnel, or grenade fragments peaked during the static years of positional battle—75 percent of all wounds, compared to 58 percent in the renewed war of movement in 1918; bullet wounds accounted for 12 percent, and "other" weapons, which would include poison gas as well as knives and bayonets, for eight. Bayonets, instruments that killed more than they wounded, might not show up in such statistics, and when killing occurred at close quarters their utility might rise. Nonetheless the positional war remained an artillery war above all, and Verdun, by its topography and its length, was the positional battle to end all positional battles.[40]

But patrols went out at night, and trenches were taken and defended and retaken and defended again, with any arms at hand. Few recorded such encounters, and when they did withheld any recollections of battle intoxication. More often they expressed revulsion. War had ceased to be a contact sport. "An awful hand-to-hand struggle" was the term used by an infantryman to describe what happened when they overran a German trench. It came down to shovels and in his case a revolver at point-blank range. "The first Boche I killed at point-blank range," he noted, implying that it was not the last one. Two weeks before he had been assigned to a

20-man unit of "moppers-up," supposed to follow the assault wave and while it moved on eliminate the last traces of resistance. They were given daggers, revolvers, rifles, and clusters of grenades, together with the simple instruction: "no mercy."[41]

Perhaps the silence about such encounters, especially if they involved knives or bayonets but firearms at point-blank range as well, signified repression, dissimulation, and guilt. Maurice Genevoix, who later devoted himself to the memory of Verdun, also struggled with his own. In 1914, in the sector, he shot four Germans with his revolver in the back or in the head, as they retreated during the night. He included the episode in his published memoir in 1916, omitted it in 1925, restored it in 1949, this time with three German victims, and then again in 1961 but with two Germans possibly rather than three, because he had hardly seen them—until, interviewed on television in 1977, he expressed with some anguish the forlorn hope that he had not killed them. However fogged his memory became over time, the episode, he wrote, had left an indelible emotional imprint on him.[42]

Habits of conscience might yield guilt-ridden narratives of face-to-face killings or better yet suppress them altogether, but the official culture did little to encourage such pieties, striving instead to stamp out the quality of mercy from the field. Genevoix first excised his episode for the record not during the war, in 1916, but later, in the 1920s. The question is whether so many could have conspired to silence their acts in this war, when so few had in earlier ones.

More plausibly, face-to-face killing with bayonets or firearms or more primitive instruments left fewer traces in recollections after the battle because it happened less often during it. Intimate killing had so marked Genevoix because it happened so rarely: on only two occasions in the entire war, he wrote, had he sensed the physical presence of the men he fired on. In May 1916 an artillery lieutenant doubted reports that the *poilus* atop Côte 304 had repulsed German attackers with the blades of their bayonets; every infantryman he had talked to denied that bayonets were ever used. The same month in a long and frank critique of the high command's understanding of conditions at Verdun, a major noted how reluctant men were to advance from trench to trench "up until the moment of the bayonet." He used the term almost idiomatically, never denying its connotation but never employing it literally. It had become a metaphor for fighting at close quarters, whatever the weapon and whatever the frequency, but without any intimation of glory. Ordeals with knives, bayonets, and rifle butts no longer yielded narratives of valor and dexterous handling, unlike earlier contests with the same weapons or more distant *gestes* with swords, lances, or battle axes. By Verdun war had shed most of the vestigial trappings of close-quarter killing.[43]

By contrast, killing at mid-range with rifles, machine guns, and grenades left a more robust corpus of reminiscences. A visible but indistinct enemy, one whose collective presence presented a target but whose individual features remained obscure, became less personal as well as less proximate. Machine gunners fired into groups of attackers perhaps 150 feet away on le Mort-Homme, or onto distant figures building siege trenches as far as 2500 yards from the ruined cupolas of Fort Vaux, at the extreme limit of their range, or into the woods at night, or onto a makeshift enemy position from the casemates of Fort Douaumont.[44] But they never fired at a human face. And men coming under machine-gun fire rarely saw the gunners either—they were too distant, or too well hidden in craters, earthworks, or ruined basements.

Grenades and flamethrowers, the weapons that made one German observer on the scene discern a return to the warfare of the Renaissance, full of new projectiles, were no more discriminating in their human targets. Like machine guns, they were meant to decimate groups at a distance. Grenades, much more versatile and less vulnerable than flamethrowers, were fast becoming the weapon of choice in some situations, highly effective against a dispersed or sheltered foe, just out of reach. They killed by fragmentation, flamethrowers by incineration, and sometimes the two complemented each other: the Germans threw grenades and flames through the woods north of Verdun in February as they approached the French machine-gun nests and blockhouses, and sent both through apertures on the superstructure of Fort Vaux as they stormed it in June. "Cowardly weapon," one of their French adversaries called the flamethrower, but the idea dated to antiquity, and the French, like their British allies, adopted it as quickly as they had poison gas.[45]

At long range, when the enemy, now completely depersonalized, was visible through binoculars or not at all, killing became anodyne and routine. This variety, more lethal as well as more voracious than short- or medium-range killing, now dominated the battlefield—its instrument, artillery, was taking more and more lives and demanding more and more men. Most of them never saw the enemy. Nestled miles behind the front lines, hidden from ground view and camouflaged from the air, the artillerists relied on intelligence from their observers on the ground and in the air to pinpoint their target and calibrate their fire. They divined their enemy's whereabouts from his rockets and the angles between his artillery flashes, and above all from aerial reconnaissance, sometimes now transmitted by radio in real time. In each battery, into each piece, a *chargeur* loaded a shell, a *pointeur* turned horizontal and vertical directional wheels, a *tireur* closed the *culasse*, pulled a *cordon tire-feu* on command; the barrel recoiled violently and returned; and almost at once the sequence resumed, with shells brought by night from depots farther back and carried on foot to the gun crews.

With batteries firing simultaneously, the valley shook; but the impact on the enemy could only be imagined. A second lieutenant, killed in the Bois Fumin in June, had watched in Belgium in August 1914 as 75 mm field guns began firing onto Germans as they left their trenches. From afar they resembled ants that suddenly scattered, their formations dissolving as they ran this way and that, victims of the punctual projectiles. The distant gunners obeyed no sudden animus then nor suffered the pangs of conscience later, the same that many years afterwards afflicted some men who had killed at close quarters.[46]

"We see dying far more frequently than killing," Norton Cru wrote. "I've seen many comrades die and am certain never to have seen a man kill." Others might have, he explained, but they would have to acknowledge how rarely. Perhaps he exaggerated; but Genevoix, who had retrieved with such struggle his own memory of the kind, tended to agree. He declared that in this war one killed, mostly, without seeing one's victim. In combat, ironically enough, emotion was secondary, even superfluous; it thrived more as a luxury of peaceful moments, when men might absorb the ambient animosities and identify the culprit, the reason for their circumstances. "We could not do otherwise"—confessions of unwilled and increasingly mechanistic behavior made their way into print, to be picked up and repeated by commentators decades later in one form or another: they did not need to hate in order to kill.[47]

How many deliberately avoided killing, shrank from violent combat in the obscurity of a crater or shell-hole, is unknowable. The failure to fire that so shocked American military specialists after the Second World War that they drastically revised their training methods, and that left unmistakable traces of its presence in earlier wars, was hardly unknown in this one. But few talked about it, at Verdun or anywhere else. Priests and chaplains might wonder whether their calling allowed them to kill, and others might recoil at what war had made of them—"they gave us grenades to lacerate, daggers to cut throats. . . . Germania, Germania, what have you made of us!"—but evasive behavior, firing over the heads of the enemy or not firing at all, left few traces. They lacked the freedom at close range and the inclination at long range to decline acts of war; only at medium range did the possibility present itself, and then only in solitude.[48]

Acts of homage or contrition tempered the killing on both sides. When the Germans buried Colonel Driant with due deference on the edge of the Bois des Caures or handed Commandant Raynal an officer's saber after taking him prisoner in Fort Vaux, they displayed an imminently obsolete and pre-modern decorum. In February, near the spot where they buried Driant, they removed what documentation they could find from French as well as German corpses, placed blankets over them, and buried them by fours in the hard, frozen earth; they removed their caps, said a silent Our Father, placed a makeshift cross over each mound, and hurried away before shells began falling again.[49]

Such acts might answer to religious as well as chivalric dictates, and might appear from the distance of time, like so many others, shot through with inconsistent and even contradictory visions of the enemy. Soldiers might kill only to bury with Christian humility, and rob a corpse only to return a letter, an object, a photograph to the man's family if they could. In March, in the Bois d'Haumont, a newly arrived French lieutenant felled a German sniper from his hideout in the trees. The body was that of a Hessian guards corporal, 22 years old like himself. Two letters from a younger sister told of a package sent to him on January 1 and of her prayers that God preserve him. Whether the lieutenant kept or returned these he did not say, but he held onto the helmet and the dagger and other "precious trophies," whether as amulets for his own protection or as merchandise for his own enrichment he did not say either. He and his men buried the young corporal, and planted a cross on the mound at their captain's insistence, but inscribed on it words addressed more to their enemy than to their deity: "The French respect the dead."

In this sequence of profanation and veneration the line between hostility and respect vanished. On the edge of the Avocourt woods in March, the infantryman who had killed his first German "at point-blank range" expressed no remorse; but he removed the dead man's cap and later sent it to his mother.[50]

Like deference to the enemy dead, fraternization with the enemy living alternated with acts of war; like close-quarter killing, it often dared not speak its name. The reason was different, however: the hierarchy vigorously discouraged it. Yet it had left traces at Verdun and all over the Western Front since 1914, during the many quiet moments when tacit truces held and barter and exchange and even conversation stirred furtively between the lines.

"Imagine that one of these days the generals found us breaking bread with the Boches!" In November 1914 Hertz, the ethnographer, thought that the words he had just overheard clashed oddly with what people were reading at home in the newspapers. A month later, at Christmas, a sergeant later killed at Verdun listened in Picardie as German mandolin players accompanied French soldiers singing "Minuit, Chrétiens." They had been shelling each other all day, and started again an hour later.

In January 1916, German officers, taken prisoner the month before at Hartmanswillerskopf in Alsace, divulged transgressions that can hardly have surprised their interrogators. In spite of all the threats and prohibitions, they said, intermittent rapports between French and Germans went on from trench to trench, when no officers were around. Ten days later fraternization had so vexed the German high command that it declared any attempt to leave the trenches without authorization tantamount to high treason.[51]

Such sociability among foes more typically graced the quiet sectors of the front, such as Verdun for most of 1915. But there, in the spring of 1916, General Gallwitz, in command of the German attack group on the left bank of the river, learned from French prisoners digging graves near Romagne that their fellows nearby were routinely exchanging notes and scraps of paper with their adversaries. A lowly machine-gunner confirmed it. In April, on the southern slopes of the Côte du Poivre, he and two or three others in his company swapped cigarettes and chocolates with the French soldiers, drank wine, showed photos, conversed as best as they could in inimical tongues: "Kapitalist kaput!" "The war great misfortune!"

"Du gut Kamerad." Their unwarlike exchanges, hardly incompatible with the hostilities that preceded and followed, contravened the orders but not the interests or the instincts of the men enjoying them; and they added another countenance that the enemy might manifest, more benign than the corpse's or the prisoner's or the combatant's that swelled at close quarters and shrank at a distance. They added the face of normalcy.[52]

In time, indulgence as well as vilification made their way into the films and novels that recalled Verdun. During the interwar years even the novelist Franz Schauwecker, a literary mouthpiece of the aggressiveness of National Socialism, wrote of his former adversaries as remarkable soldiers; Jules Romains, his pacifist French confrère, of the correct and even courteous German treatment of French prisoners.[53] The veterans of either side found ways to express kinship over enmity. The German lieutenant who had felt such a *rasende Wut*, such rage, at the "enemy" at Fleury now identified them as members of a different race but also as members of his family, the family of the front; the French *poilu* who had been made to "detest" Germany never called them "Boches" again—"I realized they loved their country as we loved ours."[54] Pierre Mac Orlan recollected a self-annihilating despair shared by French and Germans alike, a mentality that the place and the name evoked for him on each of his many returns there. Arnold Zweig declared bluntly in his pacifist novel of 1935 about Verdun that by 1916 French and Germans in the trenches had come to sympathize with each other, and that only at home, which began at the rear echelons, did handfuls of zealots strive to incite chauvinism. Periodically, the effusions returned: in Jacques Tardi's graphic novel of 2008, *1916*, the antimilitarist and deeply skeptical *poilu* denies any sentiments of hostility at all: "As for me, I can tell you I had no enemy in this whole business."[55]

In all such fanciful retellings, pacifist or chauvinistic, the nuances faded. Novels and films about Verdun rarely plumbed the subjective depths of men's perceptions of the enemy. Instead they presented an enemy in one dimension, congenial to popular imagining. Léon Poirier, the film director, went to some lengths to depict the Germans in *Verdun: Visions d'histoire* as machine-like; his German counterpart wasted little time in depicting the French as an amiable rabble.[56] They reappeared that way in the Nazi author Hans Zöberlein's autobiographical novel of 1931, as members of an alien breed, whose "lively, gesticulating, incessantly talkative bearing" instilled "no special respect for the enemy" among their German captors. "You cowardly hounds over there," he wrote in the chapter he devoted to the German attacks on Fleury, "know courage only when you can train a cannon on every infantryman! Come over here, if you have the guts."

In the same vein, the author and playwright Magnus Wehner, drawn like Zöberlein into the magnetic field of National Socialism, condemned the French colonial troops on racial grounds and the French on cultural ones—they were weak-willed, afraid of death, given to surrendering in droves.[57] In this way the crudest stereotypes enjoyed the longest lives. And historians fell into the trap: they took such constructions literally, made their purveyors into the architects of Verdun, and did not stop to ask who hated whom, and when, and for how long.[58]

For centuries men at arms killed without hating. In the middle decades of the eighteenth century the enemy might inspire the chivalric "tirez les premiers, Messieurs les Anglais ("take the first shot, good Englishmen")" of Maurice de Saxe at Fontenoy, or the sullen automatism of Frederick the Great's conscripts, or the ruthless professionalism of Hessian mercenaries. At Barbastro in 1837, during the Carlist civil war in Spain, Legionnaires on opposite sides greeted each other by Christian names, obeyed no personal or national animosities, yet bayoneted each other in the most bloody struggle one of their commanding officers had ever seen. British officers in the hedgerows of Normandy and the deserts of North Africa during the Second World War bore no ill will towards the enemy, certainly far less than they received from him, some of them claimed. And studies carried out among the American servicemen in both the European and Pacific theaters of the same war found that killing itself came low on the GI's priorities, well below survival. One even posited in a normative vein that "it is erroneous to consider that hatred of the enemy is necessary for a good fighting morale [...]."[59]

But for centuries men at arms had also discerned malignant aliens in the enemies they faced. The heretics of the sixteenth century, the counter-revolutionaries of the eighteenth, and the ethno-racial outcasts of the twentieth awakened in their persecutors a purifying zeal that strove not to defeat but to eradicate. To kill was not enough—the enemy was to disappear for all eternity, an aspiration made abundantly clear in the ritual annihilation of corpses, the killing of children, or the symbolic mutilations of reproductive organs. Such hate could rally.[60]

On the continuum from esteem to abhorrence, the enemy at Verdun floated uncertainly in the middle. Variously seen as the author and the victim of evil, the hereditary menace and the prisoner of circumstance, persecutor and fellow-sufferer, he provoked by his forced presence a mélange of resentments. Gallantry was out of the question. But so was genocide. The killing was unprecedented in scale but not in savagery. Men might utter imprecations about annihilation, yet no exterminating fury drove them. Killing the enemy sufficed. They took trophies, so plundered the bodies as to leave them without "a single button," as a sergeant commented in the Apremont forest in 1915, succumbed to a thirst for booty as old as war itself. However, they did not take body parts, a habit of some prehistoric hunter-gatherers, and some soldiers of the Second World War, and of countless other warriors in between.

When they recalled their impressions in combat at close quarters, the men often rendered a denationalized enemy, oddly bereft of the collective characteristics that they might in moments of rest have imputed to him. R. H. Tawney, the British historian, wrote of shooting Germans in their trench on the Somme on July 1, 1916, and a future German surgeon wrote of bayoneting a French soldier the year before, but neither depicted their victims in any hostile light, still less as heretical or alien beings. They were the enemy. "They did not know each other, they did not love each other, they did not hate each other—they were only soldiers, the enemies of each other," an interwar German study concluded; and it included Verdun.[61]

Among the sentiments that attended the fighting at Verdun and on the Western Front, hatred had too much company to reign supreme. In spite of an unprecedented ideological effort launched in 1914 to fix the animosities of millions for as long as the war might last, hatred, even at Verdun, cannot explain tenacity. Duty can. That duty sprang from within themselves, from allegiance rather than enmity and attachment rather than antipathy. It sprang from the group.

11

Circles of Loyalty

To MEN IN ISOLATION, the war was not only hell, it was a meaningless hell. It made sense only *en masse*—as a group manifestation—and their presence in the trenches and forts around Verdun marked not an act of individual will and still less an intellectual choice, but the conditioned behavior of social animals. Neither passion nor reason had much to do with it.

In fact, the word that observers then and later commonly used to describe the mentality of the uniformed millions was "resignation," meant to exclude chauvinism and pacifism alike and tacitly reconcile the men's acceptance of war with their aspiration to peace.

But the word could mean anything. To a career officer, a captain who knew the army well and who found himself in the Verdun sector in 1916 and 1917, it set the soldiers of the day apart. The troopers of 1914, trained, inspired, and naïve, still wearing the fatally conspicuous red leggings, had died at Sarrebourg and on the Marne and the Yser. Now came the half-trained conscripts called up in 1915 and 1916, called *bleuets* after their horizon blue uniforms, and Marie-Louises like Napoleon's late green novices of 1814 and 1815, named after his second wife, the Empress-regent who had called them into service while he was campaigning in Saxony. These ones, the captain thought, were more survivors than warriors; they had learned "moral resignation" during their long months in the trenches, and along with it fatalism, bitterness, and even cynicism of a sort, a thinly veiled contempt for discipline and hierarchy and militarist conceits.[1]

To an art historian at Verdun, plunged into his meditations when he was not in the lines, the word connoted faith rather than cynicism, a way to bear their miserable condition that drew repeatedly on Christian sentiment: "Faith, resignation. Believe, suffer without saying anything."[2]

To an ambulance driver, observing a company of machine-gunners arriving on the scene in the dark days of late February, it signified salutary fortitude. Forced to march all day, sleep on cold floors, and forgo their rations, they displayed sangfroid and a "profonde résignation" telling of inner calm, of firmness without sadness. Many in the company were Parisians, workers and shopkeepers from La Chapelle, Menilmontant, and the northern and northeastern faubourgs, men better known before the war for their spirit of revolt and their detestation of the bleak words that covered the barrack walls during military training: "In war you have to know how to suffer, obey, die."[3] Patriotism, in the eyes of the bemused driver, expressed itself as resignation.

A major, confiding his innermost thoughts to paper at the headquarters of the Second Army at Souilly, discerned apathy and fatalism in the "resigned bravery" of his men.[4] One day the postal censors used the term one way, to designate a mood equidistant from optimism and pessimism pervading the letters they read, and the next day another, to evoke a "lassitude" just short of despair: "The letters from the men who are either at Verdun or have left it all display the same weariness and horror . . . the only feeling is one of resignation." The Germans, they added, conveyed much the same impression.[5] After the war Paul Valéry, addressing Pétain, saw in the word a noble acceptance of the reality of modern war, and after him historians sometimes saw in the idea a form of stoic assent, as though the ancient philosophy advocating the transcendence of emotion had surfaced in the trenches of the early twentieth century—very nearly the opposite sense than many others had given to the "resignation" of the millions who served in them.[6]

The word's imprecision, like its vogue, betrays an aspiration to define the ties that held the men in place, as though some inner power commanded their compliance, if only a vocabulary could be found to describe it. Avoidance of duty often spoke loudly, refusal more loudly still; acceptance was mute. *Qui tacet consentire videtur*—silence is taken to imply consent—but this silence concealed an inner Babel of conflicts.

Then there were the words the men themselves used. They talked about the war—to each other, to their wives, to themselves. They talked about its length, and grasped at straws, at a rumor or a news item, to sustain the illusion that it might soon end. Surely the neutrals would now join the

Allies when word of the German flamethrowers at Verdun reached them, an artillery officer in June reflected, as though states made war to uphold chivalric protocols, and he looked hopefully at the Americans, indignant, so he had heard, at German submarine warfare.[7] In August the entry of Romania and the Italian declaration of war on Germany roused the men from their torpor and their fatalistic acceptance of another winter of war. Now toasts were raised to *la gloire des nations latines*, and cries of *vive l'Italie! vive la Roumanie!* rang out, in explosions of optimism that engulfed entire units and chased away the prospect, as the censors saw it, of serial desertions. An end to hostilities, the men wrote, was within sight, perhaps by November.[8] The Brussilov offensive in June in the Carpathians brought cries of *vive la Russie!* well into the summer, even as operations on the Somme bogged down and their English allies gave the men less and less to cheer about.[9]

Illusions expired. The failure to take Verdun dashed German hopes of an end to the war as quickly as the ephemeral vista of a swift and spectacular success had lifted them. And when Romanian military fortunes collapsed so did moods in the French Second Army. "I can't see any end to this dreadful plague," one of the men wrote to his parents in Le Havre, "and current events don't favor us . . . all this is not likely to shorten the war." In such moments the men lost all interest in the news. What point was there to reading it, when it brought so little to celebrate? A complete indifference to events had set in, a censor noted in August. No mention of the Somme, of Russia, of Italy—"we might think that not a single man reads a newspaper."[10]

What was the war all about, anyway? At the higher reaches of military and civil society the question made sense, and a surprising unanimity reigned untroubled, practically uniting the two adversaries. Both sides saw this as a war of survival. They could not but speak of Verdun, when they did, in the same transcendental idiom. "We were now engaged in a struggle in which the very existence of our nation, and not only military glory, or the conquest of territory, was at stake," Falkenhayn wrote shortly after the war. Pétain, who doubted his account of why he had attacked Verdun, nonetheless shared the same understanding of what had happened there—men had fought over plots of earth as though over national destinies.[11] Nivelle, after the failure to retake Fort Douaumont in May, reminded the men in an *ordre du jour* of "a struggle in which each people is staking its destiny."[12] In October 1916 General Castelnau spoke to British and American reporters at Chantilly and naturally linked the emerging outcome at Verdun to the meaning of the war: would the French become the slaves of the Teutons?[13] Intellectuals echoed the sentiment; Daniel Mornet, future literary historian of France and its ideas, insisted that they were living like animals at Verdun to preserve their race from bondage.[14] In the newspapers armchair generals echoed the oracular pronouncements of the men in charge. Colonel "X," in *Le Journal*, called Verdun "the trump card with which Germany played for its destiny."[15]

Perhaps the protagonists betrayed different national anxieties—the greatest military power in Europe feared for its world position in the coming century; the grandchildren of Sedan brooded over invasion and mortification. General Gallwitz, while at Verdun, fretted over the coming rise of Japan and the United States; Hohenborn, the Prussian Minister of War, over Germany's place in the sun.[16] Perhaps the more fanciful imagined a struggle between a cosmopolitan but superficial French "civilization" and a nation-bound but profound German "kultur," a climactic confrontation of the sort that a few thinkers had prophesied between the Enlightenment and Romanticism.

Few among the elites trying to expound upon Verdun ever said so very precisely. Verdun was perhaps the duel à mort, as *Le Journal* called it in March. The war correspondent of the *Frankfurter Zeitung* was writing the same week that at Verdun a closed and encircled Mitteleuropa met the open world of continents and seas, in a confrontation between the two warring faces of the "civilized world." Colonel "X" thought Verdun marked the encounter between Germanic mass and French heroism, between collective and individual courage. Uncertain constructs, springing from the same certitude: this was an existential battle in an existential war.[17]

How much of all this traveled to the front with the officers and the men and accompanied them into their trenches, shelters, and subterranean galleries? A battalion commander in the Prussian grenadiers reflected on his threatened countrymen as he watched French shells land on them in the forests of Romagne and Mangiennes, sending spinning columns of smoke and dust high into the sky. A great people, he thought, threatened by a suffocating grip, cried out in rage: "We're not dead yet!"[18] How much easier for his invaded counterparts to speak the language of the wronged!

The most missionary in spirit did not stop there, seeming to prefer the principle to the practice and the abstract to the concrete. It was right against might, they said, or justice against arrogance, or innocence against aggression. "Für Deutschland," the Prussian grenadier wrote to his people at home; "for civilization and right," one of the French *poilus* wrote to his.[19] Germany, in the letters of her defenders, constituted a self-sufficient cause, the supreme value requiring no higher or legitimating ideal. "Show that you are German, that you can bear grief," a young soldier wrote to his parents from le Mort-Homme. "German parents, who give the most precious they possess for the most precious [of all], our glorious Fatherland . . . for the new, greater, better Fatherland I happily give my young life,"—as indeed he did, a week later.[20]

The French formulations varied—they spoke of a clash of civilizations, or of cultures, or of civilization and barbarism, but they usually rested on the certitude that France, unlike her foe, was fighting for ideals rather than conquests. These turns of phrase had flourished elsewhere, in the speeches and papers of the towns and the hinterland, and many had sprung to the lips of the soldiers of Verdun when they had set out in 1914. "Right was yielding to Might," one of them had already written in his diary at the end of August 1914, as his retreating compatriots—"the defenders of the oppressed, the liberators"—abandoned the Belgians to the Prussians. The same month in Alsace a French cavalry officer attended the burial of a dragoon, in a cemetery festooned with red, white, and blue. He listened to his colonel speak of duty and of "the war of civilization, liberty, and right against barbarism, enslavement and treachery." By Verdun he was in the infantry. Much had changed. But the cause had not.[21]

And yet the *lingua franca* of higher purpose did not preclude a deepening disenchantment with the conduct of the war and with the war itself. At Verdun a former cavalry officer, already aware that chevaliers had lost their place, despaired of his leaders ever grasping the new nature of war. The infantry officer who had first pitted right against might on the Belgian border now also decried a war that threatened to destroy humanity: "You'd need to be mad to do what they're doing. Such massacres! Such scenes of carnage and horror! . . . men are mad!" And many—even most—who articulated or parroted the national mission were career officers, priests under arms, schoolteachers, professors in uniform, the educated and the literate. They came to the front equipped with the intellectual and linguistic habit of endowing sordid reality with higher meaning, unlike *les obscurs*, *les sans grades*, those who made up the mass of *la grande muette*, the army.[22]

Officers on the spot asked themselves the same question. Whatever they believed themselves, they could not be certain of the convictions of the others. On le Mort-Homme in May a French artillery officer confided to his diary that the survival of civilization and the containment of barbarism were at stake. No doubt, he reflected, the Senegalese and Annamites among them knew nothing of such a sacred cause. "But," he added, "isn't it the same with us, for many soldiers? In general everything works mechanically, by discipline. How many are moved by elevated motives?"[23] In 1915 Robert Hertz had already fretted over the seeming agnosticism of men around him, their indifference to the values that moved him mightily.[24]

A year later others did too. In Champagne, just before moving on to Verdun, an officer found himself having to defend the very idea of national dignity, derided by the men as "stupid pride [*amour-propre*]," and in Verdun he overheard men grumbling that their leaders were bent on killing them, that they would only cease when the money ran out.[25] At Verdun early illusions of imminent peace—resting among the Germans on their attack, among the French on their defense—gave way to gloomy speculations and prognostications of another winter, of a war without end. But mostly there was silence about it, the silence that a worried government kept trying to sound.[26]

They might at times have mistaken silence for subversion rather than consent. Expressions of higher purpose, of idealism and sacrifice and the cause behind the carnage, found their way so rarely into the mail that the censors singled them out, as though to rejoice in their advent. A chasseur, they noted in July, had waxed lyrical: "Justice marching before us will keep leading us to Victory." That autumn a nameless *poilu* assured his correspondent that he was fighting for justice and right against the crass materialism of German culture.

But by then the postal censors of the Second Army were reading some 7,000 letters a week and such rare transports looked singular and quaint among the usual vocabulary of distress—the "hell" or "place of death" in the men's letters and the "indifference," the "dark mood," the "tonelessness" in their own analytical reports. Yet even rarer were expressions of outright hostility to the patriotic project itself. Donors to the war effort in France or Germany were "unthinking or wretched," a dispirited *poilu* wrote in July. It was enough to weep or go mad, he added. "Ubi bene, ibi patria"—where I am at ease, there is my country—another wrote in December, tempted to cross the border into neutral Spain and desert. Clearly from the Spanish border area, perhaps a Basque, the man had jettisoned his patriotism and was sorely tempted to cross the border into neutral land and desert. A dangerous sentiment to commit to paper, even in Latin, but hardly the main reason why so few did: coded language is just as rare, and disaffection that stopped short of sedition did not hesitate to speak its name in letter upon letter.[27]

Censors scrutinized the correspondence of the men for precisely such expressions of antimilitarism or defeatism, and when they found them they seized the letters and pursued their authors. More often, however, they found apathy or skepticism, an indifference to the utterances and deliberations of the generals and still more of the statesmen who ran the war. The soldiers of the Second Army took no interest in rumors about the secret committee of the Chamber in June, even though the vulnerability of Verdun had provided the pretext for Joffre's critics to convene it. Week after week the anxious censors noted nothing in their dutiful rubric called "politique"—nothing to justify the suspicions of the high command or to suggest that anything mattered other than the material conditions for themselves at the front and for their own at home. Once in a while the men let slip a suggestion that a deputy should be at the front, a hope that an Allied conference consist of more than "toasts and promises," a preference for deeds over "fine speeches." If they talked or wrote about the war it was about the prospects for an end to it. Russia elated, during her offensive in the spring; England embittered, until hers on the Somme in July briefly reprieved her; Romania raised hopes in August only to dash them in December. But mostly they said nothing. Of 300 letters from men of the 71st Infantry Division that the censors read one week in July, not one mentioned the Allied offensives or the Russian successes.[28]

When hopes of an imminent end did not sustain them, the men carried on as though by habit. Once the initial scare had passed, and the drama of the city under siege faded into the routine of the endless battle, the attentions of the rest of the country and the world drifted from Verdun. At other points on the front the men no longer talked as much of it or of the hopes it had raised. "The men seem so sure of German failure here," the

censors concluded in the spring, "that the battle no longer grips them."
Other news from other fronts took its place, feeding transitory enthusiasms. Pacifists in the army and at home continued to hold up Verdun
from time to time as a place of massacre and folly. "After 19 months of
campaigning," one of the men wrote from his sector to a pacifist university
professor in Bordeaux, "however hardened I've become, I never contem-
plate without stupor and terror the immense cemeteries of Argonne and
Verdun. And they envisage, and demand, and magnify in advance new
holocausts. How can they justify such extermination?"

Apart from isolated moments like the recapture of Fort Douaumont,
Verdun had stopped making news. At times it seemed that the only
occasional talk of Verdun came from the men who were there. And the
Somme provoked even more detachment, to judge from the letters of
those watching from afar; what rhetoric had once filled their pages now
faded away.[29]

These soldiers—no rarefied warrior caste but mediocre commoners—
the nation itself, as one of them put it, saw no need, felt no urge, to
justify their presence here. It was self-explanatory. On both sides an
obligation to defend the nation that gave them their identities at birth
ruled inwardly and rendered vain their loud detestation of the war, like
some silent master tolerating the antics of his servant. The French had
the added insult of invasion to avenge, but had the war of movement left
the armies facing each other in neutral Belgium or German-ruled Alsace
French determination would not have been much weaker. Sometimes
educated French, usually officers, spoke the language of universalism and
abstraction, the awkward yet sincere language that the British and Americans would adopt as well, but a more elemental tribal imperative governed
the assembled hosts on the Meuse: das Vaterland, la Patrie, and the attachments that underlay them.

Pierre Renouvin, who had not asked how the enemies at Verdun saw each
other, did not ask either how they saw themselves. If hate did not suffice
to motivate them in combat and sustain them in repose, did love—of
their unit, their home, their country, or their God? During the Second
World War a study of American airmen concluded that "the men seem
to be fighting more *for* someone than *against* somebody." The same could
hold true of the First.[30]

Most did not dissect their own national fidelity. Their constancy was mute, expressed by a refusal to countenance defeat, by the repeated assurance given to friends and relatives that the Germans would never take Verdun; and by the Prussian grenadier's bewildered reflection that were Germany to go down here life and world history would lose all meaning. Only two out of 500 in the units around him, an artillery officer noted, wanted peace at any price. How had the fiction of the nation taken so deep a hold on the men at Verdun that most did not bother to explain it?[31]

Long before sociologists asked whether men fought for their units or for their countries, and whether their willingness to throw their lives away in combat sprang from any identifiable attachment, skeptics had doubted the power of patriotism to drive soldiers to brave death. Even before the Franco-Prussian war the officer and theorist Ardant du Picq had stressed camaraderie over all else, and had worried that the dispersion on the modern battlefield might fracture the solidarity he deemed so vital to morale. In one of the few passages he ever wrote about his experience of the Great War, Marc Bloch, the great medievalist, seemed to pick up where the military theorist had left off. He doubted that courage sprang from patriotism: "I think that few soldiers, save some of the most intelligent and noblest of heart, think of their country when they fight bravely: more often a sense of individual honor moves them, and it can be very strong as long as the milieu keeps it up. . . ." Alain (Emile Chartier), the philosopher, journalist, and eventual pacifist, who had volunteered for the artillery in the war and refused promotion from the ranks, later said much the same. Courage, he said, sprang not from duty to one's country but from duty to one's comrades and to oneself.

At Verdun those who thought about the matter could reach the same conclusion. An artillery sergeant thought that way: "Let's remember that the love of country, the defense of ideals of justice, right, and humanity are very ethereal, utterly intangible by most *poilus*. Their actions require motives that are more proximate and thus more keenly felt. And hence the great influence of their leader." And a second lieutenant, alone on the side of the Côte de Froideterre, reflected on how courage required an audience, as though he sensed the knowing gaze of Ardant du Picq.[32]

No doubt. However, combat, even if the most important act in war, is not the most common one, and in this war men spent long stretches away from the front lines, or in a half-world between violence and tranquility.

In such intervals no supreme sacrifice demanded immediate explanation. Which group attachments then commanded their assent to their plight? A single infantry company, under examination, reveals a cluster of smaller fellowships made of personal ties and common interests and shared resentments, sometimes so strong as to interfere with the formal authority system. And whatever the formal primary group—squad, platoon, company, or other—wider loyalties imported by its members can fracture as well as cement their union. Like "the enemy," "the group" is an elusive entity, one given to changing faces under observation, and hardly self-evident as an answer to the why of endurance and of sacrifice.[33]

A small unit at rest could resemble an extended family, and its members sometimes spoke of each other that way. In moments of separation or loss, in the aftermath of combat or of some sudden descent of shell fire, they might grieve as though for a blood relation, when the carapace of fatalism did not block such emotion. A corpse might leave them indifferent, but a dead comrade would shake them: "in war one can get used to the idea of one's own death, but when it strikes someone else of our own it seems an unjust fate."[34]

Among the Germans the experience of having traveled together to the far corners of Europe since 1914 could deepen their sense of kinship. On a single day in June a Bavarian soldier lost six of his friends from the same squad, cut down by French artillery during their attack on Fleury before they had even set eyes on the enemy. They had fought together in Serbia, on the borders of Greece, in Champagne, before coming to Verdun to die. "We had shared joys and suffering in foreign lands with them and lived their deaths almost like those of family members," he noted, and a sense of rage seized him. When units broke up, the parting of ways among the men could be wrenching. When his own company, reduced to debris at Verdun, was dissolved and its members dispersed among others, a lieutenant observed something akin to grief—the men lost their appetite, many cried. The ties were too strong. He managed to keep some survivors with him in his new company.[35]

The men conspired when at play to divert their attention from the war, in the way that recreation in peacetime took their minds off work. Oblivion at the front gained from collaboration, and when the men sang or played cards or dominoes it seemed to an observer that the nearby enemy had vanished from their mental universe. "This ability to forget," he wrote, "is something of a marvel." Thirty miles from Verdun, as hope of avoiding its "hell" dwindled, the Bavarian soldier watched his fellows dance to the melodies of a harmonica-player. It absorbed them; sweat trickled down their faces. "Verdun, bloody Verdun!" he noted in his diary. "None of these frolicking dancers thinks of the slaughterhouse ahead." Alcohol helped: "We're devoured by fleas, but when we can find wine we quickly forget our little miseries."

So did the entertainments that the army organized, the *matinées récréatives* in barns, with actors recruited from the regiments, and violins, cellos and pianos, and comic singers who grimaced and sang off-key, deliberately, to the hilarity of their audiences. At first the dreamworld pained by contrast with bestial reality, a spectator noted, but soon a sense of well-being set in, and for a moment he felt happy. Parcels, when they arrived, promoted an ephemeral and primitive communism, their coming awaited, their contents shared. The rich and the cosseted, the beneficiaries of the most generous relatives at home, lost out; but the group gained.[36]

The most observant among the French recorded, more in admiration than derision, a vanity resting on the esteem of one's fellow soldiers that could sustain men when all else might fail. Poorly lodged, exposed to the elements, infested with lice, harassed by promotion-hungry officers, as one of them acknowledged, they would still clean and polish their weapons out of *amour-propre*, the mainspring of their compliance. Fear drove the men, another observed—fear of shame, fear of loss of face, the same vanity, as another put it, that precluded their lagging behind their fellows in combat and that turned the individually meek into the collectively assertive.[37]

An impersonal, abstract variant of *amour-propre* attached itself to the unit and went by the name of *esprit de corps*. Usually a regiment, sometimes a battalion, rarely a company, the object of such devotions had to boast the size and the age to inspire pride in its history and fidelity to its emblems. *Esprit de corps*, when alive and breathing, instilled a competitive spirit that moved the regiment to outshine the next, and that took vicarious pleasure when the division or the army rewarded the collective feats with citations and decorations. Some talked about it, and took pride in the prowess of their team, in ways that recall the rival intoxications of a sporting event. Mixing regional pride with *esprit de corps*, a soldier enthused over how his regiment had retaken le Mort-Homme: "No unit has ever fought as well as ours, the regiments of Marseille and the 311th . . . they were marvelous! . . . No, never, I swear it, have we seen such courageous men! Count on it, people will be talking of this whole thing for a long time to come."

Rather than exult over the exploits of their band, however, most celebrated more practical gratifications. They were enlisted men, in an army no longer peopled by professional or long-serving soldiers, an army in which the regimental identity counted for less than in others, notably the British. In the early summer soldiers writing home from Verdun explained that any citation for their regiments meant, to them, two more days of leave. And some of the celebrations of *esprit de corps* are retrospective, tinged with nostalgia or undisguised didactic intent. Eleven years after Verdun a Prussian major explained that he was writing his recollections of the battle to recapture the spirit that bound together officers and men in his battalion, united in their will to protect Germany from her enemies. He wished to inspire the new generation to "conquer Germany's future." A French chasseur recalled how his major's wife—la Comtesse d'Aquin—had paid for a new battalion pennant, embroidered with its insignia, and how he had proudly worn it for the next two years, and how they had never ceded an inch at Verdun, or Douaumont, or Cumières, or le Mort-Homme. The chasseurs—he had served under Driant, in 1914—were a proud lot. However, he was writing all this 55 years later, without any notes.[38]

In fact, the written traces of formal *esprit de corps* left at the moment of Verdun are meager, flashes on a dark surface. It stirred. But it was only one form of collective sentiment, one of the ways in which *amour-propre* could attach itself to ever more abstract entities.

The least abstract of all, hearth and home, family and village, seemed at moments to ground soldiering in a craving for the homage of their kith and kin. "Tant pis," a trooper of the heavily engaged 20th Corps wrote home in March, "we'll carry on till the end. . . . And if we don't come back you can be sure we didn't die as cowards and my children will be proud of it later on." Even when they declined in their letters to record the graphic details of the inferno, out of modesty, deference, or an instinctive sense of the unmentionable, the men at the front found subtler ways to associate their blood relatives with their lives of drudgery and danger. The sights evoked them on the way to the front lines through the nocturnal ruins of Verdun. "Each ruined home reminds of our own."

Incongruously enough, parcels from home with cheeses and pâtés and other delicacies, and above all letters reminded them, they said, of what they were fighting for. An almost mystical communion at times took hold of them as they opened letters—"sacred hour, silent and shining, even in the saddest shelters, even in the midst of the most tragic dangers. . . ." Art itself, the trench art that turned shell casings and the metallic detritus of war into medallions, rings, vases, ash trays, lighters, linked them as well to home as they chiseled and engraved, for they fashioned their artifacts for wives and fiancées and children as often as for money or for their fellows. Conversation as well joined the trench to the home, evoking one shelter inside of another as the farmers talked of fields and the price of wheat, shopkeepers of customers and profits, workers of skills and wages. And they might see their own losses through the eyes of the bereaved at home, the widows and the mothers, *nos Madonnes nationales*, in a wartime precursor of a postwar community of mourners. "For you, for you," the Prussian grenadier wrote, and even when he expressed the wish that the sufferings at the front remain unknown his words lack credibility.[39]

Some early historians of the war discerned a widening gulf between the trenches and the home front. The front had brutalized the men, inured them to violence, severed them from the civilized mores they had left behind; or, in a later and more refined variant, the front had alienated them, estranged them from their own homes in ways that might entail the release of pent-up anger upon returning. Yet 10 billion letters traveled between the front and the home in France during the war, and 30 billion letters, postcards, and parcels in Germany. Whatever light theories of brutalization and alienation may shed on rapports between military and civilian societies, they sit uncomfortably beside the light the volume of correspondence casts on the bonds between men and their families— bonds that the war, according to some studies, strengthened rather than stretched.[40]

Regional identities, however much a Republic on one side and an Empire on the other had diluted them since the 1870s, could still galvanize the soldiers. Prussians and Bavarians still had separate kings, and could hail their accomplishments—the taking of Douaumont by the first, the recent conquests in Serbia by the second—with almost provincial smugness.[41] The French regiment, recruited locally and regionally, brought to the front a geographical as well as a numerical identity, one it retained in the minds of its men long after they had left it. "216th Infantry Regiment," a one-time corporal at Verdun, speaking on the radio 50 years later, called his unit, and added, "boys from the Loire and Bretons, depot of Montbrison."[42]

Language helped. The Austro-Hungarian army presented the greatest Babel of tongues, but in the French army regional dialects still flourished, sometimes crucially so in extremis. During the fighting near Cumières a chasseur heard a lieutenant in one of the companies give orders in a northern patois. The battalion had been formed there, in Lille, on August 5th, 1914; the chasseur's lieutenant was Lillois, his captain was Lillois, most of his fellow soldiers were Lillois.[43]

Like the Bavarians and the Brandenburgers, the native sons of French provinces could ascribe success in combat to the soil that had bred them, a habit that struck the postal censors when they encountered it: "A soldier of the 221st admires the pluck of his comrades from the Haute-Saône and the Haute-Marne: 'they're rugged soldiers, courageous, never drained of strength.'"[44] The dimension of *amour-propre*, extending to provinces what individuals might demonstrate before each other, became at times explicit. When the Marseillais of the 311th Infantry Regiment retook some ground on le Mort-Homme in June, one of them basked above all in the esteem of the soldiers and officers from the other extreme of the hexagon: "you have to hear the *poilus* of the [département du] Nord and their officers; they say no one has ever seen soldiers like them."[45] And later that summer, after the heavy fighting around Fleury and Thiaumont, another southern Frenchman took a comparable pleasure in the exhibition of regional virtue: "I have to tell you that the troops of the Midi have shown our pals from the Nord that we're as good as each other, that we have guts." Perhaps only one in twenty letters displayed such bravado, a censor noted. Still, provincialism sometimes nourished chauvinism, as though to assert its continuing vitality in the great melting pot of the army.[46]

And faith still moved some as well, not as it had the knights of the Crusades or the foot soldiers of the wars of religion—even though the hopes of a French soldier in August that "the sacred Virgin will bring us Victory," or of a German soldier on the afternoon of the 21st of February that God would be with them recalled the literal language of more archaic enthusiasms.[47] Something resembling martial spirituality arose during the Great War, couched in the idiom of crusade, sacrifice, or martyrdom.

Its appeal in the trenches is unclear, and some observers dismissed it, but even there it returned as a social force that unbelievers too had to acknowledge.[48] The pastoral consolations of religion operated among the devout at a private level, the level at which a German theology student, a survivor of Champagne as well, put it only three weeks before he was killed. Verdun, he believed, was war at its most terrible, and he found himself transported closer to his God, his mind on the afterlife.[49]

But a collective dimension, expressed by ritual and the spectacle of sectarian truce, could stretch the domain of devotion. Among the believers the ministrations of a chaplain or the celebration of a mass might renew fervors that a military mind could only welcome. "Among many soldiers," as a postal censor of the Second Army noted, "—above all Bretons and Flemings—religious faith visibly fortifies courage: 'I went to Mass; it restored my heart.'"[50] At the front, though, unlike at home, the flock no longer consisted of the faithful alone. The chaplains moved freely about the regiments, bearing stretchers, improvising open air services in clearings in the woods, making altars out of fallen tree trunks, lecterns out of munitions crates, communion stands out of empty sacks. Village churches became hospitals, their priests ministering to the faithful in the nave as medics tended to the wounded in the sanctuaries. On Christmas Eve, in Montzéville and Dombasle, the wounded filled the churches, forcing priests to celebrate midnight Mass in nearby barns, below crossed sabers and bayonets and regimental standards. There were no Sundays in the trenches, a chaplain at Verdun acknowledged. Away from the front lines, however, dominical Masses could punctuate the weeks, sometimes at the command post of the regimental colonel or the battalion major. The war, here as elsewhere, had drawn religion out of its tabernacles, and relaxed the interdictions of peacetime segregation.[51]

Priests still lamented the indifference of the Godless. In March a divisional chaplain watched evening services on an embankment. The faithful sat on the ground, gathered around the preacher. Beyond them teemed the dismissive and the unregenerate, eating out of mess kits or playing cards. Shells flew overhead. "How many of these carefree ones," he wondered, "reflect that they are on the threshold of battle and of eternity?" But, if they worried about the souls of the unredeemed, the clerics also welcomed the uniformed newcomers who swelled the ranks of their congregations. The village priest at Récicourt had never seen such throngs in peacetime. Nearby at Brabant a chaplain, camped in the sacristy of a smaller church, received *poilus* all evening long.

And, practicing or not, atheist, agnostic, or devout, the men warmed to the ubiquitous men of the cloth, now soldiers like them. "Our chaplain is a real *poilu*," a lieutenant noted in the Bois d'Haumont in March, as he described the man of God, dirty and unshaven, hands in the belt of his muddied cassock, consoling and joking, bearing *gnole* [rotgut] and *eau de vie*, trying to convert the atheists, and winning the hearts of the officers and the men. In February, as the Germans neared Bras, a French ambulance driver watched a chaplain caring for the wounded amid the ruins of the village. Most were Moslems, from colonial regiments. "What a character, *sapristi*!," his fellow-driver, an anticlerical, exclaimed. "I now know the expression on the faces of the first Christians fed to the lions!" Just as the Masses for the dead could move even the irreligious, the exertions of the clergy could disarm their inveterate foes. Near a redoubt near Fleury one night in May a soldier watched a chaplain encourage the men—the same Père Laurent whom Premier Clemenceau, the venerable anticlerical, would decorate, and whose impression on his observer at Verdun in 1916, like that of so many others, revealed the secular impact of a spiritual presence.[52]

Such solidarities, as concrete as a comrade or as abstract as a God, could fortify each other, even dissolve into a single sense of belonging. For any soldier to act in isolation was unusual and perhaps impossible. *Esprit de corps*, when it surfaced, rested on regional as much as on regimental pride. Religious observance could nourish attachment to the unit, particularly when the dead admonished the living: when a pilgrimage to a comrade's grave renewed flagging spirits; when mourning instilled a determination to follow the example of the deceased. And sometimes the mental image of the village conjured up that of its church and of the prayers said there for the men at the front. "I imagine," a soldier noted as he read an uncle's letter, "the fervent Masses in the quiet mornings in that remote mountain village of ours." Then loyalties could conspire to anchor the soldier, even in a place like Verdun.[53]

Such primary affinities marked the survival of social habits that the front never suppressed. Their pull worked differently, with the unit perhaps inspiring most devotion during combat and the others during the extended monotony of the inactive weeks. Into the mix came the nation, more abstract than any other fealty. With its primary schools, its newspapers and its elections, its statuary and its street names, its anthems and parades, it had insinuated itself into the lives of men in ways beyond the reach of any medieval or early modern forerunners. It was the only affinity that linked all the soldiers born in the hexagon—as the French sometimes call their country, because of its shape—but without the diverse others it would have been no more than a flag. Did men fight for their unit or their country? Their region or their country? Their faith or their country? The binary reasoning with its false opposites distorts the realities. One now suffused the others: the nation made little sense in isolation from the circles of attachment that surrounded each soldier at Verdun. To imagine, as a literary critic and future author did, a dialogue with his Patrie was to imagine a conversation about its sounds and sights: "What is the German doing to my language," the country asks, "in the lands he's taken from you? What is he doing to the soil of your fathers? What is he doing to my beauties?"[54]

Marveling at how quickly songs and games could eclipse the enemy in the minds of his men, a French captain reflected on how the *gaieté foncière* of French national character became a military asset in itself.[55] Nation mingled with unit here, and when another officer admired his troops, commoners with little schooling, he also admired his country. "I need barely a few hours to grasp how good and reasonable are our people . . . the good camaraderie of those who suffer, the fine devotion of comrades-in-arms is very real."[56] The letter from home that resurrected for the artillery officer reading it his uncle, his village, and his church conjured up in the same vision the Masses said for the salvation of France.[57] The dividing lines dissolved, especially when God and nation made common cause in the minds of their subjects.

The *Gott mit uns* of the German regiments had always served as a patriotic as well as a spiritual slogan. Earlier in the war Protestant pastors as well as Catholic priests had noticed the rediscovery of religion among some of the men, and the way they associated their trust in God with their devotion to *das Vaterland*. At Verdun, a soldier who willed his life to the same fatherland also felt himself, as he wrote his parents, "protected in God's hand" and a captain linked attendance at religious services to morale and thus implicitly to German victory.[58]

Among French chaplains—at least among those who had managed inwardly to reconcile their religious with their military callings, their crucifixes with their rifles—the metaphorical even gave way to the literal, as le Mort-Homme became Le Mont Thabor, and the blood of French soldiers the blood of Christ. The cause of the nation sustained the cause of its God, an alliance easing the qualms of seminarians. "Among the Boches this war is Satanic and exceeds in horror anything imaginable. God cannot be with them." And not only among seminarians. Along the dust and smoke of the *Voie Sacrée* in June a lieutenant transfigured his troop's progress toward Verdun, elevating a convoy into a religious procession and unwittingly demonstrating that for him the nation hardly sufficed unto itself, that men lived it through their faith or their unit or much else besides.[59]

When they tried to articulate the obscure sense of duty that moved them, the men could not always easily do so. "How many soldiers," a lieutenant asked, "were fighting just because they had to, with nothing to sustain their courage but the often vague sentiment of Duty." Often they invoked the imperative in the same breath as the collective, as though an organic connection between obligation and belonging—"our duty as Frenchmen," "to serve the Fatherland in this way"—explained their continued presence in an infernal place. The Church itself, a chaplain told the men gathered in the mud and the snow to hear his sermon and receive absolution, symbolized the union of Christ in duty. The same inner call could explain why, as one of the men wrote, isolated units that might otherwise have disintegrated or surrendered instead held on, even when they felt abandoned by their own army. Whether to protect a group, sustain its gratitude, preserve a privileged position within it, or cling to its moorings, a sense of duty moved the men at Verdun; attachments they had not chosen deepened in a plight they had not chosen either. Far from competing with the modern state, such primary solidarities now became grist to its mill, the auxiliaries of its cultural and coercive powers. Determined by inner compulsion and outward conformism, the compliance by millions presents no great mystery, save to historians in an age of small professional armies, and explains the utterance heard then among them and echoed so often down the decades to come: "we've all become vicious dogs. A life of misery and no end in sight. We go along with it because we cannot do otherwise."[60]

"Vicious dogs." Just as easily the same ties could pit soldier against soldier. Group solidarities at the front could enter into conflict with each other as naturally as they could at home, act in centrifugal as well as centripetal ways, and make an army, a regiment, or even a company or platoon seethe with clannish tensions. "We argue at times," an artillery officer began guardedly, before losing all restraint. "We don't get along among ourselves. Some live in complete isolation; groups, clans exist; in a word these varied elements join together poorly and I cannot speak of friendship or fellow-feeling, there's barely a vague camaraderie." Why? he wondered, and concluded lamely that only a few antisocial sorts were to blame. But the roots of dissension lay deeper than in the accidents of personality.[61]

The war, far from dissolving tensions between soldiers into a homogeneous solution called national identity, had provided some new kinds of provocations that set them off, and the discipline of the front contained but never fully stifled the implacable resentments. In some ways it intensified them.

Some of the most bitter stemmed from class. In April, as they ate together and looked out over the cratered terrain of le Mort-Homme, two artillerists discussed their battalion commander. He was solidly middle class, the son of a railroad station director, and not for the first time one of the two, the proud descendant of Corsican bandits, reproached the other for his condescension. Why keep worrying about that now, the other wondered, with German 150 mms flying overhead. But hierarchies of rank could replicate hierarchies of class, not only between the officers and the men but also among the officers themselves. A general from the Genie (the Army engineers) visited, and a captain associated his elegance with his ignorance, as though his stylishness deafened him to entreaties to build more huts for the men. Their troglodytic lives had bred a kind of reverse snobbery.

Class resentments traveled from home to front and back again, hardly evaporating at regimental depots or disembarkation centers. Farmers and others stuck in the trenches bridled at the workers sent home to the munitions factories, recipients of state-subsidized wages as well as physical security. "The workers alone are kings," one of their rural enemies wrote, "the ones who'll die of hunger after the war because they never saved anything." At one time or another many saw the shopkeepers as war profiteers, at home or at the front—price-gougers who sold them goods at three times prewar prices and who would extract even more from them once the war ended. Workers and shopkeepers now in uniform felt the deflected envy. A sense of social belonging, to the field or the workshop, could turn into social rage.[62]

And *esprit de corps* too could mean *esprit d'antagonisme*. "Iron Regiment," one telephone operator called his 101st—a regiment from the regular army—over the phone. "Parade regiment" his correspondent from the 142nd—a reserve regiment—replied.[63] "Squabbles and nasty gossip," a sergeant wrote of the relations between the professional or standing army and the conscripted one, between *l'armée de métier* and *la nation armée*. We, he wrote of the conscripts, are the ones who have sacrificed all, we are the martyrs.[64]

Rivalry was one matter, hostility another. The soldiers of one unit might deeply resent those of another, especially if they hailed from different branches of the service. On both sides, over and over, the field artillery fired into its own front lines or paralyzed the infantry's forward movement by firing too short, blind to the rockets that went up imploring them to stop. French shells fell on French soldiers, German shells on German. Inadequate registration and visibility, poor aerial reconnaissance, the diabolical dispersion that made the same shells fired within seconds from the same gun fall at different distances, an unexpectedly swift advance by attacking troops—the artillerymen had compelling technical apologies to proffer. But they failed to impress the infantrymen. "It bears witness to the great indifference of these people," a German machine-gunner complained in May. Even when they acknowledged the difficulties of coordination, the infantryman complained that he, not the gunner, was the victim, and that he, not the gunner, was the martyr of this long war. The mere sight of an artilleryman might suggest to him privilege and immunity, and incite resentments akin to class hatred. In the streets of Ste-Ménehoulde an infantry officer observed his counterparts in the artillery walk by in their smart uniforms—impeccable black jackets, leggings with double red stripes—and thought of his mud-caked fellows in the trenches. "The war isn't equally hard on everyone," he reflected. He was more temperate than an infantry colonel on the road from Bar-le-Duc, made to stand aside with his units as the artillerymen rolled by on their way to Verdun. "Bunch of bastards."[65]

If regional sentiment could build *esprit de corps* in the units, it could also come between them, especially if lives were at stake. "They," the others, wore the same uniform but spoke with strange accents or in some barely recognizable tongue, and betrayed their origins by their carelessness, incompetence, or selfishness. "It strongly suggests the mob" an artillery officer from the Massif Central complained when he relieved a battery of *méridionaux*—southerners—near Récicourt. They were chaotic, unresponsive, and even, he went on, cowardly, not exactly reluctant to quit the scene.[66] Language divided, within or between regiments. Half-dialect, half-French, the soldiers in one regiment recalled the speech of a recruit from Béziers, who complained of their hostility to him and his fellow-méridionaux.[67] Aspersions about speech rankled, and when the inhabitants of the village of Neuvillers derided the accents of some southwestern artillerymen on their way to Verdun they drew the retort that their own French was hardly that of the Loire either (where the purest French is said to be found).

Mockery of language usually attaches itself to other disdains, and the artillery officer at Récicourt who ridiculed the dialect—"quelle bouillac," "quelle gadouille," they called the mud—also slighted the professionalism of the southerners he was relieving.[68] Prosaic habits served as surrogates for graver failings. Thanks to their inability to forgo their coffee, which they heated with wet wood that sent up columns of smoke high above the trees, the soldiers of Arras, northerners this time, had brought on enemy artillery fire outside the Tunnel de Tavannes—so another artillery officer, this one a marquis from the Orléanais, insisted.[69]

War, far from dissolving regional differences, seemed at times to accentuate them, in both armies. Soon after the Bavarians joined the Prussians at Verdun in the spring of 1916, relations between the two began to deteriorate. The newcomers began to suspect that the roughest assignments were coming their way, that they, not the Prussians, were the "fall guys," and would still be once peace returned. "I know only Germans," the Kaiser had told the parties in Parliament as war broke out. But when the Bavarians at Verdun spoke of "Germans" they sometimes meant "only Prussians." The war had thrown strangers together, Saxons and Wurtembergers, Bretons and Limousins, but concord did not spring naturally from cohabitation, and habits that before the war might have seemed odd or quaint to the outlander now provoked his ire.[70]

And the religion that bound could also divide, as Janus-faced as the other solidarities. Neither anti-Semitism nor anti-Catholicism magically vanished in the trenches, even as men discovered or rediscovered in their churches a source of consolation and solace. An infantry lieutenant with right-wing, nationalist *Action Française* sympathies demanded of his Jewish compatriots the sacrifice of their faith along with that of their blood. Only renunciation and apostasy, he wrote, could finally free him of Judaism, "still a barrier between the Frenchman from France and him." And meanwhile the Republic, in its concern to separate church and state, still kept the chaplains at the front at arm's length, much to their indignation. They took umbrage at the war on their own religious insignia, at the Prefects' interdiction on the sale to the soldiers of images of the Sacred Heart and other pious medallions as alien grafts on the truly national insignia, the *cocarde* ribbon. While we are fighting the Boches, one of the chaplains wrote, "other *Boches* are working at persecuting us"— meaning his compatriots. Sometimes such quarrels could be civil. One night another chaplain spent hours at a major's table arguing with him about "politico-religious matters" over a good Burgundy.[71]

Most of all, those who fought the war hated those who did not—those who avoided it, profited from it, talked about it, prosecuted it in comfort and safety. Even if historians have sometimes exaggerated the chasm between soldiers and civilians, even if the ties between them were strong and the continuities tenacious, *l'arrière*, *Heimat*, are words whose mesmerizing simplicity conceals plural rapports. Ties to a seat of affection at home might accompany deepening hostility to neighbors close by or outliers beyond. Between civilians in uniform and soldiers in mufti the attire might change but not the identity, nor the range of animosities that went with it.[72]

At the front duty was shadowed by detestation, attachments to hearth and home by odium for vaguely defined groups of noncombatants. At times the men deflected their dejection onto such targets. The postal censors observed that the deeper their discontent at the front, the greater their resentment of the rear. One expressed the other, perhaps in the way that earlier plagues and catastrophes had inflamed social tensions.[73]

Sometimes men returned from leave incensed by what they had seen at home or on the road. The concerts, cinemas, and theaters of Paris, seemingly surreal denials of the war, stunned newly arrived revenants from the trenches. Too many people played while they suffered. Others felt like strangers in their own land. In the spring in Bar-le-Duc, only 30 miles from Verdun, a noncommissioned officer and his men on leave felt the eyes of civilians on them in the restaurant of an elegant hotel, reading humiliating alarm and aloofness in their expressions when they sought to sit down. At such moments a gulf yawned between the *poilus* and the rest of the country, and the war, far from fusing front and home in its crucible, had done much to drive them apart.[74]

Hostile generalizations now stereotyped domestic as well as foreign foes. Women, seen as victims when they had names but as parasites when they did not, came in for some bitter typecasting. "As you say," one of the men wrote in the autumn to an obviously like-minded friend, "for some women the war could [happily] go on for ten years. It's shameful. . . ." He tried to fence in his antipathy to "some." Others were not as scrupulous. The spectacle of vanity could affront the mud-caked interloper from the war, who saw in the survival of prewar frivolities a crime against conscience: "And some things shock. I've seen women made up and outfitted, while *poilus* are suffering so and dying of hunger. . . ."

Class enemies angered them no less, whether rich or poor—munitions workers spared the ordeal of the front, and better paid as well than the soldiers at the front; shirkers of all sorts; "fat cats" with a financial stake in the war and no interest in peace, luxuriating while others died. One day, perhaps, when no one else would be left standing, they would all grasp the truth about the catastrophe they had unleashed, but for now soldiers lay buried alive to defend the speculators, for now they held on—"in a word we hold, as the bitches in Lyon say."

The language of class war at times devolved into a generalized hatred of all civil society at the rear, couched in apocalyptic predictions of reckonings to come. Just when that would happen they could not say. The hour seemed as distant as the end of the war itself: "They'll try for forgiveness for their crime. But it will be too late, they won't be able to resuscitate the thousands of victims or appease the fury of the survivors."[75]

The ideal of *Union sacrée*, at such moments, meant little more than indentured servitude. Talk of it, talk of the war in its name, provoked mockery and rancor. Most irksome of all was the press. The newspapers, with their thoughtless *jusqu'au boutisme*—diehard spirit—and gallant willingness to sacrifice the lives of others, enraged some of the men at Verdun. "The papers really do claim that the *poilu* wants to fight all the way to the end," one of them complained at the end of November, as winter set in. "Well, 99 out of 100 are like me, fed up with that crap—people who want to believe in some supposed victory should give up such thoughts." They did not recognize themselves in the ecstatic descriptions at home of surging morale even among the wounded—"the facts," a major noted drily in April from the headquarters of the Second Army, "contradict such dogma brutally enough," and he pointed to men surrendering unwounded, to feeble defenses, to feeble attacks.[76]

The press lived, in their eyes, off the war, its patriotic bombast feeding on their torments. They discerned greed in the pens and callousness in the minds of the scribblers who turned out such screeds. "Then let them go see the hideous manure in which the flowers of their rhetoric grow," one of the men suggested, finding their verbosity sacrilegious in the land of the dead at Verdun.[77]

Sometimes the men tore up the papers. Sometimes—when a major daily told of concerts in the trenches, of German shells blocking up saxophones and of men continuing defiantly to hum along—they hooted in derision. Sometimes they ignored them, wise to their factitious optimism, and counseled as much to their correspondents at home: "Burn your newspaper before reading it. You'll learn fewer lies."[78] German prisoners told their French captors that no one believed the fables of the papers at home. No idiot would write them, still less a soldier, a Bavarian wrote home, and when the wife of a *poilu* sent him copies of German articles she had come across he too found them ridiculous. A Berlin paper wrote of columns of tobacco smoke rising above the men, as though from "flames of sacrifice in their hearts." The purveyors of such heroic kitsch intended it more for civilian than military readers, but when it reached the subjects themselves it only deepened their sense of estrangement from the world behind them. A medical officer who had found himself at Verdun with his infantry regiment from the beginning—from the 24th of February—strove to exclude from his notes any impression that might even remotely resemble the sentimental trash of the home front that so sickened him and his fellow-soldiers. And a lieutenant, destined to a career in art history, as different from the army as night from day, put it more simply when he spoke of "a ditch between us and the rear is deepening and widening every day."[79]

The rear, in the minds of the men, began at the major headquarters, where, as one of the officers put it, the war had become a game of phones and paperwork. From there it merged with the high command and the government itself. Behind the anger at the press lay a chronic mistrust of those who fed it, the authors of communiqués and official news. Why believe the military correspondents in the newspapers, one of the doubters asked, since along with the generals and the colonels they were all brainwashers [*bourreurs de crânes*]? One day a French captain admired the dispatch with which the Germans protected their men, digging in and sending reinforcements as soon as they had conquered a French position. To think, he complained, that the French General Staff instructed the press to inform its readers every day that their German counterparts cared nothing for human lives. His eyes had observed what the hierarchy glibly denied, and he added in his notebook a remark that would have been seditious had it been published, "We for our part know which side harbors leaders who murder their men. . . ."[80]

At such moments attachment to fellows or to family, to unit or to homeland, to faith or to nation might resurface as so much resentment, so much hostility—the authentic voice of group belonging.

Fractious dispositions, group loyalties that brought discord as well as concord, and outbursts of anger as well as expressions of devotion: just beneath the "resignation" so commonly ascribed to the men lay an unsettled reality. They might seem apathetic, expressionless. Returning from leave to his unit at Verdun, a captain tried to sound the hearts and minds of the men. The trench walls, weakened by bombardment and by rain, were slowly crumbling. He found them silent and impenetrable, talkative only at meals. They seemed wearied by it all, by fighting but also by grief, by separation, by news of hardship at home. And they held few illusions about the world that awaited the survivors. But like him they intended and even wanted to hold on. "The enthusiasm is dead," the captain concluded, "but not the will."

Reading the mail the same month, a censor detected no evidence of warlike fervor, only a pervasive melancholy that, by now, he found normal. And almost 80 years later a veteran of the battle, by then a centenarian, said much the same: "We got used to it, because that's the way it was." Such an utterance leaves unanswered the riddle of compliance. Did he mean that he had no choice? Or that talk was idle? The man might not always be as stoical as the mask; on occasion he might drop it altogether.[81]

As long as peace seemed remote but victory still possible to the men, as long as they were passably fed and clothed, led by mostly rational commanders at the front, and supported in the war effort by mostly sympathetic civilians at the rear, they were likely to "resign" themselves to the task. In the spring of 1917 in some parts of the French army and in the late summer of 1918 in many parts of the German army such conditions no longer infallibly held, yielding mutinies, desertions, or mass surrenders. The year of Verdun was different.

But, coming when it did and seeming never to end, it fell almost between the élan of 1914, the lingering hopes of 1915, and the weariness of 1917 and 1918. So strong was the desire in the French armies for an end to the war, censors trying to read the tea leaves in the men's letters concluded in July 1916, that any kind of setback might render peace more attractive to the men than victory. Even at Verdun, which for a while became a symbolic center of the war, the solidarities came undone once in a while, in outbursts of ill-will or rage that met with consternation then and oblivion later on.[82]

Group attachments are as woven with paradox as the tissue of enmity. Both rancor and forbearance might greet the hierarchy or the war itself, and both might dwell within the same army, unit, or soldier, as latent mentalities waiting for circumstance or human error or the fortunes of war to rouse them. The men at Verdun, and still less those who wrote about them, said little about the uneasy balance between acceptance and refusal. The first sprang from deep solidarities with fellows or with home, took the form of duty, and for now prevailed over the other, made of resentments at circumstances, compatriots, and the war itself. It drove the healthy to rescue the wounded from quagmires, shell-holes, and barbed wire, the wounded and even the dying to rally the others, enlisted men to volunteer for patrols, officers for local missions—innumerable acts of ordinary heroism, transfigured by publicists then and later into feats of uncommon valor. It helped keep units together during long weeks of inactivity and inspired among them a pride that one side called *Stolz* or *Ehre* and the other *amour-propre*. It had little to do with any articulated belief about the meaning of the war or of Verdun, but it surfaced in their deeds and in the words that issued from the pens of French soldiers: "Capture Verdun or Fouilly-aux-Oies, it's all the same. Every last soldier knows that. But for us it's a matter of self-esteem: they will not have Verdun." Rejection could spring from solidarity too, express it how they would. Some men now discerned in decorations, the object of such plaudits in the press, the fraudulent rewards of the well-connected or the contemptible cravings of airmen and career officers. "I couldn't give a damn," a *poilu* wrote to his wife of decorations. "Let them give me my leave. That's all I want now, and peace afterwards. . . ." Was he so different?[83]

After the war the animosities as well as the allegiances of the trenches survived. Particular resentments between front and home could drive men to the extremes of the political spectrum, especially perhaps to the far Right. In Germany such somber after-effects proved poisonous to the frail Weimar Republic, for the high command in the last two years of the war had encouraged estrangement between the men at the front and swaths of the domestic population, in particular striking workers and Socialist deputies, ably preparing opinion for the legend of the stab-in-the-back that the Nazis would exploit to such effect. The reality of the multidimensional soldier, made of group attachments that could work their plural ways, never appeared in the evocations of the postwar years. In both France and Germany, the men of Verdun returned in print or on screen as exemplars of unshakeable union, often to reproach the country for its fragmentation and its decadence if not its ingratitude.[84]

Another word, *grandeur*, confused the significance attributed to the battle with the state of mind of the men who fought it. Poincaré set the tone even before the battle ended, when he addressed the assembled dignitaries of the Entente in Verdun in September. They had come, he began, "to offer the shared tribute of their gratitude to the good men who saved the world and to the proud city which paid with so many scars for freedom's victory," and he ended with his own tribute to "the heroic defenders" who would leave "an undying example of human grandeur."[85]

In time some of the veterans of Verdun began to speak the same way themselves. In 1929 a captain, author, and professor of literature gave a talk about Verdun at the Ecole Polytechnique. He wanted, he said, to talk about what he had seen there, about the everyday realities, but instead he spoke of great deeds, of Driant in the Bois des Caures and Raynal in the Fort de Vaux. A year earlier he had published an article called "Our Days of Glory" in the *Cahiers de la Quinzaine* deploring the indifference of the young, living lives "without enthusiasm or grandeur." But he had not spoken that way when he had published his notebooks in 1917. Then, among the first to rescue the reality of the trenches, including those at Verdun, from the heroic legends in the national press, he had presented a picture without enthusiasm and without grandeur, like another with whom he had served in the brigade—the novelist Henri Barbusse. And the *poilus* had thanked him for it.[86]

Such postwar transfigurations proceeded naturally, as men endowed experience with meaning. A major who left a grim account of his own ordeals at Verdun concluded with a talk he gave there in 1920, on the day Pétain laid the first stone of the ossuary. To relatives and friends gathered on the site where his battalion had fought and held, the major invoked duty and called to his dead comrades: "'He died at Verdun,' your children will say when they grow up and they will owe it to themselves to be worthy of you."[87] When some of the French officers later wrote histories or studies of Verdun, they imputed to the Germans the larger design of world domination, and recorded even if they did not say so the ascension of their own experience onto the stage of world history. Who can blame them? They had invented nothing, not even the grandeur that seemed to attach itself to Verdun with each successive retelling.[88]

Epilogue

"THE SLAUGHTERHOUSE OF THE WORLD": the American ambulance driver whose words begin this book had never seen anything like it. The artillery fire was the most intense he had ever heard, "as continual and rapid as the rolling of a snare drum."[1]

He arrived in August 1917. For the French the battle had already ended once, when they had retaken the forts of Douaumont and Vaux the previous autumn. Now, just as symbolically, it was ending again, on the northern hills of le Mort-Homme and Côte 304 where so many had died. For the Americans it had not yet begun. They first joined combat with the Germans in a major way in the summer of 1918, during the second Battle of the Marne, and later they took over the Verdun sector. On the 22nd of September General John "Black Jack" Pershing, the commander of the American Expeditionary Force, set up his headquarters in the same town hall in Souilly where Pétain had established his, and on the 26th of September yet another massive bombardment began along a front centered at Verdun, this one mostly from American guns—not 1,200 guns, the unprecedented number the Germans had turned onto the French on the 21st of February 1916, but 3,000, followed now by tanks as well.

And again the offensive bogged down, in terrain long rendered impassable by craters, rains, and mud. And again the defenders brought in reinforcements, forcing their American assailants to pay dearly for every foot of land they took. On the morning of the 11th of November the 26th "Yankee" Division stood a few miles north of Verdun, between Beaumont and Ville-devant-Chaumont. The infantry were preparing to go "over the top" when word spread that an armistice had been signed, and a "mysterious, queer, unbelievable" silence, as an officer later described it, settled over the land.[2]

This time the battle of Verdun truly had ended, along with the war itself.

Memory, like amnesia, begins during an event, not after it. As I have tried to show in this book, ways of telling the story of Verdun, from the triumphal to the tragic, appeared in one form or another long before the French recaptured much of the ground at the end of 1916 that they had lost at its beginning. They provided the scripts that private or public chroniclers later dusted off as needed and reworked into the creative recitals of the past that drive national consciousness and even history itself.

Sometimes unwittingly, contemporaries of the battle wrote the plot and furnished the characters, and sometimes unwittingly, others seized on them to turn lackluster attrition into an epic of good and evil. A secondary battle, begun tentatively by one side and accepted reluctantly by another, became in this way a battle for national survival, centering on a place whose millennial historical significance acquired a retroactive glow it had never enjoyed in its lifetime. An attempt by Erich von Falkenhayn to provoke premature counterattacks elsewhere on the front became a monstrous and exclusive design to bleed the local defenders white, and their carefully calibrated response became a self-sacrificing denial to the enemy of access to the heartland. The determination of the German high command to limit its forces in play emerged as the myth of betrayal, an early version of the November 1918 criminals supposed to have stabbed the German army in the back; the determination of the French to do the same, as a wise and avuncular solicitude. The power of the modern state to funnel its people and its millions into a battle without issue soon came wrapped in variants of the myth of voluntarism. A contest of materiel became a triumph of the human spirit over mechanical odds, a battle of attrition a confrontation of wills. "Prestige," a self-fulfilling prophecy that kept the forces in play and rendered withdrawal unthinkable, was converted into the natural but unintended product of the struggle— tragic victory on one side and noble failure on the other. The listless indifference to the prattle of power and press emerged as a selfless devotion to the ideals that officialdom trumpeted by every means at its disposal. The passive acceptance of duty—"resignation"—sustained by primary attachments to home and comrades, emerged in some retellings as a "crusade," in others as a stoical indifference to fate. The sullen and the sour, the marginal and the insubordinate, vanished from memory.

Such mythic retellings, neither more nor less true, only more or less functional, serve purposes that change with time and circumstance. When French heads of state spoke of Verdun, they spoke of some urgent lesson for their time. So did many journalists and popular historians. More often than not, the theme of lost virtue seemed somehow to be at the heart of the matter.

When divisions fractured the country, they spoke of lost unity and elevated the battle into a civics lesson. Assorted journalists had done no less in 1916, before the battle was three weeks old, denouncing the politics of "interests" and exalting at Verdun the "living wall," the pride of the Republic.[3] A national parable was born. An old country so well versed for so long in so many varieties of civil strife had found a moment of communion on the Meuse in 1916; she could do so again. In November 1938, in the gathering gloom after the Munich accords, President Albert Lebrun worried that pockets of selfishness now threatened the integrity of the nation in its hour of need, and he recalled Verdun as a site of sacrifice and of strength.[4] In 1956 President René Coty, a veteran of Verdun, spoke to 40,000 others gathered below the Monument aux Morts in the town on the occasion of the 40th anniversary of the battle. The country was wracked by Cold War tensions, a revolt in Algeria, and ministerial instability. Coty recalled the schisms in France just before the Great War, the Dreyfus affair, the religious passions, the wife of the prominent Radical Joseph Caillaux shooting an equally prominent newspaper editor, the pacifists, the "decadence"—France, he said, had been no less divided against itself during the Belle Epoque than it was now. And still there was Verdun.[5]

Thirty years later François Mitterrand, the president just forced for the first time in the Fifth Republic to govern with a hostile parliamentary majority and prime minister, said much the same on the occasion of the 70th anniversary: Verdun showed the French that they could transcend their differences. They could unite. Ten years later, on the 80th anniversary, President Chirac picked up the theme again, with a dash of nostalgia—worker and farmer, republican and monarchist, believer and unbeliever, had come together there. He had just inaugurated a monument at Verdun to the Moslem soldiers who had served in the French army. Sites of memory already existed for the Jewish soldiers. Verdun now served the cause of inclusion, perhaps even of multiculturalism.[6]

When aggression threatened, heads of state and others—their critics, sometimes—could invoke the spirit of intransigence, the first to echo in the music-halls before the war had ended—the "on ne passe pas" songs of "Victorious Verdun."[7] In 1938, as German aggression gathered pace, the journalist Henry de Kérillis exclaimed that France could cede no more, that it confronted a "diplomatic" Verdun, that it must recover the spirit of the defenders of 1916.[8] Coty, during his speech in 1956, passed from civic community back to warlike determination when he called in the defense of Verdun, of *la patrie en danger*, to dismiss any possibility of abandoning Algeria to "a handful of cutthroats." Four years later Pierre Messmer, the Minister of Defense, invoked it again to applaud the country's newfound confidence, incarnated in its *force de frappe*, its nuclear deterrent: France was now worthy of the dead at Verdun, able to say as they had "on ne passe pas!"[9]

When war-talk, seemingly irrational during the Cold War and irrelevant after it, lost its pertinence, they could exploit the reputation that Verdun enjoyed, however questionably, as a site of unparalleled carnage. A sense of futility had always clung to it, although newspapers at the time could not give voice to it.

Still, sometimes the *poilus* did, in private utterances, and so did more outspoken activists of the far left. Time did not quickly lift the prohibition. Most authors of schoolbooks, commentators in the media, and politicians making the pilgrimage to Douaumont on the 21st of February and other days of the year preferred to celebrate national grandeur. Any commemoration of victory, especially one as slow in coming as Verdun, was intrinsically immodest. Sometimes such commemorations rankled, and a grim reading openly mocked the celebratory one. Twenty years after the battle, in 1936, *Le Petit Journal* gloomily juxtaposed the heroic war of official eloquence with the human remains in the ossuary. The rhetoric, its reporter thought, only deflected his gaze from death and despair. This version survived as long as its brighter rivals. In 1966, during the 50th anniversary commemorations, *Le Monde* lamented that France and Germany had wasted an occasion for reflecting together about the absurdity of ritually celebrating an industrial battle of attrition and about the latter-day risk of nuclear extermination.[10]

Slowly the theme of concord, of "never again," began to eclipse that of lost virtue in the ceremonial remembrance at Verdun. Already in 1924 Henry de Montherlant concluded his *Chant funèbre pour les morts à Verdun*, a lugubrious reflection upon the victims and the ossuary then rising on the site of their sacrifice, with the thought that peace might in time become as grand as war, and become as identifiable with la Patrie as victories paid in blood.[11] Even the Nazis had played with the pacific message of Verdun—in 1936 when they were trying to lull France into a lethargic benevolence.[12] Then the theme disappeared.

But not forever. In 1964 Georges Pompidou, future president and then prime minister, sounded distinctly pacifist at Verdun. The site required that he and others in his position, he said, denounce the absurdity of war. He spoke as President De Gaulle, who had been wounded and taken prisoner there as a young lieutenant in 1916, was promoting détente with the Soviet Union and denouncing the American war in Vietnam.[13] By the end of the century, when the aging ossuary stood on an avenue renamed for the new European Army Corps, the pacific tradition expressed itself as a vague yearning for European unity, and Verdun, far from incarnating resolution in defense of the nation, had come to stand for all that the old civilization must shun. Its survival depended upon it. The orators below the Monument de la Victoire or on the steps of the ossuary saw no contradiction between uplifting the nation in one breath and reducing it in the next. Remember French unity here, Mitterrand had urged in 1986 on the 70th anniversary, only to deliver minutes later an impassioned plea to the leaders of the European Union: "Make Europe! History is waiting." Ten years later Jacques Chirac presided in his turn as doves were released into the sky, and when five Israeli and five Palestinian children gathered at the new Centre Mondial de la Paix in the Episcopal Palace to study the ways of national reconciliation, the metamorphosis seemed complete: Verdun, the symbol of war, had become Verdun, "world capital of peace."[14]

Even if the extinction of 300,000 lives crowded out the survival of the nation as a commemorative theme, the two could sometimes cohabit in the revolutionary legend, that of the people in arms. The site assembled all its elements—unanimity, intransigence, sacrifice, the cause of peace and the ideal of universal concord.

The revolutionary legend, however, like the others, shut its eyes to what had happened here in 1916. No one had won the positional battle; in the end the lines remained essentially unchanged. The attritional battle had ended in a draw, with both sides absorbing the same losses. The French had won the prestige battle, because they had prevailed without allies in a defensive battle on their own soil. From that moment on legend took flight. Next to cultural fantasies historical truths can appear sacrilegious, but to demystify Verdun is not to impugn the compelling power of the truths behind legend, nostalgia, or parable.

In any case, these pass; the battle stays. At Verdun French and German men and their machines fought each other according to the logic and the conventions of the day, without either sinister design or noble purpose, bred by nation-states that enjoyed unprecedented powers over them. Most were neither chauvinists nor pacifists. They were journeymen doing their jobs without enthusiasm, so well and so doggedly that they left behind lasting testimony to the destructive capacities of two of the most creative national cultures in history.

ACKNOWLEDGMENTS

I HAVE MANY ACADEMIC COLLEAGUES to thank in various countries for advice, support, hospitality, or all three: Professor Herrick Chapman of the New York University Institute of French Studies, Professor Jürgen Förster of the Bundesarchiv-Militärarchiv, Professor Sönke Neitzel of the London School of Economics, Professor Nicolas Offenstadt of the Université Paris I Panthéon-Sorbonne, Professor Emeritus Antoine Prost of the Université Paris I Panthéon-Sorbonne, Professor Jeff Ravel of MIT and the organizers of the Boston area French historians' group, Professor Andreas Rödder of the Johannes-Gutenberg Universität of Mainz, Professor David Stevenson of the London School of Economics, Professor Thomas Weber of the University of Aberdeen, and Professor Jay Winter of Yale University. At Brandeis, Professor Govind Sreenivasan helped with the graph on page 117, Dr. Ian Hopper with the cover. Last but not least I thank my colleague David Hackett Fischer, also of Brandeis, for his unfailing support, encouragement, and counsel on this and other projects over the years.

I would also like to thank General Jean-Claude Laparra for his help on the medical services of the German army, Colonel Frédéric Guelton, former director of the Service Historique de la Défense at Vincennes, and Colonel Xavier Pierson, Director of the Memorial de Verdun, for their kindness. At Vincennes Madame Tsao-Bernard solved many problems of access for me during a period of transition and construction there. Thanks to current or former doctoral students at Brandeis: to Daniel Becker for his technical and linguistic expertise, to Clint Walding for digging out a document at the Bundesarchiv-Militärachiv in Freiburg when I could not be there myself, and to Surella Seelig of the Brandeis Archives and Special Collections for help once again, this time with photographs. Kolja Kroeger valuably improved on my own research at the Bayerisches Hauptstaatsarchiv in Munich, and Juliette Roy gave me her mémoire de DEA about "Verdun dans la mémoire allemande (1916–1944)." To both of them I am grateful as well.

Thanks are due as well to the Brandeis University Theodore and Jane Norman Fund for faculty Scholarship and to the Brandeis University Center for German and European Studies for generous financial support.

I would like to thank Ran Halévi, director of the Gallimard series "Les Journées qui ont fait la France" in which this book first appeared, for including it and then devoting much time and energy to it at every stage. Finally, I would like to thank Timothy Bent at Oxford University Press for his work on the English manuscript. He turned a manuscript into a better book, and no author could ask for more. I am also grateful to Keely Latcham for her unfailing professionalism and assistance.

Appendix on Sources

Losses

THE PROTAGONISTS OF THE FIRST WORLD WAR never infallibly established and compared the losses in dead, wounded, and missing that they suffered; *a fortiori*, nor did the historians in their wake. Verdun is a case in point.

Just as the battle was beginning, the French army implemented a new system of recording and tabulating its losses. Until then confusion had reigned. Units had drawn up "états numériques des pertes" every five days and sent them, via their corps and army headquarters, to the Bureau of Personnel of the General Staff. Separately, the health service in the ministry of war received daily counts of entries of wounded servicemen into hospitals and other treatment facilities. But no one had centralized the data, which lay dispersed among the regimental depots, the army General Staff, and the ministries in Paris, including the bureaus in the Ministry of War that recorded deaths (Etat Civil) or injuries and illness (Service de Santé) or conveyed such tidings to the families of the servicemen (Renseignements aux Familles).

To master the administrative anarchy the 1st bureau of the General Staff asked all regimental depots to create and maintain "fiches de position" for every serviceman, recording losses as they had occurred and continued to occur, and it undertook to verify the numbers coming in from the field every five days against these and the health service's daily records of hospitalization and transport of wounded, ill, or gassed servicemen. The system relied upon the requirement that every numerical list from the field match the nominative data from other sources. Applied retroactively to losses since the outbreak of the war, it allowed the 1st bureau to establish loss figures since the beginning of the war, a task that took several months. But as a way of placing loss records on a sounder footing for the duration of the war, it was in place by the end of February 1916, just as the battle of Verdun was beginning.

The weekly, monthly, and annual états numériques des pertes that the 1st bureau drew up in this way are preserved in the Service Historique de la Défense, usually from divisional level up but sometimes from regimental and battalion level as well. They provided the basis for the loss figures made public after the war, by parliamentary commissions in the *Journal Officiel*, the Service Historique in the official history of the war, and other officials and analysts in specialized publications.[1]

In the German armies units in the field compiled *Verlustlisten* and sent them in every ten days. Most of the originals have not survived, but were published after the war by the Reichsarchiv in Potsdam in the *deutsches Jahrbuch*, 1924–1925. During the war German medical units maintained detailed records of military personnel receiving treatment at the front or in hospitals in the interior, the nearest counterpart of the French Service de Santé records. Although the originals of these appear not to have survived either, in 1923 the Zentral Nachweiseamt (Central Information Bureau) published an amended and updated version of lists published during the war, incorporating data from the medical services, which the lists from the field, published in 1924–1925 by the Reichsarchiv, did not. Finally, the official history of the German medical service in the war, published in 1934, reproduced their monthly data on the treatment of the ill and wounded in its three-volume *Sanitätsbericht*.[2]

Using such sources to compare losses between sides in any single battle can be hazardous. Sometimes the data record losses for discrete periods on the Western Front but not for individual battles. In the early 1920s neither Louis Marin, in his full report to the Chamber on belligerent losses, nor the army's chief medical officer, dissecting French losses, were able to present losses by battle. Much later, three archivists, using the statistics compiled by the Service Historique (given in summary form in SHD, 6N58), used the same figures as the Marin report, tabulated with the same limitations. On the German side, the figures compiled by the Reichsarchiv in Potsdam and published in *deutsches Jahrbuch*, 1924–1925, were given as periods on the western front, and not by battle. The fuller German loss figures issued by the *Zentral Nachweiseamt* were not broken down by battle either, but by month for the Eastern and Western Fronts, and were not always easily accessible to historians.[3]

Even when loss figures were compiled for individual battles they were rarely consistent. The *Statistics of the Military Effort of the British Empire during the Great War*, for example, gives different loss figures for the same battles. The Marin report did attempt to give loss figures for some individual battles, apparently on the basis of the numerical reports issued by armies in the field, which Marin acknowledged were unreliable unless verified against the nominal lists in the way that EMA set up in 1916. They gave, for example, a figure of 194,000 for the battle of the Somme between June 20 and November 30, 1916, while the Service de Santé gave a figure of 204,000 for the shorter period between July 1 and November 10.[4]

Finally, some of the data appeared to exclude and some to include the lightly wounded. In April 1917 GQG asked the units drawing up their *états numériques des pertes* and sending them to the Ministry of War to distinguish explicitly in future between those wounded severely enough to be evacuated to hospitals in the interior and those lightly enough to be treated at the front and released within 20 or 30 days. One month before the armistice, the reporting confusion between the two categories had still not been fully resolved. The *Verlustlisten* figures from the Reichsarchiv did not include the lightly wounded, whereas the *Nachweiseamt* figures did. Such disparities raised the risk of comparing diminished German losses excluding the lightly wounded with French losses that included them. Churchill wrestled with the problem when writing *The World Crisis* in the early 1920s. To demonstrate that German losses on the Somme were substantially inferior to those of the British, but aware of the possible disparities between reporting of the lightly wounded, he adjusted the reported German losses upwards by only two percent, while the 30 percent figure that some of his critics demanded would have brought the two armies' losses to practical equality.[5]

Verdun is no different.

Contemporary compilations of the reports from the field or the medical services, when they exist, are rarely comparable or consistent. The German *Sanitätsbericht*, for example, gives no complete data for the sector, and the French Marin report and the Service de Santé give figures at Verdun for different time periods. The matter of the lightly wounded is as murky at Verdun as elsewhere. Among the Germans, the *Sanitätsbericht* does not define "wounded." The numbers reports from the field excluded the lightly wounded altogether, while the French almost certainly included them. Churchill used German losses in Reichsarchiv lists (428,000) and French losses in the Marin report (535,000) for the months of March through June 1916 and November and December 1916 for the Western Front—not broken down by battle, not defining the wounded—to infer for Verdun what he had for the Somme: that the allies had failed at attrition. But was he right?

The *états numériques des pertes* survive in quantity in the Service Historique de la Défence in Vincennes for the Second Army at the battle of Verdun. They provide the basis for most of the losses given or estimated in the Marin report, the French official history, and the Service de Santé, and by historians since who did not trust the wild estimates often aired but rarely documented. They still give rise to small discrepancies, mostly due to time frames and possibly to recounts, but all range between 348,000 and 378,000. The German counterparts—the reports that AOK5 sent every ten days to OHL and that the Reichsarchiv used to publish the more general counts by time period on the Western Front—have not survived. In 1930, however, before their destruction, a German historian, Hermann Wendt, used them to establish the most precise comparison to date of French and German losses at Verdun. On the basis of the figures from the French Second Army, provided to him by Vincennes, and those of AOK5, provided by the Reichsarchiv, he put German losses at 336,831 and French losses at 362,000, between February 21, and December 20, 1916. But he did not consider the possibility that the German figures excluded the lightly wounded while the French did not, narrowing the gap between the two even more. How can or should his conclusions be adjusted?[6]

In 2006 a historian, James McRandle, and an economist, James Quirk, used the *Sanitätsbericht*, which did include the lightly wounded, to rectify the undercount in the *Verlustlisten* that the Reichsarchiv used. They concluded that the Reichsarchiv reports, which did not include the lightly wounded, underestimated losses by about 11 percent. Using the 11 percent adjustment to revise the field report *Verlustlisten* that Wendt used for Verdun, the figures for total German losses at Verdun would rise to 373,882—almost exactly the same as the French losses given in the French Official History at the same date of December 20 (373, 231). The loss ratio over the ten months of the battle would thus approach 1:1, and the excess of German over French casualties during the same period that

Churchill noted can only be explained by events elsewhere on the Front, including the Somme and quieter sectors.[7]

A similar conclusion emerges from examining another table in the *Sanitätsbericht*, published in 1935 by the Kriegsministerium for training and other exercises, but not used by McRandle and Quirk in their study.

The table compared German loss rates at Verdun with those in Poland and Galicia in 1914 and 1915 and on the Somme in 1916. Over 20 ten-day reporting periods, the Fifth Army at Verdun had an average of 37.7 men killed, wounded, or missing for every thousand in each unit, lower than that of the Ninth Army in Poland over nine ten-day units in 1914 (48.1), of the Eleventh Army in Galicia in 1915 over 12 ten-day units (52.4), of the First Army (54.7) on the Somme over 13 ten-day units in 1916 (54.7), but close to that of the Second Army on the Somme over 16 ten-day units in 1916 (39.1). The numbers, as the *Saintätsbericht* clearly indicated for this table, excluded the lightly wounded.[8]

Similar figures for the French Second Army do not exist, but can be roughly calculated. From archival records, French losses in the period of 20 ten-day units stretching from February 21 to September 20 totaled 321,947. Allowing for 18 divisions in line at the battle of Verdun over most of the battle—even with about 25 divisions in the Second Army not all were in line at any given moment—and an average strength of 18,000 per division, the French average loss rate per 1000 men in each ten-day period comes to 40.9. But this number would include the lightly wounded. McRandle's and Quirk's adjustment of 11 percent to the equivalent German rate (37.7) to include the lightly wounded would bring the two loss rates to near equality.[9]

These calculations are only approximate, but at least suggest strongly that German and French loss rates at Verdun were even closer than Wendt's computations showed them to be.

Memoirs and Journals

Jean Norton Cru provoked a scandal when he published his *Témoins* in 1929. He examined some 300 firsthand accounts of the war by soldiers and officers up to the rank of captain, found some excellent, others absurd, and many others in-between. Those who felt impugned counter-attacked, while most historians came to his defense. But when the book was reissued in 1993, some historians turned on it. Where the authors of journals and reminiscences had attacked his skepticism, the historians now attacked his credulity. Memory, in the eyes of the doubters, loses precision with time; it is subjective; it hides much, such as the bayonet and bloodlust, and pretends much, such as victimization or heroism; it is subjective, it exculpates its owner; all experience is structured by narrative anyway—best to search elsewhere, they argued, for the lived experience of the war, including the involuntary traces left by material and cultural productions of front and home.[10]

Yes, memory fades with time, but of some 92 published and unpublished firsthand accounts by soldiers and officers used in this work, 49 date from between 1915 and 1918 and 25 from between 1919 and 1928. (Fictional works relying on personal experience, which Cru did include, are not included in this count, but most of those used in this work were also written during or within a few years of Verdun.) Memory is subjective, but absence is not the same as omission, nor silence as dissimulation. Soldiers in that age elided sexual matters from their writings out of discretion, and if they rarely wrote of bayoneting, it is because they rarely bayoneted. "Aucun témoin digne de foi [no trustworthy witness]," Delvert wrote in his review of Cru's book, "ne parle de chocs à la baïonette,—ces chocs qui ont tordu tant de lames chez les romanciers et les hableurs [speaks of bayonet clashes—the clashes that had so many storytellers twisting blades]." Some soldiers wrote of themselves as less than willing, but need this signify the repression of inner "consent," when anger, resentment, and insubordination left their traces in other ways? And yes, a haze clouded their experience. They acknowledged it. Thirty-six hours after attacking on the slopes of le Mort-Homme, Méléra noted, his memory was confused, mixing the impression of horror with the smell of corpses. Days after counterattacking near Fort Vaux, Gaudy found his recollections obscured by a smokescreen that allowed only "visions flottantes, intraduisibles [floating, inexpressible visions]. . . ." Twenty years after Verdun Mac Orlan retained in his mind only "photographies mal fixées et mal lavées . . . des images jaunes qui s'effacent arbitrairement [blurred, poorly developed photogaphs . . . yellowing, arbitrarily vanishing images]." But such mental states, along with physical recollections confirming one and another's across accounts, are themselves the stuff of historical inquiry. Why should memory invalidate the memoir?[11]

Cru relied on his own common sense, experience, and vast reading to sort out the plausible from the implausible. Perhaps he condemned as inauthentic too many sentiments that he himself did not share. But 80 years later a historian can still spot inflated dialogues, contrived anecdotes, overwrought emotions. He can still ignore the more extravagant among them, and retain those that conspire among themselves and with other sources to recover the physical and mental world of the men in the trenches.

Postal Censors

By the time of the battle of Verdun the French postal censors had widened their scrutiny from detecting and security breaches in letters to and from the front to measuring morale in the armies. By March 1916 each army had established a *commission de contrôle postal* to read samples of the weekly or biweekly correspondence, selecting different units (regiments or divisions) in turn because of the impossibility of sampling all of them. The *rapporteurs* assessed morale by dissecting the letters according to a four-part questionnaire, progressively refined over the course of the year, about the attitude of the men to their physical conditions, to the war, to the outside world, and to the home front; they usually included extracts from the letters, and soon began tabulating the results of their questionnaires. For the Second Army at Verdun the weekly (and sometimes daily) reports survive in massive bundles in 16N 1391 and 16N 1392; the biweekly analyses performed at GQG for all armies, in 16N 1485; the letters alarming enough to be seized *in toto* for all armies, in 16N 1545 (from March to June 1916). The source, precious enough as a window into what the men were writing home, is yet subject to caveats.[12]

How representative are the samples? In 1916 the *rapporteurs* did not always provide numbers; only in 1917 did individual synthesis give way to consistent analysis, usually 500 letters per regiment (i.e., about one in five) per month, making the reports statistically less shaky than those for 1916. The evidence for the Second Army suggests that *rapporteurs*, when sampling a company, could occasionally read as many as one letter for every two men, but—more typically—several hundred per division, or perhaps one for every fifty or sixty men. Such statistically insignificant sampling yielded at best informed impressions about the moods of some men in some units throughout the battle of Verdun.[13]

Even then, how reliable are the assessments of the *rapporteurs*? Lieutenants and captains may report what they wish to see, or what they imagine their superiors wish to hear. But no such wishful transfigurations emerge from these sources—they more often report low morale than high, and do not shrink from descriptions of the men, including mental states verging on cynicism, that could and did worry their superiors: such was the purpose of tracking morale.

Finally, how spontaneous were the words that men put to paper? The postal censors never shed their repressive functions, and the men knew their letters might be read. The censors retained a repressive function, never a laudatory one, providing incentives to conceal but not to affect or pretend. "Très nombreux [Many fear the censors]," as one of the censors noted in March, "sont ceux qui craignent la censure et se réservent de raconter ce qu'ils ont vu à la prochaine permission très escomptée [and save tales of what they've seen for their next, much-awaited leaves]. . . ." Listlessness and indifference they might avow, but not angry thoughts or seditious whims, which surfaced at other moments in other ways and the absence of which in letters reveals nothing about its extent. Some of them wished as well to avoid alarming the recipients at home. Already in 1914 Maurice Genevoix had asked himself as he wrote home, "pourquoi les peiner, pourquoi les décevoir [why give them grief, why let them down]" and reined in his pencil as he wrote home. All the more reason to credit the *cafard*, the misery, and the wish that the war would end: why invent?[14]

Like all archives, the reports of the postal censors speak timidly and obliquely; they speak for some but not for all, yielding impressions that can only aspire to judgments and conclusions when other sources and other traces come to their help.

LIST OF ABBREVIATIONS

AD	Archives Départementales
AFGG	Les Armées françaises dans la Grande Guerre
AN	Archives Nationales
AOK5	Armee-Oberkommando, 5th Army
BA-MA	Bundesarchiv-Militärarchiv (Freiburg-im-Breisgau)
BHSA	Bayerisches Hauptstaatarchiv (Munich)
BNF n.acq. fr.	Bibliothèque nationale de France, nouvelles acquisitions françaises
CA	Corps d'Armée
Cdt	Commandant
DI	Division d'infanterie
EMA	Etat-Major de l'Armée
GQG	Grand Quartier Général (Chantilly)
INA	Institut National de l'Audiovisuel
MV	Mémorial de Verdun
OHL	Oberste Heeresleitung
RI	Régiment d'infanterie
SHD	Service Historique de la Défense (Vincennes)
S/lt	Sous-lieutenant

NOTES

Introduction

1. France Inter (radio), February 26, 1966 (Genevoix).
2. Ibid. (Romains)
3. Cf. e.g., *Tragödie*, vol. 13, part I, 252–57; Münch, *Verdun*, 464–65; Krumeich, "soldat allemand," in Cochet, *Verdun*.
4. Horne, *Glory*, 13–14.
5. Brown, *Verdun*, 19.
6. Coker, *Future of War*, 8; TF 1, May 11, 1995: "Verdun, symbole de la guerre."
7. Duroselle, preface to Lacaze, *Opinion*, 9.
8. Cf. e.g., Estre, *Enigme*; Horne, *Glory*; Canini, *Combattre*; Jauffret, "Quinze ans"; a search on Google Ngrams revealed sharp peaks around 1926 and 1966 of the mention of "Verdun" in a large corpus of publications.

Chapter 1

1. D'Artie, *Vérité*, I, 179; Ettighoffer, *Gericht*, 39.
2. Gaudy, *Souvenirs*, I, 92; D'Artie, *Vérité*, I, 179; Hoffmann, *Deutsche Soldat*, 232 (Eugen Ernst, February 19, 1916); Denizot, *Verdun*, 77–78; Muenier, *Angoisse*, 11; Ettighoffer, *Gericht*, 39.
3. Limosin, *Verdun a L'Yser*, 16; Hoffmann, *Deutsche Soldat*, 232–33 (Eugen Ernst, February 21, 1916); Ettighoffer, *Gericht*, 44; Denizot, *Verdun*, 78.
4. Vollbehr, *Heeresgruppe*, 46–49.
5. Grasset, *Choc*, 44 ff; SHD 24N 1834, Chrétien report, April 15, 1916; MV, journal of Charles Albert Derozières, February 21, 1916; Bernède, *Point de vue français*, 81–82.

6. Stéphane, *Relève*, 50–51, 64–68, 76–77.

7. Grasset, *Verdun*, 44 ff; Desfosses, "premier jour"; Charles Leroy, France Inter, February 26, 1966; Stéphane, *Relève*, 51–52.

8. Stéphane, *Relève*, 91.

9. Koch, *Verdun*, 16–19; Grasset, *Verdun*, 61.

10. SHD 16N 1979, report of March 11, 1916; SHD 24N 1834, summary report, April 15, 1916; Bouvard, *Gloire*, 82.

11. Grasset, *Verdun*, 61; Desfosses, "premier jour"; Koch, *Verdun*, 16–23; Huchzermeier, "Angriff"; both Koch and Huchzermeier served in the 159th Infantry Regiment, which attacked in Haumont woods on February 21, 1916.

12. Bernède, *Verdun*, 83; Leroy, France Inter, February 26, 1966; Grasset, *Verdun*, 131; Koch, *Verdun*, 45–48.

13. Genty, *Trois Ans*, entry for February 21, 1916.

14. AFGG, t. IV, vol. 1, 34–35, 134–43, and annexe 130: ordre du jour, February 2, 1916.

15. Poirier, *Verdun*; Ettighoffer, *Gericht*, 5.

16. Prost, "Verdun."

17. Hourticq, *Récit et Réflexions*, 92; D'Artie *Vérité*, I, 180; Madelin, *Verdun*, 37; *Tragödie*, vol. 13, 1, 38; Erbeling, *Verdun*, vii; Brandt, *Kriegschauplatz*, 191.

18. Poirier, *Verdun*; Paul, *Doaumont*; Brandt, *Kriegschauplatz*, 214–16; Romains, *Verdun*.

19. *Echo de Paris*, February 26, 1916; SHD 16N 1981, Rapport du Colonel Benoit, November 23, 1917.

20. Afflerbach, *Falkenhayn*, 55–57.

21. *AFGG*, t. IV, vol. 2, 155–58; Pelade, *Verdun*.

22. Gallwitz, *Erleben*, 21.

23. Herr, *Artillerie*, 85.

24. SHD 16N 1977, *Notes d'un témoin*, October 30, 1916.

25. Marc, *Pilote disparu*, 57–58, 92–93.

26. Pelade, *Verdun*; Herr, *Artillerie*, 85; Hourticq, *Récit et réflexions*, 107–18.

27. Pelade, *Verdun*.

28. Gueit-Montchal, "Commémorations."

29. In a sample of 40 radio and television broadcasts at INA from 1951 to 2006 about the battle of Verdun, 11 occurred on or immediately before or after the 21st of February; next came five broadcasts on or immediately before or after the 23rd of June; those on the 11th of November were linked to the armistice and are difficult to use for purposes of comparison.

30. "La Grande Guerre en chansons," Septième/Arte (television), November 11, 1993; Theodore Botrel, *Refrains de Guerre* (3 vols., Paris, 1915–1920), vol. 3, *Chants de Bataille et de Victoire* (Paris, 1920); *Le Temps*, February 23, 1920, February 22, 1921, February 22, 1926.

31. Cf. Preface by Fortunat Strowski in Joubaire, *France*.

Chapter 2

1. Christian Delporte, "Journalistes et correspondants de guerre," in Stéphane Audoin-Rouzeau and Jean-Jacques Becker, eds., *Encyclopédie de la grande guerre 1914–1918* (Paris, 2004) 717–29.

2. *Le Gaulois*, February 22, 26, 1916; *Le Matin*, February 23, 24, 25, 1916; *Le Petit Journal*, February 25, 1916; *L'Humanité*, February 26, 1916; SHD 6N46 résumés de la presse, February 24, 1916. The Kaiser was the Supreme Commander of the Imperial German army, but orders were issued in his name by the effective commander, the Chief of the General Staff of OHL. In the field the personnel surrounding the Kaiser were known as the "Great Headquarters" (Grosse Hauptquartier), distinct from OHL (Cron, *Imperial German Army*, 14).

3. *Frankfurter Zeitung und Handelsblatt*, February 23, 24, 1916; *Berliner Tageblatt*, February 24 and March 7, 1916; *Münchner Neueste Nachrichten*, February 24, 1916; *Vorwärts*, February 24, 25, 26, 28, 29, 1916.

4. Falkenhayn,"Verdun"; Falkenhayn, *Oberste Heeresleitung*, 183–84.

5. *Weltkrieg*, X, 2, n.1 (the authors speculated that he might have given the Christmas Memorandum to the Kaiser in successive portions); *Tragödie*, vol. 13, 1, n.15.

6. See for example Groener, *Lebenserinnerungen*, 284, Liddell Hart, *Real War*, 214–16, and Bouvard, *Gloire de Verdun*, 34–40; Afflerbach, *Falkenhayn*, 543–45; Krumeich, "Saigner"; Foley, *German Strategy*, 205–6.

7. Janssen, *Kanzler und General*; BA-MA W-10 50704, Schulenburg (1935); BA-MA W-10 50705, von Mertz, 15.11.33; BA-MA W-10/50709, Solger (1933); Hohenborne, *Briefe*, 60; Bauer, *Grosse Krieg*, 58, 71–72; Zwehl, *Falkenhayn*, 8–9; Groener, *Lebenserinnerungen*, 317; Afflerbach, *Falkenhayn*, 214 n.312 and 217.

8. Stürgkh, *Hauptquartier*, 81.

9. Foley, *Attrition*, 87–91, 103–4; Janssen, *Kanzler und General*, 28–32; Groener, *Lebenserinnerungen*, 178–81.

10. Wild, *Briefe*, 124; Janssen, *Kanzler*, 66–67, 142–46; Fischer, *Weltmacht*, 217 ff.

11. Foley, *Attrition*, 138–51; Buat, *Armée allemande*, 22–25.

12. Afflerbach, *Falkenhayn*, 55–57, 76–79; Kraft, *Staatsräson*, 156–64; Janssen, *Kanzler*, 44–50, 56–66, 74–77, 147; Fischer, *Weltmacht*, 222, 232–34.

13. Afflerbach, *Falkenhayn*, 55–57, 76–79; Kraft, *Staatsräson* (Göttingen, 1980), 156–64; Janssen, *Kanzler*, 44–50, 56–66, 74–77, 147; Fischer, *Weltmacht*, 222, 232–34; Wild, *Briefe*, 72–77, 96, 111–14; BA-MA, W-10/50705, "Falkenhayn as Feldherr," Groener, March 5, 1934; Groener, *Lebenserinnerungen*, 281–82.

14. Kraft, *Staatsräson*, passim. Afflerbach, *Falkenhayn*, 147–71, *passim*.

15. Wild, *Briefe*, 77 (July 1915), (November 4, 1915), 120 (December 11, 1915); BA-MA, W-10/50705, "Falkenhayn as Feldherr," Groener, March 5, 1934, von Tappen, June 16, 1932, von Mertz, November 15, 1933; BA-MA, W-10/50709, Solger; Bauer, *Grosse Krieg*, 100–102; Groener, *Lebenserinnerungen*, 279.

16. BA-MA, W-10/50709, Solger.
17. Madelin, *Verdun*, 1–8; Bidou, "Bataille"; Bouvard, *Gloire*, 14–19. Locally the Hauts de Meuse were (and still are) known as the Côtes de Meuse. The name Verdun would have meant "fortified village" in Celtic. I am grateful to M. Roger Chazal for pointing this out to me.
18. BA-MA, W-10 50705, Groener, March 5, 1934; SHD 1N 51, "Note of May 17, 1923, and study on "rôle historique des places fortes françaises," n.d. [1924]; Werth, *Verdun*, 14–20, 26–29; Bernède, *Verdun*, 47–62; Bichet, *Role des forts*, 17–19; Rémy Porte, "Verdun avant Verdun."
19. Porte, "Verdun avant Verdun."
20. BA-MA W-10/50704, Schulenburg"; W-10/50709, Solger; W-10/51528, Tappen conversation, 6.IX.1932, transcript dated September 19, 1932); BA-MA W-10/50705, Groener, March 5, 1934, and former Kaiser Wilhelm, February 25, 1934.
21. *Weltkrieg*, X, 26–28, 36–37; BA-MA, W-10/50705, von Kuhl, January 10, 1916; BA-MA, W-10/50709, Solger, Falkenhayn notes of January 8 and 27, 1916; Einem, *Armeeführer*, 195 (February 2, 1916); Wendt, *Verdun*, 36–43; Groener, *Lebenserinnerungen*, 290.
22. *Weltkrieg*, X, 33–34, 39–40; Koeltz, Louis (Général), "Falkenhayn."
23. Falkenhayn, *Oberste Heeresleitung*, 183–84.
24. BA-MA, W-10/50705, Groener, March 5, 1934; W-10/51523, Kuhl, November 12, 1934; W-10/51528, Tappen, September 19, 1932; somewhat confusingly and inconsistently, Groener in his memoirs,(*Lebenserinnerungen*, 285), wrote that "No one of us had imagined that Falkenhayn's theory of bleeding [the enemy] to death would have such negative consequences for us"; Falkenhayn, "Verdun" and *Oberste Heeresleitung*, 199–200.
25. Falkenhayn, *Oberste Heeresleitung*, 192, 199–200; Wendt, *Verdun*, 5–7, 12–18, and Kabisch, *Verdun*, 1–7; Foley, *Attrition*, 1–13, 21 ff; Strachan, "Cabinet War."
26. Wild, *Briefe*, 59–60 (April 3 and 13–14, 1915), 72–77; BA-MA, W-10/50709, Solger, quote attributed to Falkenhayn in meeting with Kaiser at Pless, December 3, 1915.
27. Afflerbach, *Falkenhayn*, 376–78; Alfred von Tirpitz, *Erinnerungen* (Leipzig, 1919), 352, 356, 362–68; Müller, *Kaiser*, 124–38; Wild, *Briefe* 128–29; Kraft, *Staatsräson*, 173–80.
28. Afflerbach, *Falkenhayn*, 376; Kabisch, *Verdun*, 7–21; Tirpitz, *Erinerrungen*, 368.
29. AFGG, t. 3, vol. 1, 363–64, 549; *Weltkrieg*, IX, 60–68; Falkenhayn was surprised by the scope of the French attack in Champagne (BA-MA, W-10/50705, von Tappen, June 16, 1932), and had been alarmed by it; see the exchange reported by Wild between him and Falkenhayn, *Briefe*, 91: "War die Sache kritisch im Westen?" "Ja."; Delbrück, *Ludendorff* (Berlin, 1920), 64; Pelade, *Verdun*. Some, including Pelade, believed Falkenhayn hoped to encircle the Second Army at Verdun, but there is little evidence that Falkenhayn ever mentioned the possibility.

30. Both Wendt (*Verdun*, 43) and Kabisch (*Verdun*, 51–53) cited Kuhl's account of this meeting.

31. BA-MA, W-10 50705, Knobelsdorf, January 6, 1934, and Groener, March 5, 1934; Wendt (*Verdun*, 26–33) cites a letter to him from Tappen dated July 19, 1929, in which Tappen confirms the claims made in the Christmas Memorandum on the basis of a conversation with Falkenhayn on December 8, 1915, but on September 19, 1932 (BA-MA, W-10 51528), Tappen recalled that Falkenhayn had always aimed to provoke attacks elsewhere on the front; Groener, *Lebenserinnerungen*, 284.

32. Kabisch, *Verdun*, 50–64; Janssen, *Kanzler*, Anhang 5, (288); BHSA, Mkr 1832/5, report of February 22, 1916.

33. Falkenhayn, *Oberste Heeresleitung*, "Vorwort."

34. Delbrück, *Ludendorff*, 44–50.

35. Rupprecht, *Kriegstagebuch*, vol. 2, 372; Herwig, *Germany and Austria-Hungary*, 408.

36. Drevillon, *Batailles*, 254–55.

37. See note 2 above.

38. *Berliner Tageblatt*, March 2, 7, 1916; *Münchner neueste Nachrichten*, March 12, 1916.

39. *Le Gaulois*, February 28, 1916; *Le Matin*, February 25, 1916; *Le Petit Journal*, February 24, 25, 1916; *Figaro*, February 25, 1916; SHD 6N46 résumés de la presse, February 24, 1916.

40. Schoolbooks in sequence: Bernard, *Supplément*, 60–64; Giraud, *Miracle*, 19–22; Giraud, *Histoire*, 321–22; A. Lespes, P. Chales, *Histoire* (Paris, 1924), 349–50; Jullian, *Guerre*, 576; Ozouf et Leterrier, *Cours moyen*, 216; Martignon, *Histoire*, 140; Malleterre, *Court récit*, 22.

41. Lomont, *Route de la Victoire*, 87; Reinach, *Front Occidental*, 47.

42. Hanotaux, *Circuits*, 20–21, 219–20; Malleterre, *Court récit*, 22; Malet et Isaac, *Histoire contemporaine*, 599; for Vichy see e.g. Fay et al., *Histoire*, 286, and Jalabert, *Vive la France!*, 181–83, who pass over German motives at Verdun in silence; Marc Ferro in *Le Monde*, February 19 and 22, 1966.

43. Pétain, *Verdun*, 15–22; *Le Monde*, May 31, 1966; see above, pp. 27 ff. and note 4; Becker and Krumeich, *Grande Guerre*, 215–17; Geiss et al., *Manuel d'histoire*, 196.

44. Halmburger and Brauburger, *Verdun* (film).

Chapter 3

1. Madelin, *Verdun*, 155; Grigg, *Lloyd George*, 380–81; D'Artie, *Vérité*, I, 180; Bonne, *Cours d'histoire*, 274.

2. Pierrefeu, *Quartier Général*, vol 1, 94–104; Rimbault *Marmité*, 105–9; Zwehl, *Falkenhayn*, 7–9.

3. Pierrefeu, *Grand Quartier*, 94; Delbrück, *Ludendorff*, 44–50.

4. Doughty, *Pyrrhic Victory*, 113 ff, 155–57, 168, 172; AFGG, t. 3, vol. 1, 683; SHD 6N46, *L'Homme Enchaîné*, January 2, 1916, *L'Oeuvre*, January 2, 1916; Pierrefeu, *Grand Quartier*, 104–10; Galliéni, *Carnets*, entry of January 4, 1916.

5. AFGG, t. IV, vol. 1, annex 130; Cochet "6–8 décembre"; Buat, *Armée allemande*, 22, 30.

6. SHD 6N52, *Etude sur la situation stratégique* (n.d., January 1916); SHD 1K268, GQG notes of January 17 and 19, and conseil supérieur de la défense nationale, February 8, 1916; AFGG, t. IV, vol. 1, annexe 130.

7. Ibid.

8. SHD 5N 134, notes of January 9, 15, 16, 19, 22, 27, 1916 and February 6, 14, 16, 1916.

9. AFGG, t. IV, vol. 1, 137–53; SHD 24N 1834, notes of January 30, 31, 1916; February 3–12, 14–16, 1916; SHD 16N 1979, note of March 11, 1916; Werth, *Verdun*, 81–82; Morizot, "aviation."

10. Bernède, *Verdun*, 47–62; *Kaiser's Army*, 211–14, 221–23; AFGG t. IV, vol. 1, 95–106.

11. AFGG, t. IV, vol. 1, 122; Grasset, *Verdun*, 17–19; AN C7646, Maginot, June 16, 1916.

12. Ferry, *Carnets*, 128–29; Galliéni, *Carnets*, 231, 235; Joffre, *Mémoires*, vol. 2, 160; BNF, nouv. acq. fr. 16032, Poincaré, notes of December 16 and 21, 1915; SHD 5N 136 Joffre-Galliéni letters, December 16 and 18, 1915.

13. Ferry, *Carnets*, 128–29; Galliéni, *Carnets*, 231; BNF, nouv. acq. fr. 16032, Poincaré notes for December 16, 1915–January 1, 1916.

14. AFGG, t. IV, vol. 1, 158, Herr to Dubail, January 16, 1916; SHD 24N 1834, note of February 8, 1916; Mermeix, *Joffre.*, 150; Grasset, *Verdun*, 17–19; Bernède, *Verdun*, 74–81.

15. AFGG, t. IV, vol. 1, 155, 170, 189; Joffre, *Mémoires*, vol. 2, 203; Rémy Porte, "Verdun avant Verdun"; Grasset, *Verdun*, 17–19.

16. Rémy Porte, "Verdun avant Verdun"; Pelade, *Verdun*.

17. Pierrefeu, *Grand Quartier*, 122; Serrigny, *Trente ans*, 48 ff.

18. SHD 5N 134, report (n.d., c. February 25, 1916) on withdrawal plans; SHD 16N 1981, monograph on Fort de Vaux, July 20, 1916; SHD, 24N 1672, General Aimé to 7CA, February 29, 1916; Bernède, *Verdun*, 90–93.

19. Ferry, *Carnets*, 181 (March 20, 1916), 186 (June 27, 1916); Doughty, *Pyrrhic Victory*, 271; Poincaré, *Service*, VIII (1931), 115; BNF, nouv. acq. fr., 16032, Poincaré note of December 26, 1915; Galliéni, *Carnets*, 216, 262; Keiger, *Poincaré*, chap. 7, *passim*.

20. Doughty, *Pyrrhic Victory*, 44–45; Joffre, *Mémoires*, II, 151.

21. BNF, nouv. acq. fr., 16032, Poincaré notes for November 28 and December 7, 8, 17, 1915.

22. Pelade, *Verdun*.

23. Cochet, "Chantilly"; Pierrefeu, *Grand Quartier*, 94 ff.

24. AFGG, t. IV, vol. 1, 143, 151–52, 169; t. IV, vol. 1, annexes 1, nos. 427 and 428.

25. Serrigny, *Trente ans*, 24 ff; Pierrefeu, *Grand Quartier*, 130; Pétain, *Verdun*, 37.

26. *L'Action*, February 25, 1916, *La Victoire*, February 29, 1916, *L'Oeuvre*, March 1, 1916, *L'Echo de Paris*, March 1, 1916 (all from SHD 6N46, Résumés de la presse); Renaudel in *L'Humanité*, February 28, 1916.

27. *Frankfurter Zeitung und Handelsblatt*, March 2, 1916; *Berliner Tageblatt*, February 28, March 1, 1916; *Echo de Paris*, February 26, 1916, and *Le Matin* February 25, 1916; *Le Petit Journal*, March 4, 1916; SHD, 6N46, résumés de presse for February 24, 25 and March 14, 1916.

28. Grant, *Verdun Days*, 16.

29. *La Victoire*, March 6, 1916.

30. Goethe, *Campagne de France*, 45–47; *L'Echo de Paris*, February 25 and 26, 1916; *Le Matin*, February 25, 1916; Madelin, *Verdun*, 89–90.

31. Suarès, *Ceux de Verdun* (Paris, 1916), vii; Jullian, *Leçons*, 104; Dugard, *Victoire de Verdun*, 18–19; Madelin, *Verdun*, 1–6, 41–42; Lechevalier, *Précis*, 41–42; *Le Monde*, February 22, 1966.

Chapter 4

1. Zwehl, *Falkenhayn*, 189–90; AOK 5 Kriegstagebuch, December 16, 1915, and Kronprinz Wilhelm to Falkenhayn January 4, 1916, from Wendt, *Verdun*, appendix 3; *Weltkrieg*, X, 26–28, 33–36; Wendt, *Verdun*, 50–64; BA-MA, W-10 50704, *Schulenburg* (1935), 68–73.

2. *Weltkrieg*, X, 81, 94–95; AFGG, t. IV, vol. 1, 290–91; Koch, *Verdun*, 21–23.

3. AFGG, t. IV, vol. 1, 258; SHD 16N 1981, report of November 23, 1917; Muenier, *Angoisse*, 197 (entry dated the 25th in error); Mémorial de Verdun, journal of Derozières, February 2, 1916.

4. Bouvard, *Gloire*, 58–62; Deimling, *Souvenirs*, 228 ff; BA-MA, W-10 51528, *Wetzell* (1926); Dubrulle, *Régiment*, 38.

5. AFGG, t. IV, vol. 1, 294 n.2; *Weltkrieg*, X, 94.

6. Grasset, *Verdun*, 17–19; Werth, *Verdun*, 61; Denizot, *Verdun*, 72: heavy artillery, French, 150, Germans 733; light artillery, French 131, Germans 524, to which should be added the Germans' 150 trench mortars (*minenwurfer*).

7. Louis Chagnon, "1916 ou l'année de rupture en matière d'utilisation de l'arme aérienne," *Revue Historique des Armées*, 242, (1er trimestre, 2006): 37–47; Denizot, *Verdun*, 74.

8. See ch. 1.

9. *Weltkrieg*, X, 72; Denizot, *Verdun*, 77–78; Bouvard, *Gloire*, 82, 87; Grasset, *Verdun*, 8.

10. SHD 24N 1834, report of February 23, 1916; AFGG, t. IV. vol. 1, 214–26; *Tragödie*, I, 18–22; SHD 24N 1834, April 15, 1916; Grasset, *Verdun*, 17 ff.

11. AFGG, t. IV, vol. 1, annexes 1, n.d., note of February 21, 1916; AFGG, t. IV, vol. 1, 219.

12. See ch. 3.

13. Bichet, *Role des Forts*, 25–32; Werth, *Verdun*, 95–110; Madelin, *Verdun*, 63–64; SHD, 16N 1981, note Sonnerat (n.d.) and Benoit, November 23, 1917; BA-MA, W-10 51528, *Wetzell*.

14. Cailleteau, *Gagner*, 48 ff; Zwehl, *Falkenhayn*, 187–88 (Zwehl received the French surrender of Maubeuge on September 8, 1914); AFGG, t. I, vol. 2, 477.

15. SHD 1KT 126 1, Chevriers to his uncle, February 26, 1916.
16. Werth, *Verdun*, 69–76 (from interviews); Bichet, *Role des Forts*, 57–64; Hoeppner, *Krieg in der Luft*, 50–52.
17. Grasset, *Verdun*, 72; Kabisch, *Verdun*, 67–81; AFGG t. IV, vol. 1, 230–31, 245.
18. SHD 5N136, Pech to Min. of War, December 12, 1915; Pineau, "camions de Verdun"; Ragueneau, *Stratégie des transports*, 60–63; Rémy Porte, "Verdun avant Verdun."
19. Navarre, *Services automobiles*, 16; Pineau, "épopée des camions"; Doumenc, *Transports automobiles*, 49–52; Limosin, *Verdun à L'Yser*, 50.
20. Serrigny, *Trente ans*, 46–48.
21. Pelade, *Verdun*; AFGG, t. IV, vol. 1, 262, 277, and t. IV, vol. 1, annexes 1, nos. 680 and 681.
22. Nouv. acq. fr. 16032, Poincaré note of December 4, 1915; Pedroncini, *Pétain*, 78–79, 100–101, 112–13, 131.
23. AFGG, t. IV, vol. 1, 287, and appendix I, 647; Serrigny, *Trente ans*, 546–56, 63–66.
24. *Weltkrieg*, X, 94–95.
25. Crown Prince William, *Memoirs*, 210; Wendt, *Verdun*, 80; Groener, *Lebenserinnerungen*, 291; Bauer, *Grossekrieg*, 100–102; Zwehl, *Falkenhayn*, 187–88.
26. *Weltkrieg*, X, 72; Zwehl, *Falkenhayn*, 189–90; Crown Prince William, *Memoirs*, 210–12; Groener, *Lebenserinnerungen*, 290; Hohenborne, *Briefe*, 132.
27. Zwehl, *Falkenhayn*, 187–88;Wendt, *Verdun*, 88–89, *Tragödie*, 252–57; Bernède, "autopsie"; Kabisch, *Verdun*, 82–84; Bouvard, *Gloire*, 111.
28. Groener, *Lebenserinnerungen*, 292.
29. SHD 24N 909, résumé du 25 juin 1916; *Le Matin*, May 10, 21, 22, 1916.
30. Bichet, *Role des Forts*, 33–40, 48–56; SHD 1KT 69, Nathan; SHD 16N 1981, report of November 23, 1917; Wendt, *Verdun*, 183; Raynal, *Journal, passim*; *Weltkrieg*, X, 180, 192–94, 267.
31. AFGG, t. IV, vol. ii, 49; SHD 24N 85, reports of May 29 and 30, 1916; SHD 24N 87, Mangin report, May 31, 1916; Morel-Journel, *Journal*, entry for September 14, 1916.
32. AFGG, t. IV, vol. 2, 309–13.
33. SHD 16N 1977, *renseignements tirés de l'attaque du October 24, 1916*, n.d., notes of October 30, 1916, and report from "un témoin," October 30, 1916.
34. SHD 16N 1977, report from "un témoin," October 30, 1916.
35. SHD 5N 136, Lt.-Col. Rampont, "Etude sur la Guerre" (13 février 1916); Buat, *Armée allemande*, 30–32; Ragueneau, *Stratégie des transports*, 5–6; Crefeld, "Logistics"; Cailleteau, *Gagner*, 68–69.
36. SHD 5N 126, Rampont, February 13, 1916; Cailleteau, *Gagner*, 62–65.
37. SHD 5N 126, Rampont, February 13, 1916.
38. Serrigny, *Trente ans*, 112–13; see above, pp.
39. *Le Petit Journal*, April 22, 1916.

40. *Le Gaulois*, February 29, March 1, 1916; *Le Figaro*, February 28, March 6, 1916 (from SHD 6N 46); *La Victoire*, March 6, 1916.

41. *Le Petit Journal*, February 28, 1916; *Le Matin*, April 17, 1916.

42. *Frankfurter Zeitung*, April 9, May 24, July 16, 1916; *Münchner Neueste Nachrichten*, April 16, 1916.

43. Cf. *Le Figaro*, March 13, 1916.

44. Botrel, *Refrains*, vol. 3, *Chants de Bataille et de Victoire*; Boyer, *Chanson*, 99.

45. Suarès, *Ceux de Verdun*, viii; Chaine, *Rat* (Paris, 1917).

46. Bernard, E., *Grande Guerre*, 32; Bernard, J.-A., *Supplément*, 60.

47. Krumeich, "Saigner"; Werth, *Verdun*, 345–50.

48. Cf., e.g., Wehner, *Sieben*; Werth, *1916*, 148–49; Gollbach, *Wiederkehr*, 188–90; Wehner, *Wallfahrt*, 246–50.

49. *Berliner Tageblatt*, July 14, 1936 (prominence to Brandis, who 'took" Douaumont); Schauwecker, Preface to Radtke, *Erstürmung*; Norton Cru, *Témoins*, 33–35; Petermann, *Rituale*, 117.

50. Jones, *Western Way*, 648–49, 656.

Chapter 5

1. Rupprecht, *Kriegstagebuch*, March 20, 21, 23, April 6, 1916.

2. Rupprecht, *Kriegstagebuch*, May 12, 1916; Müller, *Kaiser*, April 30–May 1, 1916; Falkenhayn, *Heeresleitung*, 185 ff; Janssen, *Kanzler*, 201, 203–4; ch. 2 above, pp.

3. Wilhelm, *Erinnerungen*, 202–3; BA-MA, W-10 50704, *Schulenburg* (1935); Pétain, *Verdun*, 79.

4. Hohenborn, *Briefe*, 39 (November 25, 1914), 141 (March 27, 1916); Wendt, *Verdun*, 96–98, 147–54, 174–76, 183 ff.

5. Pétain, *Verdun*, 25; Serrigny, *Trente ans*, 54–56, 63–66; AFGG, t. IV, vol. 2, 120–22.

6. Bauer, *Grosse Krieg*, 89–90, 100–102; Wendt, *Verdun*, 96–98, 114–18, 147–54, 183 ff; Zwehl, *Falkenhayn*, 190–93; *Tragödie*, 198–200; for Falkenhayn's dismissal, see p. 23.

7. AFGG, t. IV, vol. 2, 120–22, Joffre to Pétain, June 27, 1916; *Joffre, Journal*, entries of June 23 and July 3, 1916; Joffre, *Mémoires*, (2 vols., Paris, 1932), vol. 2, 206 ff.

8. Bauer, *Grosse Krieg*, 100–102; Zwehl, *Falkenhayn*, 186; Wilhelm, *Erinerrungen*, 2–8, 13–14; von Einem, *Armeeführer*, 269 (entry of November 26, 1916).

9. *Le Gaulois*, February 29, 1916 (re Téry); *Le Matin*, March 25, 1916 (re Castelnau); SHD 5N 364, Agence Fournier, January 17, 1917; see, e.g., photos of Nivelle and Mangin in *Le Matin*, October 26, 1916.

10. AN, 415 AP1, Pétain's letters to [Hardon], March 7 and June 25, 1916, *L'Illustration*, March 11, 1916.

11. See, e.g., AFGG, t. IV, vol. 2, 120–22; *Le Matin*, March 6 and 16, 1916, *Le Gaulois*, March 11, 1916, *Le Petit Parisien*, March 4, 1916.

12. Benjamin, "Petain", 394; Gueit-Montchal "1926–2006", in Cochet, *Verdun*.
13. *Le Matin*, March 4, 1916.
14. Wendt, *Verdun*, 114–18; Zwehl, *Falkenhayn*, 190–93; BA-MA, W-10 50705, "Falkenhayn als Feldherr," Kronprinz to Falkenhayn, 31.3.16, and Falkenhayn to Kronprinz, 4.4.16.
15. Wendt, *Verdun*, 96–98, 112–14, 174–76; Rupprecht, *Kriegstagebuch*, March 8, 1916; Wilhelm, *Erinnerungen*, 205–6; *Weltkrieg*, X, 321.
16. Wendt, *Verdun*, 122; Falkenhayn, "Verdun" (*Militär-Wochenblatt*), and *Heeresleitung*, 199; Bethmann-Hollweg to Kaiser, May 28, 1916, in Janssen, *Kanzler*, 289–90; *Weltkrieg*, X, 634–45.
17. Re losses see ch. 5, pp. and "Appendix on Sources"; Bethmann-Hollweg to Kaiser, May 28, 1916, in Janssen, *Kanzler und General*, 289–90.
18. BHSA, Kriegsarchiv, Mkr 1832/5, *Berichte des Bayerischer Militär-bevollmächtiger im Grossen hauptquartier*, April 9, 1916; Wendt, *Verdun*, 174–76; BA-MA, W-10 50705 "Falkenhayn als Feldherr," conversation of a D. von Mertz with Falkenhayn, May 8, 1916.
19. SHD 16N 1805, Pétain to Joffre, May 7, 1916.
20. AFGG, t. IV, vol. 2, 120–22, Joffre to Pétain, June 27, 1916; Guy Pedroncini, ed., *Le Journal de marche du général Joffre* (Paris, 1990), entries of June 23 and July 3, 1916; Joffre, *Mémoires*, (2 vols., Paris, 1932), Vol. 2, 206 ff.
21. Robin Prior and Trevor Wilson, *The Somme* (Yale, 2005), 25 ff; SHD 5N 134, Joffre to Briand, April 3, 1916.
22. *Weltkrieg*, X, 322–24, 382–83; Albrecht von Stosch, (bearbeiter), *Somme-Nord* I. teil: *Die Brennpunkte der Schlacht in juli 1916*, in *Schlachten des Weltkrieges* (Berlin, 1927), vol. 20, 5–6.
23. Etymologies under "prestige" in Robert, *Dictionnaire alphabétique et analogique de la langue française*, and *Digitales Wörterbuch der Deutschen Sprache*.
24. BA-MA, W-10 50704, *Schulenburg* (1935); BHSA, Kriegsarchiv, Mkr 1832/5, report of July 8, 1916; Zwehl, *Falkenhayn*, 193.
25. BA-MA, W-10 50704, *Schulenburg* (1935); Wendt, *Verdun*, 183; Zwehl, *Falkenhayn*, 194.
26. Weltkrieg, X, 634–45; *Tragödie*, 198–200; BA-MA, W-10 51512, *Tieschowitz* (1939); Wendt, *Verdun*, 183 ff.
27. Hindenburg, *Aus meinem Leben* (Leipzig, 1920), 194–95; von Einem, *Armeeführer*, 26–261, entry of October 25, 1916; *Tragödie*, 198–200; Wendt, *Verdun*, 189–92 and "Appendix on Sources" in this work.
28. Von Einem, *Armeeführer*, entry of March 2, 1916; Rupprecht, *Kriegstagebuch*, entry of January 24, 1916; Pétain, *Verdun*, 1.
29. Passaga, *Calvaire*, 73–74; Serrigny, *Trente ans*, 63–66; Pastre, *Trois ans*, 137.
30. Transcripts in AN C7646; Bonnefous, *Histoire politique*, vol. 2, 156.
31. *Le Gaulois* February 27 and March 1, 1916; Filali, *Chronique*, 95; Verneuil, *Rideau*, 242–43; *Frankfurter Zeitung*, February 28, 1916; Pierre Renaudel in *L'Humanité*, February 26, 1916.

32. *Frankfurter Zeitung* December 31, 1915 and *Leipziger Tageblatt*, December 28, 1915 (from SHD 6N50); *Le Matin*, February 27, 1916; *Le Petit Journal*, February 27, March 4, April 2, 1916; *Frankfurter Zeitung*, March 24, 1916.

33. SHD 16N 1391, contrôle postal, report of March 31, 1916; "Souvenirs et chansons de 1916", France Inter (radio), January 1, 1966; Verneuil, *Rideau*, 217; Delvert, 124; Serrigny, *Trente ans*, 82–83.

34. *Le Temps*, January 19, 1917 (from SHD 5N364) and September 15, 1916; BNF, N. acq. fr. 16038, ms. of Poincaré's speech; *Le Temps*, September 15, 1916.

35. Ibid; SHD 16N 1392, contrôle postal to GQG, January 20, 1917; "A voix haute, a voix basse Verdun, une guerre dans la guerre," *L'actualité radiophonique*, February 16, 1966; Pierre Miquel on Fr2 20h (television), February 21, 1996; the phrase "no pasaran" is also attributed to Dolores Ibárrun Gómez (La Pasionaria) at the siege of Madrid in July 1936.

Chapter 6

1. Cailleteau, *Gagner*, 74 ff; Wilson, *Myriad Faces*, 336; see ch. 2.

2. AFGG, t. IV, vol. 1, 43–52; Max Boot, *War Made New: Technology, Warfare and the Course of History, 1500 to today*, (New York, 2006), 168.

3. Herr, *Artillerie*, 1–6; Doughty, *Victory*, 120–21.

4. Herr, *Artillerie*, 9–13.

5. Brose, *Army*, 228.

6. Doughty, *Victory*, 118, 256; Herr, *Artillerie*, 54–56.

7. SHD 24N 909, Berthelot, June 25, 1916; SHD 16N 1805, Pétain to Joffre, May 28, 1916.

8. SHD 24N 909 Leconte, April 3 and 25, 1916; SHD 24N 86, Mangin, n.d., April 1916; Doughty, *Victory*, 115–16, 256, 298.

9. Notin, *Foch*, 64; SHD 16N 1977, Pétain note, November 18, 1916; Chagnon, "1916"; AFGG, t. IV, vol. 2, 407 and vol. 3, 466–68; Bouvard, *Leçons militaires*, 44.

10. Bouvard, *Leçons*, 44–45, 53; Becker, *Emploi tactique*, *passim*, and figures in Marin, *Exposé*; AFGG, t. IV, vol. 2, 389–95.

11. Lucas, *Idées tactiques*, 102–10; Cochet, "Chantilly"; Herr, *Artillerie*, 41–45; SHD, 16N 1977, Pétain note, November 18, 1916; Poncheville, *Dix mois*, 12.

12. SHD 16N 1981, note of Gen. Sonnerat, n.d., 1916; see above, note 9; Strachan, *Cabinet*.

13. Figures from Wendt, *Verdun*, 242–45. See Appendix on Sources.

14. Marin, *Exposé*, table p. 74.

15. Larcher, "Données" (March 1933).

16. *Verluste des Weltkrieges*, Table 10 (see Appendix on Losses).

17. Keeping usually about the same number (18) of divisions in line, French losses came to 180,000 in Champagne and 375,000 at Verdun—but during three weeks in the first and ten months in the second case. See Larcher "Données" (avril-juin 1933), AFGG, t. III, 365, t. IV, vol. 1, appendix II and III, 648–49, and t. IV, vol. 3, 294, and Appendix on Sources.

18. Losses for each army peaked at about 90,000 dead, wounded, and missing in late February and March, fell to about 40,000 for April, and then rose again during May and June, when two months of fierce fighting cost the French 126,000 and the Germans 105,000 casualties. They never regained that level. Over the ten months between February and December each side lost an average of about 35–40,000 a month. See Appendix on Sources and loss chart, p. 117.

19. See Appendix on Sources; Cailleteau, *Gagner*,106, 108–9; McRandle and Quirk, "Blood Test," 693, gives an amended ratio of 1.31 in German favor for the Western Front between February 1 and June 30, 1916.

20. See Appendix on Sources; SHD 24N 86, memo apparently from Mangin, n.d., April 1916.

21. Herr, *Artillerie*, 233; calculations based on SHD 16N 1805, Pétain to Joffre, May 28, 1916, on basis of a 25-km. front; Larcher, "Données" (avril-juin 1933); Larcher is clearly referring to losses for the time the divisions were engaged in the front lines, see Morel-Journel, *Journal*, entry for September 14, 1916.

22. Denizot, *Verdun*, 77–78; Canini, *Combattre*, 15; Herr, *Artillerie*, 85; Cailleteau, *Gagner*, 109.

23. SHD 5N 136, Rampont, "Etude"; AN 415 AP 1, Pétain to Hardon, April 16, 1916.

24. From Canini, *Combattre*, 51, Bernède, *Verdun*, 342, and Denizot, *Verdun*, 285. Of 115 divisions engaged at Verdun between February and December, 43 had been engaged once, 23 twice, 4 thrice, 2 four times, and 1 six times, see Pelade, *Verdun*, 7.

25. Bodart, *Losses of Life*, 147.

26. From *états de pertes numériques* in SHD 16N 528; the numbers were so high for the 72nd because it had three brigades rather than the customary two, see AFGG t. IV, vol. 1, 294 n.2.

27. According to Bodart, *Losses*, 126, out of a total of 680,000 Napoleonic troops, about 340,000 died in the campaign, in battle or from hunger, exhaustion, cold, or disease, and another 100,000 were taken prisoner. These figures are out of all proportion to the losses of the Second Army at Verdun.

28. *L'Eclair*, March 6, 1916; *Le Matin*, March 10, 11, 13, May 21, 1916; *Le Journal* March 13, 1916; *L'Indépendant des Pyrénées Orientales*, May 18, 1916, from SHD 5N 364, Min. of War to 16ème region, May 28, 1916; Reinach, *Front Occidental* (from his articles in *Le Figaro* signed "Polybe"), 125–26.

29. Comments by Abel Gance to Kevin Brownlow in 1965, in "The Waste of War: Abel Gance's *J'accuse*," essay with notes with restored version of the film, Lobsterfilms 2006 and 2008.

30. Kuhn, "manuels scolaires" *in* Cochet, *Verdun*; AN, F7 13366, report of June 16, 1916; Glaeser, "Kriegsschauplatz"; Hallynck et Brunet, *Nouveau cours*, 23–24; Giraud, *Miracle français*, 31; Giraud, *Grande Guerre*, 346; Petite, *Grande Guerre*, 124–26; Lespes et Chales, *Cours moyen*, 349–50; Devinat, *Cours moyen*, 128.

31. INA, Journal National (télévisé), June 20, 1956 and "Vivre ensemble: François Mitterrand et Helmut Kohl à Verdun", FR 2 magazine (television), September 22, 1984.

32. René Arnaud on "L'Attaque allemande du 21 février 1916," France Inter (radio), February 26, 1966.

33. *Excelsior, Le Journal*, February 28, 1916; *Le Matin*, April 3, July 1, October 14, 25, 27, 1916; *Le Petit Parisien, La Victoire*, March 12, 1916; *Le Rappel*, March 16, 1916.

34. *Frankfurter Zeitung*, February 28 and March 24, 1916.

35. Werth, *1916*, 159–60.

36. *Le Gaulois*, February 26 and March 6, 1916; François de Tessan in *L'Illustration*, April 22, 1916; *Werth*, 1916, 115–16 (but the citation from Groener's diary is not to be found in his *Lebenserinnerungen*).

37. Péricard, *Ceux de Verdun*, 54; Suarès, *Ceux de Verdun*, xxiv, xxv.

38. Poirier, *Verdun. Visions d'Histoire*; Jackson, *Dark Years*, 28; Barral, *Agrariens français*, 180.

39. Gollbach, *Wiederkehr* (Regensburg, 1978), 139, 146–47, 182–83, 219, 258–60; Beumelburg, *Gruppe Bosemüller*, (Oldenbourg,1930), an autobiographical and more subjective account than his earlier semi-official narrative (*Douaumont*, in Schlachten des Weltkrieges, Bd. 8, Oldenburg, 1923); Ettighoffer, *Gespenster*; Zöberlein, *Glaube*, 285.

40. Werth, *1916*, 101–2 (estimates of dead in *Frankfurter Zeitung*, 1932, repeated from *Vu*); Ettighoffer, *Gericht* (Gütersich, 1936), 296–97.

41. *Tragödie*, Bd. 15, 200; Kabitsch, *Verdun*, 213; Werth, *Verdun*, 391–92; Zöberlein, *Glaube*, 890; Gollbach, *Wiederkehr*, 167, 188, 210.

42. Werth, *1916*, 159–60.

43. See, e.g., Horne, *Glory*, 337; Watt, *How War Came*, 20.

44. SHD 1N 51, Note of May 17, 1923, and study on "role historique des places fortes françaises," n.d. [1924].

45. See, e.g., Doughty, *Seeds of Disaster*, Kissling, *Arming against Hitler*, and SHD 1N 54, Général Condé, *mémoire sur la défense des frontières*, n.d., April–May, 1939.

46. SHD 1N 51, "Role historique . . ."; SHD 1N 53, CSG: "Note relative à l'organisation défensive des frontières," September 27, 1928; SHD 1N 53, Col. Griveaud, January 14, 1929.

47. Doughty, *Seeds, passim*; Kiesling, *Arming, passim*.

48. Falkenhayn had a few defenders, such as Zwehl and Delbrück, see ch. 2, but most turned decisively away from what they saw as his major error, see Wallach, *Dogma*, ch. 12.

49. Guderian, *Erinnerungen*, 37.

50. Kiesling, *Arming*, 169; Guderian, *Erinnerungen*, 23–24.

51. *Pétain et Valéry*, 30; Werth, *1916*, 163–68.

52. Ettighoffer, *Gericht*, 50; Jünger quoted in Werth, *1916*, 169.

53. Bréant, *l'Alsace a la Somme*, entry for April 21, 1916.

Chapter 7

1. Re the "empty battlefield" see, e.g., Citino, *Decisive Victory*, 55.
2. Gallwitz, *Erleben*, 9–12.
3. Schlieffen, "Krieg in Gegenwart"; Brose, *Kaiser's Army*, 138–39.
4. BHSA, Mkr 1832/5, reports of May 4 and 26, 1916; Pierrefeu, *Grand Quartier*, I, 83–88; cf. also Gallwitz, *Erleben*, 3.
5. SHD 1KT102, Beaucour, 16; SHD 16N 1981, report of April 14, 1916; Norton Cru, *Témoins*, 17–18.
6. Schlieffen, *Krieg*; Pierrefeu, *Grand Quartier*, 83–88; Ardant du Picq, *Etudes*, 82–86.
7. Herscher, *Quelques Images*, 149, 161.
8. Tournassus, *Nous*, 97–100; Muenier, *Angoisse*, 5–33; SHD 1KT 110, Bros, 429–34 (March 25, 1916).
9. SHD 1KT 110, Bros, 429; SHD 1KT 126 1, Chevriers, 222, (June 27, 1916); SHD 1KT 92 1, Corti, March 11, 1916; Péricard, *Ceux de Verdun*, 92.
10. SHD 1KT 92 1, Corti, March 11 and 13, 1916; Campana, *Enfants*, March 10, 1916; Muenier, *Angoisse*, 39; Mac Orlan, *Poissons Morts*, 176.
11. Limosin, *Verdun a L'Yser*, 16; Marc, *Notes*, 57–58.
12. SHD 1KT 92 1, Corti, March 22, 1916; Hourticq, *Récits*, 85; Poncheville, *Dix mois*, 52, March 20, 1916; Bros, SHD 1KT 110, May 4, 1916.
13. Poncheville, *Dix mois*, 52, entry for March 20, 1916; SHD 1KT 110, Bros, April 20, May 4, 1916; SHD 1KT 170 1, Hemery, 21; Jubert, *Verdun*, 37.
14. Koch, *Verdun*, 1–2, 10; Ettighoffer, *Gericht*, 20–22, 27–28.
15. Thimmermann, *Verdun-Souville*, 8–10; d' Arnoux, *Paroles*, 41.
16. Péricard, *Verdun* (1933), 201; Beumelburg, *Douaumont*, 16–20.
17. Ernst, *Tagebuch*, February 28, 1916 in Hoffmann, *Deutsche Soldat*, 236–37; Genty, *Trois Ans*, entry for January 19, 1917.
18. Gaudy, *Souvenirs* vol. 1, 182; BA-MA, W-10 51549, anon., *Bericht über . . .* , 31.
19. Duhamel, *Martyrs*, 103.
20. Gaudy, *Souvenirs*, I, 171, 173, 223; Muenier, *Angoisse*, 62–63, 70–71.
21. Koch, *Verdun*, 55; BHSA, 11 Inf.-Div., Pfarrer Susann, April 15, 1916; BA-MA W-10 51549, *Bericht*, 16; Beumelburg, *Douaumont*, 20; Tragödie, 68.
22. SHD 16N 1391, contrôle postal, report of August 11, 1916; Cdt. Chatton on *L'actualité radiophonique*, February 16, 1966.
23. Morel, *Journal*, September 16, 1916; Thimmermann, *Verdun-Souville*, 8–9; Koch, *Verdun*, 45, 47.
24. Hein, *Erstürmung*, 7; Méléra, *Verdun*, 42–44, 46; Mémorial de Verdun, Comte, entry for September 4, 1916; Gaudy, *Souvenirs*, 137.
25. BHSA, 1 Bayer. Inf. Div., Bd 93, *Sanitätstdienst*, n.d., late May–early June 1916; SHD 1KT 92 1, Corti, March 29, 1916; Méléra, *Verdun*, 31.
26. Hein, *Erstürmung*, 7–8; Schürmann in *Heimatkalender*, 159 Inf. Reg.; SHD 1KT 861, Legentil: Notes de campagne, 12 avril 1915 au 11 novembre 1918; Hourticq, *Récits*, 103; d' Arnoux, *Paroles*, 41; SHD 1KT 110, Bros, 460, 536–37, 551–52; Hein, *Tornisterphilosophie*, 86–87 (written in September 1916 in the trenches between le Mort Homme and Côte 304) and appended to *Erstürming*.

27. Méléra, *Verdun*, 35; Gaudy, *Souvenirs*, 189–91, 201–5; Morel, *Journal*, entry for October 23, 1916; Cabanel, *Diables Bleus*, 2; Thimmermann, *Verdun*, 44–45.

28. Cabanel, *Diables Bleus*, 29; Thimmermann, *Verdun*, 44–45.

29. Cabanel, *Diables Bleus*, 29; SHD, 16N 1977, Notes d'un témoin, October 30, 1916; SHD, 16N 1981, "mémoire sur le Fort de Douaumont . . ." French translation of German document, n.d., early September 1916); Hourticq, *Récit*, 83, 95–103; Canini, *Combattre*, 75, 79.

30. SHD 16N 1391, contrôle postal, reports of April 8 and November 4, 1916; Morel, *Journal*, September 18 and October 9, 1916; SHD 1KT 92 1, Corti, March 29, 1916; Cazin, *Humaniste*, 23; Henri Auclair, FR3 (television), Soir 3, February 21, 1996.

31. Delvert, *Carnets*, 167–68; SHD 16N 1391, contrôle postal, reports of October 19, 1916 and November 23, 1916; Ettighoffer, *Verdun*, 125–26; Münch, *Verdun*, 121–28; Koch, *Verdun*, 72–73; SHD 1KT 110, Bros, 439.

32. Koch, *Verdun*, 72–73; BHSA, Gen-kdo I. bayer. AK, tätigkeit des I. B.A.K. in der Zeit vom 22.5–12.6 (June, 1916); Gaudy, *Souvenirs*, 192; Mornet, *Tranchées*, 31 ff; Dupont, *L'Attente*, 127–43; Raynal, *Journal, passim*.

33. Dubrulle, *Régiment*, 25–27; Thimmermann, *Verdun-Souville*, 9, 90.

34. Mémorial de Verdun, Jean Penicaud, journal de campagne, Carnet V, June 1916; Jubert, *Verdun*, 48; Méléra, *Verdun*, 35.

35. Thimmermann, *Verdun-Souville*, 8, 16, 21, 43–51; Delvert, *Carnets*, 288; Gallwitz, *Erleben*, 27; Koch, *Verdun*, 76–79; SHD, 16N 1391, contrôle postal, June 3, 1916; SHD, 1KT 170 1, Hémery, 21; BA-MA, W-10 51549, *Bericht über* [. . .], 31, 34; Schürmann in *Heimatkalender*, 159 Inf. Reg.; Eugen Ernst, Tagebuch, February 19, 1916, in Hoffmann, *Deutsche Soldat*, 232.

36. Jubert, *Verdun*, 101–6; Werth, *Verdun*, 77; Delvert, *Carnets*, 257.

37. René Arnaud on France Inter, February 26, 1966; Cazin, *Humaniste*, 213; Dupont, *Attente*, 152.

38. Poncheville, *Dix mois*, 21; Hourticq, *Récits*, 85, 100; Boasson, *Soir*, 127–28.

39. Gaudy, *Souvenirs*, 145; BHSA, 1. bayer. Inf. Div, Bund 13, Angriffsgruppe ost, May 24, 1916; SHD 1KT 861, Legentil (passage relates to Les Eparges); Dubrulle, *Régiment*, 25–27; Lafont, *Ciel*, 104.

40. France Inter, René Arnaud, February 26, 1966; René Coty on RTF, Journal parlé. Paris vous parle, June 1, 1956; Mornet, *Tranchées*, 13; SHD 1KT102, Beaucour, 18–19; he quotes Coty.

41. BHSA, 1. bayer. Inf. Div., Bund 13, reports of August 28, 1916, and I. bayer AK, June 29, 1916; Thimmermann, *Verdun-Souville*, 10.

42. SHD 16N 1981, Chrétien, April 15, 1916; BA-MA, W-10 51548, Mundt, "Persönliche Erinnerungen. . ..."; Tournassus, *Soldats*, 132.

43. Dubrulle, *Régiment*, 25–27; Hourticq, *Récits*, 95–102; Jubert, *Verdun*, 40–41; SHD 1KT 102, Beaucour.

44. Joubaire, *France*, entry for May 22, 1916.

45. SHD KT1 110, Bros, I, 429, 495–96; Péricard, *Ceux de Verdun*, 147; Mémorial de Verdun, Derozières, *Carnet*, May 22, 1916; Madelin, *Aveu*, 40–41, 43, 44.

46. Zwehl, *Falkenhayn*, 183–84; SHD, 16N 1391, contrôle postal, reports of March 31, May 26, July 27, August 8, 1916; SHD 19N 309, report of October 16, 1917 [from 19N 305]; SHD KT1 110, Bros, I, 429.

47. Baumann, *Chevoleau*, 29; Delvert, *Carnets*, 125–26; Joubaire, *France*, 200; SHD 1KT 130 1, Le Quillec, 7, 19–23; Jeanbernat, *Lettres*, 8.

48. Schneider, Jean-Jacques, "service de santé"; Laparra, "Verdun 1916: "service de santé"; Schneider, Christoph, *Medizin*, 147–63.

49. Graves, *Good-bye*, 211; Rogerson, *Twelve Days*, 5–7; Tawney, "Attack"; Wilson, *Myriad Faces*, 346–47; SHD, 16N 1485, contrôle postal, report of September 15, 1916.

50. Rogerson, *Twelve Days*, 29; Méléra, *Verdun*, 35; SHD 16N 1391, contrôle postal, report of December 1, 1916; Jünger, *Storm*, 93.

51. Ch. 6, pp ; BNF, n. acq. fr. 16038 (discours de Poincaré, 1914–1918), speech of May 14, 1916; SHD, 6N 449, Diouf and Ministry of Defence, December 15, 1936 and March 2, 1937.

52. AN F7 13371, police notes of May 27 and June 23, 1916; AN F7 13349, report on pacifist movements in France, n.d., c. January 1, 1917; AN F7 12986, Comm. Sp. Toulouse to police administrative, Paris, April 9, 1916; see transcript of secret session of the Chamber, June 16–22, 1916, in AN C7646.

53. SHD 7N 2586, 23 mars 1931, French military attaché (Berlin) to Paris, article from AJZ, n.d., 1931.

54. Beumelburg, *Bösemüller*; Zöberlein, *Glaube*; "Paris vous parle," France 1, Paris Inter (Radio) 26 juin 1960; Robert Escarpit, "Au jour le jour," *Le Monde*, May 29–30, 1966.

55. Strachan, "Soldier's Experience"; Céline, *Voyage*; Drieu, Gilles, 428 ; *Pétain et Valéry*, 114–15.

56. V. I. Chuikov, *The Beginning of the Road: the Story of the Battle for Stalingrad* (London, 1963), 132 cited in Richard Overy, *Why the Allies Won* (New York and London, 1997 [1995]), 75.

57. Bloem, *Vormarsch*, 450.

58. SHD 19 N309, report of October 16, 1917 [from 19N 305]; Fr3 Lorraine (television), February 20, 1996.

Chapter 8

1. SHD 16N 1391, contrôle postal, reports of July 14, 1916.

2. Cf. Jahr, *Gewöhnliche Soldaten*, 155, 333, and *passim*; Rousseau, *Service militaire*, 195 and *passim*.

3. See ch. 9; on disobedience see above all Loez, *Refus*, cited below.

4. Laurentin, *1914–1918*, 168 ff.

5. Werth, *Verdun*, 92–93.

6. BHSA, 1 bayer. Inf.-Div, Bund 13: reports on French prisoners, June 3, 19, July 13, 1916.

7. Cf., e.g., Grinker and Speigel, *Men under Stress*, 37: "Motivation is the nucleus of morale."

8. Useful reviews of such theories can be found in Lynn, *Bayonets*, ch. 2, and Strachan, "Training." See also chs. 9 and 10, pp.

9. Ludendorff, *Kriegserinnerungen*, 275 (his emphasis); see appendix on postal censorship archives.

10. SHD 16N 1391, contrôle postal, reports of April 28, May 12, June 10, July 1 and 14, 1916; SHD 16N 1485, contrôle postal, report of May 15, 1916.

11. BHSA, 11 Inf.-Div., Bund 2 (Feldgeistliche), Akt 2, Susann, March 28, 1916; SHD 16N 1391, contrôle postal, October 19, November 15 and 22, 1916.

12. SHD 16N 1391, contrôle postal, May 5 and October 17, 1916; Rousseau, *Guerre censurée*, 151 ff; Hertz, *Ethnologue*, 58–59, 88, 132, 137–38, 146, 213; Genevoix, *Les Eparges*, ch. 1.

13. BHSA, 11 Inf.-Div. Bund 2, Susann, entries for May 2 and 7, 1916; SHD 16N 1485, contrôle postal, report of July 15, 1916.

14. SHD 16N 1391, contrôle postal, May 12, June 3, 10, October 26, November 15, 1916.

15. Madelin, *Aveu*, 8–9, 32, 36, 61, 67 ff.; these letters also provide the basis for the reports in SHD 19N309; SHD, contrôle postal, reports of November 28 and December 1, 1916; Koch, *Verdun*, 107–8.

16. SHD 16N 1391, contrôle postal, reports of July 14, 1916, June 25, 1916, July 13, 1916.

17. SHD 16N 1391, contrôle postal, June 25, August 1, 6, 27, 26, September 2, 1916, January 20, 1917; SHD 16 N 1485, rapports de quinzaine, July 15, August 1, September 1, 1916; criticisms over "hygiene" had peaked in the spring of 1916 at Verdun, see SHD 16 N 1391, "tableaux de pourcentages" in report of August 26, 1916.

18. SHD 16N 1391, reports of July 14, May 26, August 17, October 17, 1916; Fonsagrive, *Batterie*, 31; Laurentin, *1914–1918*, 168; Pedroncini, "moral de l'armée."

19. BA-MA, W-10 51549, "Bericht über die Ereignisse. . . ., 14; BA-MA, W-10-51548, Lt. Mundt, 27–29; Bloem, *Vormarsch*, 375–76, 383; SHD 19N309, report of March 6, 1916; Werth, *Verdun*, 77.

20. Koch, *Verdun*, 21–23, 64; BA-MA, W-10-51548, Lt. Mundt, 15, 34–35, 46–47; SHD 16N 920, reports of March 10, 15, April 7, 1916.

21. Delvert, *Carnets*, 316–17; SHD 16N 1391, contrôle postal, reports of 2 November (three reports), November 3, 11, 15–18, 22, 29, 1916; SHD 16N 1392, contrôle postal, report of January 20, 1917; SHD 16N 1485, rapports de quinzaine, November 15, December 1 and 15, 1916.

22. Joffre, *Mémoires*, vol. 2, 248; Hindenburg, *Leben*, 196–97.

23. BA-MA, W-10 51548, Mundt, 26; Thimmermann, *Verdun-Souville*, 17; BHSA, 11 Inf.-Div., Bund 2, Susann, entry for May 31, 1916; *Tragödie*, vol. 15, iv, 46; BHSA, 1 Inf.-Div., Bund 12, report to 1. Inf. Brigade, June 13, 1916; Hohenborn, *Briefe*, 154.

24. BA-MA, W-10 51548, Mundt, 26; Thimmermann, *Verdun-Souville*, 17; BHSA, 11 Inf.-Div., Bund 2, Susann, entry for May 31, 1916; Dubrulle, *Régiment*, 69; SHD 16N 1485, rapports de quinzaine, December 15, 1916; SHD 16N 1391, report of July 14, 1916; Laurentin, *1914–1918*, 157–58.

25. See for example conviction tables in SHD 24N 693 (29ᵉ DI), and SHD 24N 271 (14ᵉ DI); SHD 24N 1211, 51ᵉ DI—3ᵉ bureau, Notes de service du 28, 30 mars, 1916; BHSA, 2 Inf.-Div., Bund 91, letters of 31.3.1916; I have borrowed here and in the pages that follow some from my "Obéissance et désobéissance."

26. Koch, *Verdun*, 48; Muenier, *Angoisse*, 71; SHD 16N 1391, reports of December 1, 1916; Morel-Journel, *Journal*, entry for September 14, 1916; Méléra, *Verdun*, 14–15.

27. Mémorial de Verdun, Lampo, August 18, 1916; Mémorial de Verdun, Pénicaud, carnet V, June 22, 1916; SHD 16N 1392, contrôle postal, report of January 20, 1917; Gaudy, *Souvenirs*, 189–91.

28. Delvert, *Carnets*, 185, 187.

29. SHD 1KT102, Beaucour, 10 ff; Legrand-Girarde, *Quart de siècle*, 574–75; Morel-Journel, *Journal*, 230; Delvert, *Carnets*, 247–48, 295.

30. BHSA, 1. bayer. Inf.-Div., Bund 13, 1 bayer. Inf. Rgt. "König," 28.8. 1916; ibid., 2 Inf. Rgt. "Kronprinz," 26.8.1916.

31. Koch, *Verdun*, 84; BA-MA W-10 51549, Abercron, April 15, 1933; BA-MA W-10 51523, Kewisch, August 6, 1935.

32. SHD, 1K 860, Tournès; Pastre, *Trois ans*, 114.

33. SHD, 1KT102, Beaucour; AFGG, t. IV, vol. 1, 43–52, and ch. 5 above; Morel-Journel, *Journal*, entry for September 1, 1916; Delvert, *Carnets*, 182–83, 195–96; Mémorial de Verdun, Lampo, August 18, 1916; Laurentin, *1914–1918*, 168.

34. SHD 1KT102, Beaucour; ORTF, Panorama, (television), November 11, 1967, "Charles Mangin" interview with Charles Toussaint, veteran of 5ᵉ DI; Morel-Journel, *Journal*, entry for October 23, 1916; Jen-Norton Cru, *Témoins*, 20.

35. SHD 11J905, dossiers: Léon Vincent (64ᵉ RI, July 4, 1916), Léon Remenerias (137ᵉ RI, July 4, 1916), Edouard Rivière (64ᵉ RI, July 29, 1916), Valentin Le Bocoët, (137ᵉ RI, June 10, 1916); SHD 11J 674, dossier Eugène Guillot (106ᵉ RI, 132ᵉ RI, October 26, 1916); Campana, *Enfants*, entry for March 21, 1916.

36. BHSA, 1. AK Gen. Komm., Bund 179, Otto Schachner, September 9, 1916; idem, Josef Wöger, December 6, 1916. BHSA, Militärgerichte, Akten 17 and 3652 (Strafprozesslisten) include 62 instances in the 1st and 41 in the 2nd Bavarian Infantry Division at Verdun (May 12–July 15, 1916 and May

16–July 14, respectively) of *Gehorsamverweigerung, Ungehorsam, Beleidigung, Bedrohung, Angriff auf einen Vorgeseztzen*, and *Achtungsverletzung*. SHD 24N 271, lists similar cases of "outrages envers un supérieur [offences to a superior]" for the French 14ᵉ DI at Verdun from February 21–March 3 and May 5–16. These approximate comparisons, with a German divisional strength of 17,000 and a French one of 18,000 approximately, convey a hint of the minor scope of the problem in each army.

37. SHD 11J 673, dossiers Louis Hurtebise (132ᵉ RI, August 6, 1916) and Arthur Boursin (106ᵉ RI, August 12, 1916); SHD 11J 674, dossier Adrien Pichon (106ᵉ RI, August 19, 1916); BHSA, Militärgerichte, Akt 6412, case of Johann Singer, June 29, July 1, 7, and 12, 1916; SHD 11J 672, dossier Georges Tuffin (106ᵉ RI, July 12, 1916); cf. also similar or supporting cases of individual desertions bringing substantial prison terms in SHD 11J 672, Julien Duflos, 132ᵉ RI, July 12, 1916 and Louis Drouin, 106ᵉ RI, September 16, 1916, and in SHD 11J 673, Georges Dondeine, 93 Regt. du génie, July 23, 1916, and Eugène Raguènes, 132ᵉ RI, August 12, 1916.

38. Ziemann, *Fahnenflucht*; Jahr, *Gewöhnliche Soldaten*, 74, 155, 160–61; he counts 21 cases in the 2nd Bavarian ID., but since the Bavarian divisions by now had been reduced to 10–12,000 men I have counted the number of cases from three French regiments engaged in the same area at the same time, 415ᵉ and 75ᵉ ID and 106ᵉ AL, on the basis of the registers [minutiers] in SHD 11J 1067, and arrived at 20 cases. This at best rough comparison can only give an idea of the small numbers involved on both sides.

Chapter 9

1. Offenstadt, *Fusillés*, 53; Loez, *Refus*, 235 ff; Watson, *Enduring*, 208, 215—Watson places the deserters and "shirkers' at 200,000 in the second half of 1918 and the surrenders at 385,000, but others place them higher.

2. Offenstadt, *Fusillés*; Pédroncini, *Mutineries*; Smith, *Mutiny and Obedience*; Audoin-Rouzeau and Becker, *14–18*, 122; Loez, *Refus*; Deist, "Military Collapse"; Kruse, "Krieg und Klassenheer"; Ziemann, "Fahnenflucht."

3. Hohenborne, *Briefe*, 164; Münch, *Verdun*, 316–17, 330–31; Madelin, *Aveu*, 48; Dupont, *Attente*, 252 (entry for June 26, 1916).

4. BHSA, Militärgerichte, Akten 6353 and 6354, Georg Mändl, June 3, 7, 8, 20, 1916, January 29, 1917.

5. SHD 11J 913, dossier 208 (Joseph Bertin, François Henaff, Guillaume Bernard, Arnaud Juin, Joseph Picaud, Jean Trigne), June 4, 1916.

6. Re the Mourmelon mutiny of 27 May, SHD 11J 913, Joseph Bertin, François Henaff, Guillaume Bernard, Arnaud Juin, Joseph Picaud; SHD 19N 300 (justice militaire), report of July 19, 1916; re Haudainville mutiny of 14 May, SHD 11J 1067, conseil de guerre, 27ᵉ DI, 30 mai et 3 juin 1916; SHD 11J 1075/1076, cited here are dossiers of Maurice Delauney, Henri Gilbert, André Martinetti, Louis Sylvestre, Etienne Guidicelli; AFGG, t. IV, vol. 2, annexes 1, 706, note du général André du 30 mai 1916; Colonel Goutard,

"Mai 1916. Une mutinerie à Verdun," *Almanach du Combattant*, no. 39 (1968), 83–88; Legrand-Girarde, *quart de siècle* 583–84; the total number of mutineers is uncertain, as only some were indicted and 37 convicted, according to the divisional register; re major Tournès at Souilly, see p. 186 above; Offenstadt, Fusillés, 36-40

7. SHD 24N 85, Note du Général Lebrun, May 25, 1916.

8. SHD 11J 672 (12ᵉ DI), Georges Tuffin and Pierre Jouan (106ᵉ RI, July 12, 1916).

9. SHD 11J 673 (12ᵉ DI), Marcel Salmon and Louis Freton (106ᵉ RI, August 6, 1916) and Battendier, Breteau, Libert (132ᵉ RI, August 19, 1916).

10. SHD 16N 1485, Petain (GAC) to Alby (13ᵉ CA), June 28, 1916; Bazelaire, *Souvenirs*. Some of the men who deserted may have surrendered, see below p.

11. SHDT 11J 905, conseils de guerre du 21ᵉ DI, 4 juin et juillet 1916; AFGG, t. IV, vol. 2, annexes 1, 816 (Joffre, June 2, 1916), 1122 (Robert, June 9, 1916), 1129, (Nivelle, June 10, 1916); t. IV, vol. 2, annexes 2, 1740 (Serrigny, 23 June), 1774 (Nivelle, 30 June); SHD 16N 1485, Niessel to 7 CA [Bazelaire], June 26, 1916; Denizot, *Verdun*, 146 ff; see ch. 4 above. The minutier for the events of June 11, 1916 is missing in SHD 11J 1677, making it impossible to find the court-martial dossiers.

12. SHD 11J 1075/1076, Alfred Rambaud), June 3, 1916; SHD 11J 674, Mathurin Briend, and SHD 16N 1485, Bazelaire to IIe armée, June 28, 1916); SHD 24N 623, Général Carbillet, June 11, 1915; SHD 11 J 905 (65ᵉ RI), Léonce Faure and Noël Le Gouaec, June 10, 1916.

13. SHD 16N 1485, report of June 15, 1916; AFGG, t. IV, vol. 2, 50–51 et IV, 2, annexes 1, 706 (note of May 31, 1916) et 816 (Joffre to Minister of War, June 2, 1916); SHD 16N 1391, contrôle postal, report of June 10, 1916; SHD 19N 300, report of July 19, 1916; for political opinions at Verdun, see ch. 10.

14. SHD 24N 1200, notes of 22 and February 23, 1916; Werth, *Verdun*, 97; Koch, *Verdun*, 41, 43–44; Kabisch, *Verdun*, 85–86; Serrigny, *Trente ans*, 72–77; Dellmensigen, *Bayernbuch*, vol. 2, 22; SHD 24N 85, Nivelle, April 5, 1916.

15. SHD 16N 1977, "La victoire de Douaumont-Vaux," (n.d., 1916); SHD 16N 1981, report from 40 DI, June 28, 1916 (captured German instructions).

16. SHD 16N 1977: "La victoire de Douaumont-Vaux"; 133ᵉ DI, report of January 20, 1917; Koch, *Verdun*, 134, 137 ff; Hindenburg, *Leben*, 194–95; SHD 16N 1977, rapport du 4 mars 1917 (tr. of Hindenburg memo, December 25, 1916).

17. Lipp, *Meinungslenkung*, 116–17, 123, and *passim*.

18. SHD 16N 1977, report of March 4, 1917; BA-MA, W10/51507, *Stimmung im Heere* 1916/17.

19. Péricard, *Ceux de Verdun*, 92–95; SHD, 208 11J 913, conseil de guerre of 21ᵉ DI to Minister of War, June 6, 1916 (see pp. above); Memorial de Verdun, Jean Loevenbruck, July 1917; SHD 11J673, Charles Cuvelier, July 16, 1916, and cf. also SHD 11J 674, Eugène Guillot, October 26, 1916, and SHD 11J 675, Elie Diette; AN F7 13349, letters from suspected anarchist, June 19, and July 21, 1916.

20. AN F7 13349, letter of June 19, 1916, and report on meeting of 3rd section of Parti socialiste, April 20, 1916; Deimling, *Souvenirs*, 228–38.

21. Loez, *Refus*, chap. 2, *passim*; Watson, *Enduring*, chap. 6, *passim*; Ziemann, *Fahnenflucht*; Ziemann, *Verweigerungsformen*.

22. BA-MA, W10/51507, *Stimmung im Heere*; Einem, *Armeeführer*, 273–75; Ludendorff, *Kriegserinnerungen*, 244; Watson, *Enduring*, 184.

23. See ch. 4.

24. "On les aura," in Botrel, *Chants*, vol. 3; *Tragödie*, vol. 13, part 1, 5–6; vol. 15, part 4, 200; Dollé, *Côte 304*, 11–13, 28 ff; Cru, *Témoins*, 586; Bordeaux, *Souville*, 55, and *Chanson*, II, 65–66.

25. D'Arnoux, *Paroles*, 10, 15; Jubert, *Verdun*, 14, 19–20; Campana, *Enfants*, entry for April 10, 1916; SHD 1KT48, L'huilier; SHD KT1 110, Bros, 500 (May 8, 1916).

26. "Les gas d'Mangin," in Botrel, *Chants*, vol. 3; Romains, *Verdun*, 340–41.

27. Giono, *Pureté*, 638–39; Naegelen, *Suppliciés*, 81–83; Zweig, *Erziehung*; Céline, *Voyage*, 50.

28. Jahr, *Gewöhnliche Soldaten*, 218–36; see above, pp.

29. "On les aura," in Botrel, Chants, vol. 3; France Inter, "Souvenirs et chansons de 1916," January 1, 1966, including partial words of song of 1916: "Cocorico! debout petits soldats/le soleil luit, partout le canon tonne/jeunes héros voici le grand combat/et Verdun la victorieuse pousse un cri. . . ./les échos débordent la Meuse/halte-là, on ne passe pas . . ."; France Culture, "Tours de chant,", November 10, 1997, including Michel Sardou, "Verdun" (composed in 1979) and words of the chanson de Craonne; FR 3 television, November 11, 2008, 19.20, "chansons célébrant les mutins et les fusillés de la grande guerre," and Sarkozy at Douaumont; Offenstadt, "Comparer l'incomparable?"; SHD 16N 1391, contrôle postal, report of July 3, 1916; Offenstadt, *14–18 Aujourd'hui*, 47–52.

30. BA-MA, W10/51507, "Stimmung im Heere."

31. Mac Orlan, *Verdun*, 23–25.

Chapter 10

1. Renouvin, *Crise*, 352.

2. See, e.g., Ziemann, *Front und Heimat*; Lipp, *Meinungslenkung*; Fuller, *Troop Morale*.

3. For this notion and its critics see, e.g., Becker and Audoin-Rouzeau, *14–18*; Audoin-Rouzeau, *Combattre*; Prost, "Guerre de 1914" and Cazals "1914–1918: Chercher Encore."

4. Todorov, *Abus*, 28.

5. Cazin, *Humaniste*, 18; Campana, *Enfants*, entry for March 12, 1916; SHD 1KT 108, Anonyme, 56e and 16e B.C.P., *Récit*; Caporal Audry on *L'actualité radiophonique*, February 16, 1966; Werth, *1916*, 37, writes that soldiers did not see each other at Verdun, while Canini, *Combattre*, 46, writes that they did, but the first is speaking of long and the other of close range, see below, pp. 212 ff.

6. Audoin-Rouzeau, *1870*, 108; Roth, "Allemagne et Allemands."

7. Filali, *Chronique*, 74, 98; Boutroux, "L'Allemagne"; cf. the treatment of "la croisade" in Audoin-Rouzeau and Becker, *14–18*, and of the religious idiom of Germanophobia in Becker, *Guerre et Foi*, 18–24.

8. Social scientists have long noted this phenomenon—cf., e.g., Allport, *Prejudice*, 190—and historians of German and French cultural attitudes towards one another have as well, cf. Nolan, *Inverted Mirror, passim.*

9. Colonel X in *Le Gaulois*, March 7, 1916; SHD 6N 46, summary for February 28 and March 10, 1916; *Le Matin*, February 25, 1916 (de Civrieux), August 14, 1916; *Le Petit Journal*, August 1, 1916 (S. Pichon); Nolan, *Inverted Mirrors, passim.*

10. *Le Matin*, March 25, 1916 (Louis Barthou).

11. Grant, *Verdun Days*, 126; Gide, *Journal*, vol. 1, 579.

12. Dubrulle, *Régiment*, 37.

13. Joffre, *Journal*, entry for 17/6/16; Rimbault, *Journal*, 233 (entry for December 20, 1914); Hertz, *Ethnologue*, 55–56, 69, 134, (letters of September 16, October 3, December 4, 1914); Lafont, *Ciel*, 113–14, 130, 134–35.

14. Pic, *Tranchée*, x; Hertz, *Ethnologue*, 68 (October 1, 1914); Joubaire, *France*, 229 (February 2, 1916); Mornet, *Tranchées*, 22; Thérésette, *Moine soldat*, 73–74.

15. Cazin, *Humaniste*, 183; SHD 16N 1391, contrôle postal, March 31, May 26, June 10, August 2, 4, October 18, and November 4, 1916; cf. also Delvert, *Carnets*, 273 ff.

16. Boasson, *Soir*, 2–3, 291 (April 1915 and November 23, 1917); Limosin, *Verdun à L'Yser*, 25–28 (Christmas 1915); Aumonier, *Diables Bleus, passim.*

17. SHD 1KT 110, Le Bros, May 4, 1916.

18. Muenier, *Angoisse*, 107 (February 25, 1916); Dupont, *Attente*, 196–97 (June 22, 1916).

19. SHD 16N 1391, contrôle postal, August 4 and 18, November 22 and 29, 1916.

20. Muenier, *Angoisse*, 192; SHD 16N 1391, contrôle postal, November 22, 1916; Hourticq, *Récits*, 132.

21. Rimbault, *Journal*, 233 (December 20, 1914); Doria, *Lettres*, 84–86 (January 6, 1915); Cazin, *Humaniste*, 48 (March 25, 1915); Hertz, *Ethnologue*, 126.

22. Raynal, *Journal*, 89 (June 1, 1916); Delvert, *Carnets*, 355–56 (June 5, 1916); Rimbault, *Propos*, 235–36 (February 1917).

23. Delvert, *Carnets*, 356; Antenne 2, "Chantez-le moi. Les années 1914–1918," 19/09/82 and 26/09/82; Botrel, *Chants*, vol. 3; Boyer, *Chanson*, préface; Boasson, *Soir*, 10 (July 1, 1915); SHD 16N 1391, contrôle postal, May 26 and October 18, 1916.

24. Hertz, *Ethnologue*, 113 (November 17, 1914), 126–27 (November 28, 1914); Péricard, *Ceux de Verdun*, 245–46; Péricard, *Verdun*, préface; Raynal, *Journal*, 180–81.

25. Werth, *Verdun*, 141; *Frankfurter Zeitung*, May 28, 1916; SHD 6N 50, summary for January 11, 1916); *Berliner Tageblatt*, February 28, 1916; *Münchner neueste nachrichten*, March 1, 1916.

26. Werth, *1916*, 64; *Vorwärts*, March 10, 1916.

27. *Berliner Tageblatt*, March 2, 7, 1916; *Vorwärts*, March 10, 1916.

28. Ch. 2 above, p. 43; AFGG, t. IV, ii, 417–20; Hohenborn, *Briefe*, 140 (March 8, 1916); von Einem, *Armeeführer*, 195 (entry of February 2, 1916).

29. Münch, *Verdun*, 231, citing August Heider, *Grosskampftage* (Paderborn, 1930).

30. Bloem, *Vormarsch*, 420–21; Koch, *Verdun*, 21–23.

31. Bülow cited in Joubaire, *France*, 127 (October 10, 1914); SHD 16 N 920, report of January 12, 1916; Madelin, *Aveu*, 41, 46, 69–70, including some material preserved in SHD 19N 309.

32. Hertz, *Ethnologue*, 241; MV, carnets of Caporal Ernest Béranger, carnet for April 25–May 12, 1916 (night of 7–8 May); MV, Berton; Jeanbernat, *Lettres*, October 17, 1915.

33. Gray, *Warriors*, 131–69; Guy Cohn (61ᵉ RI) on FR3 television, June 15, 1996; Münch, *Verdun*, 229–30; Mac Orlan, *Verdun*, 26; Ettighofer, "Moral," in Cochet, ed., *Actes du Colloque*.

34. Thimmermann, *Verdun-Souville*, 90.

35. Lefebvre-Dibon, *Quatre pages*, 77–78.

36. SHD 16N 1391, contrôle postal, March 25, 1916; Baumann, *Chevoleau*, 83 (Easter Saturday, 1915); Richer, *Moine soldat*, 91.

37. Koch, *Verdun*, 43–44 (February 28, 1916).

38. SHD 1KT 108, Anonyme, 56ᵉ and 16ᵉ B.C.P., *Récit*, c. May 17, 1916; Lefebvre-Dibon, *Quatre Pages*, 79; MV, Comte, November 1, 1914– December 31, 1918, September 9, 1916.

39. Audoin-Rouzeau, *1870*, 99; Westman, *Surgeon*, 93; MV, Carnets Auguste Comte, November 1, 1914–December 31, 1918, September 10, 1916; Bréant, *Alsace à la Somme*, 146 (November 26, 1914); Dubrulle, *Régiment*, 15 (February 26, 1916); Philip S. Rice, *An American Crusader at Verdun* (Princeton, 1917), 62; Leonard Smith, Stephane Audoin-Rouzeau, Annette Becker, *France and the Great War 1914–1918* (Cambridge, 2003), 28.

40. See for example Bourke, *Killing*, and Grossman, *On Killing*, *passim*; Holmes, *Acts*, 378–79; Toubert, "pertes."

41. SHD 1KT 92 1, Corti, March 12 and 29, 1916. It is almost impossible at Verdun to find any accounts betraying enjoyment at close-quarter killing or any that try to imagine the effects of killing a distant and invisible foe; Bourke, *Killing*, finds occasional examples in the British, Australian, or US armies, but more in World War II and Vietnam.

42. Genevoix, *Sous Verdun* (1916), 65–66; *Sous Verdun* (1925), 83; *Sous Verdun*, (1950), 44 n.1; *Jeux de Glaces*, 46–48; Prost, *Anciens combattants*, vol. 3, 15–16; Prost, "brutalization."

43. Genevoix, *Sous Verdun*, (1950), 44 n.1; SHD KT1 110 (Bros), 502–3 (May 8, 1916); SHD 1 K 860, Tournès.

44. SHD 1KT 108, Anonyme, 56ᵉ and 16ᵉ B.C.P., *Récit*, entries for April–May 1916; Raynal, *Fort de Vaux*, 89 (June 1, 1916).

45. Raynal, *Fort de Vaux*, 132 (June 5–6, 1916); Gaudy, *Trous d'obus*, 215 (May 17–18, 1916); Koch, *Verdun*, 19 ff; Münch, *Verdun*, 273; Pelade, *Verdun*; SHD 16N 920 report for February 29 (March 3, 1916).

46. Fonsagrive, *Batterie*, 18–19; Joubaire, *France*, 31–32; Grossman, *Killing, passim*.

47. Jean-Norton Cru, *Témoins* (Nancy, 2006 [1929]), 566–67; Prost, *Anciens Combattants*, III, 15; cf., e.g., SHD 1KT 108, Anonyme, 56ᵉ and 16ᵉ B.C.P.,*Récit*: "nous ne pouvions faire autrement, nous étions tous des sacrifiés," and France Inter commentator, actualité radiophonique, February 16, 1966: "on se bat jusqu'au sacrifice, peut-être un peu par héroisme parce que les générations de ce temps sont formés à une discipline rigoureuse mais beaucoup plus parce que on ne peut pas faire autrement."

48. Marshall, *Men against Fire*, 50 ff (in spite of dubious figures); Thérésette, *Moine soldat* 88–92; d'Arnoux, *Paroles*, 12 (in Champagne, September 24, 1915).

49. *Le Matin*, April 7, 1916; Werth, *Verdun*, 74–76; Raynal, *Journal*, 169–81; Koch, *Verdun*, 53.

50. Campana, *Grande revanche*, March 14, 17, 21, 1916; SHD 1KT 92 1, Corti, March 29, 1916.

51. Ashworth, *Live*; Hertz, *Ethnologue*, 126 (November 28, 1914); Joubaire, *France*, 151; SHD 16N 920, notes of January 12 and 25, 1916.

52. Gallwitz, *Erleben*, 41; Koch, *Verdun*, 95.

53. Munch, *Verdun*, 226, 269; Romains, *Verdun*, 210.

54. Thimmermann, *Verdun-Souville*, 120 (see p. above); Guy Cohn interviewed on Fr3 (television), June 15, 1996.

55. Mac Orlan, *Verdun*, 25; Zweig, *Erziehung*, 11; Tardi and Verney, *1916*.

56. Poirier, *Verdun*; Paul, *Douaumont*.

57. Zöberlein, *Glaube*, 22, 115; Wehner, *Sieben*, 57, 153, 229, 235; Gollbach, *Wiederkehr*, 199.

58. Cf., e.g., Ousby, *Verdun*, 68, and Todorov, *Abus*, 28.

59. Holmes, *Acts of War*, 292–93, 373–74; Stouffer, *American Soldier: Adjustment*, 184–87, 451; Stouffer, *American Soldier: Combat*, 108–12; Grinker and Spiegel, *Men under Stress*, 43.

60. Audoin-Rouzeau, *Combattre*, 213 ff.

61. Cazin, *Humaniste*, 240–41; Keeley, *War*, 99–103; Tawney, "Attack"; Westmann, *Surgeon*, 58; Ziese und Ziese-Beringer, *Generäle*, 9.

Chapter 11

1. Rimbault, *Propos*, 137–44.

2. Boasson, *Soir*, 148.

3. Muenier, *Angoisse*, 119.

4. SHD 1 K860, Tournès.

5. SHD 16N 1391, October 26, 1916; SHD 16N 1485, reports of July 15, 1916.

6. *Petain et Valéry*, 114–15; Smith, *Embattled Self*, 78.

7. SHD 1KT 110, Le Bros, I, 555 (June 20, 1916).

8. Poncheville, *Dix mois*, entry for August 28, 1916.
9. SHD 16N 1391, report of August 4, 1916.
10. SHD 16N 1391, reports of August 17, September 2, November 29–December 6, 1916; SHD 24N 1834, note of February 8, 1916; see ch. 8, pp.
11. Falkenhayn, *Heeresleitung*, 245; Petain, *Verdun*, 83.
12. Pétain, *Verdun*, 104.
13. SHD 5N 364, note re Castelnau interview, October 15–16, 1916.
14. Mornet, *Tranchées*, 48.
15. *Le Journal*, March 14, 1916 (from SHD 6N46).
16. Gallwitz, *Erleben*, 36; Hohenborne, *Briefe*, 220–21.
17. Kuper, *Culture*, 23–36; *Le Journal*, March 10, 1916; *Frankfurter Zeitung*, March 16, 1916; *Le Gaulois*, March 7, 1916.
18. Bloem, *Vormarsch*, 392.
19. Bloem, *Vormarsch*, 417; SHD 16N 1391, July 3, 1916.
20. *Kriegsbriefe*, 150–51 (Heinz Pohlmann, May 25, 1916).
21. SHD 16N 1391, October 4, 18, 1916; Payen, *Ame*, vol. 2, 164; Poncheville, *Dix mois*, 10; Joubaire, *France*), 38; Bréant, *Alsace à la Somme*, entry for August 16, 1914.
22. Joubaire, *France*, entry for May 22, 1916; Bréant, *Alsace à la Somme*, 148 ff, 186–87, 190.
23. SHD 1KT 110, Le Bros, I, 513–14 (May 12, 1916).
24. Hertz, *Ethnologue*, 126 and *passim*.
25. Tuffrau, *1914–1918*, 119.
26. SHD 16N 1391, contrôle postal, reports of July 14, May 12, July 28, August 11, September 2, October 18, November 29, 1916; SHD 19N309, extraits de lettres, March 5, 1915.
27. SHD 16N 1391, July 7 and 22, October 4, December 7, 1916.
28. SHD 16N 1391, June 25, April 8, May 5, 12, 26, June 10; see *tableaux de pourcentages* of comments in letters, e.g., March 22 and 27, 1916, and *sondage* of July 27, 1916 (71ᵉ DI); SHD 16N 1485, report of August 1, 1916.
29. SHD 16N 1485, reports of May 1, 1916 (letters 10–25 April) and 27 June (letters c. 6–24 June); AD Gironde, 1M 437, dossier on "pacifiste" Theodore Ruyssen, Professeur Fac de letters, Bordeaux, letter to him from "Le Gallio, T.R. 4ᵉ Infanterie, secteur 3," November 6, 1916; Lagrange, *Images*.
30. See ch. 9, pp. ; Grinker and Spiegel, *Men under Stress*, 45.
31. Bloem, *Vormarsch*, 445; SHD 1KT 110, Le Bros, I, 555.
32. Strachan, "Training"; Shils and Janowitz, "Cohesion"; Picq, *Etudes*, 92–93; Bloch, *Ecrits*, 149–50; Rousseau, *Guerre censurée*, 138; Jubert, *Verdun*, 40–41.
33. Kellett, *Combat*, 43, 321, 334.
34. Dupont, *Attente*, 147–48.
35. Sauer, *Heilig*, entry for June 9, 1916; Delvert, *Carnets*, entry for June 25, 1916.
36. Delvert, *Carnets*, 171 (in Champagne); Sauer, *Erinnerungen*, entry for June 4, 1916; SHD 16N 1391, reports of October 19 and November 25, 1916; SHD 1KT 110, Le Bros, I, 449–50 (April 13, 1916).

37. Delvert, *Carnets*, 143 (December 17, 1915); Rimbault, *Journal*, 199–200 (October 23, 1916); Morel-Journel, *Journal*, September 18, 1916.

38. SHD 16N 1391, June 25 and July 6, 1916; SHD 1KT 108 Anonyme, 56ᵉ BCP and 16ᵉ BCP, *Récit*; Erbeling, *Vor Verdun*, vii.

39. SHD 16N 1391, March 25, 1916; Tournassus, *Soldats!*, 123; Mornet, *Tranchées*, 42 ff; Rimbault, *Propos*, 217; Bloem, *Vormarsch*, 417.

40. Mosse, *Fallen Soldiers*, 126 ff and 159 ff; Leed, *No Man's Land*, 188–89; Fussell, *Great War*, 86–87; Hanna, *Republic of Letters*; Roper, *Secret Battle*, *passim*.

41. SHD 16N 920, interrogation of Bavarian prisoners taken March 23 in Bois de Malancourt, April 7, 1916.

42. Corporal Audry on France Inter, February 16, 1966.

43. SHD 1KT 108 Anonyme, 56ᵉ BCP and 16ᵉ BCP, *Récit*.

44. SHD 16N 1391, July 28, 1916.

45. SHD 16N 1391, June 25, 1916.

46. SHD 16N 1391, August 17, 1916.

47. SHD 16N 1391, August 17, 1916; SHD 19 N309, report of March 6, 1916 (letter extracts).

48. Becker, *Guerre et Foi*, 11, 13, 31—as Becker notes, 28, Norton Cru rejected the prevalence of such exalted themes among the men.

49. Witkos, ed., *Kriegsbriefe*, letter from Johannes Haas, May 13, 1916.

50. SHD 16N 1391, August 2, 1916.

51. SHD 1KT 102, Beaucour, 22 (March 7, 1916); Poncheville, *Dix mois*, 39–40, 187; Limosin, *Verdun à L'Yser*, 5–16, 33–36; SHD 1KT 170, Hémery, carnet.

52. Poncheville, *Dix ans*, 39–40; Limosin, *Verdun*, 5–16; Campana, *Enfants*, entry for March 14, 1916; Muenier, *Angoisse*, 177–78 (February 26, 1916); SHD 16N 1391, August 17, 1916; Gaudy, *Souvenirs*, vol. 1, 212. The Père Laurent to whom Gaudy alludes appears to be the same as the one to whom Duroselle alludes, in *Clemenceau*, 839–40; the words that Gaudy attributed to Laurent—"Allons, les gars, du courage! Vous arrivez!"—seem contrived, even though Verdun provides the most authentic part of his three volumes of souvenirs (cf. Jean-Norton Cru, *Témoins*, 312–14).

53. See pp. above; SHD 16N 1391, August 17, 1916; SHD, 1KT 110, Le Bros, I, 448 (April 10, 1916).

54. Cazin, *Humaniste*, 169.

55. Delvert, *Carnets*, 171.

56. Cazin, *Humaniste*, 26.

57. SHD 1KT 110, Le Bros, I, 448.

58. Weber, *First War*, 58; Witkos, *Kriegsbriefe*, letter of Heinz Pohlman, May 26, 1916; Werth, *Verdun*, 377.

59. Limosin, *Verdun à l'Yser*, 56–57; Baumann, *Chevoleau*, 91; *Tournassus*, Soldats, 100.

60. Campana, *Enfants*, 6; SHD 16N 1391, March 25 and November 22, 1916; Hoffmann, 242 (Wilhelm Klassen, March 11, 1916); Payen, *Ame*, 160; Dubrulle, *Régiment*, 34.

61. Pastre, *Trois ans*, 115.
62. SHD 1KT 110, Bros, I, 473 (April 22, 1916); Delvert, *Carnets*, 185, 187; SHD 16N 1391, 10 June and December 5, 1916.
63. Delvert, *Carnets*, 203.
64. Cazin, *Humaniste*, 180.
65. Delvert, *Carnets*, 179; Louis Madelin, *Aveu*, 33; Fonsagrive, *Batterie*, 62–63; Gaudy, *Souvenirs*, 215, 222; MV, Derozières, February 17, 1916.
66. SHD 1KT 110, Bros, I, 434, 444 (March 5, 29 and April 6, 1916).
67. Delvert, *Carnets*, 174 (January 20, 1916).
68. SHD 1KT 110, Bros, I, 434, 444 (March 5, 29 and April 6, 1916).
69. SHD 1KT102, Beaucour, 15, and SHD 8YE 1177 (biographical details).
70. SHD 16 N 920, interrogations, April 7, 1916.
71. Boasson, *Soir*, 35–36, 39; Baumann, *Chevoleau*, 35; Poncheville, *Dix mois*, 45.
72. See in particular Ziemann, *Front und Heimat*, 8–32, and Hanna, "Republic."
73. SHD 16N 1391, December 1, 1916.
74. SHD 16N 1391, November 27, 1916; Jubert, *Verdun*, 94–95.
75. SHD 16N 1391, October 26, November 4, 28 and 29, December 1 and 5, 1916; Madelin, *Aveu*, 64–65; Roper, *Secret Battle*, 13 and *passim*, points out that historians of gender claiming to discover "sexual antagonism" as a result of the war have ignored the intimate evidence from families and households.
76. SHD 16N 1485, contrôle postal, report of July 15, 1916; SHD 1 K 860, Tournès; Delvert, *Carnets*, 218–19; Rimbault, *Propos*, 153; Vial, *Territoriaux*, 14–19.
77. Boasson, *Soir*, 149–50.
78. Jubert, *Verdun*, 85; SHD 16N 1391, July 13, 1916; Cazin, *Humaniste*, 153–54.
79. SHD 19N309, note of April 1, 1916; Madelin, *Aveu*, 64–65; Cazin, *Humaniste*, 109; MV, Carnets of Henri Goudet, introduction.
80. Boasson, *Soir*, 149–50; SHD 1KT 110, Le Bros, I, 505; Delvert, *Carnets*, 356, also mentioned in ch. 10, p. ; SHD 16N 1391, June 3, 1916.
81. Laurentin, *1914–1918*, 168 ff; SHD 16N 1391, report of August 26, 1916; FR2, Journal de 13 heures, November 10, 1995.
82. SHD 16N 1485, report of July 15, 1916.
83. SHD 16N 1391, report of March 29, 1916; cf. also report of 8 April, "Je vous assure que nous avons souffert, mais pour avoir Verdun, ils ne l'auront jamais," and "Les Boches voudraient VERDUN, mais ils ne l'auront pas. Il y a ce qu'il faut pour les arrêter," etc; ibid., reports of July 6, October 17, 1916.
84. Jardin, *Racines*, *passim*; Lipp, *Meinungslenkung*, 279 ff.
85. BNF, acq. Fr. 16038, ms. Poincaré speech at Verdun, September 13, 1916.
86. Tuffrau, *1914–1918*, préface, 22, and *passim*; Jean-Norton Cru, *Témoins*, 405–6.
87. Lefebvre-Dibon, *Quatre Pages*, 109 ff.
88. SHD 1KT 1156, Padirac 9; Passaga, *Calvaire*, 26 ff; Becker, *Après la bataille*, avant-propos: "Vouloir dominer le monde et le connaître aussi mal: quelle étrange prétention!"

Epilogue

1. Philip S. Rice, *An American Crusader at Verdun* (Princeton, 1918), 56, 68.
2. Passaga, Fénelon-François-Germain (Géneral), *The Calvary of Verdun. The American around Verdun* (Paris, 1927 [tr. of *Le Calvaire de Verdun*, Paris, 1927]), 148 ff; Michael E. Shay, *The Yankee Division in the First World War. In the Highest Tradition* (College Station, TX, 2008), 202 ff.
3. *Le Gaulois*, March 11, 1916; *La Victoire*, February 25, 1916.
4. INA, speech at Luna Park by Albert Lebrun, November 12, 1938.
5. INA, Journal National, June 20, 1956 (television).
6. INA, Inter actualités de 19H00, June 15, 1986 (radio); INA, FR2 25 juin 2006, Journal 20 heures.
7. France Inter January 1, 1966, "Souvenirs et chansons de 1916."
8. Henri de Kérillis in *L'Epoque*, September 14, 1938.
9. INA, Journal National, June 20, 1956 (television); France 1, Paris Inter, "Paris vous parle", June 26, 1960 (radio).
10. Bonne, *France*, 274; "Pélerinage à Verdun vingt ans après", *Le Petit Journal*, February 20, 1936; "Verdun", *Le Monde*, May 28, 1966.
11. Montherlant, *Chant*, 120.
12. *Völkischer Beobachter*, July 14, 1936.
13. INA, Journal télévisé de 20 heures, "Voyage de Pompidou à Verdun", 28 juin 1964.
14. INA, Inter actualités de 19H00, June 15, 1986 (radio); TF1 Journal de 20h, June 16, 1996; INA, TF1, Journal de 13 heures, 11 mai 1995; cf. also Offenstadt, *14–18 aujourd'hui*, 112–20.

Appendix

1. Cailleteau, *Gagner*, 91–92; SHD, 19N 270, Gén. Hirschauer, January 15, 1918: "Importance des pertes au cours des années 1916–1917"; SHD, 5N 229, EMA 5ᵉ bureau reports of January 10 and 13, 1916, and Minister of war to Santé, January 9, 1916; 16 N 1379, EMA 5ᵉ bureau, "Rapport sur l'étude statistique des pertes de l'armée française, February 25, 1916"; 7N 552, 1ᵉʳ bureau, EMA, "Note au sujet des méthodes suivie [*sic*] pour établir la statistique des pertes françaises", May 6, 1919.
2. McRandle and Quirk, "Blood Test"; *History of the Great War*, vol. 5, 1932, 496–97; SHD, 7N 552, EMA, 2ᵉ bureau, "Les pertes françaises et les pertes allemandes comparés au cours de la campagne à la date du 1er septembre", November 27, 1916; *Sanitätsbericht, passim*.
3. Rapport Marin, *passim*; Toubert, *Etude statistique*; Guinard, Devos, and Nicot, *Inventaire sommaire*, 204–13; cf., e.g., Churchill, *World Crisis*, vol. 3, Part I, 52 n.1 and table; Larcher, "Données statistiques" and "Données statistiques (suite)."
4. *Statistics of the Military Effort of the British Empire during the Great War*; McRandle and Quirk, "Blood Test"; Rapport Marin, 75; Larcher, "Données statistiques (suite)."

5. SHD, 16N 523, GQG note of April 6, 1917; *History of the Great War*, vol. 5, 1932; McRandle and Quirk, "Blood Test." Between Churchill, his critics, and the Reichsarchiv argument and uncertainty prevailed over whether the *Verlustlisten* included or excluded the lightly wounded, but the tables published by the Kriegsministerium in 1935 (see below) clearly indicated that they excluded them.

6. SHD, 16N 528; Larcher, "Données statistiques (suite)"; AFGG, t. IV, vol. 3, appendix i, 521 (correcting for error in final total); SHA, 19 N 270, Gen. Hirschauer, "Importance des pertes au cours des années 1916–1917," January 15, 1918; Marin report, 75; Canini, *Combattre à Verdun*, 11; Bernède, *Verdun*, 342; Denizot, *Verdun*, Annexe XII, 286–87; Churchill, *World Crisis*, vol. 3, Part I, 97; Wendt, Verdun, 243–44; Pierre Renouvin, review of Wendt's *Verdun* in *Revue d'Histoire de la Guerre*, April 1931.

7. McRandle and Quirk, "Blood Test"; *AFGG*, t. IV, vol. 3, appendix I, 521 (correcting for error in the final total); Cailleteau, *Gagner*, table 106, 109–10.

8. Reichskriegsministerium, *Zusammenstellung*, Table 10: "Vergleich der Verluste in längerem Zeitraum zwischen Stellungskrieg (5 army Verdun) und Bewegungskrieg (11 army Feldzug im Sommer 1915 und 9 Armee, Feldzug in Polen 1914).

9. See SHD, 19N 270, Hirschauer, "Importance des pertes au cours des années 1916–1917," January 15, 1918. For 1916, the data and sources from Second Army did not enable Hirschauer to give losses as percentages of those engaged. At the beginning of March the Second Army had 18.5 divisions in line, the same as in early September, *AFGG*, t. IV, vol. 1, appendix II and III, 648–49, and t. IV, vol. 3, 294; Bernède, *Verdun*, 367.

10. Cru, *Témoins*; Rousseau, *Procès*, *passim*; Mariot, "Tuer"; Smith, *Embattled Self*, 12–13; Audoin-Rouzeau, *Combattre*, 69–167; Prost "Guerre de 14"; Prochasson, "Mots pour le dire."

11. Delvert, "Histoire de la Guerre"; Méléra, *Verdun*, 42–44; Gaudy, *Souvenirs*, 160; Mac Orlan, *Verdun*, 18–19.

12. Cochet, Annick, *Opinion*, I, 8–17; Jeanneney, "Archives"; Pedroncini, "Moral de l'armée."

13. From SHD 16N 1391: 23 August, 300 letters from 2 companies in 71ᵉ DI read, or 1 for 2 soldiers; 27 July, 300 letters from the 71ᵉ DI, or about 1 for fifty soldiers; 8 August, likewise for 37ᵉ DI; for the Second Army, at intervals of several days between March 22 and May 30, 848–1,621, on 11 August 3,356, and on 4 October 7,132 letters read, or very approximately 1 for a range between 50 and 100 men.

14. SHD 16N 1391, report of March 31, 1916; Genevoix, *Sous Verdun*, 125.

BIBLIOGRAPHY

UNPUBLISHED PRIMARY SOURCES

I. Archives

A. Service historique de la Défense, Vincennes (SHD)

Conseil supérieur de la guerre:

1N 50, 51, 52, 53, 54: défense des frontières, 1920–1933.

Cabinet du Ministre de la Guerre:

5N 134, 135: renseignements divers, November 1915–January, 1917.

5N 136: télégrammes d'attachés militaires, February 1916–May 1917.

5N 229: calcul des pertes allemandes, 1914–1916.

5N 364: presse concernant les généraux, 1915–1917.

Fonds particuliers:

6N 46: Fonds Galliéni: revues de presse nov. 1915–mars 1916.

6N 50: idem, revue de la presse allemande November 1915–February 1916.

6N 52: idem, étude stratégique (January 1916).

6N 59: Fonds Clémenceau: notes divers; pertes (1916).

6N 449: médaille de Verdun, 1936–7.

Etat-Major de l'Armée:

7N 552: Pertes, 1914–1920.

7N 2586: (2ᵉ bureau), attaché militaire en Allemagne, rapports 1930–1931.

Grand Quartier Général:

16N 523: Pertes par armée. Statistiques, 1914–1918.

16N 528: Pertes (2ᵉ armée) January 1915–November 1918.

16N 920: Bulletins de renseignements, 1916.

16N 1379: Pertes allemandes et françaises, 1915–1916.

16N 1977: Opérations à Verdun et dans la Somme, 1916.

16N 1979: 45ᵉ div a côte 304 (1916).

16N 1805: Correspondence GQG–GAC, 1916–1917.

16N 1981: Organisations et fortifications à Verdun.

16N 1391–1392: Commission de contrôle postal (2ᵉ armée), mars 1916–jan. 1917.

16N 1485: Contrôle postal: rapports de quinzaine sur la correspondance des troupes (toutes armées).

IIe Armée:

19N 270: Etats des pertes, 1914–1916.

19N 300: Discipline, justice, morale 1916–17.

19N 309–310: Bulletins et renseignements, October 1915–August 1916.

Opérations de corps d'armées et de divisions:

22N 1684: 32ᵉ CA, opérations, 1916.

24N 85–87: 5ᵉ DI, opérations, 18 fév.–20 juin 1916.

24N 271: 14ᵉ DI pertes; justice militaire, 1914–1918.

24N 632: 29ᵉ DI, opérations, 1915–1916.

24N 693: 32ᵉ DI, renseignements sur l'ennemi, 1916.

24N 909: 40ᵉ DI, opérations, 21 fév.–26 déc. 1916.

24N 1060: 43e DI, opérations, 1 fév.–31 juillet 1916.

24N 1200: 51ᵉ DI, pertes; justice militaire 1914–1918.

24N 1211: 51ᵉ DI, 102ᵉ brigade, 1916–1918.

24N 1672: 67ᵉ DI, opérations, January 16–September 26, 1916.

24N 1834: 72ᵉ DI, opérations, 3 août 1914–4 juillet 1916.

Fonds privés:

1KT 48: Colonel André L'Huilier, 151ᵉ RI.

1KT 69: Témoignage de Pierre Nathan sur la journée du June 23, 1916 (12 juin 1967).

1KT 92 1: Claude-Louis Corti, Journal du 157ᵉ RI.

1KT 102: Marquis de Beaucour, Souvenirs de Guerre 1914–1918 (1969).

1KT 108: Anonyme, 56ᵉ puis 16ᵉ B.C.P., Récit des opérations qui se déroulèrent sur Verdun, en Argonne, en Champagne 1914–1918 (ms. Photocopié, fév. 1971).

1KT 110: s/lt. Le bros, Gaston Joseph, carnet de route (236e RAC).

1KT 126 1: Comte Lucien Fischer de Chevriers, 7ᵉ RA, lettres à sa famille.

1KT 130 1: André Le Quillec, "Un fantassin de la classe 16 en 1914–1918. Mémoires retracés en 1966".

1KT 170 1: Carnet de route du Lt. René Hemery du 48ᵉ RI, 5 août 1914–23 juin 1919 (ms. Copié par son fils, 1978).

1K 268: Fonds Joffre.

1K 816: Papiers Fernand Leduc.

1K 860: Documents de René Tournès, Cdt. du 3ᵉ BCP, écrits de sa main probablement à Souilly, 20–31 mai 1916.

1KT 861: Legentil (743 RI), Notes de campagne, 12 avril 1915 au 11 nov. 1918.

1KT 1156: Robert de Foulhiac de Padirac (Lt.-Col.), Mémoires.

de guerre (1924; ms. photocopié).

1KT 1170 1: Journal du Maréchal des logis Andre Petit classe 1900.

Conseils de Guerre:

Registres de jugements: 11J 1067, 1655, 1677.

Dossiers d'instruction: Dossiers 11J 905, 913, 672, 673, 674, 675, 1075/76.

B. *Archives du Mémorial de Verdun*

Journaux, lettres, carnets: Jean Loevenbruck (caporal, 151ᵉ RI), Charles Albert Derozières (82ᵉ RAL), Eugène Berton (brancardier), Auguste Comte (78e RH puis 288ᵉ RI), Jean Pénicaud (s/lt., 2ᵉ RA lourde), Lucien Gissinger (174ᵉ RI), Pierre Maurice Lampo (maréchal des Logis, 3ᵉ groupement d'art. d'Afrique), Jules Herique (Col.), Henri Goudet (médecin auxiliaire, 70ᵉ RI), Gaston Bollery (mitrailleur, 11ᵉ DI), Ernest Béranger (caporal, 50ᵉ RI).

C. *Archives Nationales [AN]*

C7646: Comité secret de la Chambre, June 1916.

Série F7 (police générale–syndicats, socialisme, pacifisme):

13366, 13371, 13349 (Paris).

12986 (Haute Garonne), 12987 (Gironde), 13023 (Haute Vienne).

13072, 13073 (Congrès socialistes).

D. *Archives départementales du Rhône*

4M 234: Etat d'esprit de la population.

4M 260: Partis politiques 1906–1925.

E. *Archives départementales de la Seine-Maritime*

1M 323, 325 (censure).

F. *Archives départementales de la Gironde*

1M 435, 437, 438: pacifisme.

4M 153: rapports hebdomadaires au prefect.

G. *Bibliothèque nationale de France (Richelieu)*

Nouv. acq. fr. 16038: discours de Poincaré, 1914–1918.

Nouv. acq. fr. 16032: Raymond Poincaré, notes journalières, October 16–December 31, 1915.

H. Bundesarchiv-Militärarchiv, Freiburg (BA-MA)

W10 50704: Die Führung Falkenhayns. Forschungsarbeit von Graf von der Schulenburg (1935).

W10 50705: Falkenhayn as Feldherr (1933).

W10 50709: Forschungsarbeit von Dr. W. Solger. Die OHL in der Führung der Westoperationen Ende 1915 bis Ende August 1916 (1933).

W10 51507: Die Entwicklung der Stimmung im Heere 1916/17 (1936).

W10 51512: Gedanken zum "Ruckblick" für die Zeit von Herbst 1916 bis zum Frühjahr 1918. Forschungsarbeit von v. Tieschowitz (1939).

W10 51523: Die OHL und die Kämpfe um Verdun 1916. Schriftwechsel A-K. Ergänzungsakte zu Bd X.

W10 51528: Vorbereitung und Durchführung der Schlacht bei Verdun 1915–1916. Schriftwechsel N-W, Ergänzungsakte Bd X.

W10 51537: Kritiken und Bemerkungen zur Darstellung der Schlacht von Verdun in Weltkriegswerk. Zu Bd X.

W10 51548: Lt. Mundt, Persönliche Erinnerungen.

W10 51549: Schlacht bei Verdun 1916. Schriftwechsel K-W. Ergänzungsakte zu Bd. X.

I. Bayerisches Hauptstaatsarchiv, Abt. IV, Kriegsarchiv, Munich (BHSA).

Mkr 1830, 1832/5: Berichte des Bayerischer Militär-bevollmächtiger im grossen Hauptquartier, February 11, 1916–May 15, 1916.

11.Inf.-Div., Bund 2 (Feldgeistliche): Akt 2, Kriegstagebuch des katholischen Feldgeistlichen Pfarrer Susann.

2.Inf.-Div., Bund 91 (Feldgeistliche): Akt 2, Feldgeistliche und Seelsorge 1914–1918; Bund 118, Feldjustiz.

1.Inf.-Div, Bund 12, 13: Generalkommando I. Bayer. Armee-Korps Bund 194 (Feldjustizbeamter), Bund 179 (Justizpflege).

Militärgerichte Akt. 3652: 2.Bayer.Inf.Division 2c. Strafprozessliste (1916).

Militärgerichte, Akten 6353 and 6354: Georg Mändl, June 3, 7, 8, 20, 1916, January 29, 1917.

II. Unpublished Theses

Cochet, Annick, *L'Opinion et le moral des soldats en 1916 d'après les archives du contrôle postal* (thèse de doctorat, 2 vols., Paris X-Nanterre, 1986).

Roy, Juliette, *Verdun dans la mémoire allemande (1916–1944)* (Mémoire de DEA, Université Paris-IV, Sorbonne, 2003–2004).

Schneider, Christoph, *Medizin an der front. Die verwundetenversorgung der Ersten bayerischen Infanterie division im Ersten Weltkrieg anhand der kriegstagebücher des Divisionsarztes. Zulassungsarbeit für das Staatsexamen im Fach Bayerischer Geschichte an der Ludwig-Maximilians-Universität München* (Munich) 1995.

III. Audiovisual
A. Films
Poirier, Léon, *Verdun. Vision d'Histoire* (1927, 1929; spoken version, *Verdun. Souvenirs d'Histoire, 1931).*
Paul, Heinz, *Douaumont. Die Hölle von Verdun* (1931).
Renoir, Jean, La Grande Illusion (1937).
Brauburger, Stéphan, et Halmburger, Olivier, *Verdun. Aux portes de l'enfer* (2006). Re-diffusion sur Arte, 4 November 2008.

B. Archives de l'Institut Nationale de l'Audiovisuel (INA)
Radio:
Albert Lebrun at Luna Park, November 12, 1938.
France 1, Paris Inter, "Paris vous parle," June 26, 1960.
L'actualité radiophonique, "A voix haute, à voix basse. Verdun, une guerre dans la guerre" February 16, 1966.
France Inter, "L'Attaque allemande du 21 février 1916" February 26, 1966.
France Culture, "Le Pont des Arts: Ailleurs, ailleurs: à Verdun," November 11, 1978.
France Inter, actualités de 19 heures, Mitterrand à Verdun, June 15, 1986.
Television:
Journal National, "Paris vous parle," June 20, 1956.
Journal télévisé de 20 heures, "Voyage de Pompidou à Verdun," June 28, 1964.
Journal télévisé, "Spéciale Verdun," February 22, 1964.
Antenne 2, Journal de 20 heures, June 12, 13, 1976 (60ᵉ anniversaire).
FR 2 magazine, "Vivre ensemble: François Mitterrand et Helmut Kohl à Verdun," September 22, 1984.
Antenne 2, February 21, 1988 (Arthur Conte).
France 2, Journal, March 30, 1994 (Michel Giraud).
FR3, June 15, 1986 (voyage de Chirac à Verdun).
TF1, Journal de 13 heures, 11 mai 1995 ("classe de la paix" à Verdun).
TF1, Journal de 20 heures, 16 juin 1996 (Chirac à Verdun).

PUBLISHED PRIMARY SOURCES
I. Newspapers and Periodicals
French: *L'Action, L'Echo de Paris, L'Eclair, L'Epoque, Excelsior, Le Figaro, Le Gaulois, L'Homme Enchaîné, L'Humanité, L'Illustration, Le Journal, Le Matin, Le Monde, L'œuvre, Le Petit Journal, Le Petit Parisien, Le Rappel, Le Temps, La Victoire* German: *Berliner Tageblatt, Frankfurter Zeitung*

und Handelsblatt, Leipziger Tageblatt, Münchner Neuste Nachrichten Völkischer Beobachter, Vorwärts.

II. Fiction and Poetry

Beumelburg, Werner, *Gruppe Bosemüller, der Roman des Frontsoldaten* (Oldenburg, 1930).

Céline, Louis-Ferdinand, *Voyage au bout de la nuit* (Paris, 1952 [1932]).

Chaine, Pierre, *Mémoires d'un rat* (Paris, 1917).

Drieu La Rochelle, Pierre *Gilles* (1962 [1939]).

Ettighoffer, P. C., *Gespenster am Toten Mann* (Gütersicht, 1937).

Genevoix, Maurice, *Sous Verdun, août-octobre 1914* (préface d'Ernest Lavisse, Hachette, 1916).

——. *Sous Verdun* (Paris, 1925).

——. *Jeux de Glaces* (Namur, 1961).

——. *Les Eparges* (Paris, 1923).

Hein, Alfred, *Der Erstürmung des "Toten Manns," am 20. mai 1916 und die Tornister Philosophie* (Berlin-Leipzig, 1936).

Montherlant, Henry de, *Chant funèbre pour les morts de Verdun* (Paris, Grasset, 1925 [1924]).

Naegelen, René, *Les Suppliciés* (Paris, 1966 [1927]).

Romains, Jules, *Prélude à Verdun* (*Les Hommes de bonne volonté*, XV, Paris, 2003 [1938]).

——. *Verdun* (*Les Hommes de bonne volonté*, XVI, Paris, 2003 [1938]).

Suarès, André, *Ceux de Verdun* (Paris, 1916).

Tardi, Jacques and Jean-Pierre Verney, *1916* (Paris, 2008).

Wehner, Josef Magnus, *Sieben vor Verdun. Ein Kriegsroman* (München, 1930).

——. *Die Wallfahrt nach Paris. Eine patriotisches Phantasie* (Munich 1933).

Werth, Leon. *Clavel Soldat* (1919).

Zöberlein, Hans, *Der Glaube an Deutschland. Ein Kriegserleben von Verdun bis zum Umsturz* (München, 1935 [1931]—Zentralverlag der NSDAP).

Zweig, Arnold, *Erziehung vor Verdun* (Berlin and Weimar, 1935).

III. Schoolbooks, Children's Books, Popular Histories

Bernard, Eugénie, *La Grande Guerre racontée aux enfants* (Paris, 1925).

Bernard, J.-A., *Histoire de la Grande Guerre (1914–1920). Supplément à l'Histoire Contemporaine* (Paris, 1920).

Bonne, E. E., *France et Civilisation: Petit Cours d'Histoire à l'usage des candidats au CEP* (Paris, slnd, [1930]).

Devinat, E., *Histoire de France: Cours moyen* (Paris, 1926).

Dugard, Henry, *La Victoire de Verdun 21 février 1916–3 novembre 1917* (Paris, 1918).

Hallynck, P., Brunet, M., *Nouveau cours d'histoire primaire supérieure* (Paris, 1935).

Fay, Bernard, et al., *Histoire de France des origines à nos jours. 2ᵉ partie: de 1610 a nos jours* (Paris, 1943).

Giraud, Victor, *Le Miracle français: Trois ans après* (Paris, 1918).

———. *Histoire de la Grande Guerre* (Paris, 1919).

Jalabert, Pierre, *Vive la France!* (Paris, 1942).

Jullian, Camille, *La Guerre pour la Patrie: Leçons du Collège de France 1914–1919* (Paris, 1919).

Lechevalier, Auguste-Ernest, *Précis historique de la guerre de 1914, cours moyen-supérieur* (Cuverville-en-Caux), 1919.

Lespès, A. and P. Chales, *Histoire de France, Cours moyen. Programme de 1923* (Paris, 1924).

Leterrier, L. and R. Ozouf, *Histoire de France, Cours moyen—classes de 73 et 83 des lycées et collèges* (Paris, 1953).

Lomont, A. (Inspecteur de L'enseignement primaire), *La Route de la Victoire: Histoire de la Grande Guerre, août 1914–novembre 1918* (Paris, 1922).

Malet, Albert and Jules Isaac, *Histoire contemporaine (de 1815 a nos jours), 3e année.* (Paris, 1935).

Peter Geiss, Daniel Henri and Guillaume Le Quintrec, *Histoire: l'Europe et le monde du Congrès de Vienne à 1945: manuel d'histoire franco-allemand* (Paris, Nathan, 2008).

Martignon, Jean, *Histoire de France Classe de 7ème 1936* (Paris, 1936).

Petite, H. Vast, *Histoire de la grande guerre* (Paris, 1919).

IV. Songs

"Souvenirs et chansons de 1916," France Inter, January 1, 1966 "Chantez le moi. Les années 1914–1918," A2, September 19, 1982.

"La Grande Guerre en chansons," Septième/Arte, November 11, 1993 Soir 3 (FR3), February 21, 1996.

"Tours de chant," France Culture, November 10, 1997.

Botrel, Théodore, *Refrains de Guerre* (3 vols., Paris, 1915–1920), vol. 3, *Chants de Bataille et de Victoire.*

Boyer, Lucien, *La Chanson des poilus. Recueil des chansons et poèmes dits par l'auteur en France et en Macédoine aux Armées de la République* (Paris, 1918).

V. Memoirs, Journals, Letters

d'Arnoux, Jacques, *Paroles d'un Revenant* (Paris, 1925).

Aumonier, P. C., *Avec les 'Diables Bleus'* (Paris, 1916).

Bauer, Max (Col.), *Der Grosse Krieg in Feld und Heimat. Erinnerungen und Betrachtungen* (Tübingen 1921).

Baumann, Emile, *L'abbé Chevoleau, caporal au 90ᵉ d'infanterie* (Paris, 1917).

Bazelaire, Georges de (Général), *Souvenirs de guerre* (Paris, 1988).

Bloch, Marc, *Ecrits de Guerre 1914–1918*, ed. Etienne Bloch and Stéphane Audoin-Rouzeau (Paris, 1997).

Bloem, Walter, *Vormarsch-Sturmsignal!-Das Ganze-halt! Kriegserlebnis Trilogie 1914–1918* (3 vols., Leipzig, 1939).

Boasson, Marc, *Au soir d'un monde. Lettres de guerre* (16 avril 1915–27 avril 1918) (Paris, 1926).

Bréant, Pierre-Louis-Georges (commandant), *De l'Alsace à la Somme. Souvenirs du front (août 1914–janvier 1917)*.

Cabanel, P. *Avec les 'Diables Bleus'* (Paris 1916).

Campana, Roger (Lt.), *Les enfants de la "Grande Revanche": Carnet de route d'un Saint-Cyrien* (Paris, 1920).

Deimling, Berthold von, *Souvenirs de ma Vie* (traduit de l'Allemand, Paris, 1931).

Desfosses, André, "Le premier jour de la bataille de Verdun vu par un caporal de la Somme," *Le Journal des Combattants*, February 16, 2008.

Dollé, André, *La Côte 304* (Paris and Nancy, 1917).

Dubrulle, Paul (Abbé), *Mon Régiment dans la Fournaise de Verdun et dans la Bataille de la Somme* (Préface d'Henry Bordeaux, Paris, 1917).

Duhamel, Georges, *Vie des Martyrs 1914–1916* (Paris, 1938).

Dupont, Marcel, *L'Attente. Impressions d'un officier de légère (1915–1916–1917)* (Paris, 1918).

Einem, Karl von, *Ein Armeeführer erlebt den Weltkrieg* (Leipzig, 1938).

Erbeling, E. (Major), *Vor Verdun. Ernstes und Heiteres in Wort und Bild: Aus dem kriegstagebuch eines Frontoffiziers* (Stuttgart, 1927).

Falkenhayn, Erich von, *Die Oberste Heeresleitung 1914–1916 in ihren wichstigen Entschließungen* (Berlin 1920).

———. "Verdun" Von *** [Falkenhayn]. *Militär-Wochenblatt. Zeitschrift für die deutsche Wehrmacht* 104, 6 (12 July 1919): 98–107.

Ferry, Abel *Carnets secrets 1914–1918*, (Paris, 1957).

Fonsagrive, F. (Lt.), *En Batterie! Verdun (1916)—La Somme—L'Aisne—Verdun (1917)* (Paris, 1919).

Gallieni, Joseph-Simon, *Les Carnets de Gallieni, publiés par son fils Gaetan Gallieni* (Paris, 1932).

Gallwitz, Max von, *Erleben in Westen 1916–1918* (Berlin, 1932), 21.

Gaudy, Georges, *Souvenirs d'un poilu du 57e regiment d'infanterie*, (3 vols., Paris, 1921–1923), vol. 1, *Les trous d'obus de Verdun février-août 1916* (Paris, 1922).

Genty, Edmond, *Trois Ans de Guerre: Lettres et carnets de route* (Paris, 1918).

Gide, André, *Journal 1889–1939*, (2 vols., Paris, 1951).

Giono, Jean, *Recherche de la Pureté* in *Récits et essais*, ed. Pierre Citron (Paris, 1989 [1939]).

Goethe, *La Campagne de France, annotée par L. Dietz* (Paris, 1868 [*Die Campagne in Frankreich 1792 von J.W. von Goethe*]).

Grant, Marjorie, *Verdun Days in Paris* (London, 1918).

Grasset, A. (Lt.-Col.), *Verdun. Le premier choc à la 72e division Brabant-Haumont-Le Bois des Caures (21–24 février 1916)* (Paris, 1926).

Graves, Robert, *Good-bye to All That* (New York, 1957 [1929]).

Groener, Wilhelm, *Lebenserinnerungen* (Osnabrück, 1957, 1972).

Guderian, Heinz, *Erinnerungen eines Soldaten* (Heidelberg, 1951).

Heimatkalender, 159 inf. Reg., 1942, 3. Jahrgang:

———. "Das I-R 159 im Weltkrieg. Verdun 1916. Bericht des Vizeweldwebels Schürmann": 40–43.

———. Huchzermeier, Hans, (Lt.), "Der Angriff auf das Sternwerk bei Verdun": 47–49.

Herscher, E. (Lt.), *Quelques Images de la Guerre* (Paris, Nancy, 1917).

Hertz, Robert, *Un ethnologue dans les tranchées (août 1914–avril 1915). Lettres de Robert Hertz à sa femme Alice* (présentées par Alexander Riley et Philippe Besnard, préfaces de Jean-Jacques Becker et Christophe Prochasson, Paris, 2002).

Hindenburg, Paul von, *Aus meinem Leben* (Leipzig, 1920), 196–97.

Hoffmann, Rudolf (Hg.) *Der Deutsche Soldat: Briefe aus dem Weltkrieg* (Munich, 1937).

Hohenborne, A. Wild von, *Briefe und Tagebuchaufzeichnungen des preussischen Generals als Kriegsminister und Truppenführer im Ersten Weltkrieg* (Boppard am Rhein, 1986).

Hourticq, Louis, *Récits et réflexions d'un combatant. Aisne-Champagne—Verdun 1915–1917*, (Paris, 1918).

Jeanbernat, Jules Barthélémy de Ferrari Doria, *Lettres de Guerre, 1914–1918* (Paris, 1920).

Joffre, Joseph, *Mémoires du Maréchal Joffre* (2 vols., Paris, 1932), vol. 2, 248.

———. *Journal de marche du Général Joffre, 1916–1919* (documents présentés par le professeur Pedroncini à partir des archives de l'armée de terre, Paris, 1990).

Joubaire, Alfred, *Pour la France. Carnet de route d'un fantassin* (Paris, 1917).

Jubert, Raymond *Verdun mars-avril-mai 1916* (Nancy, 1989 [1918]).

Jünger, Ernst, *The Storm of Steel*, (Eng. tr., New York, 1996 [1929]).

Koch, Heinrich, *Verdun 1916* (Verden/Aller 1971).

Lafont, Bernard, *Au Ciel de Verdun. Notes d'un aviateur* (Paris, 1918).

Laurentin, Maurice, *1914–1918 Carnets d'un fantassin* (Paris 1965 [*Le Sang de France*, 1919, and *La Victoire des Morts*, 1920]).

Lefebvre-Dibon, Paul, *Quatre pages du 3ᵉ bataillon du 74ᵉ R.I. Extrait d'un carnet de campagne 1914–1916* (Paris, 1921).

Legrand-Girarde, E., *Un quart de siècle au service de la France* (Paris, 1954).

"Lieutenant Marc" (pseudonym), "Notes d'un pilote disparu (1916–1917)" (Paris, 1918).

Limosin, Jean, *De Verdun a L'Yser. Notes d'un aumonier militaire* (Paris, 1917).

Ludendorff, Erich, *Meine Kriegserinnerungen* (Berlin, 1919).

Mac Orlan, Pierre, *Les Poissons Morts: La Lorraine—L'Artois—Verdun—La Somme* (Paris, 1917).

———. *Verdun* (Paris, 1935).

Méléra, Timothée-César, *Verdun (Juin–Juillet 1916). La Montagne de Reims (Mai–Juin 1918)* (Paris, 1926).

Mermeix (pseudonym of Gabriel Terrail), *Joffre. Première crise du commandement, novembre 1915–décembre 1916* (Paris, 1919).

Morel-Journel, Henry, *Journal d'un officier de la 74ᵉ division d'infanterie et de l'armée française d'Italie* (1914–1918).

Mornet, Daniel, *Tranchées de Verdun* (Paris, 1918).

Muenier, Pierre-Alexis, *L'Angoisse de Verdun. Notes d'un conducteur d'auto sanitaire* (Paris, 1918).

Müller, Georg Alexander von, *The Kaiser and his Court* (London 1961, Eng. tr.of *Regierte der Kaiser*, Göttingen, Berlin, Frankfurt, 1959).

Pastre, J.-L. Gaston, *Trois ans de front: Belgique, Aisne et Champagne, Verdun, Argonne–Lorraine: Notes et impressions d'un artilleur* (Paris and Nancy, 1918).

Payen, Joseph-Eugène (chanoine), *L'Ame du Poilu* (2 vols., Paris, 1924–1927).

Péricard, Jacques, *Ceux de Verdun* (Paris, 1917).

Petain, Philippe, *La Bataille de Verdun* (Paris 1986 [1929]).

———. *Discours de M. le Maréchal Pétain et réponse de M. Paul Valéry prononcés le 22 janvier 1931, à l'Académie française* (Paris, 1931).

Pic, Eugène, *Dans la tranchée, Des Vosges en Picardie: Tableaux du front* (Paris, 1917).

Pierrefeu, Jean de, *Grand Quartier Général. Le Quotidien d'un état-major de guerre* (2 vols., Paris, 2002 [1922]).

Poincaré, Raymond, *Au Service de la France. Neuf années de souvenirs* (9 vols., Paris, 1926–1933), vol. 8 (1931).

Poncheville, Thellier de (Abbé) *Dix mois à Verdun* (Paris, 1919).

Raynal, Sylvain-Eugène (Col.), *Journal du Commandant Raynal: Le Fort de Vaux* (Paris, 1919).

Rice, Philip S., *An American Crusader at Verdun* (Princeton, 1918).

Richer, Jean (Capitaine; Père Jérôme), *Un Moine soldat. Le sous-lieutenant Xavier Thérésette (en religion: Fr. Marcel, de Reims)* (Paris, 1917).

Rimbault, Paul, *Journal de Campagne d'un officier de ligne Sarrebourg-la Mortange—Foret d'Apremont* (Paris, 1916).

———. *Propos d'un marmité* (Paris, 1920).

Rogerson, Sidney, *Twelve Days on the Somme: A memoir of the Trenches, 1916* (London, 2006 [1933]).

Rupprecht, Kronprinz von Bayern, *Mein kriegstagebuch*, ed. Eugen von Frauenholz (3 vols., Berlin, 1929).

Sauer, Andreas (Hrsg.), *Heilig soll der Grundsatz "Krieg dem Krieg" sein! Die Erinnerungen Karl Rosners an seine Kriegserlebnisse im Jahr 1916* (Erfurt, 2008).

Schauwecker, Franz, Preface to Eugen Radtke, *Die Erstürmung des Douaumont* (Leipzig, 1941).

Stéphane, Marc, *Ma dernière relève au Bois des Caures* (Paris, 1929).

Serrigny, Bernard, *Trente ans avec Pétain* (Paris, 1959).

Stürgkh, Josef Maria Aloysius, Graf von, *Im deutschen grossen Hauptquartier* (*Leipzig*, 1921).

Tawney, R. H., "The Attack," [1916] in Guy Chapman, ed., *Vain Glory* (London, 1968), 319–25.

Thimmermann, Hermann, *Verdun-Souville. Ein Tatsachenbericht nach den Aufzeichnungen eines Offiziers vom Bayerischen Infanterie-Leibregiment* (Munich, 1936).

Tirpitz, Alfred von, *Erinnerungen* (Leipzig, 1919).

Tournassus, Jean, *Nous, soldats!* (Paris, 1918).

Tuffrau, Paul, *1914–1918. Quatre années sur le front: Carnets d'un combattant* (Paris 1998 [1917]).

Verneuil, Louis, *Rideau à neuf heures: Souvenirs de Théâtre* (Paris, 1945).

Vial, Francisque, *Territoriaux de France* (Paris, 1918).

Vollbehr, Ernst, *Bei der Heeresgruppe Kronprinz, zweites Kriegsbilder-Tagebuch von Ernst Vollbehr (Mit einem Geleitwort Seiner kaiserl, Hoheit des Kronprinzen des Deutschen Reiches und von Preussen)* (Munich, 1917).

Westman, Stephen, *Surgeon with the Kaiser's Army* (London, 1968).

Wilhelm, Kronprinz von Preussen, *Erinnerungen des Kronprinzen Wilhelm. Aus den Aufzeichnungen, Dokumenten, Tagebüchern und Gesprächen herausgegeben von Karl Rosner* (Stuttgart and Berlin, 1922).

Witkos, Philipp (hrsg.), *Kriegsbriefe gefallener Studenten* (Munich, 1928).

Ziese, Maxim and Hermann Ziese-Beringer, *Der Soldat von gegenüber* (Berlin, 1930).

VI. Official Histories and Period Military Studies

d'Artie, H. M., (aka colonel Mélot), *La vérité sur la guerre 1914–1918* (2 vols., Paris, 1930).

Becker, G. (Colonel), *Après la bataille. Idées d'avant-guerre. Evènements de Guerre* (Paris, 1919).

———. *Emploi tactique des grandes unités* (Paris, 1924).

Benjamin, René, "Petain," in Sacha Guitry, ed., *De Jeanne d'Arc à Pétain* (n.d. 1942; Monte Carlo, 1951).

Beumelburg, Werner, *Douaumont. Unter Benutuzung der amtlichen Quellen des Reichsarchivs bearbeitet* (Oldenburg, 1928).

Bidou, Henry, "La Bataille de Verdun," *Revue des Deux Mondes*, LXXXVI, 33 (mai 1916): 171–203.

———. *Histoire de la Grande Guerre* (Paris, Gallimard, 1936).

Bodart, G., *Losses of Life in Modern Wars: Austria-Hungary, France* (Oxford, 1916).

Bordeaux, Henry, *La Chanson de Vaux-Douaumont* (2 vols., Paris, 1917).

———. *La Bataille devant Souville* (Paris, 1921).

Boutroux, Emile, "L'Allemagne et la guerre," *Revue des deux mondes*, LXXXVI, 33 (mai 1916): 241–62.

Bouvard, H., *Les leçons militaires de la guerre* (Paris, 1920; Préface par le Maréchal Pétain).

———. *La Gloire de Verdun* (Paris, 1922).

Buat, Edmund Alphonse Léon, (Général), *L'Armée allemande pendant la guerre de 1914–1918. Grandeur et Décadence: Manœuvres en lignes intérieures* (Paris, 1920), 22–25.

Chambre des députés, *Exposé des motifs de la proposition de résolution tendant à charger la commission de l'armée d'établir et de faire connaître le bilan des pertes en morts et en blessés faites au cour de la guerre par les nations belligérantes*. Documents parlementaires, Chambre des députés, t. 2, annexe 633, séance du 29 mars 1920, 32–78 (rapport Marin).

Committee of Imperial Defense, *History of the Great War based on official documents. Military Operations. France and Belgium, 1916*, vol. 5 (1932), 496–97.

Cron, Hermann, *Imperial German Army 1914–1918: Organisation, Structure, Orders-of-Battle* (tr. C. F. Colton, Eastbourne, 2002 [Berlin, 1937]).

Dellmensingen, Konrad Kraft von (Generalmajor a. D.), *Das Bayernbuch vom Weltkriege 1914–1918 Ein Volksbuch* (2 vols., Stuttgart, 1930).

Delvert, Charles, "L'histoire de la guerre par les témoins," *Revue des deux mondes*, LIV (1ᵉʳ dec. 1929): 628–41.

Doumenc, A. (capitaine), *Les Transports automobiles sur le front Français 1914–1918: Notes du ct. Doumenc recueillies et classées par le Lt. Paul Heuzé* (Paris, 1920).

d'Estre, Henry, *L'Enigme de Verdun. Essai sur les causes et la génèse de la bataille* (Paris 1916).

Ettighoffer, P. C., *Verdun: Das grosse Gericht* (Gütersloh, 1936).

Glaeser, Ernst, "Kriegsschauplatz 1928" in Glaeser (Hrsg.), *Fazit. Ein Querscnitt durch die deutsche Publizisitik* (Kronberg, 1977 [1929]): 56–75.

Hanotaux, Gabriel, *Circuits des Champs de bataille de France* (Paris, 1920).

Herr, Frederick (Gen.), *L'artillerie: Ce qu'elle a été. Ce qu'elle est. Ce qu'elle doit être* (Nancy-Paris-Strasbourg, 1923).

Hoeppner, Ernst von (Gen.), *Deutschlands Krieg in der Luft. Ein Rückblick auf die Entwicklung und die Leistungen unserer Heeres-Luftstreitkräfte im Weltkriege* (Leipzig, 1921).

Koeltz, Louis (Général), "L'histoire militaire. Falkenhayn et la bataille de Verdun," *Revue de Paris*, V, (Sept.-Oct. 1937): 229–40.

Lucas, Pascal, *L'évolution des idées tactiques en France et en Allemagne pendant la guerre de 1914–1918* (Paris, 1924).

Madelin, Louis, L'Aveu. *La Bataille de Verdun et L'opinion allemande* (Paris, 1916).

———. *Verdun* (Paris, 1920).

Malleterre, Pierre (Gén.), *Pour qu'on s'en souvienne. Un court récit de la grande guerre, 1914–1919* (Paris, 1921).

Ministère de la Guerre. État-Major de l'Armée. Service historique, *Les Armées françaises dans la grande guerre*, t. IV, vols. 1–3 and annexes (Paris, 1926).

Navarre, A.-J., *Les services automobiles pendant la guerre* (Paris, 1919).

Passaga, Fénelon-François-Germain (Général), *Le Calvaire de Verdun* (Paris, 1927).

Pelade (cdt.), *La bataille de Verdun: Conférence devant l'Association des officiers de complément de l'école d'instruction d'infanterie de l'Ecole militaire, 11 juin 1922* (Paris, 1922).

Péricard, Jacques, *Verdun: Histoire des combats qui se sount livres de 1914 a 1918 sur les deux rives de la Meuse. Avec la collaboration de plusieurs milliers d'anciens combattants* (Paris, 1933).

Picq, Ardant du, *Etudes sur le Combat. Combat antique et combat moderne* (Paris, 2004 [1880]).

Ragueneau (Gén.), *Stratégie des transports et des ravitaillements* (Paris, 1924).

Reichsarchiv, *Die Tragödie von Verdun 1916*, vols. 13–15 of *Schlachten des Weltkrieges*, (36 vols, Oldenbourg, 1921–1930), vol. 13, I. teil, *Die Deutsche Offensiv Schlacht*, (Oldenburg, 1926).

———. *Somme-Nord*, vols. 19–20 of *Schlachten des Wektkrieges* (36 vols., Oldenbourg, 1921–1930), vol. 19, I. teil: *Die Brennpunkte der Schlacht in juli 1916* (1927).

———. *Der Weltkrieg 1914 bis 1918. Im Auftrage des Reichskriegsministeriums bearbeitet und herausgegeben von der Forschungsanstalt für kriegs-und-Heeresgeschichte* (12 vols., Berlin, 1925–1939), IX (1933) and X (1936).

Reichskriegsministerium, *Sanitätsbericht über das Deutsche Heer (Deutsches feld-und-Besatzungsheer) im Weltkriege 1914/1918* (Berlin, 1934).

———. *Die Verluste des Weltkrieges. Zusammenstellung aus dem III band des Saintätsberichts über den Weltkrieg 1914–1918* (Kriegsministerium, Berlin, 1935).

Reinach, Joseph, *La Guerre sur le Front Occidental. L'année de Verdun. Etude stratégique de 1916* (Paris, 1918).

Renouvin, Pierre, review of Hermann Wendt, *Verdun*, in *Revue d'Histoire de la Guerre Mondiale*, IX, 2 (April 1931): 182–83.

———. *La Crise européenne et la première guerre mondiale* (Paris, 1948 [1934]).

Schlieffen, Alfred von, "Der Krieg in der Gegenwart," *Deutsche Revue*, 34, 1 (January 1909): 13–24.

Toubert, Joseph-Henri (médecin inspecteur-général), "Les pertes subies par les armées françaises pendant la guerre de 1914–1918," *Revue d'Infanterie* 59, 348 (September 15, 1921): 305–9.

———. *Etude statistique des pertes subies par les français pendant la guerre 1914–1918* (Paris, 1922).

War Office, *Statistics of the Military Effort of the British Empire during the Great War, 1914–1920* (London, 1922).

Wendt, Hermann, *Verdun 1916. Die Angriffe Falkenhayns im Maasgebiet mit Richtung auf Verdun als strategisches problem* (Berlin, 1931).

Zwehl, H. von, *Erich von Falkenhayn, General der Infanterie: Eine biographische Studie* (Berlin 1926).

SECONDARY SOURCES

Afflerbach, Holger, *Falkenhayn. Politisches Denken und Handeln in Kaiserreich* (Munich, 1994).

Allport, Gordon W., *The Nature of Prejudice* (New York, 1958 [1954]).

Ashworth, Tony, *Trench Warfare 1914–1918. The Live and Let Live System* (New York, 1980).

Audoin-Rouzeau, Stéphane, *1870: La France dans la guerre* (Paris, 1989).

———. *Combattre. Une anthropologique historique de la guerre moderne (XIXe-XXE siècles)* (Paris, 2008).

Audoin-Rouzeau, Stéphane, Annette Becker, Leonard Smith, *France and the Great War 1914–1918* (Cambridge, 2003).

Barral, Pierre, *Les Agrariens français de Méline à Pisani* (Paris, 1968).

Becker, Annette, *La Guerre et la Foi: de la mort à la mémoire 1914–1930* (Paris, 1994).

Becker, Annette and Stéphane Audoin-Rouzeau, *14–18: Retrouver la Guerre* (Paris, 2000).

Becker, Jean-Jacques and Gerd Krumeich, *La grande Guerre: Une histoire franco-allemande* (Paris, 2008).

Bernède, Allain, *Verdun 1916. Le point de vue français* (Le Mans, 2002).

Bichet, Gabriel, *Le Role des forts dans la bataille de Verdun* (Nancy, 1969).

Bonnefous, Georges, *Histoire politique de la Troisième République* (6 vols., Paris, 1965–1973 [1956–1962]).

Bourke, Joanna, *An Intimate History of Killing* (London, 1999).

Brandt, Susanne, *Vom Kriegschauplatz zum Gedächtnisraum: Die Westfront 1914–1940* (Baden-baden, 2000).

Brose, Eric Dorn, *The Kaiser's Army. The Politics of Military Technology in Germany during the Machine Age, 1870–1918* (Oxford, 2001).

Brown, Malcolm, *Verdun 1916* (London, 1999).

Cailleteau, François, *Gagner la grande guerre* (Paris, Economica, 2008).

Canini, Gérard, *Combattre à Verdun: Vie et souffrance quotidienne du soldat, 1916–1917* (Nancy, 1988).

Cazals, Rémy, "1914–1918: Chercher Encore," *Le movement social*, 199 (avril–juin 2002): 107–13.

Chagnon, Louis, "1916 ou l'année de rupture en matière d'utilisation de l'arme aérienne," *Revue Historique des Armées*, 242, (January–April, 2006): 37–47.

Churchill, W. S., *The World Crisis* (5 vols., London, 1923–1929).

Citino, Robert M., *Quest for Decisive Victory: From Stalemate to Blitzkrieg in Europe, 1899–1940* (Lawrence, KS, 2002).

———. *The German Way of War: From the Thirty years' War to the Third Reich* (Lawrence, KS, 2005).

Cochet, François, "6–8 décembre: 1915, Chantilly: La grande guerre change de rythme," *Revue Historique des Armées*, 242, 2006, 1er trimestre: 17–26.

Cochet, François, sld, *Verdun 1916–2006: Sous le regard du monde actes du colloque de Verdun, 23 et 24 février 2006* (Paris, 2006):

———. Bärbel, Pauline Kuhn, "La bataille de Verdun dans les manuels scolaires allemands de 1920 a 2006. De l'héroïsme du soldat à l'horreur de la guerre," 285–308.

———. Becker, J.-J. "Conclusion," ibid, 381–83.

———. Bernède, Allain, "Verdun 1916, autopsie d'une bataille, le point de vue français," 39–57.

———. Gueit-Montchal, Lydiane, "1926–206: Les Commémorations de la bataille de Verdun," 351–70.

———. Krumeich, Gerd, "Le soldat allemand devant Verdun. Variations du souvenir," 77–87.

———. Offenstadt, Nicolas, "Comparer l'incomparable? La 'victoire' de Verdun et l'échec de l'offensive Nivelle dans l'entre-deux-guerres," 309–25.

———. Porte, Rémy (Lt.-Col.), "Verdun avant Verdun," 25–38.

Coker, Christopher, *The Future of War. The Re-enchantment of War in the Twenty-first Century* (Malden and Oxford, 2004), 8.

Crefeld, Martin van, "World War I and the Revolution in Logistics," in Roger Chickering and Stig Förster, *Great War, Total War. Combat and Mobilization on the Western Front, 1914–1918* (Cambridge, 2000): 57–72.

Deist, Wilhelm, "The Military Collapse of the German Empire: The Reality behind the Stab-in-the-Back Myth," *War in History* 3, 2 (April, 1996): 204–7.

Delbrück, Hans, *Ludendorff, Tirpitz, Falkenhayn* (Berlin, 1920).

Delporte, Christian, "Journalistes et correspondants de guerre," in Stéphane Audoin-Rouzeau and Jean-Jacques Becker, eds., *Encyclopédie de la grande guerre 1914–1918* (Paris, 2004), 717–29.

Denizot, Alain, *Verdun 1914–1918* (Paris, 1986).

Doughty, Robert, *The Seeds of Disaster: The Development of French Army Doctrine 1919–1939* (Archon Hamden Ct, 1985).

———. *Pyrrhic Victory: French Strategy and Operations in the Great War* (Cambridge, Massachusetts, and London, 2005).

Drevillon, Hervé, *Batailles. Scènes de guerre de la table ronde aux tranchées* (Paris, 2007).

Duroselle, Jean-Baptiste, *Clemenceau* (Paris, 1988).

———. preface to Yvon Lacaze, *L'Opinion publique française et la crise de Munich* (Berne, Paris, 1991).

Filali, Frédéric et al, *Chronique de la grande guerre dans le 2ème arrondissement de Paris* (Paris, 1994).

Fischer, Fritz, *Griff nach der Weltmacht: Die Kriegszielpolitik des kaiserlichen Deutschland 1914/1918* (Düsseldorf, 1962 [1961]).

Foley, Robert, *German Strategy and the Path to Verdun: Erich von Falkenhayn and the Development of Attrition, 1870–1916* (Cambridge 2005).

Forrest, Alan, *The Legacy of the French Revolutionary Wars* (Cambridge 2009).

Fuller, J. G., *Troop Morale and Popular Culture in the British and Dominion Armies 1914–1918* (Oxford, 1990).

Gollbach, Michael, *Die Widerkehr des Weltkrieges in der Literatur: Zu den Frontromanen der späten zwanziger Jahre* (Regensburg, 1978).

Gray, J. Glenn, *The Warriors. Reflections on Men in Battle* (New York, 1967 [1959]).

Grigg, John, *Lloyd George from Peace to War, 1912–1916* (London, 1985).

Grinker, Roy R. and John P. Spiegel, *Men under Stress* (Philadelphia, 1945).

Grossman, Dave (Lt.-Col.), *On Killing* (New York, 1996 [1995]).

Guinard, Pierre, Jean-Claude Devos, and Jean Nicot, *Inventaire sommaire des archives de la guerre, série N 1872–1919* (Troyes, 1975): 204–13.

Hanna, Martha, "A Republic of Letters. The Epistolary Tradition in France during World War I," *American Historical Review*, 108, 5 (December 2003): 1338–61.

Herwig, Holger, *The First World War: Germany and Austria-Hungary, 1914–1918* (London and Oxford, 1997).

Holmes, Richard, *Acts of War* (New York, 1989 [1985]).

Horne, Alastair, *The Price of Glory: Verdun 1916* (London, 1987 [1962]).

Jankowski, Paul, "Obéissance et désobéissance à Verdun," in Nicolas Offenstadt, ed., *Obéir et Désobéir. Les Mutineries de 1917 en perspective* (Paris, 2008), 21–40.

Jackson, Julian, *France. The Dark Years, 194–1944* (Oxford, 2001).

Jahr, Christoph, *Gewöhnliche Soldaten: Desertion und Deserteure im deutschen und britischen Heer 1914–1918* (Göttingen 1998).

Janssen, Karl-Heinz, *Der Kanzler und der General: Die Führungskrise um Bethmann-Hollweg und Falkenhayn 1914–1916* (Göttingen 1967).

Jardin, Pierre, *Aux Racines du mal: 1918, le déni de la défaite* (Paris, 2005).

Jauffret, Jean-Charles, "Quinze ans d'historiographie française sur la grande guerre, 1983–1998: essai de bilan," in Jules Maurin and Jean-Charles Jauffret, eds., *La grande guerre 1914–1918: 80 ans d'historiographie et de représentations* (Montpellier, 2002): 39–68.

Jeanneney, Jean-Noël, "Les archives des commissions de contrôle postal aux armées (1916–1918): Une source précieuse pour l'histoire contemporaine de l'opinion et des mentalités," *Revue d'histoire moderne et contemporaine*, XV (jan.-mars 1968): 208–33.

Jones, Archer, *The Art of War in the Western World* (Urbana and Chicago, 2001 [1987]).

Kabisch, Ernst, *Verdun. Wende des Weltkrieges* (Berlin, 1935).

Keeley, Lawrence H., *War before Civilization: The Myth of the Peaceful Savage* (Oxford, 1996).

Keiger, J. F. V., *Raymond Poincaré* (Cambridge, 1997).

Kellett, Anthony, *Combat Motivation: The Behavior of Soldiers in Battle* (Boston, The Hague, London, 1982).

Kiesling, Eugenia C., *Arming against Hitler: France and the Limits of Military Planning* (Lawrence, KS: 1996).

Kraft, Heinz, *Staatsräson und Kriegführung im kaiserlichen Deutschland 1914–1916: Der gegensatz zwischen dem Generalstabschef von Falkenhayn und dem Oberbefehlshabber von Falkenhayn und dem Oberbefehlshaber Ost inRahmen des Bündniskrieges der Mittelmächte* (Göttingen, 1980).

Krumeich, Gerd, "Saigner la France? Mythes et realite de la stratégie allemande de la bataille de Verdun," *Guerres mondiales et conflits contemporians*, 182 (1996): 17–29.

Kruse, Wolfgang, "Krieg und Klassenheer. Zur Revolutionierung der deutschen Armee in Ersten Weltkrieg," *Geschichte und Gesellschaft. Zeitschrift für Historische Sozialwissenschaft* 22, 4 (1996): 533–49.

Kuper, Adam, *Culture: The Anthropologists' Account* (Cambridge and London, 1999).

Laparra, Jean-Claude, "Verdun 1916: le service de santé de la 5ᵉ armée allemande," in *Soigner et sauver à Verdun: Le service de santé dans la grande guerre*. Actes du colloque, Mémorial de Verdun, 4–5 novembre 2006 (Triel-sur-Seine, 2009): 41–48.

Liddell Hart, B. H., *The Real War 1914–1918* (Boston, 1964 [1930]).

Lipp, Anne, *Meinungslenkung im Krieg: Kriegserfahrungen deutscher Soldaten und ihre Deutung 1914–1918* (Göttingen, 2003).

Loez, André, *14–18. Les refus de la guerre. Une histoire des mutins* (Paris, 2010), ch. 2, *passim*.

Lynn, John, *Bayonets of the Republic: Motivation and Tactics in the Army of Revolutionary France, 1791–1794* (Urbana and Chicago, 1984).

Marshall, S. L. A., *Men against Fire* (Norman, Oklahoma: 2000 [1947]).

McRandle, James, and James Quirk, "The Blood Test Revisited: A New Look at German Casualty Counts in World War I" *Journal of Military History* 70 (July 2006): 667–702.

Miquel, Pierre, *La Grande Guerre* (Paris, 1983).

Morizot, Alain, "L'aviation française en 1916," *Revue Historique de l'armée*, XXII, 3 (August 1966): 40–52.

Mosse, George L., *Fallen Soldiers Reshaping the Memory of the World Wars* (Oxford 1990).

Münch, Matti, *Verdun. Mythos und Alltag einer Schlacht* (Munich, 2005).

Nolan, Michael, *The Inverted Mirror: Mythologizing the Enemy in France and Germany, 1898–1914* (New York and Oxford, 2005).

Notin, Jean-Christoph, *Foch* (Paris, 2008).

Offenstadt, Nicolas, *Les Fusillés de la Grande Guerre et la mémoire collective (1914–1999)* (Paris, 1999).

————. *14–18 Aujourd'hui. La grande guerre dans la France contemporaine* (Paris, 2010).

Ousby, Ian, *The Road to Verdun* (New York, 2003 [2002]).

Pedroncini, Guy, *Les Mutineries de 1917* (Pris, 1967).

————. "Le Moral de l'armée française en 1916," in *Verdun 1916. Actes du colloque international sur la bataille de Verdun (6–8 juin 1975)*, (Verdun, 1976), 159–73.

————. *Petain. Le soldat et la gloire, 1856–1918* (Paris, Perrin, 1989).

Petermann, Sandra, *Rituale machen Raüme. Zum kollektiven Gedenken der Schlacht von Verdun und der Landung in der Normandie* (Bielefeld, 2007).

Pineau, Georges, "L'épopée des camions de Verdun," *Bulletin trimestriel de l'association des amis de l'école supérieure de guerre*, 24 (July 1964).

Prior, Robin and Trevor Wilson, *The Somme* (Yale, 2005).

Prochasson, C., "Les mots pour le dire: Jean Norton Cru, du témoignage a l'histoire," *Revue d'histoire moderne et contemporaine*, vol. 48, no. 4, 2001: 160–89.

Prost, Antoine, *Les Anciens combattants et la société française vols.*, (Paris, 1977).

————. "Verdun" in Pierre Nora, ed., *Les lieux de mémoire*, II, *La Nation*, iii (Paris 1986), 111–42.

————. "La Guerre de 1914 n'est pas perdue," *Le movement social*, 199 (avril–juin 2002): 95–102.

————. "Les limites de la brutalisation: tuer sur le front occidental, 1914–1918," *Vingtieme siècle, revue d'histoire*, 81 (jan.–mars 2004): 5–20.

Rieuneau, Maurice, ed., *Les Dossiers préparatoires des "Hommes de Bonne Volonté"* (Paris, 1987).

Roper, Michael, *The Secret Battle: Emotional Survival in the Great War* (Manchester, 2009).

Roth, François, "Allemagne et Allemands vus de France, 1860–1914," *Compte-rendu du colloque de Brive-la-Gaillarde La France et l'Allemagne en Europe: le cœur et la raison. 24–25 Nov. 2006.*

Rousseau, Frédéric, *Service militaire au XIXe siècle: de la résistance à l'obéissance: un siècle d'apprentissage de la patrie dans le département de l'Hérault* (Montpellier, 1998).

————. *La guerre censurée. Une histoire des combattants européens de 14–18* (Paris, 2003 [1999]).

————. *Le Procès des témoins de la grande guerre. L'Affair Norton Cru* (Paris, 2003).

Shay, Michael E., *The Yankee Division in the First World War: In the Highest Tradition* (College Station, TX, 2008).

Shils, Edward A., and Morris Janowitz, "Cohesion and Disintegration in the Wehrmacht in World War II," *Public Opinion Quarterly*, 12 (1948): 280–315.

Schneider, Jean-Jacques, "Le service de santé français au cours de la bataille de Verdun en 1916," in *Soigner et sauver à Verdun: Le service de santé dans la grande guerre. Actes du colloque, Mémorial de Verdun, 4–5 novembre 2006* (Triel-sur-Seine, 2009): 15–40.

Smith, Leonard V., *Between Mutiny and Obedience. The Case of the Fifth French Infantry Division during World War I* (Princeton, 1994).

——. *The Embattled Self: French Soldiers' Testimony of the Great War* (Ithaca and London, 2007).

Stouffer, Samuel A., et al., *The American Soldier: Adjustment during Army Life* (Princeton 1949).

——. *The American Soldier: Combat and Its Aftermath* (Princeton 1949).

Strachan, Hew, "The Soldier's Experience in Two World Wars: Some Historiographical Comparisons" in Paul Addison and Angus Calder, eds., *Time to Kill: The Soldier's Experience of War in the West, 1939–1945* (London, 1997).

——. "From Cabinet War to Total War: The Perspective of Military Doctrine, 1861–1918," in Roger Chickering and Stig Förster, eds., *Great War, Total War. Combat and Mobilization on the Western Front, 1914–1918* (Cambridge, 2000), 19–33.

——. "Training, Morale and Modern War," *Journal of Modern History*, 41 (2006): 211–27.

Taylor, A. J. P., *The First World War. An Illustrated History* (London, 1970 [1963]).

Todorov, Tzvetan, *Les abus de la mémoire,* (Paris, 1998).

Wallach, Jehuda, *The Dogma of the Battle of Annihilation* (Westport and London, 1986).

Watson, Alexander, *Enduring the Great War: Combat, Morale and Collapse in the German and British Armies, 1914–1918* (Cambridge, 2008).

Watt, D. C., *How War Came* (London, 1989).

Weber, Thomas, *Hitler's First War* (Oxford, 2010).

Werth, German, *Verdun. Die Schlacht und der Mythos* (Bergisch Gladbach, 1979).

——. *1916. Schlachtfeld Verdun: Europas trauma* (Berlin, 1994).

Wilson, Trevor, *The Myriad faces of War: Britain and the Great War, 1914–1918* (Cambridge and Oxford, 1986).

Ziemann, Benjamin, "Verweigerungsformen von Frontsoldaten in der deutschen Armee 1914–1918" in Andreas Gestrich, *Gewalt im Krieg: Ausübung, Erfharung und Verweigerung von Gewalt in Kriegen des 20. Jahrhunerts* (Münster, 1996), 99–122.

———. "Fahnenflucht im deutschen Heer 1914–1918," *Militärgeschichtliche Mitteilungen* 55 (1996): 93–130.

———. *Front und Heimat: Ländliche Kriegserfahrungen im südlichen Bayern 1914–1924* (Essen, 1997).

INDEX

Alain, alias for Emile Chartier, French
   author (1868–1951), 229
Ardant du Picq, Col., French military
   theorist (1821–1870), 133, 229
Artois
   compared to Verdun, 9, 148–49, 151,
      194
   French offensives in, 1915, 9, 35, 38,
      49, 201, 210
   German plans in, 35–37, 88
   and Joffre, 88
   and Pétain, 75
Asquith, Herbert, British Prime
   Minister in 1916, 99
Attrition, 21, 22, 27, 38–39, 43, 50, 60,
      109–30
   and Pétain, 73–74, 97–98
   in theory, 22, 38, 109–10, 117, 119
   See also Ausblutung; battle of materiel;
      Haig, Douglas; losses; Rawlinson,
      Henry
Aubréville, 72
Audoin-Rouzeau, Stéphane, French
   historian, 178

Ausblutung
   and Falkenhayn, 27–28, 37, 41–42, 95
   in French and German press, 44–45,
      58–59, 85
   in practice, 37–42
   in postwar accounts, 45–47, 62–63,
      76, 95
Aviation
   growth of, 118
   and Pétain, 115
   at Verdun, 10, 23, 68, 77, 113–14
Avocourt (village), 67

Barbastro, battle of (1837), 219
Bar-le-Duc, 9, 72, 92–93, 98, 242.
      See also Central Army Group;
      Voie Sacrée
Barrès, Maurice, French author
   (1862–1923), 18, 19, 61, 73, 197
Barthou, Louis, French statesman out
   of power in 1916 (1862–1934), 25
Battle of materiel, 6, 23, 82, 109–16,
      118–19, 129–30. See also attrition
Bauer, Max, Col., 76, 77

316

Norton Cru, Jean, French author
(1879–1949), 173, 215, 261

Offenstadt, Nicolas, French historian,
178
Ornes (village), 65, 143

Paul, Heinz, German film director
(1893–1983), 18
Pedroncini, Guy, French historian
(1924–2006), 178
Péricard, Jacques, Lt., French author
(1876–1944), 125, 134, 148, 149,
188, 205
Pétain, Philippe, French general
(1854–1951)
  character, 17, 61, 63, 74, 80, 90, 120
  fame, 20, 25, 93–94, 106–7, 125, 191,
  193
  and Germans, 46, 89, 199, 207
  and Joffre, 81, 92, 98–100, 103
  military thought, 38, 49, 74, 97–98,
  103–4, 115, 118, 223
  mission to Verdun, Feb. 1916, 20, 58,
  73–75, 90, 103
  and morale, 163, 172,
  threats to withdraw, 90–91, 92, 104,
  183–84
  and war of materiel, 112, 113–14, 115,
  130, 154–55
Petit Meusien (railroad), 72, 73
Poincaré, Raymond, President of the
  Republic in1916 (1860–1934), 5,
  134
  and Joffre, 53, 56,
  and Pétain, 74–75, 104
  and politics, 56–57
  and Verdun, 56, 57, 58, 104, 107–8,
  152, 165, 247
Poirier, Léon, French film director
(1884–1968), 16, 18, 125, 218
Poison gas
  effects of, 11, 68, 139, 145, 212
  limitations of, 80, 138, 145

use of, 23, 67, 79, 114, 140, 166, 168,
214
Poivre, côte du, 20, 149, 217
Pompidou, Georges, President of the
  Republic (1911–1974), 253
Port-Arthur, siege of (1904–5), 19, 85
Przemysl, Fort, 69

Rations, 11, 22, 142, 158–60, 162, 187, 188
Rawlinson, Henry, General Sir
(1864–1925), 38, 39
Raynal, Sylvain-Eugène, Cdt (major),
  203, 205, 216, 247
Regnéville (town), 65
Renaudel, Pierre, French statesman
(1871–1935), 105
Renoir, Jean, French film director
(1894–1979), 108
Renouard, Lt.-Col., 55
Renouvin, Pierre, French historian
(1893–1974), 195, 196, 228
Rip, alias for Thenon, Georges-Gabriel,
  French songwriter and librettist
(1884–1941), 107
Rivoli, Battle of (1797), 85
Rogerson, Sidney (British author), 151
Romagne, 131, 217, 224
Romains, Jules, French author
(1885–1972), 4, 18, 25, 191, 192, 218
Romania, 170, 223, 227
Rose, Charles de Tricornot de, major,
  113
Rossbach, Battle of, (1757), 4
Rotation of troops (*noria*), 136, 160,
  166, 184, 188
Rupprecht, Crown Prince of Bavaria,
  General (1869–1955), 28, 29, 36,
  103
Russia
  in 1812, 121
  and Falkenhayn, 29, 30, 31, 32, 48
  and French poilus, 223, 227
  and Hindenburg and Ludendorff, 29,
  42, 43, 48, 103